Praise for
Gary Ginsberg and FIRST FRIENDS

"Intimate... Gary Ginsberg chronicles the unelected yet undeniably powerful people who shape presidencies... advisors of presidents with all-access passes to the Oval [who] can make or break legacies."

—*New York Times*

"One of the most important roles in any administration is that of First Friend, the person a president can trust completely and be relaxed around. It's a wonderful idea for a book, and with his great research and personal feel for true friendship, Gary Ginsberg has woven together fascinating stories and memorable insights. His lessons are important not just for studying the presidency, but for understanding leadership and life."

—Walter Isaacson, #1 *New York Times* bestselling author of *Leonardo Da Vinci*

"Gary Ginsberg has brought us a fresh, fascinating, and irresistible account of nine presidential relationships that helped to change history. FIRST FRIENDS demonstrates that one of the best ways of understanding the presidents of our past is to discover their relationships with intimate friends, and the author tells us many important things we did not know before."

—Michael Beschloss, *New York Times* bestselling author of *Presidents of War*

"Gary Ginsberg takes a fascinating and utterly original look at the most crucial of questions: How do we best understand those who occupy our highest office, and the first friends who supported them?"

—Malcolm Gladwell, #1 *New York Times* bestselling author of *Talking to Strangers*

“Everyone needs a BFF, especially people in high places: someone to lean on in good times and bad. An entertaining and enlightening romp through interpersonal presidential relationships.” —*USA Today*

“Ginsberg has crafted an insightful series of biographies, showing just how these friendships thrived and survived and were consequential for the nation’s history.” —*Booklist* (starred review)

“Paints a crisp, well-proportioned portrait of an otherwise underconsidered area of presidential history.” —*National Review*

“This is... the book you want to read this summer.”
—Fareed Zakaria, *Fareed Zakaria GPS*

“What a great book! I loved it!” —Joe Scarborough, *Morning Joe*

“Readers will delight in this intriguing look at the human side of the presidency.” —*Publishers Weekly*

“I have to say, this subject is so fertile, a great subject for a book. And the examples [Gary Ginsberg] chose are phenomenal.”
—John Berman, *CNN New Day*

“Even if you’re an avid reader of presidential biographies, you’ll find yourself saying, ‘Who knew?’ all the way through FIRST FRIENDS. Gary Ginsberg combed through diaries, letters, and interviews with an investigator’s eye, teasing out personal details about the intimacies of nine presidents and their best friends. It is one of the best reads of the genre, rich with well-told anecdotes, new angles on critical historical events, and evidence of the vital importance of friendship for presidents—and all of us. This book is a joy to read.”
—Lesley Stahl, *60 Minutes* correspondent and
former CBS White House correspondent.

"FIRST FRIENDS is an overdue reminder that deep friendship has always played a priceless role in shaping the contours of history. It gives us a fresh reminder of the power of relationships."

—Tom Brokaw, former *NBC News*
anchor, journalist, and author

"Delicious, charming, and original, this examination of largely unexplored terrain—presidents and their best friends—packs a historical punch."

—Peggy Noonan, *Wall Street Journal* columnist and
bestselling author of *The Time of Our Lives*

"A fresh, well-written take on the lives of our presidents." —*Kirkus*

"The author wraps history and humanity in a sparkling package."

—Kitty Kelley, *Washington Independent Review of Books*

"This book was a wonderful surprise, for it is engaging, entertaining, and informative. Gary Ginsberg has opened an entire new genre and an important area of presidential study—their close friends. This is an insightful look at presidents from the point of view of those who can have even more influence on them than their top advisors. Gary's reporting shines fresh light on the workings of the highest political office in our government. Best of all, it is a fun read."

—John W. Dean, Nixon White House Counsel

FIRST FRIENDS

The Powerful, Unsung
(And Unelected)
People Who Shaped
Our Presidents

By Gary Ginsberg

TWELVE

New York Boston

Twelve
Hachette Book Group
1290 Avenue of the Americas, New York, NY 10104

twelvebooks.com

twitter.com/twelvebooks

First published in hardcover and ebook in July 2021
First Trade Paperback Edition: June 2022

Twelve is an imprint of Grand Central Publishing. The Twelve name and logo are trademarks of Hachette Book Group, Inc.

The Library of Congress has cataloged the hardcover as follows:
Names: Ginsberg, Gary, author.
Title: First friends: the powerful, unsung (and unelected) people who shaped our presidents / by Gary Ginsberg.
Description: First Edition. | New York : Twelve, [2021] | Includes bibliographical references and index.
Identifiers: LCCN 2021006851 | ISBN 9781538702925 (Hardcover) | ISBN 9781538702949 (ebook)
Subjects: LCSH: Friendship. | Presidents—United States—History. | United States—Politics and government. | Male friendship. | Interracial friendship.
Classification: LCC GN486.3 .G56 2021 | DDC 302.34—dc23
LC record available at https://lccn.loc.gov/2021006851

ISBNs: 978-1-5387-0293-2 (trade paperback), 978-1-5387-0294-9 (ebook)

Printed in the United States of America

LSC-C

Printing 1, 2022

To Susanna, Sam, and Alec

&

To My Parents

Contents

Preface

I was in the third grade when I saw Abraham Lincoln assassinated. It was during the sixth-grade play at Windermere Elementary School, outside of Buffalo, New York, and I was jarred and transfixed. Until then I didn't know anything about politics let alone Lincoln, but from that moment on I was obsessed with the American presidency: the people who occupied our country's highest office, their strengths and weaknesses, what made some succeed while others failed, and those who surrounded them.

Thirteen years later I found myself working on Colorado senator Gary Hart's 1984 presidential campaign. Hart had just pulled off one of the biggest upsets in Democratic Party history, beating former vice president Walter Mondale in the New Hampshire primary. As the sudden front-runner, Hart needed an advance team. A good friend recruited me, and, as a college senior with nothing better to do, I eagerly accepted.

Over the next four months, I traveled the country as a bit player, organizing events for a maverick young politician seeking to wrest the nomination from a better-known opponent. Hart would ultimately lose, but I saw how a campaign operated and the important role that close friendships can play. Two friends of Hart's in particular fascinated me. One, Billy Shore, was his chief of staff and close friend, always at Hart's side. He seemed to be Hart's alter ego, someone with the right combination of intensity yet inner calm to keep an often pensive candidate switched on. He was so in sync with the candidate that on long plane flights, depending on how Shore read his friend's mood, he would know to either keep Hart entertained for hours or remain utterly silent. The other was Warren Beatty, the famous Hollywood actor; their close friendship stretched back a dozen years to when Hart had managed George McGovern's losing

1972 presidential campaign. Beatty would appear dramatically in some of the Hart campaign's most important events and speeches. His movie star glamour always generated a buzz, but he also had the effect of elevating the enigmatic Hart into a lighter and more demonstrative personality. "Stop acting and talking like a politician" was one of his favorite refrains. Beatty's visits were infrequent—part of his mystique—but his influence on the campaign was palpable, particularly in the marathon conversations he and Hart would have late at night, Beatty's preferred time of day. He was the only one in Hart's tight circle with greater wattage and status, and he used them—as well as the fact he needed nothing from Hart—to tell him in blunt terms when something wasn't working, which was often.

In some ways, the subject of this book came about through those two formative insights: one that's universal—the realization that the presidency of the United States is larger than life—and the other personal and human—the realization that even someone aspiring to the most powerful office in the world can use a friend just like anyone else.

The more I learned and interacted with politics, the more interested I became in how people *act* around the enormous power of a presidency and how the presidency is shaped by those people. Inside the proverbial room where it happens, do they act authentically or conformingly? Can they speak difficult truths, or do they genuflect to preserve their place in the room? I also began to wonder about those with influence *outside* the room—the unseen hands who, because of their history, independence, wisdom, or intimacy with the leader often helped shape and decide the questions debated *in* the room. Those who, when the heat gets too high, the tension too palpable, the leader can call on: for a meal, a game of golf, a late-night phone call, a walk in the park—a respite so that he can then return to his duties with more clarity and perhaps even new perspective.

Of course this is what friends do, and why would it be any different for people at the highest levels of politics and government? But over the years, as my own involvement in politics and business grew and I gained access to some of those rooms, I began to observe two things more clearly. First, it truly is lonely at the top, and trust, candor, and care for people in positions of great authority and responsibility can be extremely rare. And second, in my own career, much of whatever success I've had was made possible by the true friendships I've forged.

My interest in this subject went from a mild curiosity to a revelation in June 1992, when I found myself in an apartment next to the US Supreme Court building interviewing Al Gore, who ten days later would be nominated for the vice presidency of the United States.

This was my fourth stint working for a presidential campaign, and this time I had chosen a winner—Arkansas governor Bill Clinton, who was on the verge of becoming the Democratic nominee for president.

I was one of five lawyers assigned by the campaign to vet potential VP candidates. Gore, a second-term senator from Tennessee, was among the candidates on my list. Four years earlier, after graduating law school, I had actually worked on Gore's unsuccessful campaign to be the Democratic presidential nominee. I got to know him well and admired his intelligence and commitment to the issues he cared most about. The fact that a former low-level staffer was now his primary vetter must have irked Gore, as I went about prying into every detail of his political and private lives. The task included weeks of public research and private investigative work, including traveling to Nashville to interview every important person in his life, even his wife and parents. I wrote my final memo to the senior campaign team in Little Rock detailing my findings, and waited for word.

A week or so later, I was told Gore was one of four finalists, and I should prepare for a final interview. The campaign brass shrewdly decided that someone older and wiser than a twenty-nine-year-old former Gore underling was needed for this sensitive task. They chose Harry McPherson, an old Washington hand, to join me for the last round of questioning. A Texan by birth, McPherson was best known as former president Lyndon Johnson's White House lawyer and chief speechwriter—a tall and stately man who conveyed the easy confidence of someone who had already made his name and neither needed nor wanted anything from anyone.

McPherson and I met at his Connecticut Avenue law office. He wanted a briefing to understand the essence of Al Gore. He asked me a number of questions I was ready for, then one that I wasn't: "Does Al Gore have any friends?" I hesitated before I said anything, slightly stumped.

"It's a simple question," McPherson repeated. "Does Al Gore have any friends, because it's not clear to me he does, and if that's the case, I'd be concerned."

In all the spade work I'd done over three months, this wasn't anything I'd given any thought to nor addressed in any of my vetting memos. And yet I sensed he was on to something far more important than Gore's views on the MX missile or noxious greenhouse gases. Looking back on my first-hand campaign experience with Gore, it occurred to me that I couldn't recall a Billy Shore or a Warren Beatty around. And there certainly wasn't the gaggle of friends like I'd seen already on the Clinton campaign—the famous "Friends of Bill"—who had rescued the rocky candidate during the New Hampshire primary by traveling to the state to personally reassure skittish voters of his character and integrity. Their continued efforts afterward were a key reason Clinton cited for his success in securing the nomination.

Gore was different, but I wouldn't say he was friendless. He certainly was *friendly*, as smart and earnest a politician as any I had dealt with in my nascent political career. Harry, however, couldn't get past it, drawing on the years he had worked closely with LBJ. He had come to understand and value the importance of having a First Friend—and of not having one. On a daily basis, Johnson manifested the power of personality as central to the effective functioning of the presidency. No one could cajole, flatter, berate, or bludgeon another into capitulation as well as Lyndon Johnson. Using his hulking frame almost as a weapon, he would hover over his prey, lean in, and, alternating between whispers and shouts, eventually get his way.

Yet despite LBJ's outsized personality, Harry long believed that the president was, at heart, a solitary figure. He had legions of people around him, but no true, close confidants. Harry recognized that there was a gaping hole in Johnson's life, one that could have been filled with a friend who might have enabled him to be a more successful president. Over his long agonizing debates over Vietnam, for example, Harry had theorized an intimate could have helped clarify his thinking and eased the pressure as the country divided over the war and ultimately forced his early retirement. With Gore, he worried about the same deficiency.

A week later, Gore met with us for the final interview at his parents' apartment in a building across from the Capitol. After some brief pleasantries, Harry began.

"Senator, who are your friends?" he asked.

Gore shot McPherson a look of surprise, with a hint of anger that I knew all too well from the 1988 campaign.

"Harry, what are you asking?" Gore said.

"Senator, who are your friends... the people you most like, relax with, travel with, drink with. Your friends."

A few seconds of silence ensued. Gore leaned forward in his armchair. He looked straight at McPherson and spoke in an assured, senatorial voice.

"Norm Dicks and Tom Downey," he said.

Both men were then members of the House of Representatives, and they had served with Gore during his eight years as a congressman. Harry expected to hear these names, but he wanted more.

"Who besides men you've served with would you describe as close friends? Any friends from Carthage? From Harvard? From Nashville? From DC outside of Capitol Hill?"

"Well... my brother-in-law, Frank Hunger."

McPherson was also expecting that name. "Anyone outside your family?"

Another uncomfortable silence followed. Finally, Gore repeated the same three names.

The rest of the interview was occupied with questions about his military record, House and Senate careers, legislative victories, and personal financial dealings, all of which satisfied Harry and the campaign leadership. Gore had indeed demonstrated the character and experience to be a strong VP candidate, but as we departed Capitol Hill, Harry kept returning to the question of Gore's inability to name anyone other than Dicks, Downey, and Hunger. Then he just said it out loud:

"If he can't develop or even claim one real friendship, how's he going to lead a nation?" This was Harry's bottom line on the subject. Later, I would learn he relayed this fear directly to Warren Christopher, but for reasons that never made their way back to me, it was discounted. Gore was chosen as Clinton's running mate, and he served as vice president loyally and effectively for eight years until they had a bitter falling-out over Clinton's behavior with Monica Lewinsky.

We will never know whether Gore's perceived friend deficit might have affected his presidency. He lost the 2000 election narrowly and controversially to a man who would enjoy many close friendships but nonetheless suffer through a failed war and an economic collapse that would undermine his presidency.

The point here is not to assert that a First Friend is essential to presidential success. It would be a reach—and a misreading of history—to draw that conclusion. And yet the deeper I delved into dozens of presidential friendships, the more convinced I became that those presidents who did have First Friends were almost always the better for it—and so was the country.

I finally decided to write this book two years ago in the context of the Trump administration and the strongly held perception—fair or not—that this president's friendships were transactional rather than genuine. It made me, like Harry, wonder whether the presence of a real friend during his years in the White House (family being a different matter), most critically in those fateful last two months of his presidency, might have saved him from his worst moments: softened his intemperate behavior, given him a calm that so often eluded him, and perhaps provided him with unvarnished honesty at seminal moments when everyone else seemed terrified to offend him (and those who did were ridiculed or fired).

Beginning my research in earnest, I looked to the vast trove of presidential literature and to popular culture to find clues to how First Friends over the centuries had affected our leaders and their time in office. To my surprise, there was very little. An entire library could be devoted to books that profiled those in a president's immediate orbit: his wife, senior staff, an occasional chef, sometimes the butler, and even his pets. But the role of the First Friend, the man—or more rarely, woman—who was the closest person to the president outside of his immediate family or staff, was a mystery.

To be sure, there were some occasions when a First Friend himself was a celebrated figure, like a Nathaniel Hawthorne, and became the subject of numerous biographies. There were also a handful of other instances when the friendship itself was notable enough to warrant a book, like the bond between Franklin D. Roosevelt and Daisy Suckley or Abraham Lincoln and Joshua Speed. But mostly popular culture holds no place for the First Friend: The most famous president in prime-time television history, Jed Bartlet, didn't have a First Friend outside his staff on *West Wing*, nor did Frank Underwood in *House of Cards.* Occasionally, a First Friend will appear in a movie, such as FDR's confidante Daisy in *Hyde Park on the Hudson,* or in the news, especially if there is a scent of scandal around him, as there was with Bebe Rebozo and Richard Nixon, or if the First Friend has done something to change the course of history, as Eddie Jacobson did with Harry Truman. But typically those friends were forgotten as quickly as they became famous.

Politics is also, of course, the bastion of convenient quote-unquote "friendships," in numbers perhaps exceeded only by people's lists of "friends" on modern social media. But real friendships manifest themselves in different ways and are forged for different reasons. When I think of my closest friends, some are confidants, others are sports buddies. I enjoy some friends for their wisdom and wit, others for the comfort and stability they provide. I imagine the same holds true for everyone's friends, including our commanders in chief. As much as we like to venerate our leaders, they are in the end motivated by the same need for companionship and affirmation that we all have, the same need for respite and fun we all crave, and a break from loneliness that can sometimes consume us. The crucial difference, of course, is a president's relationship with a First Friend plays out under an often-searing spotlight (or deliberately out of its gaze) and with immense, staggering stakes. Most of ours, thankfully, do not.

This book focuses on nine different relationships between a president and his First Friend. I chose those that I found most compelling and illuminating and made choices to cover the most critical periods of America's 245-year history: America's founding, the Civil War, two World Wars, the Cold War, and the one presidency to bridge the twentieth and twenty-first centuries. Identifying a First Friend was obviously a subjective choice. For a few, like John Kennedy, there were many equally compelling options; for others, like Woodrow Wilson, the choice was obvious. For the one president I include who is alive today, Bill Clinton, I was relieved to leave that decision to him. A voracious and legendary collector of friends—arguably the president who demonstrated the *greatest* capacity for friendship among his peers—I'm grateful he was able to narrow his many options to one. Our nearly two-hour conversation about Vernon Jordan was among the richest and most illuminating in this book.

The list of First Friends I profile regrettably includes only one woman and one person of color, undoubtedly reflective of the times and the lack of opportunities during much of the history I cover. Vernon Jordan speaks eloquently to that in chapter 9. I've deliberately chosen not to include First Ladies or other close relatives of the president for the simple reason that friends by nature are different from family, a subject well-trod and understood. And if I hadn't kept the definition strictly platonic, I might have included the curious case of the mistress who also doubled as First Friend to future president Warren Harding when he was a senator. (Unbeknownst to Harding, his mistress happened to be a German spy at the very moment Harding was voting on whether to approve America's entry into the First World War. Thankfully, he was able to suppress his lust long enough to vote his conscience.)

As part of my research, I consulted a number of books on the nature of friendship to better understand how it can be applied, normatively or not, to the most powerful person on the planet. The most useful construction I found also happens to be the oldest and perhaps most enduring, from Aristotle's *Nicomachean Ethics.* Aristotle describes three kinds of friendships: those based on utility (Do I get what I need from this friend?), pleasure (Do I enjoy being around this friend?), or best of all, on the essential character of each of the friends (Do we each want only good things to happen to the other?). Those relationships, the rarest but most precious of the three, can exist only if both parties possess similar virtues and values. And when one party is a politician, these "complete" friendships become even rarer, as we will see.

A president who is constantly surrounded by and attended to by family and staff, burdened by the crush of domestic and international affairs, might seem to have little need for friends. With time a precious commodity, and access to anyone in the world assured, friendship would seem more of a frivolous indulgence than an imperative. Perhaps that is the reason First Friends have been largely unexplored and their roles little understood. This is my attempt to fill that gap. Through telling these stories, my hope is to show how a First Friendship—one of the most intimate relationships in a very public life—can provide insight into the president himself, and to explore how and where these friendships have helped shape, for better or worse, not only presidencies and their legacies, but our country.

Gary Ginsberg
New York, NY

CHAPTER 1

Thomas Jefferson and James Madison

Founding Partners

On a balmy June evening in 1790, the enslaved chef James Hemings was putting the final touches on a meal that, according to his master Thomas Jefferson, would "save the Union." Jefferson had recently returned from five tranquil years in France. He'd dreamed of retreating to his Monticello plantation in Virginia, where he would farm, renovate the house, read books, and entertain friends. Instead, soon after his arrival, he had reluctantly agreed to serve as George Washington's secretary of state, a daunting task that left him with migraines for the better part of the previous month. Even worse, his position required relocating to the capital in New York and renting a small house at 57 Maiden Lane, a far cry from the spacious home he was used to at Monticello. The cramped quarters left him longing for his former life, but on this night he had no time for distraction: This dinner, from the food to the conversation, had to be executed to perfection.

He asked Hemings to prepare each course in advance, laying everything out neatly on dumbwaiters. That way, no servants would enter the dining room and potentially leak what they heard to outsiders. For his plan to work, secrecy was essential. Hemings carefully reviewed each menu item: no less than five rare wines; green salad and jelly; two main courses of Virginia ham and beef stew; an array of sweets including meringues, macaroons, and vanilla ice cream.

The lavish spread seemed fit for a crowd, but only two guests arrived that night: Alexander Hamilton and James Madison. To Jefferson's relief, the fancy food and fine wine put both men at ease, especially Hamilton. The previous day, Jefferson had encountered Hamilton in front of Washington's office, looking "somber, haggard, and dejected beyond comparison." Even his clothes, in Jefferson's recollection, appeared "uncouth and neglected." The purpose of this "little dinner" was to broach the topic causing Hamilton's distress.

Hamilton, as secretary of the treasury, had warned Jefferson that the fragile, three-year-old experiment in republican government would soon "burst and vanish." He placed the blame on none other than Jefferson's closest friend, Madison. It was Madison who was leading Southern congressmen to block Hamilton's prized fiscal proposal: to create a national bank that would pay off states' debts from the Revolutionary War. Madison strongly opposed this "assumption" of debts, believing it would give too much power to the central government at the expense of Southern states.

But in the comforts of Jefferson's home, sipping on French brandy after the main meal, Madison and Hamilton finally reached an agreement that had eluded the legislature for months. The South would support the federal assumption of states' debts in exchange for the relocation of the capital from New York City to the banks of the Potomac River, right outside Virginia.

In the words of historian Joseph Ellis, this Dinner Table Bargain should "rank alongside the Missouri Compromise and the Compromise of 1850 as one of the landmark accommodations in American politics." Months of backroom maneuvering had yielded no progress; it was only after Jefferson's dinner that the deadlocked legislature finally passed the Residence and Funding Acts. The first great political crisis of the nascent republic had been averted, a deadlock many statesmen had feared would destroy the country.

On a more intimate level, the dinner marked the height of a potent political partnership, the so-called "great collaboration" between Jefferson and Madison. While Jefferson portrayed himself as a neutral mediator that June night, he had already sided firmly with Madison on the need to rein in the "monarchist" Hamilton. This alliance between Jefferson and Madison was by no means assured. Only a few years earlier, any "great collaboration" would have better described the partnership between Madison and Hamilton, now sworn enemies. At the outset of the Revolutionary era, it was Madison and Jefferson who differed vastly both in how they related personally and how they thought politically. Now, in 1790, fifteen years into their complex and layered friendship, the two patriarchs had managed to find common ground. The story of that convergence reflects the story of America's own shifting political tides. As their friendship evolved and deepened, Jefferson and Madison jointly developed our nation's highest ideals and, with them, the hybrid foundation for our democracy.

In popular American history, Jefferson is typically portrayed as the dominant player in his partnership with Madison, more charismatic, vigorous, and ultimately successful. In a literal sense, the depiction is accurate: The six-foot-three-inch Jefferson did tower over the five-foot-four-inch Madison. While Jefferson appeared more intense and manly, Madison looked colorless and fragile, never weighing more than one hundred pounds. The physical differences translated to temperamental ones as well. The fundamentally optimistic Jefferson exuded charisma, while Madison was a chronic worrier often paralyzed by shyness. Madison's delicate health stemmed from hypochondria, defined then as a disease afflicting those who studied too much. Plagued by a slew of physical ailments and depression, Madison once confessed to a friend that he anticipated dying young. With his dark clothes and feeble voice, "little Jemmy" (as his colleagues nicknamed him) in no way came across as the commanding, self-confident figure that Jefferson was.

These superficial differences have only enhanced the impression of Jefferson's singular status. The popular image is of Jefferson perched heroically atop his Windsor chair, quill pen poised to write that epic phrase "all men are created equal." Madison, though recognized as the "Father of the Constitution," still tends to be consigned to the role of Jefferson's trusty lieutenant, a junior member forced to rely on a senior leader for his own later prominence. In some ways, this characterization rings true. Madison did serve largely as Jefferson's political wingman, especially amid the divisions of the 1790s, then as his secretary of state and ultimately his presidential successor. Later in life, a pattern seemed to emerge: Jefferson would communicate the overarching vision, while Madison would manage the messy details, offering advice and quietly editing Jefferson's speeches and writings.

But appearances can also be illusory; in this case, they surely don't tell the true story of a friendship that was in fact much more equal than popular lore has long held. Madison's readiness to linger in Jefferson's shadow masked and even distorted the extent to which he actually possessed independent power in the relationship—one that lasted for half a century and encompassed nearly 1,250 letters. Those letters ranged from casual notes to more extended essays, such as Madison's seventeen-page description to Jefferson of the Constitutional Convention. Their closeness was apparent in how easily they switched between sharing the meaningful and the mundane. Plots against Hamilton might be interspersed with jokes about "the mystery of the missing pecans" that Madison had tried sending unsuccessfully to Jefferson in France. Occasionally, the two men would even write in code to conceal gossipy tidbits about their famous contemporaries. They also shared more blunt assessments of their enemies, such as one December 1784 letter, in which Jefferson expressed their mutual wish for Patrick Henry's downfall: "What we have to do I think is devoutly pray for his death." Such candidness and cattiness showed how much they considered themselves equals, with mutual respect and devotion for one another. Their seamless collaboration, wrote John Quincy Adams, resembled "a phenomenon, like the invisible and mysterious movements of the magnet in the physical world."

As Adams recognized, Jefferson and Madison's magnetic attraction partly stemmed from their opposite charges. Their contemporaries repeatedly pointed out that the two giants were not simply dissimilar in looks but in abilities. Jefferson was more imaginative and creative; Madison was more prudent and systematic. Jefferson wrote with greater eloquence and facility, Madison with heightened persuasion and analysis. Jefferson was lofty in his thinking; Madison was anchored in reality. In short, their partnership embodied the human equivalent of checks and balances. For Jefferson to be Jefferson—big thinking and idealistic to the max—he needed as his stabilizer and actualizer the more practical, cautious Madison.

For all their contrasts, Jefferson and Madison were bound by one vital feature: They were proud sons of Virginia. Indeed, their determination to broker the Dinner Table Bargain stemmed first from an unflinching loyalty to their native state. They viewed the location of the District of Columbia on the Potomac as proof of Virginia's centrality to national governance. As Joseph Ellis points out, though their stance reflected a certain provincialism, Virginia in the late 1700s did possess one-fifth of the country's population and contributed one-third of its trade. When John Adams quipped that "in Virginia all geese are swans," he meant to capture the conviction among the Virginia gentry that their state had stood at the forefront of the Revolutionary War. Both Madison and Jefferson held deeply to this belief, and it persisted even through all their disagreements.

Of course, their faith in Virginia's superiority rested on an uncomfortable fact: Both were wealthy Southern farmers who possessed large plantations that relied heavily on slave labor. Though they claimed to detest slavery, they never ceased to own slaves or to temper their paternalistic and racist judgments. Though Madison entertained ideas about gradual emancipation and exporting freed slaves to Africa, he never fully reconciled his economic interests with his theoretical musings. His four-thousand-acre Montpelier estate, less than thirty miles from Jefferson's Monticello, was tended by more than one hundred slaves, none of whom he ever freed. Most notoriously, it was Madison who proposed during the Constitutional Convention that slaves, as property, should be counted as only three-fifths of a person.

And Jefferson—the same man who famously proclaimed that "all men are created equal"—could just as easily insist on the inferiority of Black people, describing them as being "incapable as children." One of the largest slaveowners in Albemarle County, Jefferson held 607 slaves over his lifetime. It was the kind of contradiction that seeped into Jefferson's own family as well. James Hemings, the slave who cooked Jefferson's legendary 1790 dinner, was the older brother of Sally Hemings—another of Jefferson's slaves, the mixed-race half sister of his wife and likely the mother of six of his twelve children. One of those six children, James Madison Hemings, was named after Jefferson's best friend.

This mixture of intimacy and inhumanity defined the personal and political lives of both Jefferson and Madison. It hovered in the background of their existences and formed the subtext of nearly every discussion the two men shared about the emergent nation's future.

So much of how we can understand Jefferson and Madison's friendship today must be learned through subtext—the deeper meaning hidden beneath the surface of their words. Unlike other First Friends, they were often separated by long physical distances. Consequently, their bond had to develop mostly through the written word—letters—not by casual get-togethers in favorite haunts. Both were prolific writers at a time when print culture dominated; political arguments were made and disseminated through letters as much as by newspapers, broadsides, and pamphlets. Yet none of this dissemination—no matter how urgent—was ever instant. Months might pass before even the most important news could be received. Political gossip had to traverse undeveloped terrain or linger aboard slow-moving ships. In short, most communication required patience, investing each letter with considerable weight and gravity.

When Jefferson and Madison wrote one another, their words were not particularly effusive or evocative. For both men, words needed to be carefully chosen and considered, often alluding to an emotion but rarely stating it directly. This restraint was also partly a function of who Jefferson and Madison were: two serious, highly intellectual philosopher-statesmen, the only First Friends who would both go on to serve as president. Born and bred into leadership, their primary way of signifying trust and closeness was through abstract meditations on democracy, government, and human nature. Though occasionally there were glimmers of shared jokes and stinging opinions, most of their correspondence initially appears rather dull and formal by today's standards.

To appreciate this particular friendship, we must accept it then as a product of its own time with its own peculiarities. Through it, we can also better perceive the intricate nature of our national experiment. For two such powerful men during the Revolutionary era, personal identity was inseparable from national identity. As Jefferson and Madison first clashed then grew into intimate friends, they were also working out the contours and character of America itself.

Born in 1751, James Madison was the oldest of eleven children, surrounded by brothers and sisters to play with on the rich, red soil of their family's Piedmont plantation. From the beginning, Madison's life benefited from the privileges of inheritance. His father, James Madison Sr., was the wealthiest man in Orange County, himself the beneficiary of a long line of English ancestors who had accumulated fortunes in Virginia more than a century before. As his family grew, the senior Madison had a mansion built on his vast lands and proudly named it Montpelier, meaning "Mount of the Pilgrim." With ample space and supportive parents, the young Madison enjoyed a largely happy childhood. But what marred those early years—what gave him a sobering view of reality—was his frail health, including a digestive disease that forced him to stick to a bland diet of gruel. From an early age, Madison knew intimately the fragility of his own body and of life itself.

The one benefit of Madison's bad health was that it encouraged his studiousness (though his studiousness would also worsen his health). Before reaching his teens, he was already reading the works of Greek and Roman philosophers—Virgil, Homer, Ovid, Plato, Plutarch—as well as the great Enlightenment thinkers like Locke and Montesquieu. He was so precocious that at age eleven his father sent him away from home to attend an advanced boarding school in neighboring King and Queen County. After five years of intense study, he returned home for two more years of private lessons with a local minister. By 1769, the eighteen-year-old Madison was ready for college, but his father wanted to get him away from Virginia's unhealthy tidewaters. So rather than the College of William and Mary, which most Virginians—including Jefferson—attended, Madison left for the College of New Jersey (now Princeton).

Arriving in Princeton in 1769, Madison soon showed how much his classical education had overprepared him for college. He easily aced all the exams needed to skip his entire freshman year. He then started a rigorous study regimen, one that the college's new president, the Reverend John Witherspoon, believed would demonstrate the school's superiority over its rivals to the north at Harvard and Yale. Madison more than lived up to Witherspoon's high standards, cramming three years of college into two (in part by going weeks at a time sleeping only five hours a night).

But cruising through college proved to be a near-fatal mistake. Soon after completing his studies, the young man collapsed, too ill to make the three-hundred-mile journey back home. Instead of relaxing after this scare, Madison plowed ahead, lingering at Princeton for another year to take more classes. In the fall of 1772, he finally returned home—twenty-one years old, worn out by his declining health, and loath to become a farmer in the remote hill country. He began suffering from seizures, which kept him home for three more years. While recuperating, he read books, wrote to college friends, and contemplated his uncertain future. He began studying law, but he lacked passion for the subject and never intended to practice. The next common choice for any Princeton graduate—the ministry—seemed equally dreary.

In 1774, with better health but still directionless, Madison decided to embark on a trip to Pennsylvania to visit his friend William Bradford, who came from a prominent Philadelphia printing family. There, Madison witnessed something he'd never seen before: riotous street demonstrations in support of the Boston Tea Party, when a group of colonists had protested British taxes by dumping chests of tea into Boston Harbor. For the first time in his life, Madison felt truly inspired, marking the beginning of his fascination with Revolutionary politics. Once back in

Virginia, he asked Bradford to send him regular updates on the political scene. Aimless until then, Madison had finally found his life's mission in the ferment that would become the American Revolution.

When war broke out at Lexington and Concord in 1775, Madison joined the Orange County militia as a colonel, elected because of his father's local importance. Before he could even take the battlefield, it became clear that the sickly Madison was far better suited to safer confines, like a legislative body. In less than six months, he resigned from the militia to accept a more fitting, elected position in the House of Delegates during Virginia's Convention of 1776, a moment that forever altered the course of his life.

In April 1776, the twenty-five-year-old Madison ventured into Williamsburg and took his seat among this illustrious body of politicians. It was here that he would soon meet Jefferson, an impressive, reddish-haired man eight years his senior. Jefferson had already made a name for himself after writing the "Summary View of the Rights of British America" two years earlier, in 1774. That pamphlet propelled him to prominence in the Revolutionary cause, highlighting his exceptional ability to articulate the colonial yearning for independence. While Jefferson stood on the brink of penning an even more revered document, the Declaration of Independence, Madison could boast of little else than untapped potential. Fifty years later, Jefferson recalled his rather humdrum first impression: "Mr. Madison came into the House in 1776, a new member and young: which circumstances, concurring with his extreme modesty, prevented his venturing himself in debate."

Jefferson wasn't exaggerating in describing Madison's first venture into public life. Throughout the proceedings, as Virginia adopted a new constitution, Madison kept his mouth shut, more than happy to let established politicians like Jefferson dominate the spotlight. It certainly didn't help that his many ailments left him with a weak and reedy voice; it was so incapable of projecting that he wouldn't even attempt to speak in public until he turned thirty years old. But Madison's silence foreshadowed the style for which he would soon become celebrated: He watched closely, quietly took everything in, studied intently, until one day when his genius would catch everyone off guard.

Later that fall, when the Virginia legislature began a debate over religious freedom, Madison was awed by Jefferson's eloquence in arguing his case for the separation of church and state. From Madison's standpoint, Jefferson was as (if not more) articulate than one of his heroes, the dynamic Patrick Henry, known for his uncompromising motto, "Give me Liberty or Give me Death!" Madison entered politics as a rapt observer of firebrands like Henry and Jefferson, stirred by their charisma but sensitive to their untouchable status—and his own inadequacies. As Madison would recall decades later, Jefferson paid scant attention to him at the time because of "the disparities between us." Jefferson seemed to be everything Madison was not: tall, dashing, and outgoing, with a rare gift for coining pithy phrases and witticisms. Little did Madison know then, but even at that very moment, the student was evolving into the master.

Before "little Jemmy" met that hallowed author of the Declaration, Jefferson was just a scrawny daydreamer growing up in Virginia's Blue Ridge Mountains. He idolized his father, Peter, a strapping frontiersman who had served in the House of Burgesses. Peter Jefferson's main focus seems to have been trying to transform the lanky boy into a robust Virginian man like himself. At one point, Peter sent young Thomas into the woods with a gun to fetch a wild turkey. Jefferson fired his shots but each one missed—until he stumbled across a turkey trapped in a pen. He tied the unlucky bird to a tree and shot it point-blank. Despite this failed attempt, Peter continued his project to toughen up his son. But Thomas remained a bookworm, reading everything he could find in the family's small library.

When Peter Jefferson died, fourteen-year-old Thomas was left reeling, unable to rely on books for concrete solutions. There were, though, the familiar benefits of inheritance to soften the blow. As the older son, Jefferson received his father's Shadwell plantation, totaling more than five thousand acres of land—a blessing that eased his worries over money and allowed his imagination to blossom.

In 1760, at the age of seventeen, Jefferson enrolled in the College of William and Mary. As a country boy, he began his college years feeling self-conscious around the scions of Virginia's leading families. To compensate, he cloaked his insecurity with diligence. As one friend recalled: "He used to be seen with his Greek grammar in his hand while his comrades were enjoying relaxation." According to family legend, he would sometimes study fifteen hours a day, building the same strong foundation in classical and Enlightenment thought that Madison would. In 1762, he was introduced to George Wythe, one of colonial America's most renowned lawyers, who took Jefferson under his wing and honed his legal mind and writing talents.

For five years, Jefferson studied law under Wythe just as the legal profession was gaining greater standing. Wythe taught Jefferson invaluable lessons about how to fill his time: reading law in the morning; exploring political philosophy and political economy in the afternoon. According to fellow attorney William Wirt, Jefferson absorbed from Wythe an "unrivaled neatness, system, and method in business." He also learned to write. His goal was to be able to recap legal cases as succinctly as possible, "never using two words where one will do." After countless hours studying and writing, Jefferson grew more and more convinced that law could be used to structure and shape society.

After he had completed his studies with Wythe, Jefferson joined Virginia's House of Burgesses, establishing his reputation as a highly respected lawyer and a strong advocate for Virginia's legal reform. His social life skyrocketed in turn; he began mingling with members of Williamsburg's most elite circles. Friends orbited around him, drawn to Jefferson's warmth and good humor. One of those friends happened to be Madison's cousin, who (confusingly) was also named James Madison. Then, in 1770, Jefferson began courting a twenty-two-year-old widow named Martha Wayles Skelton, one year his junior and the daughter of John Wayles, also a successful lawyer who made handsome profits as a slave trader. The father disapproved of his daughter's new beau, but the increasingly serious couple ignored his opposition.

Giddy with passion and full of resources, Jefferson finally began to tackle a project he'd been fantasizing about for years: the construction of a mansion on an 857-foot summit a mile outside Charlottesville. Jefferson inherited the peak from his father and, as a teen, had wandered on the slopes dreaming of one day building a house there. He spent months sketching and planning, then recruited a year's worth of slave labor to transform his one-room cottage into something much more regal: a neoclassical villa with a shining dome and snow-white columns. Jefferson christened the estate "Monticello," meaning "little mountain" or "hillock."

In creating Monticello, Jefferson was not just preparing for his future with Martha but straining to secure the approval of Martha's father. His hard efforts paid off. On November 11, 1771, John Wayles finally gave his permission and only two months later, on New Year's Day of 1772, the young couple wed. When John Wayles died a year later, Jefferson and his new bride found themselves with even greater riches: 11,000 additional acres and 142 slaves. With this massive inheritance, Jefferson now was set for life, free to be a gentleman farmer and needing only his family, his fields, and his books.

At the very moment the world opened itself up to his brilliance and ambition, Jefferson retreated. At heart a homebody, Jefferson became deeply ambivalent about being a lawyer, preferring instead to remain a farmer. The irony is that while the reserved Madison steadily ascended the ranks of Revolutionary leaders, the more sociable Jefferson often preferred a simpler, quieter existence. In 1774, for the first of many times, he took steps toward abandoning his profession so that he could lead an idyllic life on his hilltop. He gave up his busy law practice, hoping to prove his steadfast loyalty to Martha as she struggled through multiple pregnancies. Day after day, month after month, Jefferson devoted himself to her, only occasionally fulfilling his legislative duties. He saw himself willingly and happily living the rest of his life on Monticello—reading his favorite books with Martha, doting on their babies, far from the tumult of Virginia politics.

Until, that is, events on the horizon forced Jefferson to descend from his sheltered hilltop world.

The Revolution that ignited in Boston in April 1775 spread across the rest of the colonies, turning local clashes into full-scale war. For Madison, this moment finally gave him the opportunity to prove himself—to show Virginia's political elders what a remarkable mind and keen judgment he truly had. Jefferson, meanwhile, did not share Madison's excitement, confessing to his cousin John Randolph that he longed for the day when "this unnatural contest" with Britain would end. Only then, Jefferson wrote, could he "withdraw [himself] totally from the public stage and pass the rest of [his] days in domestic ease and tranquility."

Unfortunately for Jefferson, the word "tranquility" turned out to be overly optimistic. The strains of childbirth had so weakened Martha that Jefferson needed to curtail his public responsibilities, even refusing an appointment as commissioner to France. For the ensuing months, he split his time between the Continental Congress and Monticello, torn between his loyalty to the Revolutionary cause and his romantic wish to simply stay home.

In the end, a quiet domestic life was never a realistic option. Especially after the acclaim he received for authoring the Declaration of Independence, Jefferson could do little to avoid the drama engulfing the land. By 1779, he was elected governor of Virginia, a triumph that coincided with a hiccup in Madison's own ascent. In the first real political contest of his life, Madison had lost his race for re-election to the 1777 session of the Virginia House of Delegates. He had refused to accede to the local tradition of plying voters with whiskey and beer as they gathered first to drink and then vote. His opponent, a tavern owner, showed no such reluctance. A decision Madison thought noble was instead interpreted as cheap, teaching Madison an expensive lesson. But all was not lost. In less than six months, his former colleagues in the House appointed him to the Council of State, a newly formed body to ratify decisions made by the governor.

Working together daily, Jefferson soon noticed that Madison's unassuming presence belied his shrewd political skill, and he began turning to him as his primary confidant and friend. As Madison remembered years later, it was during this time, three years after their initial meeting, that "a friendship was formed, which was for life."

Their increasing closeness could not have come at a better time for both men and for the cause to which they were committed. As Madison achieved greater renown in state politics, fighting for such causes as religious freedom, Jefferson entered the lowest point of his life, both publicly and privately. Foreshadowing criticism of dilettantism that would dog him years later, many leaders disapproved of how Jefferson split his time between Monticello and politics. But Madison remained sympathetic and loyal, providing Jefferson with a constant stream of news from Philadelphia, where he began serving in 1780 as Virginia's youngest delegate to the Continental Congress. For the next few years, as Jefferson grappled with problems at home and as Virginia governor, Madison emerged as an unwavering source of emotional support. It is no coincidence that during this period, Madison began signing his letters "your sincere friend" rather than his usual "your obedient servant."

The first great challenge that Jefferson faced as governor unfolded just after New Year's Day in 1781. British troops, led by the traitor Benedict Arnold, stormed into Virginia and destroyed the capital in Richmond. Braving harsh winter weather, Martha hastily packed some things and fled with her infant girl. Meanwhile, Jefferson frantically tried to rally the state's militia, but only two hundred men showed up. Vastly outnumbered, he could do nothing but sit powerlessly on his horse near the James River, watching as Arnold ravaged buildings, looted homes, and burned property. Only a few months later, in April, Jefferson and Martha's newborn daughter died, devastating both parents. They had no time to grieve; in May, the British again invaded Virginia with seven thousand men.

In the midst of these dual crises, Jefferson did the unthinkable: He informed his council and state legislature that he would not accept a third term as governor. He had done his duty for two years; now, more than ever, he needed some time to himself. Many outsiders, including Jefferson's former friend and Virginia's ex-governor Patrick Henry, condemned Jefferson for shirking his duties at the worst possible time. Madison himself urged Jefferson to reconsider, confessing that he was "lamenting that the state... in the present crisis" could not afford "to lose the benefit of your administration." Jefferson ignored even Madison's pleas, and whisked Martha and the children away to Monticello.

But the mountain hideaway was not as impervious as Jefferson believed. On June 4, Jefferson received news that Lord Cornwallis had ordered a British strike force to invade Charlottesville with the specific goal of capturing him—the ultimate prize as the state's governor and the Declaration's author. This attack presented a final, unforgiving reflection of Jefferson's failed governorship, as Virginia again could do nothing to block Cornwallis's dragoons from entering the state. Despite this reality, Jefferson had already resolved that he would no longer try to manage the war. His sole priority was simply to escape with his family to the last remaining refuge, Poplar Forest, where he owned a small plantation. They hid there, in the woods, for the next few months.

Finally, in October 1781, with pressure from both the French and an American army led by George Washington, the British under Cornwallis were forced to retreat, ultimately surrendering at Yorktown. America had won the Revolutionary War. Madison joined the jubilant celebrations in Philadelphia, but Jefferson enjoyed no such reprieve. While out for a morning ride in Poplar Forest, he had been thrown from his saddle and broken his wrist. During his six-week recuperation, he received a letter from a friend revealing that an investigation was being launched, led by Patrick Henry, that would assess his conduct as governor. The implication was that Jefferson had failed to properly defend Richmond from invasion by Arnold and Cornwallis and, even worse, that he was a coward. Jefferson, unused to being ridiculed, believed that his reputation had been damaged forever.

When the Virginia Assembly met in late fall, Jefferson stood ready to defend himself against all accusations. Henry gleefully read a list of charges, but they went nowhere. Without any debate, the assembly passed a resolution affirming its faith in Jefferson's "ability, rectitude, and integrity as chief magistrate of this commonwealth." Madison, meanwhile, showed how deeply he understood Jefferson's sensitive nature and especially his fear of rejection. Rather than penning a gushy letter to express his sorrow over Jefferson's embarrassing situation, he simply sidestepped the topic altogether. In the midst of the investigation, Madison blithely wrote to Jefferson about western expansion, then signed off: "With great respect and sincere regard." Once again, subtext was key: By focusing on what was "important"—thus ignoring the elephant in the room—Madison was implicitly showing his confidence in Jefferson's innocence and his faith that his friend would be redeemed. The Assembly ultimately agreed in returning a not-guilty verdict.

But if Madison thought that the vindication would heal Jefferson's wounded pride, he was wrong. Rather than resuming his duties, Jefferson claimed that this whole ordeal had ruined his appetite for future public service and that "these injuries...will only be cured by the all-healing grave." He then retreated to Monticello once again, announcing in a note to his distant cousin Edmund Randolph, "I have retired to my farm, my family and books, from which I think nothing will ever more separate me."

Freed of responsibilities, it seemed at first as if happiness had finally returned to Jefferson's life. On May 8, 1782, Martha gave birth to another baby girl. But the labor was an arduous one, especially since she had never fully recovered from having to flee Richmond and Monticello. Martha died four months later on September 6, 1782. Already ashamed over being investigated by his peers, Jefferson was shattered by his wife's death. For three weeks, he went into isolation at Monticello, consumed by grief and guilt. He shut himself in his room, pacing back and forth in despair, then burned every single letter to and from Martha.

A concerned Madison went into action, determined to get Jefferson away from Monticello, now a haunted place. He began lobbying the Confederation Congress to send Jefferson to Paris, where Benjamin Franklin, John Adams, and John Jay were negotiating a peace treaty with the British after the surrender at Yorktown. Madison knew that such a trip would not simply benefit the nation; it would place Jefferson in a new setting that would soothe his grief and perhaps moderate his attachment to home. After Madison's repeated encouragement, Jefferson grimly accepted the appointment. In January 1783, he arrived in Philadelphia to lodge with Madison while awaiting his departure to Paris.

While living with Madison at Mary House's upscale boardinghouse, Jefferson noticed something surprising: Madison had begun courting a fifteen-year-old woman named Catherine "Kitty" Floyd. Kitty was the daughter of a Continental Congress delegate from New York, William Floyd, who roomed at the same boardinghouse and was an acquaintance and political supporter of Jefferson. While most men during that era married by their midtwenties, the thirty-two-year-old Madison was still a frustrated bachelor. He had never been an appealing catch, given his introverted nature and a bald spot he tried to conceal by brushing downward his last few strands of hair. The wife of a fellow Virginia delegate compared him to the stylish European emissaries visiting Philadelphia and found him wanting: "Mr Madison, a gloomy, stiff creature, they say is clever in Congress, but out of it there is nothing engaging or even bearable in his manners—the most unsociable creature in existence."

Luckily, Madison could rely on Jefferson to tone down at least some of this awkwardness. With frosty winter weather delaying his departure to Paris, Jefferson continued to linger in Philadelphia, encouraging his friend's blossoming romance. He effectively served as a middleman, passing on Madison's "compliments" to Kitty and then relaying how Kitty had responded. In April 1783, Jefferson returned briefly to Monticello after Congress withdrew his appointment as a peace commissioner; the Treaty of Paris had been negotiated before he could leave. His disappointment was short-lived, however, since the Virginia legislature elected him a delegate to the Confederation Congress only a month later. While easing back into affairs of state, he continued pushing Madison to propose marriage, even admitting his hand in convincing her to marry him: "I often made it the subject of conversation, more, exhortation with her," Jefferson wrote. Consequently, "I... was able to convince myself that [Kitty] possessed every sentiment in your favor which you could wish."

But only a few months later, on August 11, 1783, Madison wrote a coded letter to Jefferson disclosing devastating news: Kitty had fallen in love with a more age-appropriate, nineteen-year-old medical student named William Clarkson. Jefferson tried his best to console the crushed Madison, admitting that "no event has been more contrary to my expectations," yet reassuring him that "the world still presents the same and many other resources of happiness, and you possess many within yourself." But it was now Madison's turn to grieve. For weeks afterward, he did his best to avoid social situations and wrote letters only to his family and closest friends.

For the rest of his life, Madison never got over Kitty's brutal rejection, even after he married Dolley Payne Todd more than a decade later. When he was nearly eighty years old, he stumbled across two letters he had written to Jefferson about Kitty. Rereading those letters so upset him that he passionately scribbled out all the references to his long-lost love and pushed the papers to the bottom of his files.

Their shared emotional torment bonded the two friends tightly, but the world was moving forward fast, with little time to indulge their grief. Though heartbroken, Madison was not one for self-pity. He remained an attentive friend, aware that Jefferson's anguish over losing Martha persisted despite his resumption of various public duties. After masterfully orchestrating the Congress' ratification of the Treaty of Paris shortly after New Year's Day 1784, Jefferson felt readier than ever for, in his words, "a change of scene." The Confederation Congress now agreed to add Jefferson to its mission in Europe, joining Franklin and Adams in helping to fortify the nation's new alliances. The day after his ambassadorship was made official, Jefferson told Madison that he intended to stick to the same principles that informed his public life thus far: "I shall pursue there the line I have pursued here; convinced that it can never be the interest of any party to do what is unjust, or to ask what is unequal."

In July 1784, at a turning point in both of their lives, Jefferson finally moved to France, where he would stay for the next five years. Before his departure, Jefferson asked two things of Madison: first, to care for his favorite nephew, Peter Carr, whose father had died a few years before; and second, "to continue to favor me with your correspondence" as the new nation embarked on creating a government.

Madison's moment to emerge from Jefferson's shadow finally came in May 1787, when he began serving as a delegate to the Constitutional Convention in Philadelphia. Always the overachiever, he arrived in Philadelphia a full eleven days before the Convention's start date. None of the other members of the Virginia delegation had come yet, slowed by heavy rainstorms that turned the dirt roads into muddy bogs. As Madison waited, he experienced a bittersweet sense of déjà vu. Once again, he was staying at Mary House's boardinghouse, where he and Jefferson had lived together when his ill-fated romance with Kitty began.

Now both Kitty and Jefferson were gone, but Madison comforted himself knowing that he could still communicate with one of them. The two friends began exchanging gifts that marked their current obsessions and endeavors. Jefferson mostly sent books about political philosophy, European governments, and failed democracies, as well as contraptions like a telescope that retracted into a cane, phosphoretic matches, a pedometer, and a box of chemicals to further indulge Madison's growing interest in chemistry. Madison dispatched various wildlife unique to America, including sugar maples, Pippin apples, and pecans. One thing he failed to procure was Jefferson's request for a live opossum.

Interspersed between the plants and animals, gizmos and gadgets, they also shared the latest political news. Jefferson described his fascination with France, which was undergoing its own revolution that had not yet turned violent. Madison provided the insider details of the upcoming Convention, barely concealing his anticipation. "Nothing can exceed the universal anxiety for the event of meeting here," he confessed to Jefferson. He tackled this anxiety as he always had: by immersing himself in the books that Jefferson sent his way, books that enabled him to conceptualize the idealized contours of a new centralized government.

At the same time, Jefferson continued to envision a life beyond politics, proposing that upon his return, they become neighbors in Virginia's mountains. He had identified a large property adjoining Monticello, reassuring Madison that it was "all within two miles, all of good land." Though moved by Jefferson's "affectionate invitation," Madison deferred, reflecting, as Noah Feldman writes, "Madison's quiet sense of independence, even from Jefferson... He intended to become master of his own house." Though their correspondence remained as open and candid as ever, the two men would soon find themselves separated by more than just an ocean.

Hints of tension in their friendship began to emerge even before Madison's work on the Constitution formally began. In August 1786, an armed uprising erupted in Massachusetts among farmers who had fought in the Revolutionary War. Led by Daniel Shays, a former captain in the Revolutionary Army, these veterans were protesting the poverty and debt crisis caused by the state's heavy taxes. By the beginning of 1787, the protest had flared into uncontrolled violence, as the Shaysites attempted to overthrow the Massachusetts government. The federal government found itself unable to muster the troops needed to stifle the revolt, leaving Massachusetts to fend for itself.

For many observers, including Madison, Shays' Rebellion seemed to prove the necessity of replacing the weak Articles of Confederation and creating a newly empowered federal government. Madison viewed the Shaysites as dangerous rebels whose populist rage threatened to topple the republican experiment. But Jefferson—watching from afar—expressed blithe approval, writing to Madison, "I hold it that a little rebellion now and then is a good thing, and as necessary in the political world as storms in the physical." From Jefferson's perspective, the "tree of Liberty" occasionally required "the blood of patriots & tyrants" as fertilizer. The divergence could not have been more dramatic, serving as a stark foreshadowing of what was to come.

Neither Madison nor Jefferson allowed their contrary opinions of Shays' Rebellion to interrupt the flow of their correspondence, which remained constant and increasingly frank, until the business of drafting a new federal constitution could begin during the summer of 1787. Madison would have happily continued to provide Jefferson with regular updates, but the conferees agreed that no details of their deliberations should be discussed with anyone outside the room until the convention ended. That rule deprived Jefferson of news for nearly half a year, but it enabled Madison to evolve into the ideal narrator. Madison not only had come more prepared with more concrete ideas than any other delegate, but he also placed himself (literally) at the center of the convention itself. He sat in the exact middle of the front row, and from that desk he kept the most complete set of notes of each day's proceedings. Once the convention concluded in September 1787 with the signing of the Constitution, the friends freely resumed their correspondence. And it was this set of pivotal correspondence that highlighted for the first time their divergent views about the American character, republican government, and democracy itself.

For Jefferson, nearly four thousand miles and an ocean away from his home country, sweeping constitutional reform lacked urgency. As a supreme idealist—someone who fantasized about spending his days on a secluded farm—Jefferson held an almost instinctive hostility to any form of authority outside of the individual. In modern parlance, it's possible Jefferson would have identified as a kind of libertarian—and many libertarians today view him as their chief intellectual ancestor. He saw centralized political power as dangerous and wanted as many decisions as possible to be made by "the people" at the state level.

But for Madison, positioned in the thick of the drama, nothing could have been more urgent for the republic's survival than total reform. The solution, Madison believed, lay in creating a strong national government with adequate checks and balances: a unitary executive with limited powers, appointed by electors chosen by the people; a large legislative body elected by the people, with significant and enumerated powers; a smaller but more senior body chosen by the elites; and a judiciary appointed by the executive subject to agreement of the Senate. Ultimately, nearly all of Madison's original conceptions were incorporated into the ratified Constitution.

On October 24, 1787, Madison sent Jefferson a detailed analysis of what had transpired in Philadelphia. Before enumerating the specifics of what was won and lost in the final agreement, he extolled the sheer improbability of what had been achieved: The "task," he wrote, was "more difficult than can be well conceived by those who were not concerned in the execution of it." Given how complicated the subject matter and opinionated the conferees, "it is impossible to consider the degree of concord which ultimately prevailed as less than a miracle." Over the next sixteen pages, Madison laid out the shape of the new government to the one person whose opinion he most valued.

Jefferson's response, written two months later, shows how far the two friends occupied opposite ends of a great political divide. The issue separating them was the very role of the government Madison was laboring to create. Jefferson expressed his central worries about the Constitution as it stood: "I own I am not a friend to a very energetic government.... After all, it is my principle that the will of the Majority should always prevail." But Madison's whole point was that majority rule posed the biggest threat to democracy, and that the Constitution's main job was to curb such factions. In short, Jefferson feared that the Constitution overreached in curtailing liberty, while Madison felt that the document did not go far enough in containing popular passions.

In the same letter, Jefferson told Madison that he agreed with the idea of dividing power into three branches, governed by the idea of "checks and balances." But he raised objections to key parts of the Constitution, especially one particular omission: "Let me add that a bill of rights is what the people are entitled to against every government on earth, general or particular, and what no just government should refuse or rest on inference." Jefferson's insistence on a bill of rights echoed the position of George Mason, another close friend, who was at that moment arguing that delegates like Madison were attempting to establish a "modern aristocracy" without regard for "the people." Jefferson agreed with Mason that it was only through a bill of rights that liberty could be preserved and tyranny avoided.

Madison disagreed; he opposed making the inclusion of a bill of rights the precondition for ratification, as his friend suggested. He doubted that mere "parchment barriers" could protect against encroachments on liberty, and they might even encourage the government to violate any rights not explicitly mentioned. After all the hard work he had invested, Madison felt convinced that the way he had structured the Constitution was plenty sufficient to protect individual rights.

But Jefferson would not relent, even if he had to operate from the sidelines. He began searching for outlets that would circulate letters—written by him but without his name attached—stressing the necessity of a bill of rights. When Patrick Henry heard that Jefferson's letters were making the rounds, he seized the chance to sow more discord and impede ratification in divided states. At the Virginia Ratifying Convention, Henry invoked Jefferson's name in an attempt to discredit the Constitution: "This illustrious citizen advised you to reject this government till it be amended." Henry knew full well what embarrassment and inner conflict this announcement would cause for Madison. During the debates, though, Madison betrayed no ill will, insisting that he knew better than anyone where Jefferson's true feelings lay: "I believe that were that gentleman now on this floor, he would be for the adoption of this constitution."

Outwardly, they maintained their First Friend status. Deep down, however, Madison bristled at Jefferson's covert maneuvering, which might have contributed to his decision to keep his own secret as well. Without telling Jefferson, he had begun working in the fall of 1787 on *The Federalist Papers* with Hamilton and John Jay, a project that would become famous for its eloquent defense of the Constitution. Not until a year later, a mere two months before its official publication, did Madison mention the *Federalist Papers* to Jefferson.

Though Jefferson had heard about the *Papers* from other participants, he respectfully waited for Madison to reveal the news to him directly. And when Madison finally did, Jefferson responded graciously, with admiration and pride for the feat Madison had accomplished: "I sincerely rejoice at the acceptance of our new constitution." Jefferson still insisted that the key element in need of "retouching" was a bill of rights, that "half a loaf is better than no bread." But he knew to tread lightly at this delicate point in their friendship.

Perhaps Jefferson also knew that Madison's pragmatism would ultimately prevail and that he would see the merit in a bill of rights. Though initially wary of doing anything that might throw ratification into doubt, Madison eventually came around to his friend's view after realizing he needed to show flexibility to win his race for Congress against his friend James Monroe. Having suffered the indignity of losing a Senate seat to two anti-Federalists in an earlier vote of the Virginia state legislature, Madison could ill-afford to lose another race now for the House. Nor could he deny any longer that constitutional revisions would be necessary to placate anti-Federalist opposition; unity, he concluded, would be better than perfection. So he ran for the House in part on support for a Bill of Rights—and won easily. On June 8, 1789, fulfilling his campaign promise, Madison proposed a series of constitutional amendments to be considered by the First Congress. When ten of those were finally ratified, Madison became widely hailed as "the Father" not only of the Constitution but also of the Bill of Rights.

The pivotal years of drafting the Constitution and Bill of Rights could have marked the first serious rupture between Madison and Jefferson. What preserved their friendship was their mutual awareness that the Constitution was far from finished in 1789. In a sense, their ability to come to an agreement about the Constitution stemmed from an understanding that their own friendship operated in a similar fashion. Just as Madison calmed Jefferson's idealism and Jefferson inspired Madison's, so too did America have to strike the proper balance between self and society, unrestrained freedom and political order.

Considering how fully the Madisonian and Jeffersonian worldviews differed in 1789, it is shocking how quickly things would change, a testament to the tectonic shifts occurring across the American landscape. In what would be the greatest plot twist of all, Madison—in less than a year—would become the most ardent Jeffersonian of his era.

After five years in France, Jefferson returned home to a fractured nation. Insiders expected him to plunge right back into the political storm, especially given his recent drive to influence the Constitutional Convention from afar. But Madison knew his friend and what motivated him better than anyone. He appreciated fully Jefferson's persistent streak of domesticity and how it would pull him back to Virginia. Even before Jefferson landed on American shores, Madison had tried gauging his interest in accepting an appointment in Washington's administration. Jefferson stalled, claiming that his sole "object is a return to... retirement." But Madison wasn't deterred. Shortly after Jefferson's arrival, Madison visited him at Monticello to goad him back into public life, just as he had done after Jefferson's humiliation as Virginia governor and Martha's tragic death. Madison's persuasiveness prevailed once again. A few months later, Jefferson found himself living at 57 Maiden Lane in New York, poised to negotiate the momentous Dinner Table Bargain.

With that extravagant and carefully orchestrated meal, Jefferson and Madison signaled the rebirth of their "great collaboration," now mightier than ever. But that collaboration was so durable in 1790 precisely because of the preceding years of divergence. Only by working through their differences over the Constitution and Bill of Rights could Madison and Jefferson emerge stronger in their conviction of what they held in common.

The simplistic explanation for Madison's conversion is that Jefferson simply won him over once back in America. But that explanation does a disservice to Madison's independently brilliant mind—and his deep-seated resolve to prove himself equal to his famous friend. By the time Jefferson returned from France in September 1789, Madison had vastly matured. He had spent the last five years in the weeds of policy making, confirming his bona fides as an impressive statesman and a supreme intellectual. He was no longer just Jefferson's admirer or student; he was a veteran of the constitutional battles of the 1780s. Few other Revolutionary leaders possessed as sophisticated an understanding of the new American republic and its levers of power as did Madison. Any evolution in his thinking arose from his own considered judgment, with Jefferson providing some—but far from all—of the influence.

In the six months prior to the fateful dinner on Maiden Lane, Madison had already begun moving closer to Jefferson. The key moment came in January 1790, when Hamilton submitted his *First Report on the Public Credit* to Congress. The report outlined Hamilton's fiscal goals, which echoed Madison's own arguments at the Constitutional Convention and in *The Federalist Papers*. In fact, before 1790, Madison had collaborated far more with Hamilton as a nationalist than he had with Jefferson. It was actually Madison who had first promoted the assumption of state debts in the 1780s—now a key tenet of Hamilton's fiscal proposal. It was Madison who had joined with Hamilton under the pseudonym "Publius" to write *The Federalist Papers*. And it was Madison who had proven to be the most outspoken defender at the Constitutional Convention for a powerful national government.

But now, in Madison's words, "I deserted Colonel Hamilton, or rather Colonel H. deserted me." After considering Hamilton's fiscal plan more deeply, Madison feared the prospect of the federal government exercising economic control over all thirteen states, including his beloved Virginia. In his view, this consolidation of power would not just pervert the legacy of the Revolution; it would translate to economic advantages for a narrow subset of the population centered in the northeast. Both Madison and Jefferson, despite their privileged backgrounds, believed they represented the common man: yeoman farmers who formed the basis of republican decency and agrarian society. Hamiltonian Federalists, in their eyes, were Anglophiles who protected the financial interests of merchants, bankers, businessmen, and other members of the urban elite. So as nationalism surged under Federalist rule, Madison found himself inching closer to his roots, ones that his best friend had never relinquished.

The new rift between the two friends and Hamilton defied expectations, as the three had been expected to form a fierce trio within Washington's unofficial Cabinet (officially Madison was a US congressman from Virginia). But Madison and Jefferson quickly realized that they were outliers in the administration, with the president increasingly swayed by Hamilton's recommendations, especially the establishment of a national bank. As tensions escalated, Jefferson sarcastically told Washington, "Mr. Madison and I have wondered whether we should resign, since Mr.

Hamilton is taking over both our jobs." Such not-so-subtle hints did little to diminish Hamilton's influence; the Federalists steadily secured most of Hamilton's pet causes. Jefferson—who often recoiled from conflict—seemed overwhelmed by the fight ahead, confessing to Madison, "Hamilton is really a colossus." But he now had a fierce ally on his side. He recognized how resilient the soft-spoken, diminutive Madison truly was, and how potent their combination could be in checking Hamilton's worst abuses. In one letter to Madison, Jefferson praised his tireless commitment to undermining their mutual foe: "There is nobody but yourself who can meet him."

Their relationship during this period reached new heights. They schemed and strategized, and in between dined and mused generally about life. In one letter Jefferson deigned "to make a proposition" to Madison "... to come and take a bed and plate with me. I have four rooms of which any one is at your service. Let me intreat you, my dear Sir, to do it, if it be not disagreeable to you. To me it will be a relief from a solitude of which I have too much." He even touted the advantages of his vast library to further entice his friend.

Madison declined the lodging offer, but he did agree to a second proposal from Jefferson to take a vacation. In May 1791, they embarked on a month-long trip through New England and upstate New York, looking for, in Madison's words, "health, recreation and curiosity." They spent most of their time studying plants, fishing, and wandering over Revolutionary War battlefields.

But even on this supposed vacation, they couldn't refrain from politicking. Privately, they met with anti-Federalist leaders, including the newspaperman Philip Freneau, a classmate of Madison's from Princeton. The two friends were consciously strengthening their coalition and beginning to breathe life into a formidable new force: the Democratic-Republican Party (a faction of which later became today's Democratic Party). By October 1791, they had persuaded Freneau to help establish a mouthpiece for their fledgling party—the *National Gazette* newspaper, an obvious counterweight to Hamilton's own *Gazette of the United States.*

The catch was that Jefferson, as secretary of state, was using the *National*

Gazette to launch a mud-slinging campaign against the very administration he still worked for. So he had to find ways to be as discreet about his involvement as possible. Rather than writing articles for the press himself, he recruited Madison to do much of the dirty work. In a letter on July 7, 1793, he urged Madison to go on the offense: "For god's sake, my dear Sir, take up your pen, select the most striking heresies, and cut him to pieces in the face of the public." Madison willingly obliged, penning a series of scathing articles signed with the name "Brutus." These dynamics foreshadowed the nature of their alliance for the next two decades, with Madison often working behind the scenes and Jefferson trying to float above the fray.

Still, Jefferson could not avoid the emotional wear of statecraft. By December 1793, he had grown so worn out from constantly battling Hamilton that he resigned from Washington's Cabinet and retired to Monticello. There, he focused on developing a crop rotation system and also established a nail factory operated by his teenage slaves. But just as in the past, Jefferson's quasi-farmer life masked the fact that one foot still remained in politics—with Madison as his vital link. In fact, Jefferson now found it even more advantageous to exert influence from outside the administration, and Madison as always was his willing accomplice.

In a letter to Jefferson during his brief retirement, Madison divulged personal news that delighted his best friend: He had at last shed the embarrassment of his "single state" by marrying the vivacious, twenty-three-year-old widow Dolley Payne Todd. Jefferson already knew of the romance and approved. Ten years after having his heart broken by a teenager, Madison at forty-three had finally found his life partner. But in a nod to his equally important alliance with Jefferson, he was careful to note that marriage would not in any way interfere with their business, adding: "I shall always receive your commands with pleasure." In that same letter, Madison hinted at his own interest in retiring, but Jefferson wouldn't hear of it: "But this must not be, unless to a more splendid and more efficacious post." Unless Madison were considering running for president, Jefferson implied, he must not entertain any ideas other than remaining as leader of the opposition party. So over the next several years, with guidance from

Jefferson, Madison worked within Congress to strengthen the young party and sharpen its platform.

Jefferson's semi-absence from politics did not last long. At first, he uttered his usual protestations when Madison urgently wrote in March 1795 that he should seek the presidency: "You ought to be preparing yourself... to hear truths which no inflexibility will be able to withstand." The fifty-one-year-old Jefferson responded that he had no such interest, despite rampant rumors that he aimed to succeed Washington. "The little spice of ambition, which I had in my younger days," he claimed, "has long since evaporated." Years later, however, Jefferson admitted that his attempt at permanent retirement left him a shell of his former self. From the confines of Monticello, he realized how fully politics formed the core of his being: "From 1793 to 1797 I remained close to home, saw none but those who came there, and at length became very sensible of the ill effect it had upon my own mind.... I felt enough of the effect of withdrawing from the world then, to see that it led to an antisocial and misanthropic state of mind, which severely punishes him who gives into it: and it will be a lesson I shall never forget as to myself."

Thus, by December 1796, in a stunning turnaround, Jefferson returned to politics as the standard-bearer for the Democratic-Republican Party—and Madison again played the role of his shrewd operative, charting Jefferson's political comeback. In those days, electors didn't vote for tickets, and candidates for president did not select a running mate. Instead, before the 12th Amendment was ratified in 1804, the system provided for each state elector to cast two votes, not distinguishing between president and vice president. The candidate with the most electoral votes would then be declared president, with the runner-up becoming vice president. The election of 1796 thus was the first truly contested election in American history after George Washington refused to run for a third term, pitting two parties against each other: the Federalist candidates John Adams and Charles Pinckney against the Democratic-Republican candidates Jefferson and Aaron Burr. The Constitution thus made it possible for two leaders of opposing parties to serve concurrently as president and vice president.

As Jefferson worried over the possibility of not winning the presidency, Madison advised him to accept whatever came to pass: "You *must* reconcile yourself to the secondary as well as the primary station, if that should be your lot." And when Jefferson did finish a close second in the election, he eventually swallowed his pride and agreed to serve under his bitter rival, Federalist president John Adams.

Working together in the same administration only worsened the divisions between Adams and Jefferson and their respective parties, as became obvious in June 1798, when the Federalist-dominated Congress passed the Alien and Sedition Acts. One of the most controversial aspects of the Acts made it illegal to criticize the government's policies in its impending war against France. Not coincidentally, this meant that prosecutions were targeted primarily at newspaper editors favoring Jefferson and Madison's new party, the pro-French Democratic-Republicans.

For Jefferson, such prosecutions amounted to a "reign of witches," with Federalists exercising monarchical powers to suppress free speech and press. Meanwhile, Madison had recently retired from Congress, tired of the constant infighting and deflated by what he viewed as Federalism's constitutional abuses. After twenty-three years in public service, he was enjoying life at Montpelier as a gentleman-farmer. But the uproar over the Acts—which Madison denounced as "a monster that must for ever disgrace its parents"—roused him back to action.

While both deplored the Alien and Sedition Acts, the friends did not blindly agree on how to undercut them. In October 1798, Jefferson invited Madison to Monticello and showed him drafts of what would become known as the Kentucky Resolutions. Jefferson's resolutions made a radical argument (though toned down when adopted later by the Kentucky legislature): that the Acts were "void" and that states could "nullify" such unconstitutional laws. In effect, Jefferson repudiated the belief that the president, Congress, or the Supreme Court were the final arbiters of constitutionality.

Madison, of course, did not fully agree—even though he had been inching closer to a states' rights position over the last decade. A month after meeting with Jefferson, Madison wrote his own Virginia Resolutions, which employed more restrained language to argue for the right of states to *announce* that a law was unconstitutional but not the right to *nullify* a law outright. Under Madison's purposefully vague language, states could "interpose" against the Acts using all "necessary and proper measures" to protect their rights, but they couldn't consider the Acts utterly "void & of no force."

Such fine distinctions, however, were papered over amid the country's heightened polarization. Despite Madison's conciliatory language, seven state legislatures rejected both the Kentucky and Virginia Resolutions, with three issuing condemnations over the threat the Resolutions posed to the Union. Still, the outcry over the Alien and Sedition Acts persisted, with the Adams administration plagued by accusations of federal overreach. Amid this continued opposition to the Acts, Jefferson's and Madison's Resolutions did serve as useful campaign documents, helping rally together Democratic-Republicans just in time for the presidential election of 1800.

After nearly a decade of consolidating their Democratic-Republican forces, the two friends could finally rejoice when the so-called "Revolution of 1800" ushered in a major political realignment, with vice president Thomas Jefferson defeating incumbent president John Adams. This win occurred only after the House of Representatives cast thirty-six ballots to determine whether Jefferson or his running mate, Aaron Burr, who both received the same number of electoral votes, would become president. Ironically, it was none other than Hamilton who played the decisive role in throwing his support behind Jefferson, viewing him as the lesser evil. On March 4, 1801, Jefferson became the first president to take the oath of office at the new capital on the Potomac, the prize he had secured from the Dinner Table Bargain over a decade before (although not the first to reside in the White House, as Adams had beaten him by four months). One of his first decisions as president was to appoint Madison as secretary of state.

In his inaugural address, carefully edited by Madison, Jefferson ironically sought to heal the same political wounds that he had helped stoke throughout the 1790s. Glossing over the animosity of the previous decade, Jefferson proclaimed: "We are all republicans; we are all federalists," evoking a theme candidates would use to great effect for the next 220 years. Aside from being a call for unity, those words carried another layer of unintended meaning. Jefferson and Madison would soon discover how much they, when faced with the realities of power, acted like the Federalists they had once condemned. Both men ended up overturning few of the institutions they had criticized in the 1790s. Even Hamilton's prized national bank, the source of so much discord during the Dinner Table Bargain, remained untouched. Yet again, the "checks and balances" in their own friendship provided a fitting guide for how to act as presidents: accommodating their seemingly fixed principles to circumstance and experience.

The most striking illustration of the necessity for compromise occurred midway through Jefferson's first term. During debates over the Constitution, Jefferson had proudly told Madison that he was no fan of "energetic government." But in 1803, he pulled off one of the most energetic uses of federal power ever: the historic Louisiana Purchase from France, doubling the size of the nation with 827,000 square miles of land west of the Mississippi River. In October 1802, that vast region had come under French control after Napoleon Bonaparte reached an agreement with Spain's King Charles IV. Jefferson and Madison viewed that agreement as a crisis in the making. After his time abroad, Jefferson was more than familiar with France's imperial ambitions, and he worried about the military dangers of that country controlling the Mississippi River.

He and Madison worked feverishly to try to resolve this issue through diplomatic channels, but the Federalist Party increasingly clamored for war. Fearing the prospect of disunion, Jefferson recognized the need to take more visible action than just backroom maneuvering with Madison. So in January 1803, he enlisted his political ally James Monroe to join Minister to France Robert Livingston in an attempt to acquire some of the Louisiana territory from Napoleon. Before Monroe's departure, Jefferson told him (no pressure): "All eyes, all hopes, are now fixed on you,... for on the event of this mission depends the future destinies of this republic." Monroe's instructions, written by Madison and approved by Jefferson, allowed up to $10 million to be spent on New Orleans and all or parts of the Floridas.

When Monroe reached Paris on April 12, however, the political equation in France had already changed. Napoleon's grand scheme to reestablish French presence in the New World had started to unravel after a rebellion of slaves and free Black persons in Saint Domingue (now Haiti). Even worse, a new war with Britain appeared unavoidable. France's treasury minister, François de Barbé-Marbois, advised Napoleon that Louisiana would be rendered worthless without Saint Domingue and that France would likely lose the territory in the event of war with Britain. Reluctantly, Napoleon concluded his best option was just to sell the territory, and that was what he did, for $15 million. Including New Orleans, it was a stretch of land that would ultimately encompass fifteen states. It was, as Jefferson later described, "a fugitive occurrence"—such a steal that in today's dollars it equates to less than fifty cents an acre—something beyond both his and Madison's wildest dreams.

The deal was officially announced on July 4, 1803, a day for Americans to celebrate not just their independence from Britain but their tangible progress toward world influence. The deal was not universally popular, though. Ironically, it was the Federalists who continued to ramp up their criticism of Jefferson, arguing that purchasing such a huge expanse from a foreign government was not allowed under the Constitution. The Federalists were certainly correct in the most literal sense: The Louisiana Purchase *did* clearly test Jefferson's principles, forcing him to expand his strict interpretation of the Constitution and his idealistic pronouncements on limited federal power. He admitted as much to Livingston: "Perhaps nothing since the Revolutionary War has produced more uneasy sensations through the body of the nation."

Jefferson tried to sidestep Federalist criticisms by proposing a constitutional amendment that would allow for the government to purchase and incorporate new territory into the Union. In other words, since a provision for this particular power didn't exist, it could be written in—and Jefferson could still claim to be adhering to the Constitution's plain words, not overstepping his bounds. Madison, however, disagreed about the need for such an amendment, reverting to his earlier flexibility over what the Constitution permitted under its treaty-making provisions. Once again, Jefferson was left persuaded by his friend, agreeing that they needed to push for ratification now, before the deadline passed.

Heeding Madison's advice, the president rationalized the position of the Democratic-Republicans—now suddenly supportive of broad presidential powers—in his usual sentimental, slightly exaggerated terms: "It is the case of a guardian, investing the money of his ward in purchasing an important adjacent territory; and saying to him when of age, I did this for your good." With those paternalistic words, Jefferson and Madison managed to overcome Federalist opposition and convince Congress to ratify and fund the Louisiana Purchase. After only two days of debate, the Senate approved the treaty by a vote of 24 to 7, and it was signed shortly thereafter.

The Louisiana Purchase was as much a political triumph for Madison as it was for Jefferson. As Jefferson's chief advisor, Madison supervised the entire transaction, with French Foreign Minister Charles Talleyrand noting that it was the inhibited Madison who actually "governed the President" in foreign affairs. Madison also played a chief role in ensuring that a durable Senate majority would pass the Louisiana Treaty, making it more immune to criticism. And for the next six years, he would continue to stick with Jefferson, as new events unfolded that challenged much of what they professed to believe.

With successes like the Louisiana Purchase, Republican ideas soon gained sway over national politics. In response, opponents decided that one of the easiest ways to weaken Jefferson's popularity was to dig up the sordid details of his private life—which inevitably involved Madison. Because Madison and Dolley lived with Jefferson in the White House at the beginning of his term, stories began circulating that the president had commenced a sexual relationship with his best friend's wife. Added to that incendiary (and false) claim was the more accurate charge that Jefferson had fathered several children with his slave Sally Hemings.

Both these accusations also converged into an even more twisted reality: On January 18, 1805, Sally gave birth to a son who would be named James Madison Hemings. Dolley, present at Monticello for the birth, pled Sally for the honor of naming the baby after her husband in exchange for a "fine present." Sally agreed—but no present ever arrived. And a year later, Martha Jefferson Randolph, one of Jefferson's daughters with his deceased wife, gave birth to her own son and also named him James Madison Randolph. It was this type of intimate (if perverse) connection—Jefferson's slave son and free grandson, both named after Madison—that illustrates the complex layers sustaining their legendary political partnership.

Naturally, then, after Madison won the overwhelming support of Republican congressmen to be their presidential nominee in 1808, the election emerged as a referendum on Jefferson's own stewardship of the nation. In attempting to discredit Madison, the Federalists repeated their familiar criticisms of Jefferson: that Madison was a Francophile; that the Virginians exercised far too much control over national politics; that the Democratic-Republican fear of centralized power encouraged mob rule. None of those arguments worked. Madison secured 122 electoral votes over Federalist candidate Charles Cotesworth Pinckney's meager 47—and now followed his friend in becoming president of the United States.

On March 4, 1809, Jefferson cheerfully attended Madison's own presidential inauguration, sitting alongside his comrade at the front of the Capitol hall. When it came time for Madison to deliver his inaugural address, the newly sworn-in president could barely contain his nerves. But he managed to pull himself together, conscious of the fact that his election represented an endorsement of Jefferson's own vision. As the writer (and contemporary observer) Margaret Bayard Smith recalled, "Mr. Madison was extremely pale and trembled excessively when he first began to speak, but soon gained confidence and spoke audibly." As his friend listened proudly, Madison delivered a short but clear speech announcing his intention to continue governing with Jeffersonian principles.

During that evening's ball in Long's Hotel, someone remarked on how happy Jefferson looked in comparison to his solemn successor, as if Jefferson "were the one coming in, and he the one going out of office." Jefferson replied, with more than a little relief: "There's good reason for my happy and his serious looks. I have got the burden off my shoulders, while he has now got it on his." For Jefferson, the presidency would soon be a distant memory. At long last, he could spend the rest of his days in Virginia as "the Sage of Monticello." But part of his happiness also arose from seeing Madison in this new, glorified light, as Smith wrote: "I believe... that every demonstration of respect to Mr. Madison gave Mr. Jefferson more pleasure than if paid to himself. I do believe father never loved son more than he loves Mr. Madison."

As the festivities ended and Madison entered the White House, he faced an uncomfortable fact: His dear friend and predecessor had left *him* with an impending war on his hands. Back in 1807, Jefferson and Madison had imposed a trade embargo against Britain and France as a way to stay out of their ongoing war. Incensed by this policy of neutrality, the two European countries had begun attacking American ships. Ultimately, the embargo ended up harming American sailors and merchants more so than it did Europe. So shortly before leaving office in 1809, Jefferson lifted the embargo. But hostilities still simmered.

On his way back home, Jefferson wrote a letter to the new president, acknowledging this tricky situation: "If peace can be preserved, I hope and trust you will have a smooth administration." Aiming to ease Madison's stress and affirm his continued support, Jefferson concluded his letter with a heartfelt expression: "I salute you with sincere affection and every sympathy of the heart."

It was a touching note, but it could do nothing to stave off reality: Madison was about to have anything but a "smooth administration." Soon after he took office, the British navy continued its aggression, reneging on a peace agreement and then forcing American sailors pulled from seized ships to serve on its behalf in its war against France. From Monticello, Jefferson watched in horror as one of his greatest fears—British power over America—loomed once again. Though he hoped that armed conflict with Britain could be avoided, he also advised Madison to prepare for the worst.

On November 5, 1811, the president sent his war message to Congress, urging the nation to defend its hard-fought independence. Jefferson responded with tender words of encouragement: "Your message had all the qualities it should possess, firm, rational, and dignified.... Heaven help you through all your difficulties." Those words arrived just in time: Before his first term ended, Madison found himself the nation's first wartime president. His presidency—not to mention the future of the embryonic country—rested on him winning what he soon dubbed "our second war of independence."

For all the rousing rhetoric of Madison's war declaration, the truth was that the nation was far from ready for war. Congress had not provided sufficient funds or other necessities for a standing army, while several states blasted "Mr. Madison's War" as a foolish exercise and refused to contribute their militias. American forces attempted to fight back on land and sea, but the ordeal proved to be a grueling and unpopular one. As war raged throughout 1812, Madison managed to win re-election over Federalist candidate DeWitt Clinton, but he still faced a barrage of criticism over the international debacle. At one point, New England even threatened to secede from the Union.

By 1814, the war looked all but lost. British troops stormed into DC, ransacking the city while laying waste to the White House. Dolley Madison stayed behind at the mansion just long enough to save Gilbert Stuart's famous painting of George Washington. Only after General Andrew Jackson won a resounding and unexpected victory over the British in the Battle at New Orleans in early 1815 could Americans finally rejoice; they had won a second War of Independence over their bitter adversary.

Madison left office in 1817 more popular than he had arrived, so successful that his former enemy John Adams was forced to acknowledge that Madison had "acquired more glory, and established more union, than all his three predecessors, Washington, Adams, and Jefferson, put together." Jefferson himself agreed with Adams's assessment, writing after the signing of the Treaty of Ghent, which ended the war, that "the cement of the Union is in the heartblood of every American." There could be no better evidence of shared historical purpose for Jefferson: that the presidency of his beloved First Friend marked the end of half a century of hostilities with Britain, thus ensuring a more perfect Union.

Jefferson and Madison's friendship was defined not just by the boisterous times but by the calmer ones, the moments when they withdrew from the swirl of politics and immersed themselves in books, walks, and lighthearted conversation. In retirement, they launched one final collaboration: establishing the University of Virginia. The university fulfilled Jefferson's lifelong dream of founding an academic temple dedicated to letters and science. As always, Madison stood loyally by his side, helping to hire the faculty and prepare books for the library.

For years, Jefferson had struggled to secure funding for the university, a struggle that would then be echoed in his own finances. In February 1826, he was forced to sell all of his property except for Monticello due to financial difficulties. He used the poignancy of the moment to write his best friend about the depth of his gratitude amid such great loss: "The friendship which has subsisted between us, now half a century, and the harmony of our political principles and pursuits, have been sources of constant happiness to me throughout that period." After that emotional note, the friends saw each other one last time, at the university's Board of Visitors meeting in April. Jefferson died a few months later on July 4, the fiftieth anniversary of the Declaration of Independence and of his friendship with Madison.

In his will, Jefferson gifted Madison a gold-headed walking stick, which Jefferson considered "the most elegant thing... I have ever seen." Both men understood the symbolism of such a gift. As Jefferson had written to Madison that February, "You have been a pillar of support through life. Take care of me when dead, and be assured that I shall leave you with my last affections." And Madison did take care of Jefferson after death, serving as rector of the university, as well as guarding Jefferson's sterling reputation when speaking to biographers and historians.

Madison, who as a sickly young man had always predicted his imminent demise, ultimately outlived most of his contemporaries. In June

1836, Dr. Robley Dunglison, Jefferson's personal physician, traveled from Baltimore to attend to the ailing Madison. Dr. Dunglison offered him stimulants to extend his life until July 4, so that he could die on the same day as Jefferson a decade later. As much as he was tempted to share one final thing with his friend, Madison refused.

After his burial at the family plot in Montpelier, Madison's family released a note he had written entitled "Advice to My Country." With Jeffersonian eloquence, the small man with the quiet voice now articulated his dying wish for the republic—the core truth that transcended whatever once separated the two partners:

"The advice nearest to my heart and deepest in my convictions is that the Union of the States be cherished and perpetuated."

CHAPTER 2

Franklin Pierce and Nathaniel Hawthorne

The Cost of Closeness

On the edges of the lawn outside the New Hampshire State House in Concord stands a statue honoring the only US president the state has ever produced. Sculpted in bronze by Augustus Lukeman, the statue rises above eye level, a dignified figure adorned in a bow tie and flowing cape. At its granite base, the inscription praises the man's achievements as a soldier and lawyer but remains utterly silent on his presidency. The statue's honorable place on that lawn belies the controversy of its unveiling in 1914, nearly a half century after the man's death of complications from alcohol abuse. That it took so long to commemorate him speaks to New Hampshire's ambivalence about its not-so-favorite son: Franklin Pierce.

Pierce's presidency has been broadly viewed as one of the least notable in the annals of the office. (One 2014 study found that only 7 percent of Americans could name him as president; only Chester A. Arthur was less recognizable.) His turbulent term began in 1853, when the nation, already a political and social tinderbox over the issue of slavery, elected the very man who would strike the match to ignite it. Full of promise when he entered the presidency, Pierce left the White House dispirited and despised. His fall from grace stood as the supreme paradox in a life defined by them. A gregarious, hard-drinking man of vast ambition, Pierce married a somber Calvinist woman who supported the temperance movement and wanted nothing more than to live a quiet life. An avowed patriot, his policies would all but assure that his beloved country would be pitched into the Civil War. A Northerner, he sided with Southerners on the issue of slavery. And a man who wanted everyone to like him, he was disliked by almost everybody by the end of his presidency.

Eighty miles to the southeast, down the Merrimack Valley into Massachusetts, stands another statue in Salem. It honors Franklin Pierce's dearest friend, Nathaniel Hawthorne, the only First Friend better known today than the man he befriended. Erected sixty-one years after Hawthorne's death, the statue—like Pierce's, cast in bronze and sitting on granite—was the first memorial to the town's most famous author, "Salem's Great Romancer." Linked inextricably to Pierce, Hawthorne possessed his own share of paradoxes. He enjoyed immense literary fame but could never translate his popularity into financial success. He moralized about the sins of the Puritan past but supported slavery. And, most significant, he remained Pierce's stalwart defender until the very end, even as he faced ostracism for his political views and scorn from his abolitionist peer group for publicly attaching himself to such an inept president. In short, Hawthorne learned the hard way that sometimes having a friend in high places can pose a terrible burden and exact tremendous costs.

Hawthorne once wrote, "Our most intimate friend is not he to whom we show the worst, but the best of our nature." To outsiders, such words rang insincere, given that Pierce seemed to show only the very worst of his nature. But those words testified to Hawthorne's utter loyalty to Pierce precisely when the nation stood on the brink of determining its moral character—one that many believed Pierce had sullied forever. Though widely condemned as a stunning mediocrity, to Hawthorne, his friend was simply a patriotic man plagued by inner turmoil—as morally conflicted as any of Hawthorne's transgressive characters. Ultimately, theirs would prove to be among the most tragic of First Friendships, ravaging their reputations and leaving a trail of ignominy behind them.

Franklin Pierce was born on November 23, 1804, in a white clapboard house built by his father, Benjamin. That house stood as solid evidence for Benjamin Pierce that he had survived (and would thrive) after the turmoil of the American Revolution. Back in 1775, when hostilities broke out at Lexington and Concord, Benjamin had immediately dropped his plow and walked off his father's farm to join the colonial army. A decade later, he left the war with distinction, having served bravely at the Battle of Bunker Hill and under George Washington's command. He moved to Hillsborough, New Hampshire, where he purchased fifty acres of land

and married his sweetheart, Anna Kendrick. Benjamin then immersed himself in politics, soon emerging as a prominent Democratic-Republican legislator. Now, with a new home and a new son (their fifth of what would be eight children), the Pierces set out to raise their family in post-Revolutionary America.

Years later, Franklin would reminisce fondly about his family's homestead, a symbol of simpler times: "I shall never cease to remember my birthplace with pride as well as affection." The house's spacious second floor boasted an ornate ballroom and parlor, which Benjamin Pierce sometimes used as a training space for the local militia he helped form. Mostly, though, he transformed the site into a public tavern, made possible by his liquor license. Though Hillsborough was located in New Hampshire backcountry, a land studded with hills, the Pierces' impressive home stood right on the highway. The tavern quickly became a popular gathering spot for eminent politicians and other travelers bringing news of the outside world. Inside those walls, the Pierces entertained guests, threw dances, and argued politics. Later, when Benjamin Pierce twice served as New Hampshire governor, he would also use the grand room as his campaign headquarters.

The young Franklin thus came to associate his family's tavern with both politics and play—those two elements inseparable from each other. He grew accustomed to the house as a social center, full of noise and excitement. But the tavern could also encourage self-destruction; his mother, though far more affectionate and easygoing than his father, often drank to excess when facing a depressive episode. Eventually, the mature Franklin would inherit these psychological troubles, turning to the tavern as a place not only where political deals happened but also where political stress could be forgotten.

Those dark secrets, however, remained hidden among the privileged gentry of Hillsborough. Like the town's other ambitious parents, Benjamin and Anna strived to give their children the best education possible at local schools. If he learned how to read and write from the state's best teachers, Franklin learned about politics at home from his father, a domineering man who had helped put Jefferson's devotees in control of New

Hampshire politics the same year as Franklin's birth. Growing up, Franklin learned that the Federalists were no better than the despised British whom his father had battled during the Revolution. He would sit by the fireside, listening intently to Benjamin's wartime stories and absorbing lessons about the sanctity of the Revolution and their hard-won liberty. And when the War of 1812 began, eight-year-old Franklin watched in admiration as two of his older brothers left to fight and his father traveled to the capital to oppose Federalist legislators. Throughout the war, Franklin regularly headed to the post office down the road to check for letters and newspapers.

The War of 1812 left an indelible mark on the impressionable boy, even after it ended and his parents sent him to an academy in Hancock for more advanced studies. The boy soon grew homesick for his father's "elegant mansion," so one Sunday he decided to trudge twelve miles back toward the hills. After feeding Franklin dinner, his father drove him partway to Hancock before kicking him out of the chaise and ordering him to walk the remaining distance in a rainstorm. Later, Pierce would recall this moment as a "turning point" in his life, when he learned the difference between reality and fantasy, the importance of not ruffling feathers and of doing what he was told.

After that, every time he was allowed to return home—including later from Phillips Exeter Academy—he couldn't wait to slip inside his father's tavern. Amid the hubbub, Franklin imbibed Benjamin Pierce's lessons about Federalist treason, the fragility of the Union, and the need for firm loyalty to Democratic-Republican values. As Hawthorne later wrote, Pierce clung to his faith "in all the simplicity with which he inherited it from his father. It has been the principle and is the explanation [of his career]."

In contrast to Pierce's loud and lively childhood, Nathaniel Hawthorne learned early about loss, loneliness, and guilt—recurring themes of his future literary works. Born on America's twenty-eighth birthday, July 4, 1804, Hawthorne belonged to the sixth generation of a staunchly Puritan family from Salem, Massachusetts. His early ancestors included John "Hathorne," a leading judge for the Salem witch trials (Hawthorne later changed the spelling of his name to hide his ancestor's shameful past). While Pierce grew up idolizing his father, Nathaniel was only four years old when his father, a sea captain, died of yellow fever while on a voyage to the West Indies. The boy's childhood would be shadowed by his mother's grief. Now dependent on relatives, she took Nathaniel and his two sisters to live with her extended family in Salem, where they slowly tried to piece their lives back together. But soon after Nathaniel's ninth birthday, his leg was hit during a game of "bat and ball." Though several doctors could find nothing wrong, the mysterious injury kept him bedridden for a year. A highly imaginative child, Hawthorne spent this recuperation period reading and writing avidly.

Three years later, in 1816, Nathaniel's life took a turn for the better when his uncles built his family a house in Raymond, Maine, then a part of Massachusetts. In this new setting, the twelve-year-old boy came to love the wildness of nature, embracing the solitude of "scattered clearings" and reveling in the freedom of exploring the "primeval woods." Once he reached age fifteen, Hawthorne had to leave behind this self-contained world and return to Salem for two years of prep school. Despite feeling homesick for his beloved Maine, the intense studies fired his creative mind. Soon he began producing his own handwritten newspaper called *The Spectator*, which featured news stories, essays, and humor pieces—a small foreshadowing of greater creations to come.

In 1821, at his uncle's insistence, Hawthorne attended Bowdoin College in Brunswick, Maine, just thirty miles east of Raymond. Known for educating the sons of the elite since its 1794 founding, Bowdoin also offered a relatively inexpensive tuition rate for the financially strapped Hawthornes. While Harvard cost $600 for first-year students, Bowdoin charged only $34. Bowdoin's prerequisites for new students included knowledge of Latin, ancient Greek, geography, and algebra, as well as a certificate of "good moral character." Hawthorne fit all of these qualifications, passed the entrance examination easily, then enrolled the same day.

That day proved momentous in Hawthorne's life for one other reason.

Earlier in the morning, during his 120-mile ride from Salem to Bowdoin, the stagecoach swung by Portland, Maine, to pick up another passenger. That passenger was none other than Franklin Pierce, returning to college for his second year. Two other incoming Bowdoin students also jumped onto that stagecoach: future naval reformer Horatio Bridge and future congressman Jonathan Cilley, both of whom became close friends of Pierce and Hawthorne (Cilley would die in 1838 in a duel Pierce tried to avert with a fellow congressman). Years later, Bridge recalled that serendipitous journey: "drawn by four strong, spirited horses, and bowling along at the average speed of ten miles an hour. The exhilarating pace, the smooth roads, and the juxtaposition of the insiders tended, in a high degree, to the promotion of enjoyment and good fellowship, which might ripen into lasting friendship."

Pierce operated as the ebullient center of attention in any social situation, as his travel mates undoubtedly witnessed that day as they traveled to Bowdoin and for the remainder of their time on the bucolic campus. Hawthorne, on the other hand, seemed as reserved as Pierce was outgoing, an introverted man with an aversion to looking people in the eyes. "I cannot remember that I ever heard Hawthorne laugh," recalled John S.C. Abbott, another Bowdoin classmate. Hawthorne's taciturn manner and constant watchfulness made him an enigma, even to close friends such as Oliver Wendell Holmes, who admitted that talking to Hawthorne "was almost like love-making, and his shy, beautiful soul had to be wooed from its bashful prudency." Cilley found Hawthorne even more impenetrable, living "in a mysterious world of thought and imagination which he never permits me to enter."

Pierce's vivacity, matched with Hawthorne's reticence, produced an alchemy that worked for both men. Profoundly insecure and prone to self-criticism, Hawthorne relished Pierce's company because Pierce modeled precisely who he could never be, someone who lived boldly and "moved confidently in the world, engaging in manly pursuits," in the words of biographer Peter A. Wallner. Hawthorne himself admitted as much: "It contributes greatly towards a man's moral and intellectual health, to be brought into habits of companionship with individuals unlike himself, who care little for his pursuits, and whose sphere and abilities he must go out of himself to appreciate."

Though unquestionably bright and well educated, Pierce did not share the same devotion for his studies as his best friend, far preferring hunting, fishing, and other nonacademic pursuits. Halfway through his college years, Bowdoin ranked Pierce lowest in his class, a distinction he earned by skipping classes to go for walks in the woods, or bursting into his friends' rooms during evening study sessions to engage in "furniture-breaking wrestling matches." Ignoring school regulations, Pierce also regularly frequented Ward's Tavern near the edge of campus, a place that reminded him of home. Not until his third year at Bowdoin did he finally settle down and apply himself, moving up to an admirable fifth in his class. As Hawthorne would later explain:

> During the earlier part of his college course, it may be doubted whether Pierce was distinguished for scholarship. But, for the last two years, he appeared to grow more intent on the business at hand, and, without losing any of his vivacious qualities as a companion, was evidently resolved to gain an honorable elevation in his class. His habits of attention, and obedience to college discipline, were of the strictest character.

Despite his apparent nonchalance, Pierce also progressed because he gravitated toward people whose intellects surpassed his own. The lure of such cerebral companions drew Pierce into Bowdoin's thriving literary culture, composed of two societies: the Peucinians and the Atheneans. He enthusiastically joined the Atheneans, the less elitist of the two, and successfully recruited Hawthorne to sign up as well. Pierce even prevailed on Hawthorne to take a committee position, an experience the shy novelist would later describe as his "first and last appearance in public life." Pierce, on the other hand, eventually became president of the Atheneans and emerged as a standout student leader. He also organized Bowdoin's first military company, another homage to his father, and again attempted to draft the decidedly unmilitary Hawthorne. The company would march up and down campus with "Captain" Pierce at the head and an awkward Hawthorne trailing in the rear ranks. Throughout their college years together, the friends pulled one another in directions that often seemed uncomfortable or foreign but that tightened their bond and shaped them into the men they would become.

The two remained in close touch even after Pierce graduated in 1824. Before heading back to Bowdoin for his final year, Hawthorne visited Pierce in Hillsborough, where they hiked, hunted, and fished. On the day of Hawthorne's departure, the friends walked beneath a stand of thick, towering walnut trees. Hawthorne took out a pocket knife and etched the initials F.P. and N.H. into one of them. Decades later, after both men had become famous, the walnut tree would attract countless tourists wishing to glimpse that evidence of their friendship.

Upon returning to Bowdoin for his final term (and his first without Pierce by his side), Hawthorne finally found his life's calling. "I do not want to be a doctor and live by men's diseases; nor a minister to live by their sins; nor a lawyer and live by their quarrels," he wrote passionately to his mother. "So I don't see that there is anything left for me but to be an author." It was a bold professional choice at a time when few (one estimate put the number at a dozen) tried to make a living by writing fiction. But Hawthorne certainly fit the archetype of the tormented artist of the Romantic era. For the next twelve years, he isolated himself in "my lonely chamber" at his mother's house, focused solely on perfecting his craft. "Here I have written many tales, many that have been burned to ashes, many that doubtless deserved the same fate," he confessed. But the outside world would soon provide plenty of fodder for Hawthorne's writing—and, as his dearest friend ascended the political ladder, pull Hawthorne out of his self-imposed isolation.

Fresh out of college, Franklin Pierce ventured into the political world that he had first glimpsed at his father's tavern. He certainly looked the part: a robust and attractive young man—"Handsome Frank," as some called him, with auburn hair, blue-gray eyes, and a square jaw. He also stood out for his convivial, charming, and magnetic personality, which enabled him to make friends easily. And with his innate gift for public speaking, a skill he had honed at Bowdoin, Pierce became known for his ability to deliver a speech without so much as glancing at his notes. It surprised no one then when he shot to political stardom shortly after graduating from Bowdoin.

In 1828, Pierce won his first public office as Hillsborough town moderator. His real political baptism came later that year when he and his father campaigned hard for General Andrew Jackson, a hero from the War of 1812 whose humble origins and rural roots attracted ordinary farmers and the working class. Jackson's insistence that government must be made more representative of "the people" aligned perfectly with the Pierces' Jeffersonian values. Though Jackson lost New Hampshire on his way to the White House, the experience of stumping for him enabled Pierce to clarify his political stance and, in the process, help secure his future. His devotion to Jackson even led people to nickname Pierce "Young Hickory of Granite Hills," a reference to Jackson's moniker "Old Hickory" and to Pierce's beloved home state.

The following year, Pierce won a seat in the New Hampshire legislature, a proud moment that coincided with his father's second term as governor. By 1831, at age twenty-six, he began serving as the youngest-ever Speaker in the New Hampshire House. During this time, Pierce emerged as a faithful member of the state's Democratic Party, trumpeting popular rule by farmers, craftsmen, and small businessmen. Echoing both Jackson and his father, Pierce wrote to a friend that "the citizens are convinced that Jeffersonian principles are the principles for a free people, and I trust they have no notion of renouncing their faith." New Hampshire Democrats like Pierce articulated a creed that supported the "common man": building an agrarian society; protecting state sovereignty; limiting centralized government; removing concentrated economic power from the hands of special interests; and hewing closely to the Constitution.

Campaigning on these principles, Pierce easily won election to the US House of Representatives in 1832, at the age of twenty-nine. The timing of his move to Washington could not have been more fortuitous, right when Jackson had secured his second term as president. Pierce as a congressman garnered a reputation for being a "doughface"—a Northern man with Southern principles, someone who bucked the trend of his region by accepting the continuation of slavery for the sake of national unity. Throughout his time in the House, Pierce strongly supported Jackson's policies and voted the Democratic Party line on nearly every issue.

Continuing his rapid ascent, Pierce moved up to the Senate in 1837, seemingly destined for national prominence. Their old friend Bridge was more cynical in a letter to Hawthorne, describing Pierce's Senate win as "an instance of what a man can do by trying. With no very remarkable talents, he at the age of 34 fills one of the highest stations in the nation." Bridge's premonition proved more correct than even he could have known. Washington in the 1830s was an uninviting place, with putrid swamps, constant political intrigue, and shabby living quarters. Many politicians, overexerted and homesick, sought escape in alcohol—and Pierce was no exception. Before long, the Washington grapevine pulsed with stories of his drunken escapades and frequent carousing. Because of his late nights, Pierce was often absent from his Senate seat and drafted no notable bills.

When he *was* present, Pierce proved more of a follower than a leader, reflexively adhering to his party's Jacksonian stance. Only one cause awakened his zeal: opposition to the abolitionist movement. He continued to believe that the Union must be preserved by striking compromises between proslavery and antislavery forces. Many of Pierce's Washington friends were Southerners, including future Confederate president Jefferson Davis of Mississippi, who would become Pierce's closest political ally. Even as fellow Northerners began voicing their disapproval of him, Pierce remained convinced that he had taken the wiser stance: North and South must be regarded as "absolutely inseparable," and such inseparability could be maintained only through honorable concessions.

Like Pierce, Hawthorne also viewed abolitionism as a challenge to several of his deeply held concerns. Many of Hawthorne's own friends were loyal southern Democrats who did not believe the slavery issue should undermine the bonds of Union. Furthermore, as someone who would ultimately benefit from Democratic patronage, Hawthorne had little incentive to appear at odds with the party leadership. Hawthorne viewed Jackson as the rare leader who would aid a sorely overlooked segment of society: poor, working-class whites. The issue, he told a friend, was not about race but class: "I have not... the slightest sympathy for the slaves; or, at least, not half as much as for the laboring white, who, I believe, are ten times worse off than the Southern negroes." To push for ill-advised social reforms was simply reckless, in Hawthorne's view, meddling with one institution in order to replace it with something far more dangerous. Together, Hawthorne and Pierce clung to these convictions, even as vast historical forces challenged the friends to abandon them.

Despite his proclivity for the bottle and general mediocrity in the Senate, Pierce still appeared to be on a fast track to the presidency. But the truth was far more complex, for Pierce remained a man veering between extremes, as if walking along a tightrope strung between his political ambitions and his pliable nature. In November 1834, he had married Jane Means Appleton, the daughter of a former Bowdoin president. Franklin and Jane seemed like total opposites in both personality and ideology. The Appleton family were Whigs, a party that arose in opposition to Andrew Jackson during the 1830s. Jane was also an ardent supporter of the temperance movement, even though she married into a family notorious for being heavy drinkers. Unlike her affable husband, Jane was a reclusive and morose woman who hated living in Washington, complaining that the city's suffocating humidity worsened her fragile health. She refused to move permanently to the capital, even after Franklin became a US senator. Above all, Jane believed that slavery should be abolished, while Pierce never wavered from his stance that whites should be free to hold human property.

The tension between Jane and Franklin was exacerbated by a string of unfathomable tragedies. The couple lost their first son three days after Jane gave birth in 1836. Seven years later, they lost a second son at the age of four to epidemic typhus. Not surprisingly, then, they doted on their third son, Benjamin or "Bennie," who was born in 1841. The following year, Pierce made the rare decision to depart the Senate before his first term ended, in part under pressure from his wife. Despite being a devout woman, Jane found her faith provided little comfort, and she lived in constant fear of what horror would befall them next. After the birth of her second son in 1839, she had found an excuse to move back to New Hampshire. Lonely in Washington, tempted by the bottle, and frustrated by the direction the newly empowered Whigs were taking the country, Pierce finally gave up and resigned his seat in February 1842, a full year before his term expired.

He returned home to New Hampshire, settling back into the old Pierce homestead in which he had grown up. In Concord, Pierce built a prosperous law practice, proving to be a master at swaying juries with his oratorical flourishes. People from across New Hampshire would fight for a seat in the courtroom to watch him in action—a popular form of entertainment at the time.

Even as a famous trial lawyer, however, Pierce couldn't fully resist the allure of politics. When he resigned from the Senate, Pierce made a promise to Jane he would never again run for political office. Left unsaid was whether that included accepting political appointments. Just months after his return, he interpreted his promise narrowly, accepting an offer to become chairman of the State Democratic Committee. He bought a house located just down the street from the New Hampshire statehouse and dug into party work when he wasn't tending to his law practice. The focus of his causes, however, changed under Jane's influence. Pierce suddenly stopped drinking, even becoming president of the state temperance association, and he led an effective drive to outlaw liquor in Concord. His approach to state politics also foreshadowed one he would take as president. Subordinating his own views to party unity, Pierce valued moderation and compromise above all.

As Pierce's legal career blossomed, Hawthorne also began making a name for himself. In 1829, four years after graduating from Bowdoin, he published his debut novel, *Fanshawe*, but insisted on anonymity because he doubted its literary value. The novel was set in a small country college much like Bowdoin, and one of its chief protagonists, Edward Walcott, greatly resembled Pierce: a man with handsome features and the social grace that enabled him to move easily through "polished society" despite his "youthful follies [that] sometimes, perhaps, approach[ed] near to vices." Then, in 1837, Hawthorne finally achieved a hint of literary prominence with the publication of *Twice-Told Tales*, a collection of eighteen short stories. The collection nearly sold out, earning the author praise for his "fine moral tone" and "the sedate, quiet dignity displayed in his diction." Yet, despite the positive reviews and early strong sales, Hawthorne ultimately earned little to no money from the endeavor, foreshadowing a trend that would recur throughout his literary career. Nor did it lead to any of the stable editorial jobs that he craved. His life suddenly seemed to be at a standstill precisely when it should have been skyrocketing.

Still a US senator at the time, Pierce recognized his friend needed a boost, and he schemed with his old Bowdoin classmates Cilley and Bridge to help Hawthorne secure a federal appointment to serve as historian on a South Sea expedition recently authorized by Congress. Hawthorne eagerly accepted the offer, confiding to poet Henry Wadsworth Longfellow (another Bowdoin pal) that he felt secluded and in need of adventure: "I have not lived, but only dreamed about living." Though Bridge warned Hawthorne not to get his hopes up, he reassured him that Pierce would never rest until he had helped his friend. Through no fault of Pierce's, the job never materialized, leaving Hawthorne even more frustrated and broke.

Hawthorne did, however, find more success in his romantic life. In 1838, he met the transcendentalist and illustrator Sophia Peabody, and they became engaged the following year. Two years later, just before Pierce left the Senate, Hawthorne (still unwed) ended up moving to Brook Farm, a utopian commune founded by Unitarian minister George Ripley, where he would meet the transcendentalists Ralph Waldo Emerson and Henry David Thoreau. Though Hawthorne did not agree with transcendentalism, he thought that living at Brook Farm would help him save money to marry Sophia and also give him time to write. Very quickly, though, Hawthorne realized he had made a big mistake. His designated job was to shovel and transport manure, an ordeal that left him with blistered hands and little time for writing. The solitary Hawthorne also detested the required social activities. According to another resident, Georgiana Kirby: "No one could be more out of place than he in a mixed company.... He was morbidly shy and reserved, needing to be shielded from his fellows." After just six months, Hawthorne left Brook Farm—disillusioned, exhausted, and still broke.

His misery at Brook Farm, however, convinced him that he should move forward with marrying Sophia. They married in July 1842, then moved to Concord, Massachusetts, to settle down. They would go on to enjoy a long and happy marriage, but Hawthorne continued struggling to make ends meet—that is, until Pierce intervened. In 1844, Pierce and Bridge came to visit Hawthorne; the sight of them entering the home, recalled Sophia, resembled that of "two ministers of providence" who had arrived to save the couple from financial ruin. Bridge immediately loaned the newlyweds $100, while Pierce started discussing possible job opportunities in the federal government.

Since Hawthorne was a Jacksonian Democrat, Pierce knew he could help his friend by exploiting his political connections—crucial during a time when public offices were still awarded according to the spoils system that had flourished under Andrew Jackson. This time, the job would not fall through. Pierce happened to be campaigning hard for James K. Polk, a friend from Congress who was launching a dark horse bid for the presidency. It took more than a year, but once Polk landed in the White House, Pierce made sure to secure Hawthorne a position as surveyor for the Customs Collection District of Salem and Beverly. The post didn't make Hawthorne rich, but it finally gave him financial stability and, more important, the opportunity to continue plying his craft. Through Pierce's generosity, Hawthorne likely avoided falling into even deeper despair—a twist of fate that would be repeated in years to come.

Meanwhile, Polk also tried to reward Pierce with several patronage positions, including an appointment as US attorney general. Pierce turned down the summons, instead asking Polk to give him a commission to fight in the Mexican-American War, which had just erupted in April 1846. Knowing how vital military service had been to his father's political rise, Pierce quietly began eyeing his own return to politics, no matter what he had sworn to Jane. And President Polk did not hesitate to repay Pierce's past campaign favors.

Less than a year after the Mexican-American War broke out, Pierce began serving as a brigadier general in charge of volunteer regiments from New Hampshire, some 2,500 men all told—even though his sole military experience dated back to his unofficial role as "Captain" of the Bowdoin Cadets. Dispatched to the Mexican port of Vera Cruz, he led his troops on a harrowing, 150-mile journey through enemy territory to reinforce General Winfield Scott's forces with much-needed troops, supplies, and munitions. Much of the time, though, freak injuries and illness kept him from fighting in the most critical battles. During the Battle of Contreras, Pierce was thrown off his horse, then passed out in pain from his injured leg—a detail his political opponents would later seize upon by nicknaming him "Fainting Frank." Nonetheless, in late 1847, Pierce arrived home to a hero's welcome and resumed his law practice, reinstating his promise to Jane that he would never again pursue public office.

An increasingly heated political landscape would make it all but impossible for Pierce to keep this promise. By the start of the 1850s, the Democratic Party was facing deep sectional divisions over what to do about slavery as the nation expanded westward. Northern Democrats tended to argue for free soil in the western territories or for eradicating the institution altogether, while Southern Democrats sought to preserve their way of life by extending slavery to new lands. In an attempt to avert this crisis, Congress passed the Compromise of 1850, which admitted California as a free state in exchange for no federal restrictions on slavery in the Utah and New Mexico Territories. Additionally, the compromise banned slavery in Washington, DC, while passing a more stringent Fugitive Slave Act, which required Northerners to return escaped slaves to their owners.

For the time being, the Compromise of 1850 preserved the Union. But a mere two years later, in June 1852, the still-warring Democrats gathered in Baltimore to choose a presidential nominee. Though the 288 delegates agreed on a platform pledging support for the Compromise of 1850, they ended up deadlocked over the three leading candidates: Stephen Douglas, James Buchanan, and Lewis Cass. They balloted 48 times before nominating Pierce, who epitomized the meaning of a dark horse candidate, having sat out national politics for the past decade. With his devotion to the Democratic Party, his reputation as a moderate, and his service in the Mexican-American War, Pierce had emerged as a Northerner who would defer to whatever the largely Southern party leadership dictated.

For the first two days of the convention, Pierce idled at a telegraph office in Concord and nervously tracked the deliberations by wire. When news of his unexpected nomination finally reached New Hampshire, he felt as stunned as anybody. His wife—who had no idea her husband had even been pursuing the candidacy—fainted, prompting eleven-year-old Benjamin to express his hope that his father would lose. In a letter to his mother, Bennie wrote, "I hope he won't be elected, for I should not like to be at Washington. And I know you would not be either."

But Bennie's wish would be snuffed out by none other than Pierce's anemic opponent. The Whigs nominated General Winfield Scott, Pierce's commanding officer during the Mexican-American War. Nicknamed "Old Fuss and Feathers," a reference to his obsession with military tradition and decorum, Scott left even many Whigs uninspired by his candidacy. Despite his exemplary military career, his staid, long-winded messages on the campaign trail carried all the excitement of the dried beans his soldiers once ate. Faced with such a weak competitor, Pierce did virtually no campaigning at all. Even though the electorate barely knew him, he followed the counsel of party elders to do and say as little as possible, spending most of his time in Concord. But the Democrats still fought hard for Pierce, with one witty campaign slogan proclaiming, "We Polked you in 1844; we shall Pierce you in 1852." The Whigs responded by taking a stab at Pierce's alcoholism and questionable war record, calling him the "hero of many a well-fought bottle."

The most compelling case for Pierce's candidacy would be delivered in print, through his campaign biography. During the first half of the nineteenth century, long before massive television and social media expenditures and slick, ad-agency-created commercials, candidates relied heavily on biographers to detail their accomplishments and to define their characters to voters. Pierce considered several writers before selecting one who could craft his life story with true skill and flourish: Nathaniel Hawthorne.

Ironically, twenty-three years earlier, shortly after the publication of his first novel, *Fanshawe*, Hawthorne had written Pierce, who was still Speaker of the New Hampshire House:

> I sincerely congratulate you on all your public honors, in possession and in prospect. If they continue to accumulate so rapidly, you will be at the summit of political eminence by that time when men are usually just beginning to make a figure.... It's a pity that I am not in a situation to exercise my pen in your behalf.

Now Hawthorne had the chance to do just that—and from a position of greater prominence.

Despite having never written a work of nonfiction, Hawthorne certainly knew how high the current stakes were amid a time of intense partisanship. He also knew that this moment offered a rare opportunity to finally achieve financial security for himself and his family. Over the previous three years, Hawthorne had published his two most popular novels to date—*The Scarlet Letter* and *The House of the Seven Gables*—yet like all of his previous works, their literary success didn't translate into financial riches, leaving Hawthorne sorely frustrated. So without wasting any time, he volunteered his talents for *The Life of Franklin Pierce* in a letter to the candidate:

> It has occurred to me that you might have some thoughts of getting me to write the necessary biography. Whatever service I can do you,

> I need not say, would be at your command; but I do not believe that I should succeed in this matter so well as many other men. It needs long thought with me, in order to produce anything good, and, after all, my style and qualities, as a writer, are certainly not those of the broadest popularity, such as are requisite for a task of this kind.

Though the letter reeked of false modesty, Hawthorne sincerely hoped he could help his friend win the presidency, in part because of what it would mean for him. If the campaign biography proved a success, as Hawthorne suspected it would, then he would be guaranteed a stipend that far exceeded what he could ever make as a writer. Even better, whatever job he landed would come with few onerous duties, allowing him time to write without financial pressures. Given these calculations, the subtext of Hawthorne's self-effacing letter suggests how much he in fact wanted to write the campaign biography—as both a gesture of friendship and an investment in his own future. A delighted Pierce did not hesitate to accept.

Hawthorne's decision to take on the project immediately raised hackles among the members of his New England family, neighbors, and literary peers, all of whom disapproved of Pierce's support for Southern slaveowners. Now that Hawthorne had become an acclaimed novelist, it also seemed foolhardy to ignore the sentiments of his largely progressive book-buying public. Well aware of the risks of assuming such an assignment, Hawthorne took some precautions. In the preamble to the biography, he made sure to downplay any perception of himself as partisan, writing that he was "so little of a politician" that he could barely "call himself the member of any party." In what would become a noticeable pattern, Hawthorne used the power of his pen not only to defend his friend but also to safeguard his own reputation.

As one would expect, the 144-page book lauded Pierce's "marvelous and mystic-influence of character" and his "high and fearless spirit." It highlighted Pierce's fidelity to his past, the ways in which he had been shaped by the valor and honor of his father, the Revolutionary War hero: "From infancy upward, the boy had before his eyes, as the model on which he might instinctively form himself, one of the best specimens of sterling New England character, developed in a life of simple habits, yet of elevated action." Explaining away the candidate's own lack of civil or military accomplishments, Hawthorne portrayed his friend as a modest man, comfortable with making "little noise" and slipping "into the background."

In attempting to explain why Pierce hadn't authored any important legislation while in Congress, Hawthorne wrote that his friend "rendered unobtrusive, though not unimportant, services to the public." Despite the fact that Pierce as a senator had gained more of a reputation for partying and drinking, Hawthorne claimed that his friend had stayed inconspicuous out of deference to more established intellects in the chamber: "With his usual tact, and exquisite sense of propriety, he saw that it was not the time for him to step forward prominently." Hawthorne's sanguine characterization seemed perfectly engineered to calm those who worried that Pierce might be a leader who would overturn the status quo.

Hawthorne's romanticizing carried over to the most delicate and controversial issue swirling around Pierce's candidacy: slavery. Rather than tackling the morality of the institution itself, Hawthorne pitted the drive to abolish slavery against Pierce's devotion to preserving the Union. While abolitionism would tear the country apart, Hawthorne alleged, Pierce had made the difficult decision of stomaching slavery because he "dared to love... his whole, united, native country" rather than "the mistiness of philanthropic theory." Hawthorne entirely skirted the question of how, precisely, the nation should deal with slavery's sectional implications. Instead, he claimed that a wise man like Pierce "looks upon slavery as one of those evils which divine providence does not leave to be remedied by human contrivances, but which, in its own good time, by some means impossible to be anticipated, but of the simplest and easiest operation, when all its uses shall have been fulfilled, it causes to vanish like a dream." For Southerners, Hawthorne's promise—that slavery would simply "vanish" in due time—came as a relief, a way to straddle the line between moral dubiousness and economic profitability.

A few weeks after the book's publication, Hawthorne joined Pierce at

Bowdoin for the school's semicentennial celebration. Though reviews of the book broke largely along party lines, the two friends remained in a jovial mood. The outside world might not understand their friendship, but nothing could lessen their affection for one another. "I love him," Hawthorne said plainly during the trip. At one point during their sojourn, Pierce commissioned George Healey, the foremost portraitist of his day, to paint Hawthorne for the then-princely sum of $1,000. The painting would be on exhibit in Washington throughout Pierce's term and would remain in the Pierce family for more than a century.

With Hawthorne's biography and a campaign emphasizing national unity, Pierce won the presidency in a landslide, securing a whopping 254 electoral votes from twenty-seven states. General Scott received only 42 electoral votes from four states—the last gasp of the struggling Whig Party. Pierce also won the popular vote (though more narrowly), and the other Democrats sharing the ballot coasted on his success by securing substantial majorities in both the House and Senate. At age forty-eight, Pierce had capped his promising political career by becoming the then youngest president ever.

Everyone agreed that Hawthorne's best-selling biography powered Pierce to victory, but interpretations over its accuracy varied widely. While smug Democrats hailed the book as a faithful record of the facts, bitter Whigs blasted it as nothing more than political lies and hogwash. For many critics, Hawthorne's Pierce was a laughable attempt to frame an average backbencher as the blessed heir of Andrew Jackson. As the famed Massachusetts educator, committed Whig, and Hawthorne's brother-in-law Horace Mann contended, "If he makes out Pierce to be a great man or a brave man, it will be the greatest work of fiction he ever wrote." Even Hawthorne himself privately admitted that he had massaged the truth just a bit: "Though the story is true, yet it took a romancer to do it."

Hawthorne might have been a skilled "romancer," but his payment didn't seem to reflect that fact: a mere $300, with no royalties at all. The book's success also opened an unwanted line of work for the author: "I have had as many office-seekers knocking at my door...as if I were a prime minister." By this time, Hawthorne grew increasingly impatient about gaining fairer compensation. After all, he had assumed an outsize burden: defending Pierce's anti-abolitionist views and Southern sympathies even though doing so would clearly alienate his Northern neighbors. In a letter to a friend, Hawthorne complained that "the biography has cost me hundreds of friends, here at the north... in consequence of what I say on the slavery question." Pierce seems not to have grasped how much of a toll writing the biography had on his friend. But for the sensitive Hawthorne, the project had not been a particularly pleasant one—rushed to publication, a product less of studied inspiration than of manipulation. In its own way, *The Life of Franklin Pierce* proved just as much a tale of redemption as Hawthorne's classic novel *The Scarlet Letter*. In light of the effort it demanded, Hawthorne now had one expectation: "Pierce owes me something."

Hawthorne got what he was hoping for (and thought owed) in the spring of 1853, when Pierce appointed him US consul in Liverpool, England. The moment echoed what had happened nearly a decade earlier, when Pierce had used his connections to pull Hawthorne out of financial ruin. Funded by fees on heavy American trade through Liverpool, this foreign service position was considered the most lucrative at the time, second in prestige only to the embassy in London. Though it required few duties and provided a steady income for Hawthorne to focus on his writing, he still insisted that the job fell short of his economic needs: "A man might be comfortable with this in a New England village, but not, I assure you, as the representative of America in the greatest commercial city in England." Those words did not go unheeded by Pierce; in 1855, Congress would approve a much higher $7,500 annual salary for the unsatisfied consul.

Putting aside all the politics, spoils, and coming conflicts, the novelist maintained great faith in his friend's abilities to lead the nation. As he wrote their old classmate Bridge in 1853:

> I have come seriously to the conclusion that he has in him many of the elements of a great ruler, and... he may run a great career. His talents are administrative; he has a subtle faculty of making affairs

> roll onward according to his will, and of influencing their course without showing any trace of his action.

Hawthorne concluded, with confidence, that Pierce "is deep, deep, deep luck withal! Nothing can ruin him."

That prediction would soon prove to be among the worst Hawthorne ever made.

Tragedy struck two months before Pierce's inauguration, just as he was turning his attention to assembling his Cabinet. On a snowy day in January 1853, Franklin, Jane, and eleven-year-old Bennie were returning to Concord, New Hampshire, from Andover, Massachusetts, after attending the funeral of Jane's favorite uncle. Husband and wife sat side by side, with Bennie in the seat behind them. Just minutes into the short trip, the two-car locomotive derailed and plummeted down a twenty-foot embankment, landing on its roof. The train car, the *New York Times* reported, "broke in pieces like a cigar box." Franklin and Jane Pierce escaped any serious injury, but Bennie was killed. As one witness recounted in horror, the boy "one minute so beautiful, so full of life [was] struck so violently as to remove the upper portion of his head." Even worse, Pierce could not prevent Jane from seeing their son's mutilated body in the wreckage. So stricken with grief and guilt (why didn't she have Bennie next to her?), Jane did not attend the boy's funeral, where twelve of Bennie's schoolmates carried his casket.

Now having lost all three of their sons in childhood, the Pierces felt they might never recover. Though in the brutal grip of his own grief, Franklin did all he could to comfort his devastated wife. During this time, one family member hailed Pierce for being "one of the noblest and most tender-hearted of human beings." Privately, however, Pierce struggled to overcome his anguish and face his impending duties. In a letter to Jefferson Davis sent the day after Bennie's burial, Pierce confessed, "I presume you may already have heard of the terrible catastrophe upon the railroad, which took from us our only child, a fine boy 11 years old." After lamenting his wife's precarious state, "crushed to the Earth by the fearful bereavement," Pierce added, "How I shall be able to summon my manhood and gather up my energies for the duties before me it is hard for me to see." Adding to Pierce's burden, Jane began confiding to friends that she believed Bennie's gruesome death had been God's punishment for her husband's vanity in seeking the presidency.

Pierce took Jane's criticism to heart: At his inauguration on March 4, 1853, he would not swear on the Bible, afraid that God was punishing him for his sins. Jane did not accompany her husband to the ceremonies, and no inaugural ball had been planned. Eighty thousand people crowded into Washington, though only twenty thousand braved the snow for the ceremonies. Among those battling the frigid weather was Hawthorne, who had traveled from Massachusetts to witness the moment when his friend would ascend to the presidency.

Standing in the East Portico of the Capitol, a grieving Pierce proceeded to recite his 3,319-word inaugural address purely from memory, beginning with an allusion to Bennie's death and a humble plea to his audience: "You have summoned me in my weakness. You must sustain me by your strength." He continued, revealing his deep insecurity over winning the highest position in the land: "It is a relief to feel that no heart but my own can know the personal regret and bitter sorrow over which I have been borne to a position so suitable for others rather than desirable for myself." He did not, however, hold back in setting the tone for his administration, emphasizing the importance of saving the Union by respecting the Compromise of 1850. Despite being a New Englander, the new president clearly stated his support for slavery. "I believe," Pierce said, "that involuntary servitude, as it exists in different States of this Confederacy, is recognized by the Constitution. I believe that it stands like any other admitted right."

These formed the cornerstones of his administration: strict adherence to the Constitution and strong support for states' rights. Pierce urged his compatriots to look to "the founders of the republic" and their "comprehensive wisdom" for how best to deal with slavery. Otherwise, the new president vowed, "to every theory of society or government, whether the offspring of feverish ambition or morbid enthusiasm, calculated to dissolve the bonds of law and affection which unite us, I shall interpose a ready and stern resistance." His position, however controversial, would not budge. In closing, Pierce expressed his ultimate (naïve) wish: "I fervently hope that the [slavery] question is at rest, and that no sectional or fanatical excitement may again threaten the durability of our institutions or obscure the light of our prosperity."

Unfortunately for Franklin Pierce and for the country, the question was far from being "at rest." The issue of slavery cut through America like a cleaver, and it would persist through all four years of Pierce's calamitous single term in the White House. Bennie's death only exacerbated Pierce's self-destructive tendencies. The grieving father arrived in Washington tired, depressed, and demoralized. Observers noted a change in his appearance, a solemn quality that differed markedly from his youthful amiability. His sorrows, combined with his new responsibilities, made him even more resistant to change than he might have been. His wife's inconsolable state did not help the situation either. Jane secluded herself in the upstairs bedroom for the next two years, with one writer describing her as "the shadow in the White House." Refusing to take part in Washington life, she wore black mourning clothes every day and wrote letters to her dead sons that she then tossed into the fireplace. Jefferson Davis's wife, Varina, stepped in to relieve Jane of her duties and took charge of hosting Washington society. According to one journalist, "The President's house assumed a somber, melancholy aspect.... every echo of the merry laugh had died from the walls." The contrast could not have been more tragic between the vivacious home in which Pierce had grown up and the gloomy White House where he began his disastrous term.

Robbed of any ability to forge a buoyant vision for the nation, Pierce came to rely heavily on the guidance of others. Though he had never possessed a firm backbone, Pierce now became even more pliant than usual, awarding patronage plums to those who would tell him what he wanted to hear. When his vice president, William Rufus King, died from tuberculosis only six weeks into his term, Pierce never replaced him. Instead, he depended on a select inner circle of slaveholding interests to counsel him. Convinced that giving the South a central role in his administration would help maintain national unity, he appointed Jefferson Davis as his secretary of war, who joined an alliance of Southern planters and Northern businessmen in his Cabinet, all of whom opposed abolitionism. Not once during his entire term did Pierce change a single Cabinet member.

It soon became obvious that Pierce lacked the political gravitas required to tamp the building discord. No matter how auspicious his past may have seemed, the truth was that "Young Hickory" shared nothing in common with his assertive idol Jackson. "Pierce, poor fellow, has no hold on the nation," observed Pennsylvania politician J. Glancy Jones. "He is the accidental head of an organization, without any cohesive power." For the next four years, Pierce stood at a moral crossroads and repeatedly chose accommodation to proslavery interests—even as such accommodation destroyed the very Union that he professed to revere.

Pierce did not just remain loyal to the ideology of his party; he also badly underestimated the depth of the abolitionists' commitment. In 1854, he lent his support to the Kansas-Nebraska Act, the handiwork of Democratic senator Stephen Douglas from Illinois. The controversial legislation reopened the issue of slavery that had seemingly been settled with the Compromise of 1850, and it effectively nullified the Missouri Compromise of 1820, which prohibited slavery north of latitude 36°30'. Pierce applied the coup de grace by adding language to the act that expressly declared the Missouri Compromise "inoperative and void." Instead, the act endorsed the notion of popular sovereignty, allowing those in the Kansas and Nebraska territories to decide for themselves whether to permit slavery within their borders. Soon pro-slavery "border ruffians" and impassioned abolitionists like John Brown rushed into the region. Shooting ensued as they vied for control, all but insuring that the nation would descend into wider war. As violence raged in "Bleeding Kansas," Pierce remained unmoved, sticking to his rigid definition of limited government intervention in matters pertaining to individual states.

But he also wasn't shy to exercise federal power in certain situations. At exactly the same time as the passage of the Kansas-Nebraska Act, Pierce made a point of enforcing the controversial Fugitive Slave Act. Article IV of the Constitution included a clause requiring that Northern citizens cooperate with Southern masters in returning runaway slaves, an issue that had long sparked conflict between the regions. In Boston, an intellectual and abolitionist hotbed, activists sought to subvert this clause by moving escaped slaves to Canada or to Northern free Black communities. One fugitive slave was Anthony Burns, who had fled Virginia as a nineteen-year-old, only to be arrested a year later in the clothing store where he had found work. Burns's arrest quickly became a cause célèbre among abolitionists, especially in the wake of Harriet Beecher Stowe's *Uncle Tom's Cabin*. They organized rallies and marched on the courthouse where the trial was held, and the city of Boston even proposed buying Burns's freedom.

Rather than recognizing a chance to placate the sectional divide, Pierce moved sternly to enforce law and order. As Black and white protestors gathered around the courthouse, Pierce sent in a large contingent of US Marines, monitoring the situation closely with Secretary of War Davis. Within days, a group of activists stormed the courthouse in an attempt to rescue Burns, but amid the melee, a federal marshal was killed. In a cable to his US attorney in Boston, Benjamin Hallet, Pierce ordered Hallet to "incur any expense deemed necessary... to insure the execution of the law." Shortly after that order, marshals escorted Burns from the courthouse to a ship anchored in Boston's Long Wharf and bound for Virginia. Some 50,000 Bostonians crowded the streets—booing and shouting "Kidnappers!" as a shackled Burns trudged past.

Boston abolitionists viewed this entire episode as a disgraceful display of federal overreach, a selective interpretation of "states' rights" on the part of a heartless Pierce. The poet Walt Whitman did not hold back: "The President eats dirt and excrement for his daily meals, likes it, and tries to force it on the states." In the eyes of antislavery forces, the president—someone who had grown up in New Hampshire, close to Boston—had bitterly betrayed and disrespected his own Northern roots.

By making an example of Anthony Burns, Pierce all but assured that the nation would be pulled into the vortex of civil war. "The old Democratic party is now the party of slavery," Maine senator Hannibal Hamlin proclaimed. Together, the Kansas-Nebraska Act and the Anthony Burns affair realigned the parties, spurring a coalition of antislavery Democrats, Free Soilers, and former Whigs to band together to form a new political powerhouse: the Republican Party. From this pressure cooker, an obscure lawyer and former Illinois congressman came out of political retirement to protest the morality of slavery—Abraham Lincoln.

Hawthorne, by now situated 3,500 miles away in Liverpool, observed the rising bitterness from afar but managed to avoid much of the drama. Instead, he dutifully filled his eight-hour workdays tending to issues of maritime law, providing safe passage home to American seamen, and resolving delicate matters that befell Americans traveling through the city. The job proved more tedious than he expected, taking him "to prisons, police-courts, hospitals and lunatic asylums." Eight hours a day he labored at his "stingy" desk; he rarely left Liverpool at all. The only saving grace was that he finally acquired money he could "bag." After four years, Hawthorne calculated, he would be able to return to America financially secure.

Hawthorne wasn't sorry to be missing the action across the ocean. "If anything could bring me back to America this winter, it would undoubtedly be my zeal for the Anti-slavery cause," he noted sardonically in December 1855. "But my official engagements render it quite impossible to assist personally." Despite Pierce's failures, Sophia Hawthorne remained an ardent supporter, characterizing the president as "an incorruptible patriot [who] loves his country with the purity and devotion of the first of our early patriots." She continued: "... The personal homage and love he commands, the enthusiasm of affection felt for him by his friends, are wonderful. His gentleness is made beautiful by a granite will." Nathaniel shared his wife's sentiments. Like her, he agreed with Pierce's support for the Kansas-Nebraska Act and his approach to solving the Burns affair.

He was mystified, however, by the country's extreme reaction: "I find it impossible to read American newspapers (of whatever political party) without being ashamed of my country."

Even from a distance, Hawthorne did not leave his friend to struggle alone. As Pierce's popularity continued to plummet, Hawthorne's support never wavered. Late in Pierce's term, Hawthorne sent him some words of encouragement: "What a storm you have had to face! And how like a man you have faced it!" Years afterward, Nathaniel's son Julian recalled that his father made a point to be vocal in his affection for Pierce just when public denunciation reached peak volume. As a writer, Hawthorne knew that though words might seem "so innocent and powerless," they could be "potent for good and evil [when] in the hands of one who knows how to combine them." In the ensuing years, amid intensifying national conflict, Hawthorne would repeatedly wield his pen in his friend's defense—to the disappointment of many.

As late as 1863, Hawthorne continued to repeat his familiar argument: What critics might perceive as Pierce's ineptitude was actually his resolute commitment to the ideals of the Founders. This quality should be admired, Hawthorne argued, not condemned: "It would ruin [this] noble character... for him to admit any ideas that were not entertained by the fathers of the Constitution and the Republic." It was far more admirable, Hawthorne reasoned, to display loyalty to America's sacred values than to "[adapt] one's self to new ideas, however true they may turn out to be."

But whether it was Pierce's integrity or his inflexibility that limited his effectiveness, even Hawthorne would have found it hard to deny that his friend's presidency was proving an abject disaster. On the single most important issue of his term, Pierce had failed: By 1856, the country stood far closer to war than it had in 1852.

Despite all the failures and hardships of his four years as president, Pierce continued to believe he deserved reelection in 1856. But the first indication of his misplaced hopes came when the slogan "Anybody But Pierce" began to circulate among fellow Democrats. Soon his inability to quell the violence raging in the Kansas Territory rendered him even more unpopular. Without much drama or fight, Pierce became the first elected president not to be renominated by his own party, losing on the relatively early nineteenth ballot after failing to lead any of the previous rounds. He lost to James Buchanan, who as the US ambassador to England had been able to avoid the debate over slavery for the previous three years. As the *New York Times* wrote shortly after Pierce's rejection, "He was taken up [in the public eye] because he was unknown. And now he is spurned because he is known." At precisely the time the country most needed a leader who could heal divisions and advance a prudent, sweeping vision, Pierce did not just retreat but further fanned the flames of sectionalism.

Pierce's loss naturally meant the end of Hawthorne's position in Liverpool. When word arrived that Pierce had lost his party's renomination, ending Hawthorne's own political life, his diligence for his consular responsibilities waned. He started to travel, got involved in the publication of a friend's book that was so panned the author went mad, and indulged himself in pleasures denied the previous three years. As his term ended, Hawthorne submitted to Buchanan (whose presidency would be as reviled as Pierce's) a letter of resignation, then began plotting his family's future. Neither Hawthorne nor Sophia had any interest in returning to an America that now confounded them. They decided instead to stay in Europe, making a slow trek to Rome, where they ultimately settled in January 1857.

Meanwhile, in the wake of his public repudiation, Pierce and his wife returned as private citizens to Concord. This time, he did not receive a hero's welcome; in a sharp rebuke, the city chose not to give him the customary parade. Compounding his disgrace, in the presidential election, New Hampshire voted for the Republican candidate, John C. Fremont. But Pierce didn't need the public's rejection to notice how broken he was by his single term in the White House. He could see it in the mirror, with one reporter describing the once "Handsome Frank" as "a wreck of his former self... his face wears a hue so ghastly and cadaverous that one could almost fancy he was gazing on a corpse." Another observer echoed this observation, saying that Pierce had left office "a staid and grave man, on whom the stamp of care and illness was ineradicably impressed." It was rumored that amid such widespread scorn, the ex-president hopelessly muttered, "There's nothing left . . . but to get drunk."

And reunite with the one man whose friendship he could still count on. In 1858, the Pierces traveled to Rome to visit the Hawthornes. The two men hadn't seen each other in five years. When Pierce arrived in Rome, the author was struck by how ravaged he looked, not just his graying hair and furrowed brow, but "something that seemed to have passed away out of him, without leaving any trace."

Pierce may have surfaced from the presidency a destroyed man, but the depth of his friendship with Hawthorne remained unchanged. The timing of his visit proved fortuitous for Hawthorne, whose fifteen-year-old daughter, Una, had fallen seriously ill. Hawthorne derived comfort from the presence of his dear friend, someone who knew intimately about a parent's grief and worry. When Una's condition reached its lowest point, Pierce stayed by Hawthorne's side in his apartment on Piazza Poli, acting as a "divinely tender" companion, in Sophia's words. To get some fresh air, the friends went for long walks through the cobbled streets, and even discussed the possibility of Pierce staging a political comeback. With the aid of Pierce's compassion, Una slowly recovered. In his journal, Hawthorne wrote with gratitude: "I did not know what comfort there might be in the manly sympathy of a friend. I shall always love him the better for the recollection of these dark days." Three decades after they had first met at Bowdoin College, Pierce and Hawthorne in this shared moment as fathers became closer than ever.

Following their lengthy European travels, the Pierces returned to New Hampshire and a country on the brink of war. After winning the 1860 election (albeit with 40 percent of the popular vote), Abraham Lincoln sought to preserve the Union at whatever cost. In March 1861, he tried to strike a conciliatory tone in his inaugural address, declaring, "We are not enemies, but friends. We must not be enemies." By this point, however, seven Southern states had already seceded. Five weeks later, a South Carolina militia fired on Fort Sumter, and the eventuality Pierce most dreaded—the Civil War—erupted.

Pierce had left office nearly a half-decade earlier, but the turmoil he had engendered in just one term continued to damn his reputation. Jefferson Davis, his former secretary of war, one of his closest aides, and the man Pierce had recommended for the 1860 Democratic presidential nomination, was now president of the Confederacy. When the press leaked some of Pierce's correspondence with Davis, including one letter in which Pierce seemed to encourage secession, his already wretched legacy was sealed. As if the linkage with Davis were not enough, Pierce continued to insist on the constitutionality of "involuntary servitude" and declared his support for the Confederacy. And, hyperpartisan as ever in defense of the Democratic Party, he railed against the policies of the rising Republican Party. He even had the temerity to criticize Lincoln's Emancipation Proclamation of 1863 as unconstitutional, an interference "with states' rights and the right of private property." Repeatedly, Pierce blasted Lincoln's handling of the Civil War, describing it as "fearful, fruitless [and] fateful" on the exact day that news arrived of Union victories at Gettysburg and Vicksburg.

Yet, even in his repugnance toward Lincoln, Pierce remained a man of irreconcilable contradictions—the very contradictions that Hawthorne appreciated and respected so fully. When Lincoln's son Willie died in 1862, Pierce penned a heartfelt letter, writing not as a political foe but as a father who had worshipped his own father yet lost all three of his children: "Even in this hour, so full of danger to our Country, and of trial and anxiety to all good men, your thoughts, will be, of your cherished boy, who will nestle at your heart, until you meet him in that new life, when tears and toils and conflict will be unknown."

That empathetic gesture, however, was overshadowed by Pierce's far more divisive actions. Later, after Lincoln's assassination in April 1865, Pierce would refuse to hang a flag in mourning. An enraged mob converged on his home, but in one last display of oratorical prowess, he stubbornly defended his public service and war record: "It is not necessary for me to show my devotion for the stars and stripes."

Echoing Pierce's penchant for provocation, the reserved Hawthorne was no less controversial on the issue of slavery and the justness of war. In a lengthy satiric essay, "Chiefly About War Matters By A Peaceable Man," for the *Atlantic Monthly* in July 1862, Hawthorne, with Pierce's encouragement, decided to travel to DC to see for himself the effects of war on the country. During his visit, he met with Lincoln, members of his Cabinet, and his generals. Then, once back at home with pen in hand, Hawthorne took aim at everything the magazine's northern progressive readership held dear.

The article spared no one, nor their polite sensibility. He referred to Lincoln as "Uncle Abe" and described his "homely," "unkempt," and "coarse" appearance. He attacked the justness of the war while questioning the wisdom of freeing the slave into a hostile new world. Not unaware of the effect it would have on the magazine's pro-Union readership, he asked the magazine's publisher to carefully read it and recommend changes. The publisher suggested Hawthorne remove some of his most offending passages, including his Lincoln language. He acquiesced. But then he cleverly inserted footnotes for other incendiary passages, written in the voice of a scornful editor attacking the very points he was making in the article (e.g.,"We do not thoroughly comprehend the author's drift in the foregoing paragraph, but are inclined to think its tone reprehensible").

Though satirical, the article revealed a man clearly out of step with the prevailing sentiments of his community—torn over the propriety of slavery and the costs of a war to end it. "If ever a man was out of his right element, it was Hawthorne in America," wrote Edward Dicey, a reporter Hawthorne had earlier befriended during a tour of a battlefield. "Nobody disliked slavery more cordially than he did," Dicey also observed, "and yet the difficulty of what was to be done with the slaves weighted constantly upon his mind."

But he continued to follow Pierce's lead, prompting many to denounce the two friends for being complicit in the sins of slavery. In 1863, Hawthorne published a book called *Our Old Home*, a collection of pieces he wrote while serving as the US consul in England. He insisted on dedicating the book to Pierce and celebrating the former president's undying faith in the "grand idea of an irrevocable Union." Most of his friends, his editor, and his publisher all strenuously objected. One large book dealer warned he wouldn't carry the book if it included the dedication. Hawthorne didn't listen or even care. The dedication sealed his fate as an outlier if not persona non grata among his literary peers and the intellectual elite of his native New England. As Hawthorne lamented at the time, "My friends have dropped off from me like autumn leaves." Henry David Thoreau likened Pierce to the devil and viewed Hawthorne as scarcely better. Longfellow publicly ended his connections to Hawthorne. Ralph Waldo Emerson also followed suit. When Hawthorne personally sent Emerson a copy of the book, Emerson ripped out the pages containing the gushing, heartfelt dedication, "To A Friend":

> And now farewell, my dear friend; and excuse (if you think it needs any excuse) the freedom with which I thus publicly assert a personal friendship between a private individual and a statesman who has filled what was then the most august position in the world.

The social ostracism did nothing to weaken the friends' fierce bond. As they came under ever harsher criticism, Pierce and Hawthorne grew even more stubborn, feeling that they formed a two-man club against the world.

When *Our Old Home* was published, both men knew that the prime of their lives had passed. Hawthorne's health was in marked decline, and Pierce worried deeply over his friend's state just as his own wife's life hung in the balance. On December 2, 1863, Jane died of tuberculosis, at the age of fifty-seven. She was laid to rest alongside her three deceased boys in Concord, New Hampshire. Hawthorne had had a difficult time warming up to Jane Pierce—many people did—but he did not hesitate to visit her gravesite on that frigid day, despite his own feeble health. When Pierce noticed Hawthorne shivering, he turned up the collar of Hawthorne's coat in a futile defense against the cold. In that moment, as Hawthorne biographer Brenda Wineapple writes, "Probably not even Pierce's wife loved him as Hawthorne did." Later, Pierce recounted how his friend's presence expressed "in his glorious face and wonderful eyes a depth of unutterable sympathy and sorrow."

Five months later, Hawthorne's health took a precipitous turn for the worse. Hoping a trip to the country might benefit his friend, Pierce arranged an outing to the White Mountains of New Hampshire. "I would not trust him now in any hands except such gentle and tender hands as yours," Sophia Hawthorne gratefully wrote to Pierce. The friends met in Boston, then traveled to Pierce's home in Concord, waiting until the weather improved to head north to the mountains. They set out for the town of Dixville Notch on May 18, 1864, with Pierce noting that Hawthorne seemed unusually quiet that day, except for when he spoke about the recent death of William Thackeray, the British novelist. "[What] a boon it would be, if when life draws to a close one could pass away without a struggle," Hawthorne mused.

When the coach arrived in Plymouth, New Hampshire, Pierce and Hawthorne checked into the elegant Pemigewasset Hotel. Hawthorne ate a little food before turning in for the night. Pierce's own room was just down the hall. At midnight, Pierce got out of bed to check on Hawthorne, who seemed to be sleeping peacefully on his side, his right hand pressed against his cheek: "Like a child," Pierce said. Three hours later, Pierce woke up again and checked on his friend. Hawthorne remained in the exact same position. Pierce edged closer, leaning over the bed. Hawthorne's color looked normal but he didn't appear to be breathing. Pierce took his friend's wrist and laid his fingers on it, detecting no pulse. "The great, generous brave heart beat no more," Pierce later told a friend. Just as he had wished only the day before, Hawthorne died "without a struggle." Incidentally, his death fulfilled a passage from his own book *The Blithedale Romance*: "Happy the man that has such a friend beside him, when he comes to die!" As he gathered Hawthorne's belongings, Pierce looked into Hawthorne's handbag. The former president found a photo of himself.

Pierce accompanied the body back to Boston, and the funeral was held three days later, on May 23, 1864. Even amid mourning, old political wounds had not healed. Hawthorne's other friends, mainly members of the New England literati, continued to shun the former president, keeping a respectable distance from him throughout the entire service. Pierce was left heartbroken that they excluded him from serving as a pallbearer, pushed aside in favor of more illustrious names, including Emerson, Longfellow, Louisa May Alcott, John Greenleaf Whittier, Louis Agassiz, and Oliver Wendell Holmes. Most of the funeral attendees viewed Pierce not as Nathaniel Hawthorne's closest friend but as Jefferson Davis's corrupted buddy—no better than an "archtraitor," in Harriet Beecher Stowe's opinion. Emerson explored his deeply conflicted feelings later that day in his diary:

> I have found in his death a surprise and a disappointment. . . . Lately, to be sure he had removed himself the more by the indignation his perverse politics and most unfortunate friendship for that paltry Franklin Pierce awaked,—though it rather moved pity for Hawthorne, and the assured belief that he would outlive it, and come out right at last.

As Emerson suggested, Hawthorne did not "outlive" his "unfortunate friendship" with Pierce. Nor did he witness the end of the Civil War that he and his friend helped stoke. Rather, Pierce would be left behind to grapple with the contested legacy they left behind and, unlike his friend, would not be forgiven for his perceived betrayals.

Pierce did not forget the Hawthorne family even after the death of their patriarch. He remained in touch with Sophia, put Julian through

Harvard, and gave the young man his silver-tipped cane. But his connections to his best friend's family could not assuage Pierce's deep isolation, made all the worse by the snubbing of Northerners. "I need not tell you how lonely I am, and how full of sorrow," Pierce confessed to Bridge after Hawthorne's death. With the dual losses of his wife and his best friend, Pierce relapsed. Drinking only hastened his descent, and by October 1868, Pierce reportedly weighed less than one hundred pounds. His once-strong outdoorsman's body—as much his trademark as his handsome face—began to fail him. He sought comfort by joining St. Paul's Episcopal Church in Concord; the Episcopals were the only denomination that welcomed him, since the others—Presbyterians, Methodists, Congregationalists, and Baptists—had all publicly denounced slavery.

Even in the late stages of the Civil War, Pierce maintained that the Union be held above all else. His father had fought in the Revolutionary War, his brothers had fought in the War of 1812, and he had fought in the Mexican American War. Pierce was nothing if not steadfast. He stayed in touch with Jefferson Davis, even after Davis's imprisonment following the Civil War. He seethed when the Republican-controlled House of Representatives impeached President Andrew Johnson, who had enacted a lenient Reconstruction policy on the defeated South. But he continued to insist that his unpopular position stemmed from a place of goodwill, a desire to protect the Union at all costs. When General Ulysses S. Grant, a Republican, won the presidency in 1868, Pierce genuinely hoped that Grant's campaign slogan—"Let Us Have Peace"—would fulfill its promise.

Pierce did not live to see whether that promise would come to pass. His health got progressively worse, and by the fall of 1869, his doctors knew that he was not going to recover. Six weeks before his sixty-fifth birthday, Pierce died alone in his home from cirrhosis of the liver. He was interred in the family plot at Old North Cemetery, alongside his wife and children—a man whose legacy remained as contested during his life as after it.

The press greeted the news of Pierce's passing with little sympathy. *Harper's Weekly* dismissed his entire presidency as one that "outraged humanity, liberty, and the better sense of the country." The *National*

Anti-Slavery Standard agreed: "A more pliant and submissive servant the slave power never had than Franklin Pierce." Even in his own home state, the *Granite Free Press* concluded that "his administration was one of the most deplorable failures ever recorded." The *New York Times* sidelined his obituary to the third page.

Even with the generosity of historical hindsight, these interpretations of Pierce's presidency have barely budged in the decades since. For no matter how much Pierce waxed lyrical about national unity, he in the end failed to preserve just that, bringing the nation closer than ever to the precipice of war. But if discord defined his life, Pierce's resting place was in Concord, a name honoring the kind of harmony that had always eluded him. Sixty miles to the south sits Hawthorne's own gravestone in Concord, Massachusetts—a final if unwitting show of solidarity by one of history's most defiant duos.

CHAPTER 3

Abraham Lincoln and Joshua Speed

Room Over the Store

In January 1841, just a few weeks shy of his thirty-second birthday, Abraham Lincoln had reached a new low in a brief lifetime already full of setbacks and disappointments. Bedridden at the home of a friend in Springfield, Illinois, Lincoln was so distraught over a broken romance that the two men now caring for him feared he might well be on the verge of suicide. Not wanting to take any chances, they hid all razors, knives, and "other such dangerous things."

His descent into "hypo"—Lincoln's name for his condition, hypochondria—had come abruptly. Only months earlier, Lincoln had been in high spirits for a change. His nascent legal practice was starting to gain traction, he was the vibrant center of a social life that gave him immense satisfaction, and his political future, anchored by his stirring oratory and personal warmth, seemed limitless. "He was the favorite of all," one friend remarked. ". . . He loved all of them as they loved him."

But beneath Lincoln's veneer of bonhomie and stability lay a man who had struggled with depression for many years, most likely due to a succession of losses during childhood that left him feeling unloved and untethered. Those who knew him best as an adult were well aware of his dark moods and debilitating sadness; they were always on guard. Now two events—unrelated but in rapid succession—conspired to overwhelm Lincoln at the very moment he seemed to have his life on track.

Earlier that fall, Lincoln had begun courting Mary Todd, a new arrival to town. They were an "odd couple," admitted Todd's sister, who first introduced the two. Lincoln "could not hold a lengthy conversation with a lady—was not sufficiently educated and intelligent in the female line to do so." But Lincoln, she added, was "charmed with Mary's wit and fascinated with her quick sagacity—her will—her nature—and culture." Despite lacking both a steady income and prior intimacy with a woman,

Lincoln steeled his nerves and proposed to Todd. And, despite her own family's objections, she accepted.

What should have been a time of joy, however, soon turned to agonizing misgivings. Almost as soon as he got up from his bent knee, Lincoln began to question the wisdom of his proposal. Did he know her well enough? Was he marrying too far up? Consumed with doubts bordering on dread, Lincoln impetuously decided to break off the engagement and wrote a letter to his fiancée about his change of heart. But before sending it, he showed it to the one person in his life he trusted enough to share his deepest fears and darkest secrets. "Burn it," his best friend told him. "Once [you've] put your words in writing... they stand as a living and eternal monument against you." Instead, he advised Lincoln to rely on his "manhood" to see her in person.

Lincoln heeded his friend's advice, telling Todd to her face what he had written earlier: "I don't love you." She immediately broke into tears, and just as quickly the six-foot-four-inch, onetime suitor was on his knees, kissing the five-foot-two-inch crying woman. The engagement was now postponed, neither on nor off.

In the midst of this painful romantic saga, Lincoln had to confront another, even more devastating development, this time not of his own making: His best friend, roommate, and soulmate—the one who had just advised him on Mary Todd—had decided it was time to leave Springfield for his hometown in Kentucky. For the past three and a half years, Abraham Lincoln and Joshua Speed had shared not only their most intimate emotions and thoughts, but also a bed. Now the other half of the bed would be empty—just like, Lincoln feared, his life itself. When he heard about Speed's plan to return home "that fatal first of Jany. '41," the news simply overwhelmed him.

That Lincoln could be so devastated by the prospect of losing a friend speaks to how few intimate relationships he had enjoyed over the first three decades of his life. Popular lore long held that Lincoln from birth was gregarious and fun-loving, full of yarns and good cheer that attracted legions of friends. But the reality, as historians like David Herbert Donald have unearthed, was a reserved man unable to forge close friendships—perhaps only six, including Speed, in his fifty-six years. Partly accounting for this dearth of companionship, his law partner and friend William

Herndon described Lincoln as "the most shut-mouthed man" who ever lived.

With the realization of Speed's planned departure, the already fragile Lincoln collapsed. Some historians believe that even without the aborted engagement, Lincoln would have become unhinged—simply by the thought of losing the one man who gave meaning and stability to his life. "That threatened the ground of his being," the historian Charles Strozier writes. For the next few precarious weeks, Speed and a local doctor cared for Lincoln as he hovered between life and death. It was then that the room had been cleared of anything sharp.

Lincoln would of course survive, going on to become one of America's greatest leaders. But without Speed's timely and compassionate intervention, Abraham Lincoln might very well have been lost to history.

The Sangamon River is shaped like a sickle and courses for 264 miles right through the belly of Illinois. For six years beginning in 1831, when he was just twenty-two years of age, Abraham Lincoln lived alone on a bluff overlooking the Sangamon in a small settlement named New Salem. A year earlier, Lincoln had moved to Illinois with his father, stepmother, and eleven other family members to escape "insecure titles" the family held in Indiana and a new outbreak of "milk sickness" that years earlier had killed his mother. Life in Illinois turned out to be just as bad for the Lincoln family as it was in Indiana. Flooding at his new home a few months later forced Lincoln to set out on his own and seek gainful employment for the first time in his life. His prodigious talents working a barge caught the eye of a New Salem storeowner who offered him a job in his store. Lincoln eagerly accepted, and he soon found himself living alone miles away on a different bank of the Sangamon.

When he first arrived in New Salem in the spring of 1831, he was by his own admission a "strange, friendless, uneducated, penniless boy." In a town of just one hundred people, he worked variously as a storekeeper, postmaster, and surveyor, ingratiating himself into the small community with his sharp wit and physical strength. His gift for splitting rails and chopping down trees impressed his neighbors, and in a town with numerous illiterates, so did his ability to read and write.

Within a year of his arrival, Lincoln had made his mark in town, especially when the leader of an out-of-town gang that frequently terrorized New Salem citizens challenged Lincoln to a fight. Lincoln insisted it be a proper wrestling match instead of a brawl. He followed all the rules in fighting Jack Anderson to either a draw or a victory (the history is still muddled). His neighbors already admired his physical gifts; now they saw in him a moral courage for taking on the town bully with such exactitude. From that point forward, his neighbors marked him for future leadership.

Seizing the moment, Lincoln decided in March 1832 to run for the Illinois House of Representatives despite being only twenty-three years old. Before his campaign could even begin, however, the Black Hawk War broke out, and Lincoln instead joined a local, all-volunteer militia to fight Native Americans. Within days, his fellow soldiers elected Lincoln their captain, an honor he would later say exceeded even his presidential nomination. Over the following eighty days, Lincoln served three tours of duty but never quite faced any battles (he would later poke fun at himself for his "charges against wild onions"). Still, he earned the respect of both his men and his commanding officer, John Todd Stuart, a Springfield lawyer who would later play an important role in his life.

Upon returning home, Lincoln threw himself back into his legislative campaign, but missing three months left him little time to become known across the larger district. Undaunted, Lincoln made his case to voters in his honest and direct way:

> Every man is said to have his peculiar ambition. Whether it be true or not, I can say for one that I have no other so great as that of being truly esteemed of my fellow men, by rendering myself worthy of their esteem. . . . I was born and have ever remained in the most humble walks of life. I have no wealthy or popular relations to recommend me. My case is thrown exclusively upon the independent voters of this county, and if elected they will have conferred a favor upon me, for which I shall be unremitting in my labors to compensate.

Those voters who knew him supported him overwhelmingly, but as he feared, his long absences away from the campaign trail—as well as his lack of money and influential friends—doomed his chances of victory. He won more than 90 percent of the vote in New Salem but lagged far behind in all the other precincts, finishing eighth out of thirteen candidates—the only time he would ever lose a direct election. Two years later, in 1834, he ran again for the Illinois House, and this time he won, beginning a four-term, eight-year stint of service.

Over that time period, Lincoln cemented his standing in the Whig Party, which had emerged in the 1830s to oppose President Andrew Jackson, whom members pilloried as "King Andrew." The Whigs fervently supported a program of economic modernization that encompassed the Second Bank of the United States, protective tariffs, and internal improvements. Though they did not formally endorse anti-slavery, northern Whigs hewed closer to abolitionism than did Jacksonian Democrats.

Lincoln envisioned himself as following in the footsteps of influential Kentucky statesman and Whig leader Henry Clay, who had played a pivotal role in passing the Missouri Compromise of 1820. That legislation had averted the sectional crisis by barring slavery north of the 36°30' parallel except for Missouri. Echoing Clay, Lincoln in the late 1830s began endorsing a middle-of-the-road, "free soil" stance on slavery: He did not support outright abolition but he did oppose extending slavery westward. As he proclaimed in 1837, "[The] institution of slavery is founded on both injustice and bad policy, but... the promulgation of abolition doctrines tends rather to increase than abate its evils." And like Clay, who founded the American Colonization Society, Lincoln advocated for the "return" of freed slaves to Liberia on the west coast of Africa.

Partly due to his growing preoccupation with these charged political issues, Lincoln made the fateful decision to pursue law as a profession while serving out his term in the Illinois House. Mentored by his former commander and new friend, John Todd Stuart, he dove into every law book he could find, most of them provided by Stuart. Exceedingly driven to learn the law, Lincoln would sometimes walk the fourteen miles from his home in New Salem to Stuart's office in Springfield to borrow more books. When he started studying law, Lincoln only had a single year of formal schooling under his belt. Largely self-taught as a reader and writer, Lincoln pursued his legal studies in much the same way—through a combination of hard work, perseverance, and innate gifts.

Lincoln was admitted to the Illinois bar in the spring of 1836 and took a position as Stuart's junior partner in Springfield, a town of 1,200 that had just become the Illinois capital. It was a minor move geographically but a daunting one professionally and personally. On April 15, 1837, Lincoln set out on a borrowed horse, with seven dollars in his pocket and saddlebags packed with a pair of underwear, other clothing items, and a well-worn copy of his legal bible—William Blackstone's *Commentaries on the Laws of England*. Lincoln had already hired a cabinetmaker to build him a bed for his new home—a spare room in Stuart's law office. When he arrived in Springfield, he tied up the horse in front of a dry goods store on the corner of Washington and Fifth. He then walked into the store and immediately came face-to-face with its storekeeper: a pleasant, twenty-two-year-old Kentuckian with the social grace and education that one might expect from a young man who came from a well-to-do family.

There was no way to know it at that moment, but Lincoln's fortunes were about to change dramatically. Two weeks earlier, asked by a friend why he was so down, Lincoln responded that he had nothing to look forward to nor anyone to keep him company. Within a matter of hours, he would have both.

Joshua Fry Speed's ancestors had distinguished themselves for hundreds of years. His great-great-grandfather prospered as an eminent historian and cartographer in sixteenth-century England; his grandfather James Speed became one of Kentucky's largest landowners; and his father, John Speed, oversaw a large plantation filled with slaves who harvested the hemp fields. Joshua was one of thirteen Speed children to grow up on those bountiful lands, shaped by the hierarchical systems upon which plantation life depended.

Like Lincoln, Speed as a child suffered from depression, as did many other members of his immediate family. And he was often sick, losing months at his elite private schools to return home for medical care. After becoming estranged from his father, he decided after one illness to set out on his own with no particular idea of what to do. He headed to Louisville at the age of seventeen for a job as a clerk at a wholesale store. Then, three years later in 1834, when a downturn hit the city, Speed moved north to Springfield, Illinois, by then a fast-growing community and a destination for prominent businessmen. With its new hotels and bustling retail stores, Springfield seemed to hold a promising future.

Partnering with a first cousin who lived in Springfield, Speed established a dry goods shop in a two-story brick house at the corner of a town square. He named it Bell & Co. With money likely advanced by his father, with whom he had since patched up his differences, Speed and his cousin opened with $12,000 worth of dry goods, groceries, mattresses, and books. By 1837, when Lincoln strode into that store for the first time, Speed was comfortably ensconced in the economic and social life of the vibrant town.

Greeting Lincoln as he entered the shop, Speed was struck immediately by his customer's ungainly appearance, with limbs as long as cornstalks, disheveled clothes, and gray eyes that reflected gloom. *This man has the saddest face I've ever seen*, Speed recalled thinking. Lincoln inquired about the cost of a mattress, sheets, blankets, and a bedspread. Seventeen dollars, Speed told him. Lincoln replied that the price was reasonable but still beyond his means.

"If you will credit me until Christmas, and my experiment here as a lawyer is a success, I will pay you then," Lincoln bargained. "If I fail in that, I will probably never be able to pay you at all."

Speed had never met Lincoln before, but he surely knew him by reputation as the legislator widely credited with moving the Illinois capital to Springfield earlier that year. He had also seen Lincoln on the stump in a particularly electrifying moment during his 1836 reelection campaign. The speaker preceding Lincoln had been a tart-tongued political operator, George Forquer, who had left the Whigs to become a Democrat, a switch that enabled him to secure a coveted position in the local government. Forquer lived in one of the finest homes in town, complete with a lightning rod—the only one around. Vowing to "take Lincoln down," Forquer delivered a cutting, sarcastic speech. Then Lincoln's turn came, and he did not hold back:

> I am not so young in years as I am in the tricks and trades of a politician; but live long, or die young, I would rather die now, than, like the gentleman, change my politics, and simultaneous with the changes receive an office worth $3,000 per year, and then have to erect a lightning-rod over my house to protect a guilty conscience from an offended God.

Hearing Lincoln eviscerate Forquer with this "lightning rod" remark, Speed was left awed by Lincoln's ability to turn a phrase. Later, Speed would write that he had never heard a more compelling or persuasive speaker than Lincoln, a man whose mind was nothing less than "a wonder."

By the time Lincoln appeared in his store, Speed himself was becoming more politically involved. Just hours before Lincoln arrived that day, the local paper had reported that Speed would act as secretary of a public meeting to discuss attracting a railroad to run through Springfield. Fascinated by his earnest, melancholy customer, and also sensing that a relationship with such a rising star would benefit him in both politics and business, Speed presented Lincoln with an option that would eliminate the need for a seventeen-dollar expenditure.

"I have a large room with a double bed, which you are very welcome to share with me if you choose," Speed offered.

Lincoln asked where the room was.

"Upstairs," Speed replied.

Lincoln collected his saddlebags, ascended the winding staircase, and surveyed the chamber. He left his saddlebags in the room, came back down, and smiled gratefully at the storekeeper.

"Well, Speed, I'm moved," he stated.

Abraham Lincoln and Joshua Speed, who shared the same home state of Kentucky and very little else, slept together in that double bed for four years. It was the start of an enduring, intimate friendship—a decade before Speed would become one of the most successful businessmen in

Louisville and two decades before Lincoln would become one of the most beloved presidents in history.

These sleeping arrangements have long prompted speculation that Lincoln and Speed were more than just friends. Speaking at a 1999 conference, the playwright, author, and gay activist Larry Kramer declared that Lincoln was a "totally gay man," and he claimed to have discovered a revealing diary and trove of letters in the floorboards of the room Lincoln and Speed shared. Kramer's sensational charge garnered major headlines but withered under scrutiny, and Kramer eventually admitted it was all a fabrication. Still, his claim spawned a virtual cottage industry that sought to establish Lincoln's homosexuality, fueled in large part on this single data point that he shared a bed with a man for four years.

But the overwhelming weight of evidence reveals no hint of a sexual relationship. Most persuasively, a thorough reading of the verified letters between Lincoln and Speed offers no suggestion that the relationship was anything other than platonic. In fact, what is most striking about the letters is a lack of *any* colorful or playful language that could be interpreted to support the theory they were lovers. Furthermore, the men who occasionally shared the room upstairs with them or belonged to their informal social club downstairs never reported seeing or hearing anything that would have given rise to this suspicion. And as historian Donald notes, even respectable lawyers when riding the circuit "tumbled unceremoniously into bed together." In the nearly two centuries since Lincoln and Speed last slept in bed together, no one—despite repeated and persistent attempts to prove the contrary—has conclusively determined they were anything other than very close friends.

What is not in doubt is the respect Speed felt for Lincoln upon first meeting him. A man without a trace of artifice or false pride, Lincoln had stated very plainly that he might not be able to cover the $17 for the goods he hoped to purchase. There was something about this unkempt beanpole of a man, a sensitivity and a kindness cloaked by gloom, that told Joshua Speed he could completely trust him. And so Speed had offered Abraham Lincoln his bed. Neither man's life would ever be the same.

From the moment Lincoln first walked into Bell & Co., he and Speed forged a friendship unequaled in its intimacy by any other person, including their wives. They were rarely apart except when at work—Speed at the store, Lincoln at his law office down by the courthouse. They even made sure to eat all their meals together. When Lincoln was arguing in court, Speed would often saunter down to the courthouse to watch his friend. In the evenings, the two men would preside over a rolling social club made up of friends from Springfield who were increasingly attracted to the lively banter, mostly coming from Lincoln himself. As Speed recalled, "Mr. Lincoln was a social man, though he did not seek company; it sought him. After he made his home with me, on every winter's night at my store, by a big wood fire, no matter how inclement the weather, eight or ten choice spirits assembled, without distinction of party. It was a sort of social club without organization. They came there because they were sure to find Lincoln."

Afterward, Speed and Lincoln would retire to their room upstairs, where they would converse about books, poetry—the more depressing the better—and, of course, politics. Both were Whigs and for a time in general agreement on the issues of the day. During his nearly four years as Speed's roommate, Lincoln emerged as one of the best-known young men in Springfield, gaining a reputation for his eloquence articulating Whig positions in court. His future law partner, Herndon, took note of Lincoln's boundless ambition, calling him a "little engine that knew no rest." And while Lincoln seemed destined for greatness, Speed himself also played a central role in civic life—albeit more in the shadows. He acted as a booster for the town of Springfield, held positions with Lincoln on many key Whig committees, and helped strengthen the Whig Party in Illinois.

Apart from his rising legal career and his standing as an effective Whig legislator, Lincoln stood out for his vast store of clever anecdotes, his ability to engage intelligently on most any issue, and his deft use of self-deprecation. Once when riding a train, as Lincoln told the tale, a stranger insisted on speaking to him.

"Excuse me, sir, but I have an article in my possession which rightfully belongs to you," the man said.

"How is that?" Lincoln asked.

The stranger took a jackknife from his pocket.

"This knife was placed in my hands some years ago with the injunction that I was to keep it until I found a man uglier than myself," the stranger said. "I have carried it from that time to this. Allow me now to say, sir, that I think you are fairly entitled to the property."

That episode did not offend Lincoln in the least. Years later, when a critic accused him of being "two-faced," Lincoln replied, "If I had two faces, would I be wearing this one?"

By laughing at himself, Lincoln endeared all around him—including Speed—with his humility and honesty. In *Reminiscences of Abraham Lincoln*, Speed wrote that Lincoln possessed a sweet and tender disposition that expressed itself most dramatically whenever he encountered anyone in distress, man or beast. These qualities emerged one day on a trip the two took with a group of friends out to the country. Along the road, Lincoln noticed two baby birds, too young to fly, on the ground. A fierce wind had kicked up and knocked their nest out of a tree. Lincoln stopped and hitched up his horse while the others rode ahead to a creek. It took some time, but Lincoln found the nest. He gently placed the young birds safely inside and tucked it back in a tree. When his friends found out why Lincoln had fallen behind, they laughed.

"Gentlemen, you may laugh, but I could not have slept well tonight if I had not saved those birds," Lincoln said. "Their cries would've rung in my ears."

Yet behind Lincoln's easy laugh and conviviality was a man far more prone to depression and darkness than was apparent to his growing legion of admirers. Shortly after moving to New Salem in 1831, Lincoln had fallen in love with Ann Rutledge, a woman of "exquisite beauty" and mind. For most of the three years he courted her, she was engaged to another man who lived in New York. Time and distance weren't kind to that relationship, and by 1835 Ann abandoned any hope of marrying him and agreed instead to marry Lincoln. But before they could tie the knot, Ann came down with typhoid fever. Lincoln stood at her bedside three weeks later when she took her last breath. The death of his first love left Lincoln so shattered that friends later described him as "suicidal" and needing to be "locked up by his friends" to keep him safe from himself.

Lincoln's extreme reaction to Ann's death and his inability to cope with it would not have surprised anyone aware of the debilitating losses he had suffered and the circumstances he had endured before setting out on his own for New Salem at the age of twenty-one.

As every American student learns in grade school, Abraham Lincoln was born in a Kentucky log cabin on February 12, 1809. Measuring 16 by 18 feet, the cabin had only one door, one window, a stone fireplace, and a dirt floor. Three other people lived there: Lincoln's father, Thomas; his mother, Nancy; and his sister, Sarah. That pitiable arrangement marked the start of Lincoln's isolated childhood in the near wilderness, growing up bereft of friends with "absolutely nothing to excite ambition for education," as Lincoln recalled. Over time, his scorn grew deeper for his near-illiterate father, who had no desire to learn or to write beyond "bunglingly sign[ing] his own name." Once he reached age seven, his family crossed the Ohio River into Indiana, where Lincoln would live out the rest of a lonely childhood.

In 1818, when he was nine, Lincoln's mother died of fever. He had adored her, calling her his "angel mother." If he loved too deeply, he learned, that love could be snatched away. Underscoring that lesson, Lincoln later suffered yet another abrupt loss when his sister died during childbirth. After this string of tragedies, Lincoln entered adulthood with no close friendships and in a delicate emotional state he couldn't shake. It would be Joshua Speed who assumed the central role in pulling Lincoln out of his depression.

Five years after Ann Rutledge's death, Lincoln felt ready to fall in love again. Through Speed's intercession, he met twenty-one-year-old Mary Todd, an educated, witty, and cultured woman who came from a wealthy family in Lexington, Kentucky. Mary had grown up in a household steeped in politics. Her father used his wealth to host many political functions during her youth, including one event when she met Henry

Clay. Like Lincoln, she too became an outspoken supporter of Clay's liberal ideology and, in her sister's words, a "violent little Whig" who embraced party politics with uncommon zeal. In 1840, hoping to escape a stepmother she loathed, Mary moved to Springfield to live with her sister Elizabeth. Speed, who happened to be Elizabeth's friend, pushed Lincoln to meet Mary Todd sometime after she arrived, and once he did, he was left enchanted. Elizabeth later recalled Lincoln listening to Mary and "gazing on her as if drawn by some superior power, irresistibly so."

Eventually, the couple became engaged. But Lincoln's doubts about his worthiness and readiness to make such a permanent commitment caused him to pull back from the engagement—only then to be racked with guilt over Todd's heartbreak.

His angst worsened when Speed revealed his plans to leave Springfield for his family homestead in Farmington, Kentucky. Speed's father had died in March 1840, and Speed needed to comfort his mother and siblings, as well as help settle the family's affairs. Facing life without both Todd and Speed proved too much for Lincoln to bear. "He opened up to Speed in a way that he did with nobody else," Strozier writes. "Lincoln was very guarded with his personal relationships. He never had another friend like Speed, before or since."

By January 1841, Lincoln's life, as well as his mental health, seemed to be unraveling fast. Only sporadically fulfilling his legislative duties, he had become bedridden with "hypo." In a letter to John Todd Stuart, a law partner who was now serving as Springfield's congressman, Lincoln confessed his "deplorable state":

> I am now the most miserable man living. If what I feel were equally distributed to the whole human family, there would not be one cheerful face on the earth. Whether I shall ever be better I cannot tell; I awfully forebode I shall not. To remain as I am is impossible; I must die or be better, it appears to me.

Speed's unshakable loyalty and fundamental kindness empowered him to be, when necessary, brutally honest with his friend. When Lincoln would utter such grandiose, self-pitying remarks, Speed refused to indulge him and pressed him to show more strength in moving beyond his illness. If not, Speed warned, he was heading for full-blown insanity or even death. Lincoln replied that dying didn't worry him at all, except that he was convinced he had left such an insignificant mark on the world that he would quickly be forgotten once gone.

In view of Lincoln's condition, Speed delayed his return to Kentucky and continued to watch over his friend. If his attending doctor wasn't there, Speed almost certainly was. He had come to understand Lincoln better than anyone, so his presence became one of the only comforts the sick man had. As January turned to February, the pall hanging over Lincoln finally began to lift. Feeling stronger and more focused, he returned to his law practice and to his work in the Illinois legislature. Despite Lincoln's improvement, Speed stayed in town in case of a setback.

By May 1841, confident that Lincoln had sufficiently recovered, Speed finally left for Kentucky after his friend promised to come for a long visit. Three months later, Lincoln took his first-ever vacation to stay with the Speed family—a trip he would remember as one of the happiest times of his life.

The Speeds lived in a fourteen-room brick mansion, situated on their 550-acre Farmington plantation and designed to mimic Thomas Jefferson's Monticello estate. Such opulence was foreign to Lincoln, but he warmed to his welcome from the entire Speed family. Joshua's mother, Lucy Speed, took a special liking to Lincoln, even as she noted his deep sadness. Near the end of his visit, she presented him with an Oxford Bible, saying it was the best cure for depression he would ever find. Not a churchgoer but nevertheless a profoundly spiritual man, Lincoln was moved by the gift. Two decades later, he would send Mrs. Speed a photo of himself after his election as president: "To my very good friend Mrs. Lucy G. Speed (from) whose pious hands I received an Oxford Bible twenty years ago."

After a three-week stay, Lincoln headed home in September 1841 to Springfield. Needing to tie up some business affairs in Illinois, Speed accompanied him. They boarded a steamboat named *Lebanon* in Louisville and took the Ohio River down to St. Louis. Along the way, the boat stopped to pick up a slave trader, who herded a dozen slaves onto the ship, likely on their way to the slave-trading hub of New Orleans. Born and raised in Kentucky, Lincoln had certainly seen slaves before and witnessed their ill treatment. Both his father and mother had firmly opposed slavery and belonged to a Separate Baptist congregation, which believed that human bondage violated Christian teachings. When the Lincolns had moved across the Ohio River to the free state of Indiana, they joined thousands of other anti-slavery Southerners fleeing southern states like Kentucky.

But Lincoln's visit to the Speeds' plantation and his experience aboard the *Lebanon* left a deeply disconcerting impression. At Farmington, he had seen not just slaves, but slaves at work, including one who was ordered to serve him during his stay. He had also observed between forty-five to sixty slaves laboring in the fields. Already disturbed by those images on the Speed plantation, Lincoln was left even more troubled when confronted with the realities of the slave trade on the *Lebanon*. He later wrote to Mary Speed, one of Joshua's sisters, describing his horror over seeing those bodies shackled "six and six together... strung together precisely like so many fish upon a trot-line." Lincoln lamented that these captives faced a life of "perpetual slavery where the lash of the master is proverbially more ruthless and unrelenting than any other where [sic]." His letter to Mary Speed provides the earliest evidence of his evolving thoughts about slavery.

For now, though, Lincoln had more immediate matters to face. Disembarking as planned in St. Louis, he and Speed took a stagecoach to Springfield. Before long, the two friends found themselves ironically reversing roles in a brand-new romantic entanglement. Speed had become engaged to a woman from back home in Farmington, Fanny Henning. This time around, it was Speed who was beset with doubts, and Lincoln who urged him to the altar.

Lincoln had met Fanny on his visit to Farmington and told his friend that she was "one of the sweetest girls in the world." Applying the same logic that helped him not too long ago, Lincoln urged Speed not to succumb to his inner bogeymen and turn away from a woman he truly loved. As his friend prepared to return to Kentucky on January 1, 1842, Lincoln handed him a letter. The date was highly significant to Lincoln. It marked the one-year anniversary of his "Fatal First"—the day he broke off his engagement with Mary Todd. With a tone of deep care and gratitude, the letter began:

> Feeling, as you know I do, the deepest solicitude for the success of the enterprize [sic] you are engaged in, I adopt this as the last method I can invent to aid you, in case (which God forbid) you shall need any aid. I do not place what I am going to say on paper, because I can say it any better in that way than I could by word of mouth; but because, were I to say it orrally [sic], before we part, most likely you would forget it at the verry [sic] time when it might do you some good.

More than anyone else, Speed had ministered Lincoln through one of the most painful and precarious times of his life. As this letter bore witness, for both men—but particularly for Lincoln—that agonizing experience had enriched and deepened their bond, and Lincoln now wished to aid Speed just as Speed had aided him.

How much of Speed's new struggle arose from witnessing Lincoln's own a year earlier is uncertain; but what is clear is how Lincoln and Speed, now at the ages of thirty-two and twenty-seven respectively, were finding it difficult to commit to marriage, in all likelihood because each man harbored fears about whether he would be able to consummate a marital bond. In five letters that he wrote to Speed in January and February of 1842—"the most intimately personal letters that Lincoln ever wrote," according to Donald—he continued to offer quiet encouragement to his friend about the upcoming marriage. At one point, apologizing for his boldness and his "rude intrusion upon your feelings," he told Speed, "You know the Hell I have suffered on that point and how tender

I am upon it." Speed's angst over his ability to perform on his marriage night churned nearly to the moment he said "I do" on February 15, 1842—three days after Lincoln's thirty-third birthday.

After Speed had described his "indescribably horrible and alarming" worries, Lincoln tensely waited for word on how Speed had fared on his wedding day and night. When a letter finally arrived, sent the morning after Speed's marriage, Lincoln opened it with "intense anxiety and trepidation." Luckily, Speed shared only favorable reviews, and Lincoln wrote back: "I tell you, Speed, our forebodings for which you and I are rather peculiar, are all the worst sort of nonsense." A month later, Speed marveled how much marriage had transformed his life for the better.

On February 25, Lincoln wrote two more letters: one to the happy couple and the other to his friend alone—not wanting to alert the new bride to her husband's previous doubts. In that letter to Speed, he proclaimed his "confident hope that every successive letter I shall have from you (which I pray here may not be few, nor far between), may show you possessing a more steady hand, and cheerful heart, than the last preceding it. As ever, your friend LINCOLN."

Having watched his best friend embrace his marriage and the intimacy that accompanied it, Lincoln felt empowered to do the same. With some discreet prodding from mutual friends, including Speed, Lincoln and Mary Todd began to see each other again, wisely keeping it quiet to avoid being influenced by others. The romance rekindled, Lincoln proposed again, and on November 4, 1842, Abraham Lincoln and Mary Todd became husband and wife.

Speed never doubted that their marriages were inextricably intertwined, a point he later made to Herndon: "If I had not been married and happy—far more happy than I ever expected to be, [Lincoln] would not have married." But while their romantic decisions might have been linked, their busy careers, new families, and fifty-mile separation would nudge Lincoln and Speed apart for much of the next eighteen years.

It had been no easy decision for Speed to depart Springfield in May 1841 and return to Kentucky. Aside from leaving behind his business and political connections, Speed felt deeply guilty over abandoning Lincoln. He also had no desire to help manage the family's so-called "farm," which was actually one of the largest and most profitable plantations in the entire state. Once he arrived in Kentucky, though, Speed happily adapted to plantation life. He and Fanny moved into the "Pond Settlement," a thousand-acre plot of land roughly thirteen miles from Louisville, where the Farmington plantation was located. They would live there for the ensuing nine years, with Joshua focused on farming, planting corn, and overseeing his slaves when he wasn't helping out at Farmington.

Lincoln and Speed initially tried to maintain their friendship, but the gulf between them gradually widened, even if neither could fully articulate why. Speed's "farm" no doubt caused some awkwardness, a source of handsome profits as wealth (and the price of slaves) increased across the South in the 1840s and 1850s. When Lincoln wrote to Speed in 1842, shortly after the move, he discreetly avoided using words like "plantation" or "slaves." But his disapproval pervaded the letter: "As to your farm matter, I have no sympathy with you. I have no farm nor ever expect to have; and, consequently, have not studied the subject enough to be much interested with it."

Lincoln mostly tried to skirt these issues, though, by sharing details about married life and updates on Mary's health. In March 1843, with Mary five months pregnant, Lincoln wrote about the possibility of naming the upcoming child Joshua in his best friend's honor. He also noted that he was awaiting "with impatience . . . your visit this fall." But when fall came, Speed never visited, and when Lincoln and Mary's first child arrived on August 1, they named him "Robert," not "Joshua."

The growing distance between Lincoln and Speed likely arose from the divergence in their new lives, values, and priorities. But there were also more practical reasons, stemming from the legal work that Speed had pushed upon Lincoln after leaving Springfield. Speed wanted Lincoln to help collect his leftover debts in town and to secure favorable judgments for him in court. At a time when he needed income to support his new family, Lincoln had agreed to settle Speed's financial matters with little to no pay. But his resentment grew as he tried to juggle Speed's work with his own thriving law practice. As he increasingly postponed his duties for Speed, Speed was not shy in expressing his annoyance. It appears Lincoln took offense and did not write Speed any letters between July 1843 and October 1846.

Though this silence may simply reflect a gap in the historical record, it is clear that by October 1846, their rift was real. That month, the two exchanged angry letters over Lincoln's handling of the estate of Speed's recently deceased uncle, James Bell. In reply to Speed's incensed letter, Lincoln wrote curtly: "You, no doubt, assign the suspension of our correspondence to the true philosophical cause, though it must be confessed, by both of us, that this is rather a cold reason for allowing a friendship, such as ours, to die by degrees." After that, the friends stopped corresponding again for a full year, and Lincoln had Herndon deal with all of Speed's lingering business affairs. Aside from a short visit that Lincoln and Mary paid to Speed and Fanny in October 1847, the two men barely wrote one another until the mid-1850s.

Ironically, this nearly decade-long silence may have indirectly strengthened their friendship. As the two men drifted apart, they also found the independence to forge their own identities and sharpen their political thinking. Unbeknownst to them, they tracked parallel routes during that extended separation. After serving four terms in the Illinois House and opening his law practice with Herndon, Lincoln in 1847 moved on to the US House of Representatives. And at the same time as Lincoln entered Congress, Speed himself dove into politics, serving one term in the Kentucky House of Representatives, from 1848 to 1849.

During his single term, Speed squarely confronted the slavery crisis in his state just as the Mexican War was coming to an end. Disputes over slavery's status in lands won from Mexico raised the stakes of the issue within Kentucky. While abolishing slavery had never been part of the equation in Kentucky, debate still raged over whether (and how) to restrict it there. Back in 1833, Kentucky had tried to strike a balance by passing the controversial Non-Importation Act, which limited the importation of slaves into the state. Every year since then, the question of repealing the act came before the Kentucky legislature. During his term, Speed voted with the majority to repeal the 1833 law. In a significant victory for proslavery forces, Kentucky after 1849 could once again import slaves without restriction.

Despite an eventful first term, Speed ultimately found legislative work dull and tedious. As he confided to his sister, "My mind has been forced to act upon subjects foreign to my usual habit of thought." Once his term ended in 1849, he gladly left the House and returned to his plantation. Around the same time, Lincoln also made a similar decision. After completing one term in the US House of Representatives, he retreated from public life and resumed his law practice in Springfield. Soon afterward, he and Mary faced a devastating tragedy, when their second son, three-year-old Eddie, died of tuberculosis on February 1, 1850. They would welcome their third son, Willie, that December, but Eddie's death continued to cast a dark shadow over their lives.

Lincoln managed to pull himself together and focus on his legal career, but he still nursed a lingering sense of frustration over having left politics. A disconnect arose between his aspiration to be a leading Whig politician in the tradition of Henry Clay, and the stark reality of his work as a small-town lawyer at the country's periphery. Meanwhile, once back in the comforts of his Louisville home, Speed had arrived at an opposite, though complementary, realization: He had no interest in assuming a conspicuous role in politics and far preferred to operate behind-the-scenes, just as he had done back in Springfield with his old companion Lincoln.

Those twin realizations would soon prove crucial, as Lincoln in due time would need the backroom counsel of his dear friend more than ever.

Ironically, it was during the mid-1850s, as the politics of slavery increasingly tore apart the country, that Lincoln and Speed would resurrect their correspondence and mend their friendship. The catalyst came in 1854, when Democratic senator Stephen Douglas of Illinois—who, coincidentally, had once courted Mary Todd—introduced the Kansas-Nebraska

Act. This legislation not only reopened the issue of slavery that had seemingly been laid to rest with the Compromise of 1850; it also canceled the Missouri Compromise of 1820, which had prohibited slavery in all Louisiana Purchase states north of the 36°30' parallel. The Kansas-Nebraska Act reversed this principle, determining that new states north of the boundary should, through popular sovereignty, determine the legality of slavery in their own territories. The act's passage soon triggered the "Bleeding Kansas" violence that presaged the Civil War, as both proslavery and antislavery settlers rushed into the region. Watching the violence unfold, Lincoln grew increasingly disgusted by the direction of national affairs under Franklin Pierce (see chapter 2).

Several months later, in October 1854, Lincoln delivered a noted speech in Peoria, Illinois, in which he detailed his objections to the Kansas-Nebraska Act. He blasted the entire notion of popular sovereignty, particularly its repeal of Clay's Missouri Compromise. Most significantly, he attacked the morality of slavery itself, calling it a "monstrous injustice" and contending that slaves—as humans—possessed natural rights as surely as white men: "If the negro is a man, why then my ancient faith teaches me that 'all men are created equal'; and that there can be no moral right in connection with one man's making a slave of another." That captivating speech resurrected Lincoln's political career, signaling his return to the electoral stage just as his cherished Whigs faced looming obsolescence.

The drama swirling around the Kansas-Nebraska Act also led to the resumption of Lincoln and Speed's correspondence. As the Whig Party disintegrated, Speed was left unsure about which party to join. Though he would eventually become a Democrat, Speed at this point could not decide where he stood as both a slaveowner and a Unionist—a discrepancy that mirrored the inner conflict of many Kentuckians. It was in this context that Speed broke the decade-long ice, writing a letter to Lincoln on May 22, 1855, in which he finally broached the topic of slavery. Without hesitation, Speed claimed that he would rather see the Union dissolved than to surrender his constitutional right to own human property. He would soon be surprised by Lincoln's sharp response—so different now from the more reserved Lincoln of an earlier time.

Lincoln's reply on August 24, 1855, marked the first meaningful explication of his evolving position on slavery, in line with what Speed probably sensed was in Lincoln's heart but written more forcefully and without subtext. In framing his reply, Lincoln already knew the facts and history of Speed's slaveholding: Even though he now lived in Louisville, back at his thousand-acre "farm" Speed at various times kept between ten and eighteen slaves. When he didn't need them as servants, he hired them out for work elsewhere. As his colleagues noted, Speed regularly—in three different business partnerships—"engaged in brokering, selling and hiring enslaved African Americans."

This time, Lincoln did not avoid mentioning such facts, bluntly writing: "You know I dislike slavery; and you fully admit the abstract wrong of it." He then referred to Speed's talk of dissolving the Union, saying that though "I acknowledge your rights... under the constitution, in regard to your slaves," he did not believe Speed could ignore one plain fact that tested one's humanity: "poor creatures hunted down" and "carried back to their stripes, and unrewarded toils."

Lincoln then reminded his friend of the shackled slaves they had witnessed during their trip aboard the *Lebanon*, nearly fourteen years before: "That sight was a continuous torment to me; and I see something like it every time I touch the Ohio, or any other slave-border." And yet, in those ensuing years, Lincoln wrote, "I bite my lip and keep quiet."

In his original letter to Lincoln, Speed had tried both to mend the breach and anticipate Lincoln's moralizing. He insisted that despite his own slaveowning, as a Christian man, he would "rejoice" if those within the Kansas territory voted to reject slavery and become a free state. He appeared to be suggesting that he opposed the extension of slavery into new territories—a stance ostensibly closer to Lincoln's at the time. However, Lincoln replied that such sentiments meant little if Speed and those who shared his views continued to vote for candidates who made certain that slavery endured:

> No such man [who was against the spread of slavery] could be elected from any district in any slave-state.... The slave-breeders

> and slave-traders are a small, odious and detested class, among you; and yet, in politics, they dictate the course of all of you, and are as completely your masters as you are the masters of your own negroes.

Despairing over the nation's "pretty rapid" descent into "degeneracy," Lincoln further wrote: "We began by declaring that 'all men are created equal.' We now practically read it 'all men are created equal except negroes.'" If that came to pass, Lincoln concluded, he would prefer "emigrating to some country where they make no pretence [sic] of loving liberty—to Russia, for instance, where despotism can be taken pure, and without the base alloy of hypocracy."

This letter represented a significant departure for Lincoln, a rare moment in which he committed his opinions on slavery to paper. It was also significant for what it communicated about the status of his friendship with Speed. Despite their coldness over the past few years, Lincoln still implicitly trusted Speed—at least enough to know that his controversial thoughts would not be leaked to the newspapers. Lincoln made a point of ending his emphatic letter with warm feelings and his "kindest regards to Mrs. Speed." "I have more of her sympathy than I have of yours," he admitted. For the first time in at least a decade, the two friends had corresponded frankly with one another about the most fraught issue of their day. And ironically, as the nation inched closer to war, their friendship finally began to heal and strengthen.

Lincoln's correspondence with Speed during this contentious time testified to how much his thinking had matured and evolved over the past decade. In the aftermath of his Peoria speech, Lincoln pulled himself out of political retirement and shot to the forefront of a new anti-slavery force: the Republican Party. With the Whigs now defunct, the new Republican Party had cobbled together various northern factions—not just former Whigs but also members of the Free Soil, Liberty, and Democratic Parties. At first, Lincoln approached the Republican project with caution, fearing that it would become a vehicle for an extreme abolitionist platform. As he wrote to Speed in 1855, "I think I am a Whig, but others say there are no Whigs, and that I am an abolitionist.... I do no more than oppose the *extension* of slavery."

But with the nation in a state of constant upheaval, Lincoln moved steadily closer to his emancipationist views. In 1857, the Supreme Court ruled in *Dred Scott v. Sanford* that Black persons were not citizens and therefore possessed no rights under the Constitution. Lincoln denounced the controversial ruling as a violation of the Constitution and as proof of a Democratic conspiracy to perpetuate the "Slave Power." He echoed this impassioned argument in the summer and fall of 1858, when he ran for election to the US Senate and participated in a series of seven debates against incumbent senator Stephen Douglas. Nominally, the two men were competing for the Illinois Senate seat, but ultimately the debates contributed to the larger national conversation raging over slavery, and they enabled Lincoln to hone his moral position on the issue. With his ringing (and prophetic) declaration that "a house divided against itself, cannot stand," Lincoln shot to the forefront of the Republicans' antislavery cause.

Though Douglas ended up keeping his Senate seat, Lincoln would gain a much more coveted prize. Almost immediately after losing the 1858 Senate contest, he began collecting newspaper transcriptions of his debates with Douglas. He then gave his clippings to the powerful Republican operative Oran Follett, whose publishing firm released them in book form in 1860—right in time for Lincoln's presidential campaign. The book proved to be a blockbuster success, selling out in just a few months, and helped convince the Republican Party to nominate Lincoln for president at its 1860 convention in Chicago.

Hearing the news, Speed quickly sent his congratulations as "a warm, personal friend, though as you are perhaps aware a political opponent." He expressed his confidence that if Lincoln were elected, he would "honestly administer the government—and make a lasting reputation for [himself]." Speed pointedly avoided promising that he would vote for his friend—he likely voted for one of the two Democratic candidates that fall—but jokingly added that Lincoln *could* count on Fanny Speed's vote (women would not gain suffrage until 1920). Taking the ribbing in his good-natured way, Lincoln poked back at his friend: "I scarcely needed to be told Mrs. Speed is for me with her nature and views. She could not well be otherwise."

Election day fell on November 6, 1860, two days after Abraham and Mary's eighteenth wedding anniversary. Lincoln won the presidency with 180 Electoral College votes but less than 40 percent of the popular vote. The Southern Democrat John C. Breckinridge and Northern Democrat Stephen A. Douglas divided the vote of their party, while John Bell of the Constitutional Union Party took another sliver of the total. Despite far surpassing Lincoln's popular vote total, Breckinridge, Bell, and Douglas combined could muster only 128 electoral votes among them.

It was the most rancorous election in American history, but Speed didn't get caught up in its vitriol. In a congratulatory letter to Lincoln "upon your elevation to the highest position in the world," Speed wrote: "As a friend, I am rejoiced at your success—as a political opponent I am not disappointed. The result is what I expected." Despite not voting for his friend, Speed offered his help to maneuver through the political minefield that was Kentucky, recognizing the daunting challenges ahead: "How to deal with the combustible material lying around without setting fire to the edifice of which we are all so proud and of which you will be the chief custodian is a difficult task."

But Speed also emphasized that he would give his observations only as a "private citizen seeking no office for himself nor for any friend he has." If Lincoln wanted to use Speed's Kentucky connections and his status as a slaveowner and Democrat to preserve the state's place in the Union, he would have to do so on Speed's terms. And the president-elect gratefully accepted—recognizing that Speed's viewpoints on slavery, though diverging from his own, represented a significant cross-section of the Kentucky population.

In Lincoln's view, Kentucky was a tinderbox—a border state whose politics were curiously split between a pro-Union legislature and a

Confederacy-leaning governor. Though a slave state, Kentucky nonetheless was in no rush to leave the Union with its southern neighbors. Still, with animosity toward abolitionism running deep in the state, Lincoln had won just 1,365 votes—barely 1 percent—of all those cast. Aware of this uphill battle, the president-elect was determined to keep all four border states—Delaware, Maryland, Missouri, and Kentucky—in the Union, since they could tilt the advantage against the North if they joined the Confederacy. Kentucky in particular represented the linchpin of Lincoln's border-state strategy due to its large population and strategic position on the Ohio River, between the North and the Deep South. This central location made it an ideal staging ground from which to launch military invasions into enemy territory.

Given these tricky calculations, Lincoln wasted little time reaching out to his oldest friend. Less than two weeks after the election, they met in Chicago's Tremont Hotel, a stately, five-story brick building and the most luxurious hotel west of New York City. When they settled into Speed's room, it had been nearly a decade since the two friends had last laid eyes on each other. Just like the old days in their room above the store, Lincoln immediately flung himself down on the bed, looking worn out but wasting no time getting to the point.

"Speed, what are your pecuniary conditions—are you rich or poor?" he asked.

The message was clear. Despite their differing viewpoints over slavery, and Speed's earlier protestations, Lincoln wanted Speed in his administration, and ideally in his Cabinet, to increase the diversity of views. At bottom, Lincoln approached politics as a pragmatist, and he recognized that Speed's political stance—though in conflict with his own—needed to be considered and respected, another illustration of his desire to assemble a "team of rivals" in order to consider all opposing viewpoints. Having a slave state like Kentucky remain pro-Union would represent a crucial victory for Lincoln when secessionist sentiment reached fever pitch. And Speed had all the qualities of someone who could help pull it off: trustworthy, widely respected across partisan divides, a Democratic slaveowner who nonetheless agreed with Henry Clay's pro-Union ideals.

Speed was flattered by the offer. But Lincoln was such a polarizing figure in Kentucky that accepting the offer might subject Speed and his family to opprobrium and ultimately financial hardship.

"I do not think you have any office within your gift that I can afford to take," Speed replied.

Even without an official job title, Speed soon emerged as an indispensable behind-the-scenes operative for Lincoln. Heeding Speed's advice, Lincoln sought to reassure Kentucky that he hoped for peace and that any impending war would be fought not to eradicate slavery but simply to preserve the Union. Shortly before his inauguration, the president delivered a speech in Cincinnati directed at his "Fellow citizens of Kentucky—friends—brethren" across the Ohio River. "We mean to leave you alone, and in no way to interfere with your institution," he vowed. With his deep ties to the state's Whig Party, his wife's Lexington family, and his connections to Kentuckians in Springfield, Lincoln remained acutely aware of the volatile situation there.

Once the Civil War erupted at Fort Sumter on April 12, 1861, Lincoln faced even greater pressure to tamp down tensions in Kentucky. During the early months of the war, he privately confessed, "I think to lose Kentucky is nearly the same as to lose the whole game." It now became imperative to fortify pro-Union forces in the state to guard against a secessionist uprising. So Lincoln authorized the delivery of five thousand muskets in a clandestine operation led by Lieutenant William "Bull" Nelson, a mountain-sized man charged with getting guns into the hands of Union loyalists. Nelson boarded a train for Louisville, guns in tow, with explicit instructions to work closely with Lincoln's man on the ground in Kentucky, Joshua Speed, who had enlisted the help of his older brother James. The Speeds connected Nelson with a host of leading Unionists in the capital city of Frankfort to distribute the weapons.

Speed remained a key ally throughout the rest of 1861, doing his best to keep Kentucky armed and in the Union. In the late summer he wrote to the president, prodding him to send another shipment of guns, and then traveled to Washington to secure additional funds for the Kentucky militia. The militia's commander, General William Sherman, had repeatedly failed to obtain more money from Simon Cameron, Lincoln's first secretary of war. Thanks to Speed, the president overruled Cameron and released $100,000 to the militia. But Speed remained in a most delicate spot. Kentucky's governor, Beriah Magoffin, was a steadfast Confederate sympathizer, as were many of Speed's friends and business associates. Seeking to raise seventy-five thousand troops at the start of the war, Cameron sent Magoffin a telegram asking for four militia units.

"Your dispatch received," Magoffin replied. "In answer I say emphatically Kentucky will furnish no troops for the wicked purpose of subduing her sister Southern states."

Speed's position grew even more precarious when Union general John Fremont declared martial law in Missouri and freed all slaves owned by those aiding and abetting the Confederacy. This proclamation went even further than Congress' First Confiscation Act, which applied only to freeing slaves forced into Confederate military labor. Fremont's order thus sent a revolutionary message: The war to save the Union was necessarily a war against slavery.

Mindful of Fremont's political sway and charisma, Lincoln initially responded with caution, urging the general to "conform" to the First Confiscation Act. Not doing so, Lincoln warned gently, would "certainly alarm our Southern Union friends and... perhaps ruin our rather fair prospects for Kentucky." Speed, meanwhile, immediately viewed the Fremont declaration with alarm, recognizing that it posed an urgent and highly delicate predicament: If this became a war to liberate the slaves rather than to save the Union, Speed knew, Kentuckians would want no part of it.

So Speed wrote Lincoln a series of letters, warning that the Fremont proclamation would unleash violence and insurrection and lead to the possible extermination of slaves themselves: "So fixed is public sentiment in this state against freeing negroes & allowing negroes to be emancipated & remain among us—That you had as well attack the freedom of worship in the north...—as to wage war in a slave state on such a principle—." Not content merely to correspond, Speed then traveled to Washington to meet Lincoln in person. He also asked a prominent Unionist and Kentuckian, Joseph Holt, to reassure the state that "this is no war upon individual property and the institution of slavery." Ultimately, Lincoln removed Fremont from his post and had the proclamation withdrawn. Thanks to Speed's timely and wise intercession, Kentucky never left the Union.

As discreetly as possible, Speed continued to help Lincoln, whether by alerting Washington when more munitions were needed or by working to elect pro-Union candidates to Congress and the state legislature. He even made recommendations for positions the president needed to fill, nearly all of which Lincoln accepted. As the war raged on and Lincoln's morale sagged, Speed sought to cheer him up: "I sent you some Kentucky hams—six—did you get them?" he closed one of his letters. Nobody had Lincoln's ear, or stomach, quite like Speed. For Thanksgiving that fall, Lincoln had as his guests Joshua and Fanny Speed.

The happiness of that Thanksgiving soon gave way to tragedy. Only three months later, on February 20, 1862, Lincoln's third son, Willie, died of typhoid fever at the White House. Having already lost one son in 1850, the death of a second son left permanent marks on Lincoln and Mary (their youngest son, Thomas, would survive his father, but die at age eighteen, in 1871). Elizabeth Keckly, a former slave close to the family, later recalled observing the president stand "in silent, awe-stricken wonder" beside the bed where a lifeless Willie lay. Lincoln's private secretary John Hay echoed Keckly's remarks, noting that the president changed profoundly after Willie's death, though "he gave no outward sign of his trouble, but kept about his work the same as ever."

Just as he had done after his first son's death, Lincoln again transcended his personal pain to ensure the welfare of his country. Pushing aside his depression, he busied himself with what would become the crowning achievement of his presidency.

In July 1862, Joshua and his brother James, a prominent attorney, came to Washington just as Lincoln began preparing the Emancipation Proclamation. Before even showing a draft of his speech to his top advisors,

Lincoln read it to the Speed brothers. If the president expected them to rally around his plan, their reaction certainly left him disappointed. The objection from James, who had already freed most of his slaves and once called slavery "the greatest national sin," was mainly over process: freeing slaves should be done by the states, not the federal government. Joshua, still a slaveowner, didn't disagree with Lincoln that slavery needed to end eventually. His argument was over the tool: Freeing slaves by presidential fiat—just like the clunky Fremont proclamation earlier—might cause a massive backlash in Kentucky that could compromise Unionist support.

Despite the opposition of his friend, Lincoln announced the Emancipation Proclamation on September 22, 1862, and it took effect on January 1, 1863. Ironically, the Emancipation Proclamation came a full year after Fremont's own Missouri Proclamation. The key difference, however, was timing. A year earlier, Lincoln continued to believe that a war fought to emancipate slaves would be far too risky, particularly in terms of losing the support of the crucial border states, especially his beloved Kentucky. By the summer of 1862, however, Lincoln increasingly perceived that his moral ideals needed to align with political realities—that preserving the Union and freeing the slaves were inextricable goals. In this momentous shift in his thinking, Lincoln finally diverged fully from Speed, convinced that it would be impossible to maintain the Union without outlawing slavery. Ignoring the moral dubiousness of slavery, Lincoln now saw, would ultimately undermine the character and resilience of the nation itself.

One year after the issuance of the Emancipation Proclamation, in a conversation Speed had with the president, Lincoln reflected on how the proclamation was consistent with their conversations nearly a generation earlier. As Speed remembered, Lincoln expressed his hope that the Speed brothers would, soon enough, see "the harvest of good of the act which he would erelong glean from it." The president also reminded Joshua about his depression in the winter of 1841, when his only objection to dying was doing nothing "to make any human being remember that he had lived."

"I believe," Lincoln later told Speed, "that in this measure my fondest hopes will be realized." The proclamation, by connecting his name to something that will "redound to the interest of his fellow man," had finally given Lincoln's life meaning. Both Speed brothers in time came to share Lincoln's vision.

As the deadliest war in American history continued to grind through 1864, Lincoln appointed Joshua's brother James as his new attorney general. Lincoln had developed a fondness for James on his first visit to the Speed plantation in 1841, and a separate friendship flourished between them as the years went on. They bonded over a shared love for the law and their increasing agreement on political issues. The position opened when Lincoln's first attorney general, Edward Bates, quit out of frustration that he was wielding so little authority. When Lincoln explained James's appointment to a friend, he said: "I will offer [the post] to James Speed, of Louisville, a man I know well, though not so well as I know his brother Joshua. That, however, is not strange, for I slept with Joshua for four years, and I suppose I ought to know him well."

Early in 1865, Joshua Speed was preparing to leave Washington for Kentucky when Lincoln asked to see him. It would be their last time together. The president had spent much of the day hearing appeals from the dozens of people who waited to see him every day. The last of them, Speed recalled, were two women from western Pennsylvania petitioning Lincoln to release a man imprisoned for avoiding the draft.

One was the mother and the other the wife of the prisoner. When the president agreed to free the man, the younger woman rushed forward and knelt before him in gratitude. Lincoln asked her to stand up, clearly uncomfortable with her awkward display. The older woman then said, "Goodbye, Mr. Lincoln, we will never meet again till we meet in Heaven."

"I am afraid that I will never get there," Lincoln replied, "but your wish that you will meet me there has fully paid for all I have done for you."

Once the women had left, the president sat down in a chair and pulled it close to the fireplace. He took off his boots and watched his feet steaming in front of the flames. Looking drawn and haggard, Lincoln told Speed he didn't feel well, that his hands and feet were always cold.

"I suppose I should be in bed," Lincoln said.

Speed chided him for not resting enough, saying he should not be spending so much time and energy on seeing petitioners. Lincoln told him that he was very much mistaken—that a simple act of forgiveness and kindness had brought those two women immeasurable happiness.

"Speed, die when I may, I want it said of me by those who know me best... that I always plucked a thistle and planted a flower where I thought a flower would grow."

With that, the old friends said goodbye. Joshua Speed never saw Abraham Lincoln again.

Lincoln's assassination on April 14, 1865, generated an outpouring of grief and mourning unequaled in the country's history. For nearly three weeks, from his funeral in Washington to his final burial in Springfield, Illinois, millions of Americans left their homes and farms to assemble by the rail tracks as the train carrying Lincoln's coffin passed slowly by. There is no record of how Speed first heard or reacted to his friend's death. His brother James, as a Cabinet officer, had been at Lincoln's bedside when he died on the morning of April 15. But Joshua had stayed home in Louisville, where he organized his own private memorial service rather than participating in any of the official ceremonies. When after years of squabbling the city of Springfield finally decided to erect an obelisk monument above the graves of Lincoln and his two young sons, Speed and sixty members of his extended family helped provide money for it. In the following years, he also exchanged detailed letters with Herndon, who had begun working on a biography of their mutual friend.

Despite Lincoln's untimely passing, the early postwar years brought tangible success for Joshua Speed. His relationship with Lincoln gave him a social cachet that translated into enhanced business opportunities. Doors opened that allowed him to make more profitable investments, purchase more desirable tracts of land, and even buy a hotel. Companies that witnessed his wartime leadership helping to keep Kentucky in the Union sought his wisdom; public service organizations sought his participation. The experiences he had shared with Lincoln, those that had transformed him, made him stand out in a world grappling with the reverberations of the Civil War.

On that enduring issue of race, Speed's views finally moved closer to Lincoln's in the aftermath of his death. The war's end and the start of Reconstruction did nothing to mollify the bitter divisiveness the issue engendered. In its wake, Jim Crow laws were enacted across the South that replaced physical bondage with legal segregation. The killing may have ended, but racism—and the institutions that supported it—remained as strong as ever. Watching all this from his native Kentucky, Speed gradually developed a more progressive view toward Black persons. At the end of 1865, Speed released his two remaining slaves when the Thirteenth Amendment emancipating slaves became law (though Kentucky was one of only three states that didn't ratify the Amendment until the twentieth century).

Joshua Speed's final years were marred by an increasingly futile struggle with Type 2 diabetes, which he had first developed in his early forties. Confined to a wheelchair, he traveled to spas and the Caribbean seeking relief from the debilitating disease, but to no avail. He died on May 29, 1882, at the age of sixty-eight—shortly before the Civil Rights Cases of 1883 proceeded to curtail the rights of Black persons yet again, challenging the legacy his best friend left behind.

CHAPTER 4

Woodrow Wilson and Colonel House

The Man and the Opportunity

Years before there existed a modern Department of State or US Foreign Service, long ahead of the Central Intelligence Agency or National Security Council, and decades prior to the National Security Agency or even the Office of Presidential Personnel, there was Colonel Edward Mandell House.

Over seven turbulent, historic, and ultimately bloody years from 1912 to 1919, a man who had never held public office, negotiated a global agreement, met a single foreign dignitary, nor evinced any particular interest in international affairs was entrusted by the president of the United States with helping determine whether America would be at peace or at war. Unknown outside of his home state of Texas and untested outside of his narrow business and political interests, House also helped determine presidential appointments, proclamations, policy positions, and marriage announcements. If you coveted a senior position in the administration, he was the man to impress. Once appointed, if you wanted to know whether you held favor or not, he was the man to ask. If you needed insight into Wilson's mood, he was the man to consult. And if you happened to be the president, and you wanted to know if you should run for reelection, reprimand a foreign ally, or replace your private secretary, his was the advice you sought to guide your decision.

He was born Edward Mandell House, but by the time he reached the pinnacle of power, people knew him as Colonel House, a moniker bestowed by one of his political patrons, Texas governor James Hogg, despite his complete lack of military experience. For nearly all of President Woodrow Wilson's two terms in office, Colonel House, as slight in his physique as he was shrewd and secure in his abilities, would serve unofficially as First Friend, diplomat in chief, day trip companion, sympathetic ear, campaign manager, and personnel director. With the possible exception of Robert Kennedy fifty years later, no other advisor would ever again exercise as much clout as Colonel House. All the more incredible is the fact that this man had not even talked to Wilson until the year before his election to the presidency. Within two weeks of their meeting, according to House's diary, their connection felt so complete that when "the Colonel" asked whether his new pal realized how short their acquaintance had been, Wilson replied, "My dear friend, we have known one another always."

All his life, from his birth into Texas privilege in 1858 until his death in 1938, House sought to be a person of consequence. Aware of his physical limitations, he decided early on that he was better suited to a life "behind the man" than to be the man himself. Of average height and trim build, with a gray mustache that offset sparkling eyes, House never needed fame but he craved power. The Colonel prized a special kind of power, however—the quiet kind wielded far from the glare of public accountability but exercised with cold efficacy in the rooms that mattered. His life can be appreciated best as a play in four acts that take him from mischievous child to global protagonist.

In Act I, House emerges as the youngest of three sons born to a wealthy Houston entrepreneur, a rambunctious, pugilistic kid who falls off a swing at age twelve, suffers a concussion, possibly contracts malaria, and becomes convinced thereafter that his body cannot withstand either hot weather or physical challenges. Even so, he believes at a young age that his destiny stretches as wide as the Texas prairie. If the physical feats of Sam Houston or Stephen Austin are now beyond him, House aims for eminence in his own, more nuanced way. He goes off to Cornell, but returns home when his father becomes ill. After his father's death, House joins his family's banking and real estate empire, grows it through shrewd deals, and watches his standing in Texas soar. In early 1881, he meets Loulie Hunter, daughter of a prosperous cotton grower; by August they marry. A year later they have their first of two daughters.

In Act II, House becomes the modern-day "political fixer," the nucleus of a political machine based in Austin that will dictate Democratic Party politics for almost two decades. He's especially intrigued by how candidates and voters can be manipulated. What motivates men to run for office? What kind of candidate is most amenable to outside advice? How can someone influence a strong-willed man? What House learns most of all is that having a well-oiled political organization is the key to political success, and so he organizes—in the thousands—volunteers, poll watchers, and fund-raisers. Through its patronage, financial resources, and relentless coordination, his machine facilitates the election of four consecutive Democratic candidates to the Texas governorship, from 1894 to 1906. Now known as "the Colonel," he's everywhere but nowhere. Everyone in Texas is his friend because, as he counsels his charges, "make friends of your enemies and better friends of your old ones." He raises money, lots of it, and doles it out generously to his operatives. He displays such discretion that he earns the sobriquet of a "Sphinx in a soft felt hat." At any point House can become a US senator simply by raising his hand, but never does.

Eventually, even the sprawling state of Texas isn't big enough for House, who in Act III sets his sights on New York City and the world at large. He takes an apartment in Manhattan for the winter, travels to Europe in the spring, spends the summer on the North Shore outside Boston, and then returns to his New York apartment in the autumn when the weather cools. The Colonel obsesses over the passage of time: Will he ever become a man of national or global consequence? He realizes he needs to attach himself to someone on the rise who will recognize his unique abilities and use them to change the country or even the world. Several candidates catch his attention during these years, but as a Democrat in a decade dominated by Republicans, the pickings are slim.

Now in his midfifties, the Colonel fears time is running out for his climactic fourth act. The 1912 presidential election looms, and the long ascendant Republican Party is riven and looking vulnerable at last after nearly two decades in power. This is his moment, and House knows it. But whom will he find? Who will find him?

House finally finds his man in 1911: a taciturn, flinty former president of Princeton University turned first-term governor of New Jersey and budding presidential candidate. A man who has everything going for him except a best friend to help sharpen his thoughts, ease his fears, win the presidency, run the country, and maybe even shape the world.

Thomas Woodrow Wilson always wanted to be a statesman. With his Calvinist upbringing, he dreamed of doing momentous things that would ensure eternal salvation and satisfy an innate need to direct events. One family servant recalled a very young Tommy remarking to his father at the dinner table: "Papa, when I get to be a man, I'm going to have a lofty position."

Born in Virginia in 1856, Wilson spent his entire childhood in the South, first in Augusta, Georgia, and then in Columbia, South Carolina. Whether because of dyslexia or some other undiagnosed disability, he didn't learn to read until age ten. But Tommy caught up fast, with words stirring his passion. Prodded by his father, a Presbyterian minister, Tommy became highly proficient at essay writing, almost always on "real world" political subjects. In 1875, he headed north to attend the College of New Jersey, the former name of Princeton University. "Father, I have made a discovery; I have found that I have a mind," he wrote his parents soon after enrolling. And he continued to dream of greatness, often ending his debates by declaring, "When I meet you in the Senate, I'll argue that out with you." Shortly after graduating from Princeton, he dropped his first name, Thomas, in favor of his second, reportedly to highlight his connection to James Woodrow, head of Columbia Theological Seminary in South Carolina, and also because he found "Woodrow" more dignified.

After Princeton Wilson decided to give the law a try, graduating from the University of Virginia law school. But when he started to actually practice it, he found the profession tedious and not to his liking. Now twenty-seven years of age, Wilson finally resolved his career indecision by choosing academia. He received his PhD in political science from Johns Hopkins in 1886. While there, he poured all of his energies into his first book, *Congressional Government*, which advocated for the imposition of British parliamentary methods to reform the US Congress. The book was such a success that Johns Hopkins awarded him his doctorate even though he never completed its requirements.

His singular opportunity came when Princeton recruited him for its faculty in 1891. So much excitement greeted his arrival on campus that more than half the junior and senior classes signed up for his first course. His teaching legend grew, and so did his national fame. A little over a decade later, in 1902, Princeton named him its president, and Wilson could finally feel his dreams of greatness becoming reality. Just before his inauguration, he confessed to his wife, "I feel like a new prime minister getting ready to address his constituents." As Princeton's president, Wilson introduced the preceptorial system—still in place today—whereby students learned in small seminars instead of crowded lectures. And he even helped save college football by reforming its rules to make it safer.

In academia, there's a saying that its politics are so vicious because the stakes are so small. Never was that adage more true than at Princeton in 1907, when Wilson became mired in a dispute that would end his halcyon days there. Wilson believed that Princeton's famous eating clubs were antithetical to his egalitarian vision of campus life and hatched a plan to eliminate them in favor of residential colleges. But a proposal he thought sound instead generated fierce resistance from faculty, students, and alumni who called it "un-American" and contrary to Princeton's spirit and history. When the matter finally came to a faculty vote in the spring of 1908, even Wilson's closest ally, Professor John Grier Hibben, opposed him. The episode did not just uncover a philosophical split; it opened a deep personal wound that would have immense and lasting consequences for Wilson's psyche.

A Presbyterian minister like Wilson's father, Hibben had joined the Princeton faculty a year after Wilson and immediately became part of his tiny circle of family and friends. They grew so close that twice over the following decade Hibben would manage Wilson's affairs when he came down with serious health issues that required him to take leaves of absence. Hibben even served as acting president of the university when Wilson decamped to Europe to recuperate. Wilson's dependence on Hibben became so great that once, when his friend was about to embark for an extended stay in Europe, Wilson wrote to his wife: "Doesn't that make you feel a little blank? It does me, very.... What shall we do without them?"

So when Hibben sided with the opposition on Wilson's plan—in fact seconding the offending motion—it dealt a devastating blow to Wilson both personally and professionally. Wilson excised him from his life, immediately and completely. According to Wilson biographer John Milton Cooper, "nothing up to that time had ever hurt Wilson so deeply.... His daughter Margaret would later tell a family friend, 'The two major tragedies in Father's life were his failure to carry over the League of Nations and the break with Mr. Hibben.'"

Soon after the defeat of his initiative, Wilson became convinced it would be best to put Princeton behind him. His timing proved propitious. After losing the White House in four straight elections, the Democratic Party at that very moment was searching for a fresh face. Woodrow Wilson appeared as their man: young, prominent, a Southerner not defined by Dixie, a stirring orator, and a distinguished man of letters. Once Wilson indicated his interest, party leaders rallied around him, confident that the neophyte candidate would be malleable to their political needs. With the 1912 presidential election still two years away, they could test Wilson's political abilities by drafting him for governor of New Jersey. He accepted the nomination at the same time he resigned from Princeton (Hibben succeeded him), showed impressive mettle and charisma on the stump, and won the race easily.

He needed only four months as New Jersey's new governor—a period of remarkable legislative achievements—to convince the Democrats that he would be a formidable candidate. As early as February 1911, Wilson had begun meeting with advisors to map out a presidential campaign. In May he began stumping across the nation, and in July his headquarters opened in New York City. By the summer, the Wilson presidential campaign was in full swing.

As his drive intensified, however, what Wilson truly required was someone who would be to him on the campaign trail and hopefully later in the White House what Jack Hibben had been to him at Princeton. Somebody who would ground him, nurture him, and comfort him—but also guide him, challenge him, and reassure him. The lack of intimate friendship in his life loomed large, at the very moment he needed it most.

As Wilson lay the groundwork for his presidential run in 1911, House continued his search for a candidate to back. That spring, he wrote a letter to one of Wilson's early supporters outlining the governor's prospects in Texas. As he suspected, the supporter forwarded the letter to Wilson with the notation that the author was "an exceptionally able man, well-to-do financially and, I think sound politically." Not taking any chances, House also asked two other journalists friendly with Wilson to talk to the candidate and tout House as an "eminent and effectual" politician. Meanwhile, the Colonel exerted just enough organizing effort in Texas to prove his increasing interest in the candidate and to ensure that if Wilson won the Lone Star State, House "could eventually claim some reward."

After months of maneuvering and years of longing, the man—and the opportunity he so long craved—were finally joined. The moment had come.

The meeting occurred on November 24, 1911. The only historical record of the fateful encounter comes from House's pen, and not surprisingly, it bursts with excitement. Describing the meeting as a "delightful visit" and a "perfectly good time," House then reflected on how fateful it all felt: "the chance I have always [wanted]; never before have I found both the man and the opportunity." They liked each other immediately. "We talked and talked. We knew each other for congenial souls at the very beginning," House later recalled. By the end of their hour-long session, Wilson was as smitten as the Colonel. "Each of us started to ask the other when he would be free for another meeting, and [we were] laughing over our mutual enthusiasm," House remembered. Five days after that first visit, the new friends met again. The Colonel later claimed that the meal went on "for hours" during which they "talked about everything." Of Wilson, he said: "I never met a man whose thought ran so identically with mine." The match was made.

From this auspicious beginning, the two men embarked on a historic, eight-year journey that would shape America and its role in the world for the next century, for better or for worse. Their dramatic and legendary relationship would play out across a canvas stretched over Washington, London, Berlin, Moscow, and, most fatefully, Paris. The questions it would encompass were as momentous as entering a world war and as trivial as reviewing the Wilsons' household finances. By its stunning if inevitable end in 1919, the friendship had grown so charged and so public that House would spend the last two decades of his life quarreling with Wilson partisans over who held responsibility for the successes and failures of his eight-year presidency.

What was never in doubt was the near absolute confidence Wilson placed in House to conduct many of his most important responsibilities during the first six years of his presidency. Their shared conceptions of America's moral and military role in a chaotic, splintered world would serve as the guiding principle of American foreign policy for the next hundred years—through two world wars, a cold war, and a war on terror. Ultimately, Wilson delegated an unprecedented measure of authority to a private citizen that under today's rules would never be allowed. That decision still stands as a cautionary tale of a president who in the end grew too reliant on a single friend—a man he barely knew before empowering him—and lived to regret it.

As a political operative of the highest order, House by nature possessed unparalleled cunning. Nothing could be simple. Angles had to be examined and tested, options however remote considered. So as fall turned to winter and winter to spring in 1912, House still played all his cards, even if he had professed his love and support to Wilson, and Wilson to him. He went back to Austin, fell ill, and watched as the hands of Wilson's political rivals strengthened or weakened.

His most immediate role in the Wilson campaign orbit was to win the backing of William Jennings Bryan, who remained popular and a potential presidential threat to Wilson. House perfectly played his hand, intimating to Wilson and his advisors that he alone could bring Bryan along and that his intervention was working, even if such claims exaggerated the actual influence he had over the Great Commoner. Aside from controlling Bryan, House also aimed to deliver Texas's delegates to Wilson, and in this endeavor too he might well have exaggerated the role he played. As political scientists Alexander and Juliette George wrote in 1954, "The Colonel was wondrously skilled at indirectly conveying the idea that he was almost magically efficient and had mysterious and powerful resources at his command" to accomplish any given task.

Still, House refused to commit fully to the Wilson campaign until Wilson clinched the nomination, and by the end of the primaries, Wilson still lagged far behind the delegate leader, House Speaker Champ Clark of Missouri. Keeping all his options open, House skipped the Democratic Convention in Baltimore and headed to Europe, claiming to Wilson that he needed to avoid the summer heat. But he might just as well have been calculating that if Wilson won, House could claim that his help, as he predicted, wasn't ultimately needed; and if Wilson lost, the Colonel could still attach himself to the eventual nominee. That's what political operatives do.

Wilson came from behind to win the nomination on the forty-sixth ballot, setting up one of the most rollicking general election campaigns in US history. In the general election, Wilson had the fortune of running against not just one venerable Republican opponent, but two: incumbent president William Howard Taft, the official Republican nominee; and former president Teddy Roosevelt, the Progressive ("Bull Moose") Party candidate. Rounding out the field was Eugene Debs as the Socialist Party standard-bearer. With Republicans gravely split, all Wilson had to do to win was hold the Democratic base. The Colonel received the news of Wilson's nomination by telegram. Despite promising Wilson he would return to the States immediately, House continued to dally, not arriving back in New York until mid-September. Now with nothing to lose, House went all-in for his new friend, setting up shop at the Democratic Party headquarters in Manhattan while making himself available whenever and wherever the candidate needed him.

Almost immediately the Colonel discovered he had plenty of room to maneuver. Wilson's two most senior advisors, William McAdoo and William McCombs, were both political neophytes. Even better for House, they shared a mutual hatred, and they spent as much time scheming to defeat each other as they did managing the campaign. House filled the breach, conferring regularly with Wilson on tactics and strategy both in person and by phone. When Roosevelt had to suspend his campaign in October after being wounded in an assassination attempt, McAdoo advised Wilson to continue campaigning. The Colonel disagreed, arguing to Wilson that to do so would look unchivalrous and ungenerous. Wilson sided with his informal new counselor: He would stay off the road, and he suffered no harm for doing so. By the end of the campaign, House could confide in a close friend: "My relations with [Wilson] are closer than anyone knows. In writing to me he signs himself sometimes 'Gratefully yours' and other times 'Affectionately yours' and I believe that he feels it." A genuine friendship of trust and warmth was forming that would last for the next seven years.

On November 5, Wilson won the election in a landslide, trouncing his three rivals with 435 electoral votes. He heard the news while sitting at home in Princeton surrounded by his family. House and his wife, Loulie, were monitoring the same returns from the Plaza Hotel on Fifty-Ninth Street. By nine o'clock that night, with the results confirmed, both men had achieved their lifelong dreams. At fifty-six years of age, the president-elect had finally attained the "lofty position" he had yearned for since his youth. And the Colonel at fifty-four was finally the "man of consequence" he had dreamed of being ever since his days on the Texas plains. The world now opened up—theirs to conquer, together.

The two men got right to work following Wilson's election. Their first order of business played perfectly to House's strength: choosing the men (and they were all men then) to occupy the most senior jobs in the incoming Wilson administration. In the 1830s New York senator William Learned Marcy had proclaimed, "To the victors belong the spoils," a remark that led to the coinage of the word "spoils system." Ever since the Jacksonian era, one of the great perks of winning the presidency was the chance to reward family, friends, and supplicants with plum positions in the federal bureaucracy. In 1913, nine Cabinet positions existed and behind them hundreds of other jobs that offered high pay, prestige, and job security for at least four years. As historian and journalist Godfrey Hodgson notes, the president-elect had neither the "experience nor the temperament" for personnel matters. So overnight, House moved "from being a mysterious figure occasionally glimpsed closeted with the candidate to 'the man to see' " for anyone seeking a job.

Almost from the moment the election results came in, House was totally consumed with filling the Cabinet and sub-Cabinet. Whatever the Colonel might have lacked in pure intelligence he more than made up for in emotional intelligence. Reading a room, making personal connections, and evaluating people were his forte. Within weeks House emerged as *the* man in control of personnel issues, freeing an appreciative Wilson—who viewed patronage as a "nuisance"—to concentrate on other matters. "You can see so much more than other men do and report it so much better, always getting the right point," Wilson wrote from Bermuda, where he was taking a month's vacation.

The process of staffing the executive branch "cemented House's personal relationship with Wilson, and indeed the House family's relationship with the Wilson family," according to Hodgson. Upon his return from Bermuda in early 1913, the president-elect visited the Colonel at his New York apartment at least six times; their relationship deepened over leisurely meals and trips to Broadway, where they saw *Peg o' my Heart* and *Years of Discretion*. Wilson "valued [the Colonel's] opinion more than that of any other man," Wilson's wife, Ellen, told Loulie House during the transition, and this devotion showed. Of Wilson's first ten senior appointments, House was at least partially responsible for seven, including two Texas associates. The Colonel had become so indispensable in so short a time that by Christmas he dared not take his planned trip home to Texas.

House wasn't just the key voice in Wilson's choices for senior appointments. As Charles Neu writes in his authoritative biography of House, he also controlled "the flow of information" to the president-elect. The *New York Herald* perfectly captured this power in a February 19, 1913, dispatch. After describing the futility congressional leaders felt journeying to Princeton only to be stonewalled by Wilson, the journalist cited the frustration of one member who spoke for them all: "One of them said to me: 'I know that Governor Wilson was elected President... [and] will be inaugurated on March 4. Further than that I know nothing... You will have to ask either the President-elect or Colonel House.'" Wilson held House in such high esteem that shortly after the election he offered him any Cabinet post except secretary of state, by then reserved for Bryan. After the Colonel declined, Wilson pressed further, urging him to become a "member of his official family," which House again refused. Like Vernon Jordan would do eighty years later (see chapter 9), the Colonel prized his autonomy more than an official title. He was financially secure, a man who needed nothing, and such men aren't owned even by someone as powerful as the president of the United States. He could accomplish as much if not more floating outside official circles, exerting heavyweight impact with minimal accountability. House understood intuitively that this freedom would allow him to engage on matters that most interested him while ignoring those that didn't.

As the Wilsons started their new life in the White House, the Colonel opted to remain in New York. He settled into a routine well known to power brokers navigating the New York-Washington axis by frequently riding the rails that connected the two cities. By nature a solitary man, the president became even more isolated in the White House, so the calls to House came often. And never a glad-hander, Wilson from the start eschewed the obligatory schmoozing with politicians and reporters, frequently delegating those duties to House, whose soft touch, deferential demeanor, and keen political skills became indispensable assets to the new president.

The Colonel worked tirelessly those first few months of Wilson's presidency, doing whatever Wilson asked of him both in New York and in Washington. It was during this time that Wilson, the first Southern-born president since the Civil War, made the fateful decision to resegregate the federal bureaucracy—fulfilling the demands of newly empowered Southern Democrats who made up a majority of both the Congress and Wilson's Cabinet. Large departments like Treasury, Justice, and Interior began to physically separate Black workers from their white peers, eliciting howls of protest from the NAACP and the progressive press. If House, who considered himself a fervent progressive, felt or expressed any moral qualms about Wilson's decision, scant evidence exists. His diary contains only one mention, noting that he and Treasury Secretary McAdoo discussed the question and found the controversy to be "so much foolish talk." Two years later, Wilson also chose to screen *The Birth of a Nation* in the White House, lending his imprimatur to its overtly racist, inflammatory, and inaccurate storyline (he likened the film to "writing history with lightning").

After a little over a century, in the wake of nationwide protests and heightened awareness of systemic racism in America, these decisions contributed to a searing reappraisal of Wilson's legacy—his problematic mixture of progressive politics and racial conservatism. At Princeton, the faculty and student body in June 2020 successfully demanded a "public renunciation of Woodrow Wilson," including the removal of his name from the School of Public and International Affairs and a residential college on the university campus that bore his name. Other institutions and schools named for Wilson did the same.

House preferred to operate in the shadows, but Washington was a bigger fishbowl than Austin, and the national press soon took note of this mysterious man's growing influence. The fixer studiously avoided giving interviews about himself, and when confronted he minimized his role. But the more the Colonel tried to deflect attention, the more interest he generated and the more provocative his storyline became. By the end of Wilson's second month in office, *Collier's* was already describing House as Wilson's "silent partner," while *Harper's Weekly* referred to him as "Assistant President House." To *Current Opinion,* he was a cipher: "People claim to have seen him just as other people claim to have seen the sea serpent.... What is the secret of this mysterious man's power?"

Too subtle and wise to court more attention, House determined the time had come for him to make his annual European excursion. Before leaving, the Colonel reassured Wilson he would be fine in his absence:

"No one is so well equipped as you to do what you have planned. My faith in you is as great as my love for you—more than that I cannot say."

When House informed Wilson of his plans to rest and relax in Europe that summer, he was telling a half-truth; he also expected to indulge his increasing passion for foreign affairs. Much as he longed at the beginning of the century for a stage larger than his native Texas, the Colonel by the beginning of the 1910s felt a similar restlessness to expand his political horizons beyond America's shores. House watched with particular interest as leaders in Britain and Germany enacted far-reaching social and economic reforms, and he pondered whether such measures could be brought successfully to America. The Colonel even fantasized about how his formidable deal-making skills might work globally, especially in the area of world peace. If he could turn commoners into governors and gain the unquestioned trust of the president of the United States, why couldn't he be the one to broker better relations among rival nations? Precisely because of these ambitions, House had earlier in the year lobbied the president to install William Jennings Bryan as secretary of state. He strongly suspected Bryan would flounder in the role, providing House with a prime opportunity to step into the breach and become Wilson's de facto chief foreign affairs advisor.

The plan worked splendidly. Once appointed as secretary of state, Bryan proceeded almost immediately to lose Wilson's confidence. Within just weeks, the president relegated Bryan to handling low-profile Latin American issues and hatching hazy plans for universal peace. House seized the moment. Shortly after arriving in London in June 1913 (he spent the first part of the trip meeting French leaders in Paris), House expertly played Walter Page, Wilson's new US ambassador to the UK, to advance his personal agenda. He blasted Bryan to the new ambassador while making clear he planned to become the president's principal foreign policy advisor.

Disparaging Bryan also advanced House's ultimate goal during his trip: to establish a relationship with the powerful British foreign secretary, Sir Edward Grey. Page helped the Colonel secure the Grey meeting, writing a letter in which he described him as "the silent partner of President Wilson—that is to say, he is the most trusted political advisor and the nearest friend of the President. He is a private citizen, a man without personal political ambition, a modest, quiet, even shy fellow.... But he is very eager to meet you." Grey could hardly say no to such an invitation, and when the two met, it marked the launch of a friendship that would serve as the foundation for much of House's shuttle diplomacy over the following six years as the continent devolved into war.

By July 1913 when the Colonel departed Liverpool for America, he had accomplished his mission. He now occupied all the rooms that mattered—not only in America but increasingly in Europe. With the full support of the president to operate on both continents, he had become the most powerful private citizen in the country's history. He wouldn't soon relinquish that position.

Wilson came to the White House with an unusually small number of trusted associates; not surprisingly, House managed to ingratiate himself with each of them. There was Wilson's handsome and charming thirty-four-year-old personal physician, Cary Grayson, who first met Wilson in 1913. He soon became so beloved as a doctor and golfing partner that the president had him move into the White House for a short time. Joseph Tumulty, thirty-three, served as Wilson's private secretary—managing the office and his calendar, which meant direct access to him. The first time Tumulty heard Wilson speak he described it as "the happiest day of my life." He too moved into the White House for a spell, and together with Grayson he would often share meals with the president. And then there was William Gibbs McAdoo, a wealthy, progressive businessman who met Wilson in 1910 by chance on a train platform. Two years later he became Wilson's de facto campaign manager and was rewarded with the Treasury Department. In a Cabinet of ambitious men, McAdoo seemed the most ambitious. His ambition extended even to marrying the president's favorite daughter despite being twice her age. All three men supplied House with a constant stream of gossip and news, which he then used to reinforce his standing as the president's top advisor. This circle of information enabled House to influence Wilson from the outside using inside information—just the way he wanted.

The president meanwhile stayed largely above the swirl and intrigue that enveloped his White House. In fact, President Wilson acted very much like *Professor* Wilson. He wrote and typed his own speeches and responded to correspondence in his own hand. As at Princeton, he felt perfectly content to spend his time with his wife and three daughters, or alone with his books and his thoughts. He didn't need the energy of crowds, nor more than his three staff confidants and a few others to make decisions or to keep him company. But he *did* need House.

In Wilson's largely solitary world, House played an outsized role, "the only male friend of his own age with whom Wilson shared both work and personal feelings," according to Wilson biographer John Milton Cooper. His "easygoing presence, sensitive reading of moods, and availability" were reassuring to a man often beset with doubts. The Colonel catered to Wilson's vanity perfectly and delivered heavy doses of affection to a man who needed it constantly. Many of House's letters began or ended with overt obsequiousness:

> I do not think you can ever know, my great and good friend, how much I appreciate your kindness to me. All that I have tried to do seems so little when measured by the returns you have made..... I shall believe that you will be successful in all your undertakings for, surely, no one is so well equipped as you to do what you have planned. My faith in you is as great as my love for you more than that I cannot say.

With such adoring—albeit sincere—words, House gained a strong psychological hold on Wilson. "Only House seemed in possession of the intricate combination which simultaneously unlocked Wilson's affection and desire to open his mind, to reveal his thoughts and to receive advice on public business," the Georges observed. To accomplish this vaunted status, House had to walk a fine line between being a dispassionate advisor and shameless ingratiator, between hard truth-telling and soft flattery. Beyond that, he had to act indifferent to the president's attention inside the White House even while deeply craving it. And of course House had to downplay his centrality to avoid arousing jealousies or resentments among other members of the administration.

It was not simply, however, that the Colonel possessed a political acumen that the high-minded, intellectual Wilson lacked. House played the role of First Friend in all of its manifestations—beyond just the strategic or utilitarian. Emotionally, the Colonel offered a "soothing presence" to Wilson, who once told House: "You are the only one in the world to whom I can open my mind freely, and it does me good to say even foolish things and get them out of my system. You are the only one to whom I can make an entire clearance of mind." In the honeymoon years of their relationship, Wilson never sensed in House personal ambitions. "What I like about House is that he is the most self-effacing man that ever lived," Wilson wrote to his secretary of the Navy. "All he wants to do is to serve the common cause and to help me and others."

The president especially enjoyed entertaining House as a guest. When the Colonel came to Washington, Wilson almost always insisted he stay at the White House, where they would wander its halls studying the building's history. They also loved to dine together. Years later, Grayson said that House knew "to spare the President's tired nerves" by never bringing up business during meals. At bedtime the president would walk down the hall in his robe and into House's bedroom—it came to be known as "Colonel House's room"—to say good night. The two friends would read poetry, attend church (after the minister prayed for "the President and his counselor" one Sunday, House worried that more such public mentions could be the end of him), and took drives into the countryside, where they shared their philosophies of life.

One afternoon early in Wilson's first term they drove out to Rock Creek Cemetery to see the memorial "Grief," which Henry Adams had commissioned to commemorate the suicide of his wife. The two sat in front of the massive sculpture for a long time that afternoon, quietly contemplating the ancient Greek ideal of beauty and grumbling their disappointment that the current day "could produce so little that was as good." In Hodgson's words, they resembled "two inhibited Anglo-Saxon gentlemen [who] found they could overcome their instinctive constraints together and talk about life, death, and love." By 1914, Wilson depended so fully on House that when the Colonel left for a visit to Texas, Wilson wrote he was "thanking God daily" for having so "generous and disinterested a friend," and that "it grieves me to see you go"—language eerily reminiscent of how he had described Hibben a decade earlier.

The apex of the Wilson-House relationship came in the immediate aftermath of August 4, 1914—the day Ellen Wilson tragically succumbed to kidney failure after a brutal summer fighting Bright's disease. She well knew her husband's rough edges but realized how much he needed the affection of others. And unlike most First Ladies who shielded their husbands, Ellen Wilson was happy to share hers. She too supported and relied on the Colonel, even using his visits to go over the family's finances. With her death, Wilson yearned for House's companionship even more to help overcome his grief. "I simply must see you soon and am thinking every day how to manage it," the president wrote.

Wilson would have to wait three weeks for that reunion; his best friend and counselor was still en route back from Europe, where he had just concluded his self-described "Great Adventure." With rumblings of war growing louder, the Colonel had devised a daring undertaking after his return from Europe a year earlier: As the president's semiofficial emissary, he would shuttle between London and Berlin, convincing Grey and the German Kaiser that it would be more constructive to invest their time and money in such regions as Latin America, Persia, and China than to battle each other. Together with the United States, according to House's scheme, Germany and Britain would sign a tripartite disarmament pact to refunnel their money from making rifles and shells to building bridges and roads. His intelligence gathering for the trip, as Neu notes, was unusually lax by modern standards. To understand the psyche of the German Kaiser Wilhelm, he consulted a university president who had just returned from having himself spent a few hours with the German leader. After just two hours of debriefing, House was convinced he had received "nearly all the information I need regarding the Kaiser and his entourage." He also met with a diplomat with some experience in London and Berlin who told him his chances of success with the Kaiser were no better than one in a million, but the Colonel remained undaunted.

In June 1914, House arrived in Germany, where he encountered a vastly more complex and perilous scene that exceeded his meager preparations. House got his private meeting with the Kaiser—thirty minutes on a palace terrace in Potsdam. Pushing his face closer to the Kaiser's as the conversation intensified, the Colonel pressed his point: If only Germany, Britain, and America stood together, peace could be preserved. The Kaiser agreed. The British had "nothing to fear" from Germany, Wilhelm responded, pointing out that Queen Victoria had been his grandmother.

With that ray of hope from his conversation in Potsdam, House headed to London to meet with Foreign Secretary Edward Grey. At their second session, the Colonel forcefully urged his alternative to war on Grey. The Foreign Secretary was mildly receptive, telling House to relay his favorable reaction back to Germany, which he soon did in a letter to the Kaiser. That marked the Great Adventure's high point. Despite their monarch's seemingly agreeable talk, the Germans in reality were in no mood to disarm, let alone make peace. And the British had no intention either of agreeing to any summit. And when a Serbian terrorist assassinated Archduke Franz Ferdinand, heir to the Austro-Hungarian throne, in Sarajevo on June 28, 1914, House's grand plan of a great peace to liberate the "wasted places of the earth" would soon suffer its own quick death. By the time the Colonel had set sail for America on July 21, events were already grinding their inevitable way to the most catastrophic conflict in history.

As House sat down with Wilson on August 29 to express his condolences, the European landscape had shifted to battle lines. On the very day Ellen Wilson had died, the ledger of belligerents was set: the Allied Powers, Britain, France, and Russia, on one side; the Central Powers, Germany and Austria-Hungary, on the other. House's unofficial role as the president's diplomat in chief would soon become even more critical than in the previous two years. But his personal path in the Wilson orbit would veer as well, in a direction that neither friend that day could possibly foresee.

With Ellen Wilson gone and Europe now at war, President Wilson stood at a crossroads. Until the guns of August set Europe ablaze, Wilson had been content to focus almost exclusively on domestic issues, with the single exception of a revolution in Mexico that occupied a small part of his time. Indeed, the previous eighteen months had been consumed with winning one legislative victory after another to remake America's trade and tax regime, strengthen antitrust policy, create the Federal Reserve system, and conserve natural resources. Calamities beyond his control now required him to extend his focus eastward to a European continent he found bewildering. When House had peppered him all summer with letters of his comings and goings in London, Paris, and Berlin, Wilson had responded more with bemused interest than genuine engagement. "It is perfectly delightful to read your letters and to realize what you are accomplishing. I have no comments except praise and self-congratulation that I have such a friend."

But now, with thousands of men dying daily and two of the world's great democracies locked in a mortal struggle against Germany's military might, Wilson needed a coherent strategy to defend American interests. With Bryan no more than a figurehead, the secretary of state's responsibilities naturally fell to the Colonel. The president decided, House recorded in his diary, "I should keep the matter in my hands and advise him what was being done." "This could be done," he assured the president, "indirectly through me so as not to make it quite official." In taking on this unofficial role, House grappled with America's dual objectives during those first months of war: to maintain its export trade in the face of Britain's naval blockade of the Central Powers' supply routes, and to bring about peace talks to end the conflict as soon as possible. On the blockade, through House's mediation with Grey and others, the British set up programs—such as buying American cotton at prices above peacetime levels—to cut off imports to Germany and its allies without great cost to the American economy.

On the thornier question of how America should react to the conflict, the president was adamant from the outset that the United States should remain neutral at all costs. He saw himself as the one world leader capable of bringing all the warring parties to the table. Then, by exacting a peace, Wilson believed he could impose his definition of America's ideals on the world. "America seeks no material profit or aggrandizement of any kind" from the war, Wilson explained in late 1914. His only hope from the conflict, Wilson proclaimed, was the ultimate liberation of people "everywhere from the aggressions of autocratic force."

In a masterstroke for his continued involvement at the highest level, House made certain that Wilson prioritized foreign policy from that time forward—with the Colonel as his premier emissary. As House dutifully recorded: "[Wilson] spoke of my going abroad in order to initiate peace conversations. He desires me to take charge of it and to go whenever I think it advisable."

The newly widowed president desperately needed a First Friend that autumn, and House continued to play that role as well. Through the final months of 1914 and into 1915, Wilson relied even more on him, not just for political advice, but also for his company and emotional strength. In a two-month span, the Colonel visited Wilson five times at the White House, while Wilson visited House in New York once. When they weren't talking shop, the president bared his soul to House about his loneliness and despair over losing Ellen. On his single trip to New York that winter, Wilson had fallen into a particularly fragile state. That evening the two had dinner in House's apartment before setting off on a walk around Midtown Manhattan. At one point, as they strolled down the sidewalks, the president said he had wished "someone would kill him." The Colonel continued in his diary: "His eyes were moist when he spoke of not wanting to live longer.... and of not being fit to do the work he had in hand."

Imbued with Wilson's full confidence, the Colonel set off for Europe in 1915 intent on convincing the warring parties that America could mediate an end to the conflict. What both House and the president underestimated, however, was the brute nationalism driving the conflict from all sides. As casualties mounted for each of the combatants, so too did the urge for revenge. As Hodgson writes of the moment, "pacifism seemed closer to treason than to idealism." Instead, the Colonel focused on a more limited and attainable objective: guaranteeing freedom of the seas through a pact he would negotiate between the English and the Germans.

Then on May 7, 1915, a German submarine sunk the British steamliner *Lusitania*, killing 1,200 people, including 124 Americans. It also torpedoed House's initiative. He immediately sent word back to Wilson that the United States must now join the Allied forces and declare war: "America has come to the parting of the ways, when she must determine whether she stands for civilized or uncivilized warfare. We can no longer remain neutral spectators." The president disagreed, and while he eventually sent a stern note to the Germans demanding they abandon their submarine campaign against merchantmen and passenger liners, he wasn't prepared to declare war. In his view, the British were still violating America's neutral rights to send cargo to foreign ports, and more important, the American public remained decidedly against entering the conflict. But the Colonel, an Anglophile to the core, felt more convinced than ever of the justness of entering the war on the Allied side.

As he boarded his ship to return to America in early June—still "red hot" for war—two things were happening back home that would have a direct effect on House. Secretary of State Bryan resigned, acknowledging to the president the obvious: "Colonel House has been Secretary of State, not I, and I have never had your full confidence." And, more shocking, Wilson had fallen in love.

House returned to the United States facing a delicate task: He had to ensure Bryan's successor would not challenge his total control over foreign affairs. So by the time he sat down with Wilson for their first face-to-face meeting in six months, the Colonel, as usual, had it all figured out. He laid out his preference bluntly. "I think the most important thing," he told

Wilson, "is to get a man without too many ideas of his own and one that will be entirely guided by you without unnecessary arguments"—in other words, another figurehead who would leave the real work (and power) to House alone. He suggested Robert Lansing, who had been Bryan's counselor, as the ideal candidate, and the president agreed.

With that potential peril resolved, the Colonel turned to an even more tangled issue: how to win the affections of Woodrow Wilson's new love. Edith Galt had struck Wilson on first sight, when he drove by her in the presidential limousine and asked Grayson, "Who is that beautiful woman?" When they actually met months later in the White House residence, he fell in love. She was a forty-two-year-old widow with Virginian roots dating back to 1607 and a fiercely independent streak, reputed to be the first woman in the District of Columbia to obtain a driver's license. Within two months of their meeting, the president asked her to marry him, and after a few days of feigned indecision she accepted. When the president and House saw each other several weeks later, Wilson revealed his new romance. Already tipped to the engagement, the Colonel played dumb when the president sought his advice on a deeply personal issue: Would I lose public support if I proposed to her? "No," House shrewdly replied. How soon can we marry then? House—worried that moving too soon after Ellen's death would look insensitive to voters during an election year—gave a more nuanced if unwelcome answer: Wait until the spring.

While the Colonel was doing his nuanced best, Edith wasted little time bluntly turning on her fiancé's closest advisor. From the beginning, she disliked him just from the sound of his correspondence; her letter to Wilson shortly after he sought House's advice specified her objections: "I know I am wrong but I can't help feeling he is not a very *strong* character.... I know what a comfort and staff Col. House is to you Precious One and that your judgment about him is correct, but he does look like a weak vessel and I think that he writes like one very often."

Wilson responded immediately:

> About him, again, you are no doubt partly right.... House *has* a strong character,—if to be disinterested and unafraid and incorruptible is to

> be strong. He has a noble and lovely character, too, for he is capable of utter self-forgetfulness and loyalty and devotion. And he is wise.... He wins the confidence of all sorts of men, and wins it at once,—by deserving it. But you are right in thinking that intellectually he is not a great man. His mind is not of the first class. He is a counselor, not a statesman.... We cannot require of every man that he should be everything. You are going to love House some day,—if only because he loves me and would give, I believe, his life for me,—and because he loves the country and seeks its real benefit and glory. I'm not afraid of the ultimate impression he will make on you,—because I know you and your instinctive love and admiration for whatever is true and genuine.

Despite her pledge to try, Edith would never share Wilson's love for the man or regard for his skills. She hinted at this eventuality in her half-hearted response to Wilson's letter: "I am almost sorry I wrote you what I did yesterday about Col. House but I can no more keep things from you than I can stop loving you—and so you must forgive me. I know he is fine and true, but I don't think him vigorous and strong—am I wrong?" Part of the reason she was so intractable from the outset might have been her distaste at how much she perceived Wilson *depended* on House. "The relationship between them revealed weaknesses in Wilson's makeup," the Georges suggest. "Perhaps instinctively, she sought to make Wilson independent of House in order to make reality conform with her idealized image of her husband."

By late summer, Grayson was warning the Colonel that Wilson felt "anxious" to announce his engagement but would leave the date "clearly up to [House] to decide." On this singular test of his loyalty (and strength in Edith's mind), House passed. He agreed to a shorter timetable than his political instincts prescribed, with Wilson announcing his engagement in October and his marriage in January. Delighted and relieved by his counselor's advice, Wilson immediately wrote to his fiancée with the news: "I had a fine talk with House last night, which cleared things wonderfully.... He is really a wonderful counselor.... I am sure that the first real conversation you have with him, about something definite and of the stuff of judgment, you will lose entirely your impression that he lacks strength.... I am impatient to have you know him."

The future First Lady and the Colonel met the next day for lunch at the White House and then again the day after for afternoon tea. They each knew what was at stake and the roles they were expected to play, and so the charm and the flattery flowed accordingly. House spoke of how he expected Wilson "would easily outrank any American that had yet lived," while Galt described her fiancé's "delight" in finding someone "whose mind runs parallel to his own." By the end, they each reported to the president their affection for the other. The Colonel obviously had more to lose—maybe even his friendship with the president—had it gone badly, and he could breathe a sigh of relief over surviving the moment. But it wouldn't last.

During the fall of 1915, the Colonel again juggled the mundane with the profound. Two days after Woodrow and Edith announced their engagement, House hosted the president at his apartment on East Fifty-Third Street while Edith and her entourage stayed at the St. Regis. Wilson had his jeweler send over thirteen engagement rings to House's apartment for the couple to inspect. Upon arrival, the jeweler decided he wanted to hold one back because of the "unlucky thirteen," wrote House, "but I vetoed this because the President considers thirteen his lucky number." If the Colonel appeared distracted while watching one diamond slide off Edith's finger for another, he could be excused: His focus that day was on a new peace plan he had conceived that, if successful, would either end the war or at the least commit America to fight on the side of the Allies. House was convinced that Germany "had a better chance than ever of winning, and if she did win," an "unprepared" United States would be its next target. As a result House concluded that only "something decisive" could end the war and stave off an eventual attack. The decisive plan House hatched would push all the combatants to disarm with a commitment to attend a peace conference—after secretly securing the Allies' approval. If all agreed, by his calculations the war would effectively end. If the Central

Powers refused, however, America would break off diplomatic relations and enter the war on the side of the Allies.

Before dinner that night, House laid out his audacious proposal in just twenty minutes to a "startled" president, whose silence he interpreted as acquiescence. The Colonel later floated the plan to Grey, who doubted either side would agree to lay down arms. But the foreign secretary added another idea to the Colonel's quest for peace—one that would consume the Wilson administration for the next four years. "After the war," Grey asked, would the nations of the world "band together to treat the maker of war as an enemy of the human race"? Put simply, would America, in other words, support a postwar league of nations?

Undaunted by Grey's lukewarm response, House crafted a letter from Wilson to the belligerents articulating his new plan. After painstaking work, the Colonel sent his draft down to the White House, where Wilson edited it word by word. When the president got to the sentence where House declared that the United States *would* go to war if Germany refused the peace, Wilson inserted "probably." So the sentence now read, "If the Central Powers were still obdurate, it would *probably* be necessary for [the US] to join the Allies and force the issue."

This single change had the obvious effect of weakening House's diplomatic leverage when he began traversing the Continent in early 1916. It underscored existing Allied fears that Wilson's heart wasn't in their fight. And it brought to the surface larger fears that the president had no concrete plan for the postwar world. What kind of concessions would Wilson demand of the Allies? Would they have to cede territory? None of these answers would be known for another two years. Also complicating the Colonel's mediation efforts that spring was the Allies' continued refusal to allow unfettered trade and commerce on neutral seas. In response, a furious Congress and president launched the largest peacetime naval buildup in the country's history.

The Colonel's mediation plan—known to history as "the House-Grey Memorandum"—became the prevailing American stance for much of the following year. During this period, House made two separate trips to Europe to pursue his peace plan while the president stayed home to get married and run for reelection. Outwardly, the two men appeared as close as ever, but in his diary the Colonel began articulating his first notes of frustration—annoyed that Wilson wasn't paying more attention to his diplomacy and didn't sufficiently share his pro-Allied sentiments. Early hints of growing trouble came in the late fall of 1915, when House confided to his diary disquieting reports from DC of a "curious inertia everywhere." Wilson "is so engrossed with his fiancée that he is neglecting business," House wrote on November 22. "I would go to Washington, but I know I would not be very welcome at this time, particularly, if I attempted to stir him to action."

Instead, House stayed in New York the final month of 1915 and then embarked for Europe for the first three months of 1916 to pursue his doomed peace initiative. Already discouraged by how Wilson had undermined his peace initiative, he returned home to Washington that spring worried about a development far more ominous to his future than a failed trip: Edith Wilson's ever-growing prominence in the president's life and the functioning of his presidency. She now acted as his constant companion, whether on the golf course, in the car for afternoon rides, or at the dinner table. Worse, she seemed to have become his primary confidante, including on matters of state. Whatever reservoirs of intimacy Wilson possessed were now directed almost exclusively to his new wife. Sensitive to such emotional nuances, House could feel their relationship changing, and not in his favor. "The two men remained on cordial terms and collaborated on a wide range of issues," Neu concludes, "but the intensity of earlier years was dissipating."

The 1916 presidential campaign gave House a respite from the frustrations of peacemaking and a chance once again to demonstrate his wizardry at political organizing. The campaign pitted Wilson against Republican Charles Evans Hughes, the first and last sitting justice of the Supreme Court ever to be nominated for the presidency. The former New York governor had reunited the progressive and conservative wings of the Republican Party, and by early September, when Wilson accepted the Democratic renomination, Hughes was favored to win—that is, until the Colonel went to work.

With only seven weeks until election day, House arrived in New York to take charge of the president's campaign. In typical fashion, he preferred to operate out of the limelight with no official title, even though Wilson had asked him to become his campaign chairman. Holed up alone in a private New York office with a new phone number—"so that no one can reach me until I am ready"—the Colonel wrote to Wilson that he was "back and in the thick of it and... reveling in the work." His responsibilities encompassed the campaign's structure, message, finances, surrogates, schedule, press, and, not the least, managing the candidate.

At one point in mid-October, House became worried that a Wilson loss would result in too long a transition to the new president when questions of war or peace hung in the balance. So he suggested a bold idea to ensure a swift transfer of power to Hughes as the president-elect. If Wilson lost the election, he should immediately demand the resignations of his vice president and secretary of state. He then would appoint Hughes secretary of state, and Hughes would immediately become president when Wilson stepped down four months early (presidential inaugurations then occurred in March). After mulling over the idea for a few days, the president came to the same realization as House that a shorter transition of power served the national interest. Two days before the election, he informed his secretary of state of his intention to activate the plan in the event he lost.

The election was a nail-biter as it entered its culminating weekend. Swept up in "a mad whirl" of activity and sensing a dramatic finale, House finally came out from behind the curtain to make his first appearance at campaign headquarters—becoming a figure of fascination to the young campaign workers. The Colonel organized the campaign's closing event at Madison Square Garden, and then for the final forty-eight hours furiously worked the phones and party operatives to secure every last vote. The president would need every one of them. It took three full days until the final results revealed that Wilson had won, edging Hughes by 500,000 popular votes and 23 electoral votes. Wilson's selfless decision a week before to resign early if defeated would be nothing but a footnote in the tragic final years of his presidency.

With the election behind them, the two men turned their attention back to their most vexing question: how to end a war that by election day was claiming six thousand lives a day and showed no signs of ending. Reelected on the platform that "He kept us out of war," Wilson was even more adamant now that House pursue approaches that allowed America to remain disengaged—at least officially. Although Wilson had initially favored neutrality, by the spring of 1916 he began to endorse "preparedness," a halfway measure in which the United States would mobilize for war but not fight outright. Partly sensing this shift, the Germans showed no desire to cooperate, continuing to sink US ships and disrupt trade. The president began to fear there would be no choice but to declare war against Germany if the country didn't curtail its escalating aggression.

Over dinner a week after the election, Wilson told the Colonel that he wanted to write a letter to all combatants "demanding" they end the war. But with the Allies believing, however falsely, that they were turning the tide, House resisted—saying it was both the wrong time and the wrong message. The president fought back, telling House he needed to go back to London and Paris while Wilson issued his command to stop hostilities. Speaking in uncommonly blunt terms, House replied, "I should prefer Hades for the moment" when that would happen. Wilson backed down. The note he sent a month later adopted a much softer—almost feckless—tone, neither seeking a cessation to hostilities nor a peace conference. Instead, the president simply asked each combatant what terms they would accept to lay down arms, claiming each side's goals "are virtually the same."

The letter left House irate. Wilson, he lamented to his diary, had utterly failed to appreciate how vastly the war objectives of each side differed. To suggest otherwise, the Colonel raged, "destroyed all the work I have done in Europe."

As the calendar turned to 1917, the two men had reached an impasse. The surest sign of the deadlock came at House's first meeting of the year with Wilson and his wife, who by then was a constant presence at the president's side and often attended their meetings. The Colonel at one point asked the president what he intended to do with Ambassador Page in London. Wilson responded that he planned to fire him (in reality he never had confidence in him), prompting Edith Wilson to jump in, "Why don't you take his place?" The president immediately seconded the idea. House demurred, but he must have sensed their message: The same man who had practically begged House to spend more time with him in Washington was now encouraging him to move overseas—with the most important decision of whether to go to war still imminent.

Ironically, it was the onset of war that brought the men back together. On February 1, 1917, Germany resumed unrestricted submarine warfare despite knowing it risked bringing America into the conflict. House was in Washington that day meeting with Wilson, and the two men agreed to break off diplomatic relations with Germany but to not yet declare war. Roughly a month later, however, the front pages of American newspapers published the scandalous contents of the Zimmerman Telegram, which exposed Germany's secret intention to form a military alliance with Mexico if the United States entered the war. Coupled with the submarine attacks, the Zimmerman Telegram further complicated Wilson and House's calculations right before the president's second inauguration.

On March 4, only a few days after the Zimmerman Telegram revelations, Wilson attended his inaugural ceremony at the Capitol with his wife by his side. The Colonel characteristically had chosen to stay back at the White House "I never like to be conspicuously in evidence"—but joined the Wilsons for dinner that night and later watched fireworks with them from the Oval sitting room. By then the German naval offensive was in full force, sinking American ships and with them any chances America would stay neutral. House impatiently waited for Wilson to finally declare war, and he came to Washington again toward the end of March to hurry along the process. For four days they worked together on the themes and language Wilson would employ if and when he asked Congress to declare war. The Colonel then returned to New York, but just three days later Wilson asked him back to make final changes to a speech both men knew would be the most consequential of his presidency. House left DC satisfied with its content: "No address he has yet made pleases me more than this one, for it contains all that I have been urging upon him since the war began."

The day of the speech, April 2, 1917, House "killed time" with the president before joining the Wilsons on the ride to the Capitol. In the most famous and praised speech of his life, Wilson finally contended that Germany's submarine offensive and covert plotting signaled warfare against "mankind" and "all nations." He called on Congress to declare German conduct "nothing less than war against the government and the people of the United States." As cheers resounded through the chamber, the president concluded his nineteen-minute address by emphasizing the ultimate aim for bringing America into this "war to end all wars": to make the world "safe for democracy."

Afterward, the Colonel returned to the White House with the First Couple to recap the evening. "History may record this the most important day in the life of our country," House breathlessly recorded in his diary. But he also hinted at a developing dynamic that indeed would lead to their ultimate breach. "Wilson," he observed, is "too refined, too civilized, too intellectual, too cultivated not to see the incongruity and absurdity of war." What the president needed around him, House concluded, was a man of "coarser fiber and one less of a philosopher than he."

Four days later, after debating throughout the night, Congress at 3 a.m. finally assented to Wilson's request for a declaration of war.

Despite his mounting ambivalence toward Wilson, House was reenergized by America's entry into the war, giving him purpose, responsibility, and even some measure of accountability as the president's unofficial diplomat in chief. First in New York and later that summer on the North Shore of Massachusetts, the Colonel now had all the trappings of a senior administration official without the burden of title. From his crowded apartment on East Fifty-Third Street, House built both a staff and an informal outside network to help him lead the president's war effort. Cooper described the Colonel's New York home that summer as the "headquarters of the most remarkable intelligence services ever put together by a private individual."

Friends, family, journalists, and foreign officials funneled reports, rumors, and secrets circulating at home and across Europe to him. Two private telephone lines were installed to keep him in constant contact with the president, one to his New York apartment and the other to his summer home. And now when traveling anywhere, House was constantly shadowed by the Secret Service and sometimes the security services of foreign powers.

With all that support, the Colonel in effect replaced the State Department and anticipated the vital work that the OSS and later the CIA would do. House served not just as the first port of call for foreign delegations seeking to better understand the country's war aims; he also operated at the center of the country's furious efforts that summer to prepare for war. At the same time, he played a pivotal role in refinancing Britain's massive debt so the country could continue to purchase American armaments for its troops.

A letter that Wilson wrote him on September 2, 1917, marked the peak of House's wartime influence. The president asked House to "quietly gather a group of men" to determine what each combatant hoped to gain from the war. Wilson wanted to see, for example, whether any "secret treaties" made among America's allies could undermine his pledge to create a world safe for democracy. If they intended to try to preserve imperialistic dynastics, the president wanted to know *before* negotiations began over the postwar world. In effect, Wilson aimed to establish a planning group—under House's leadership—that would anticipate every question that would arise at a peace conference, build a "library of facts, figures and arguments" to answer them, and set out guiding principles to shape the peace.

The Colonel went straight to work building his team for what soon would be called "the Inquiry." He brought in his brother-in-law, his son-in-law, a young Walter Lippmann (later to become one of the country's leading columnists), a historian, and even an expert on maps. On January 5, 1918, they presented the fruits of their work. Beginning at 10:30 a.m., House laid out for Wilson at the White House the principles of a final peace agreement: freedom of the seas, open diplomacy, a communal body to ensure peace, and disarmament, among others. He then moved to the specific tactics that would achieve those final aims, namely the territorial compromises and the border adjustments each country would have to make. Describing the meeting in his diary, the Colonel said that in just two hours, he and Wilson had "re[made] the map of the world."

Three days after, standing before Congress, the president consolidated their aims, ideas, and arguments into what became known as Wilson's "Fourteen Points"—the basis of America's next two years of peacemaking and next century of vigorous international engagement. In one "remarkable" document, as Neu writes, House and the president "rall[ied] various groups both at home and in the Allied nations behind a liberal peace settlement and outline[d] a compelling vision of a new world order."

Overnight, America had finally established and fully clarified its wartime goals. Across the political spectrum, Americans praised the president's plan. Overseas the response was more mixed. But one fact remained beyond question: With the Colonel's help, Woodrow Wilson had become the only statesman on the world stage, as Neu notes, with the "stature and vision to bring about a new international order."

By the summer's end of 1918, the war had finally and decisively turned in the Allies' favor, partly due to General John J. Pershing's able leadership of the American Expeditionary Forces. As the AEF launched its first major offensive in Europe, hopes ran high that Germany would be defeated in a few months. By this point, the Colonel's renown had reached global proportions. Writing from Paris in September 1918 to House's brother-in-law Sidney Mezes, Walter Lippmann noted that only four Americans had entered the Continent's "consciousness": Wilson, Pershing, Herbert Hoover (who was providing a depleted Europe with desperately needed food supplies), and House, "the Human Intercessor, the Comforter, the Virgin Mary."

In October, when Germany first approached the United States about ending the war, House thus stood as the obvious choice for Wilson to deputize in negotiating an armistice agreement. "House knows my mind entirely," Wilson confided to one of the Colonel's British friends. "You must ask them [British leaders] to realize though how hard it is for me to spare him. On many problems he is the only person I can consult." Putting aside whatever differences they had a year earlier, the two men by then felt so in sync on how they viewed a postwar world that Wilson saw no need to give House any instructions because "I feel you will know what to do." The oddity of their relationship was not lost on the Colonel: "I am going on one of the most important missions anyone ever undertook, and yet there is no word of direction, advice or discussion between us."

After landing in France on October 25, House faced the arduous task of convincing the Allied countries to accept Wilson's Fourteen Points as the basis for peace. By not consulting with the Allies before issuing his plan, Wilson had alienated the very partners he would need to secure its passage. Worse, the Allies believed that having borne the brunt of the war's monetary and human costs, they—and not the United States—should be the arbiters of the peace.

On first hearing of Wilson's Fourteen Points, French Prime Minister Georges Clemenceau captured the skepticism of other Allied leaders when he wryly exclaimed: "God himself was content with Ten Commandments. Wilson modestly inflicted fourteen points on us.... Fourteen commandments of the most empty theory." The British especially disliked point two, calling for freedom of the seas; while the French, thirsty to extract territorial concessions and reparations from the vanquished Germans, saw no benefit from a plan that delivered neither. Still, over four days and nights of intense discussions with Clemenceau, British Prime Minister David Lloyd George, and Italian Prime Minister Vittorio Orlando, the Colonel succeeded in persuading them to accept—aided by some vague interpretations—the Fourteen Points as the basis for a settlement.

Even if House didn't obtain ironclad commitments on some of the most contentious issues, he succeeded in establishing the Wilson plan as the bedrock for the final peace. Whenever and wherever the final peace conference would be held, it would now focus on such Wilsonian ideals as self-determination, freedom of the seas, free trade, and arms reduction rather than on what the Allies really wanted: ruthless retribution. House cabled the president to report "a great diplomatic victory," but he knew much work lay ahead to build on that initial triumph. First, the victors and the Germans had to negotiate the Armistice. The talks ended on November 11, when German delegates and the French General Ferdinand Foch signed the agreement in a railway car in Compèigne, France. The Armistice signed that day bore little resemblance to Wilson's Fourteen Points, but the war had finally ended—at the eleventh hour on the eleventh day of the eleventh month of 1918.

The Colonel learned of the Armistice fifteen minutes after its signing and sent word immediately to Wilson: "Autocracy is dead—Long live democracy and its immortal leader—In this great hour my heart goes out to you in pride, admiration and love." The president received the news at 3 a.m. on November 11, addressed a joint session of Congress that afternoon, and then spent a quiet evening at home with Edith reading the Bible—no doubt pondering the difficult days ahead before a final peace would be cobbled together.

The final chapter of this most extraordinary—if decidedly peculiar—friendship would play out with the whole world watching amidst the charms of Paris and the final grandeur of Versailles. The president and the Colonel, as individuals and as a team, would be on full display. The stakes were nothing less than the future world order after more than four years of unimaginable death: 11 million soldiers and 13 million civilians lost to battle and disease.

Given such costs, Wilson displayed a moral urgency bordering on arrogance, as though he alone could right the war's shocking atrocities. To this son of a Presbyterian minister, only he had the moral superiority to save the European continent from the failings of its leaders. So, as the head of the US delegation to the Paris Peace Conference, the president would brook no dissent in pursuit of his destiny. He would stay true to all Fourteen Points regardless how impractical or unpopular the people of Europe found some of them. In his mind, Wilson would be the one to create a League of Nations, which would police relations and solve disputes between countries—thus solidifying his legacy as the man who put an end to war.

House's goals were no less ambitious. The Paris Peace Conference would be the stage on which to display his mastery of the European geopolitical situation. By that point House knew the Allied leaders better than any other American. Not only had the Colonel studied how to harness their strengths and exploit their weaknesses; he also knew their tics, how to charm them, and when to shame them. Even better, House had the backroom experience to convert the president's often overwrought language into practical approaches around which leaders could unite.

The Colonel greatly respected Wilson as a thinker and as an orator, but he also knew Wilson's limitations as a negotiator. The president believed the power of an idea—a moral truth—should dictate the outcome to any dispute. To him, the vulgar give-and-take of diplomatic negotiations was a facet of the old order he sought to replace. For House, such negotiations felt like second nature to him—whether the deft personal appeal at just the right moment or the exact practical solution that addressed a specific need. Clemenceau would capture this chasm between the two men best when he later said: "Colonel House is practical, I can understand him, but when I talk with President Wilson, I feel as if I am talking to Jesus Christ." A confident if naïve House assumed that, just as he had won every political race he managed with superior political skills, he would win the peace with his equally superior diplomatic skills. His confidence would be short-lived.

The first hints of what would cause the later split between the two men came just hours after the signing of the Armistice. The president cabled House in Paris with disquieting news: He was coming to Paris, and he intended to preside over the peace conference itself. That was certainly not the Colonel's plan. All along, he had expected that Wilson would make a short appearance at the conference's opening but then leave him in charge of the American delegation and the day-to-day negotiations. In anger, House sent his response: "Americans here whose opinions are of value are practically unanimous in the belief that it would be unwise for you to sit in the Peace Conference." Underscoring the insult, he noted that Wilson would be the *only* head of state to attend, and that Clemenceau agreed with his recommendation for Wilson to stay home. The president ended the sharp exchange with this final missive: "Your [response] upsets every plan we have made.... It is universally expected and generally desired here that I should attend the conference.... The programme... seems to me a way of pocketing me. I hope you will be very shy of their advice and give me your own independent judgment after reconsideration."

The Colonel, of course, had no choice but to back down, but he later confessed in his diary how disappointed he was not to be appointed chairman. Instead, Wilson named House one of America's five "peace commissioners" on a delegation derided by Republicans as nothing but a group of yes men. Of the five commissioners, however, the Colonel correctly assumed that he along with Wilson would serve preeminent roles: that anything important would be handled by only the two of them.

When Woodrow Wilson entered Paris in December 1918, he could be forgiven for confusing himself with the Messiah. Captain Harry Truman witnessed the moment and wrote in 1950, "I don't think I ever saw such an ovation as he received." Two million people crowded the Champs-Élysées to glimpse their American hero, many shouting "Wilson the Just" as his carriage regally rolled down the Grand Boulevard. Later that month, he enjoyed similarly rapturous receptions in England and Italy. The president had proved to be the peoples' savior, the man who delivered victory when all seemed lost and now brought them the panacea they desperately desired: a world free from war and filled with justice and democracy.

As the conference began in January 1919, though, Wilson soon noticed the discouraging disconnect between the will of the people and the aims of their leaders. Fissures quickly appeared between the Americans and the Allied countries on a host of issues, beginning with Wilson's League of Nations. Both the French and the British were willing to accept the League, but not without using it as leverage. In return, both countries wanted to keep portions of the overseas territories they had taken from Germany, as well as reparations. They also wanted to maintain strong militaries to guard against any future German rearmament and aggression.

Nevertheless, the president played to type, refusing to negotiate when the moment called for it. He held his ground, insisting on a strong League without granting any concessions. The Allied leaders soon learned what Wilson's former colleagues at Princeton knew all too well: The president was not a compromiser. He never bent, only broke. If he couldn't get his way, no one would get their way. It was all or nothing for him.

House himself noted this peculiarity in Wilson's character as early as November 1915, at a moment when his problems with Wilson first began surfacing: "Let me put up something to him that is disagreeable, and I have great difficulty in getting him to meet it. I have no doubt that some of the trouble he had at Princeton was caused by this delay in meeting vexatious problems." He "dodges trouble," House wrote, and holds "intense prejudices.... He finds great difficulty in conferring with men against whom, for some reason, he has a prejudice and in whom he can find nothing good."

If true, House's observations portended great difficulty as he and the president sat down to negotiate a complex peace agreement with equally headstrong leaders holding diverging interests.

Using all of his political skills, the Colonel went to work bridging the differences. Operating out of a suite in the Crillon Hotel, House and his staff devised language on which the League of Nations committee could agree. He personally convinced Clemenceau in a "heart to heart" talk to give up all his opposition. With the British, House and his lawyer worked painstakingly to overcome their objections, especially to Wilson's plans regarding disposition of desired German territory in Africa and the Pacific. On February 14, with the language finally settled, Wilson addressed the entire conference, reiterating his vision of the League as the solution to any future crises that threatened peace. He presented a Covenant with procedures for settling disputes and a commitment to disarmament for all its members. The League as Wilson and House first envisaged it—and the conference now affirmed—would be a transformative body, a "vehicle of life" that would sweep away the "miasma of distrust, of intrigue" that had plagued the world.

With the League locked in place for now, Wilson prepared to head home for a month-long respite. Before leaving, he deputized House to take his place at the negotiating table. In his absence, the Colonel assured him, he would make no commitments that would limit the president's future decision-making. Worried about the president's obdurate nature, the Colonel also advised him to convene a dinner upon his return for the members of both the House and Senate Foreign Relations Committees, many of whom were isolationists. That would give Wilson the opportunity to win them over to the League by outlining the plan and answering their questions. Wilson objected, but the Colonel pressed, sensing the deteriorating relations between the president and a Congress now firmly in Republican hands after the 1918 midterm elections. Still, the two men parted on warm terms, with Wilson "clasping my hand and placing his arm around me." "He looked happy, as well indeed he should be," House recorded in his diary. Neither man knew it, but this would be their last happy embrace.

The president returned to Paris a month later in a foul mood. His White House dinner—held only at the Colonel's insistence—ended up a flop. Wilson had been courteous throughout but still failed to win the support of a single Republican there. One senator afterward said Wilson seemed so disengaged from the details of the League that it felt "as if I had been wandering with Alice in Wonderland and had tea with the Mad Hatter." The president's chief foe, Senator Henry Cabot Lodge from Massachusetts, soon to chair the Foreign Relations Committee, left the dinner more determined than ever to block the League in the Senate. And that was what he did, introducing a resolution with enough support to force Wilson to make changes to his beloved Covenant.

At the same time, press reports from Paris seemed to indicate to Wilson that House was making unacceptable concessions to the Allies on the League Covenant and territorial demands. Equally infuriating, the president read numerous dispatches from Paris suggesting that as a result of those concessions, things were proceeding more smoothly with him away. Those reports proved accurate: The Colonel *had* been negotiating concessions with the British and French that broke the stalemate. The Allied leaders *did* prefer to deal with him, whose style of doing business suited theirs. And House, in a rare departure, *wanted* these developments known. Every day at 6 p.m. the Colonel hosted a gathering of American correspondents covering the conference, when by his own admission he would "talk freely" despite Wilson's preference that he stay quiet. The very qualities that had initially drawn them together—the scholarly idealist and the sage realist—now threatened to divide them.

So when Wilson met with the Colonel on the train ride from Brest to Paris on March 14, 1919—their first face-to-face meeting in a month—a fight seemed inevitable. Differing descriptions survive of their encounter, ranging from Edith Wilson's apocalyptic to House's benign. In the Colonel's brief retelling, the proud president still felt rankled by the failed White House dinner, speaking to him with "considerable bitterness" about the way in which the senators treated him. Otherwise nothing out of the ordinary occurred, as House recalled, aside from a cryptic observation that Wilson had returned "very militant" and wanted to ensure the League Covenant remained core to the final peace treaty.

Edith Wilson's account, written two decades later, presented a far more dramatic and damning depiction. In her version, she waited in the stateroom while her husband and House conferred next door. A little after midnight, House left and she entered to see that her husband "had aged ten years." Asking him what had happened, she remembered that Wilson "smiled bitterly" and then explained: "House has given away everything we had won before we left Paris. He has compromised on every side, and so I have to start all over again and this time it will be harder, as he has given the impression that my delegates are not in sympathy with me." According to Edith, the president then ruefully said, "So he has yielded until there is nothing left."

Wherever the truth lies between those two accounts, one thing is certain: The relationship between these two best friends had changed for the worse by the time House exited that rail carriage as the sun rose over Paris. For now they would continue to work together: With the treaty in the balance, each needed the other too much to break immediately. Looking back, however, the point of no return had passed. The process of excommunication had begun. And if there wasn't the Hibben-like single moment of a faculty vote to mark the breach, there was a steady withdrawal of Wilson's reliance on the Colonel. By the end of May, House would write in his diary, "I seldom or never have a chance to talk with him seriously and, for the moment, his is practically out from under my influence. When we meet it is to settle some passing problem and not to take inventory of things in general or plan for the future. This is what we used to do."

The question then arises: What exactly did the Colonel do in those four short weeks while Wilson was in Washington—and then in the last months of the conference—to warrant the president essentially cutting him off after seven years of unprecedented personal friendship and professional partnership? Did House indeed make concessions without Wilson's knowledge, thereby setting back the process while threatening the entire moral structure of the treaty itself? Or was his pragmatism necessary at that moment to break the stalemate and get the parties to an agreement? Did the Colonel lose his trademark discretion at exactly the wrong time by talking too brazenly and immodestly to reporters, or was he shrewdly and appropriately filling a seismic information gap created by Wilson's refusal to engage the press? Finally, it must be asked, was Edith Wilson really at the heart of the break, seeking once and for all to eliminate the one person who could compete for her husband's affections?

The record of the Paris Peace Conference before and after the rail carriage showdown offers fragmentary clues to these questions. Once back in Paris, the two men did continue to collaborate, even agreeing at one point to precipitate a "showdown" with Allied leaders to stir movement on open questions. To the extent House had made concessions during Wilson's absence, the president easily reversed them. Indeed, the first two weeks of their Paris reunion seemed to restore some stability to their relationship despite Wilson's undercurrent of hostility.

But the truce wouldn't last. The president fell ill in early April with a severe fever, quite likely the Spanish flu. Bedridden, Wilson asked the Colonel to take his place as head of the Council of Four meetings (with Lloyd George, Clemenceau, and Italy's Orlando). From April 4 to April 8, House used all his political skills to break the stalemate that had characterized the previous two weeks. Even as the president and his loyalists derided his approach, House moved the process along and forged a consensus exactly in line with his plan when the conference had started.

Wilson quickly made known his disgust with House's placating style. "The rift between the President & Col. House seems to be widening," Press Secretary Ray Stannard Baker recorded in his diary. "The Colonel compromises everything away." Edith Wilson echoed Baker's view, writing that she "exploded" at her husband in describing House's behavior: "Oh, if Colonel House had only stood firm . . . none of this would have to be done over. I think he is a perfect jellyfish." Wilson reportedly replied, "Well, God made jellyfish, so, as Shakespeare said about a man, therefore to let him pass, and don't be too hard on House."

House felt equal disgust toward Wilson, describing in his diary throughout the second half of the conference how out of touch the president was with what other leaders needed from the treaty and how ineffective a negotiator he was proving to be. "He seems to do his best to offend rather than to please," he wrote. "He speaks constantly of teamwork but seldom practices it." Wilson's obsession with keeping others out of deliberations maddened House and the other now anemic commissioners. In various entries the Colonel characterized Wilson as "stubborn," "angry," and "the most prejudiced man he ever knew." He now saw his friend in an ever harsher light: "I am quite sincere in believing that the President will rank with the great orators of all time. In truth, I believe that it is as an orator that he excels rather than as a statesman. . . . The President's actions do not square with his speeches. There is a *bon mot* going the round in Paris and London, 'Wilson talks like Jesus Christ but acts like Lloyd George.'"

The denouement in House's relationship with the First Couple came when he visited the elegant Wilson residence in the Eighth Arrondissement on April 21. As he did most days during the conference, House arrived to brief the Wilsons on events. At some point in the conversation Edith Wilson showed the Colonel a news story bylined by a reporter known to be close to House. The article dismissed the president while praising House as the "brains of the Commission." She demanded an explanation, implying that House had something to do with the portrayals: "Colonel, have you been reading these awful articles on Woodrow, or have you been too busy?" His face turning red, House could only reply: "Has the Governor seen the article?" Hearing he hadn't, House grabbed the offending article from Edith and fled the room. That marked not just House's last conversation with Edith, but the last time he would ever pay a visit to the First Couple.

By the summer of 1919, the Allies had unanimously agreed on at least one objective: They had to finalize the treaty. The Europeans needed the Americans to rebuild their continent, and Wilson needed the Europeans both to empower his beloved League of Nations and then to help win its approval in the US Senate, now controlled by Republicans who had swept the midterm elections the previous November. By way of compromise, Allied leaders gave Wilson the amendments he needed to his Fourteen Points before presenting it to the Senate. In return, Wilson accepted a treaty that fell far short of his goal of being magnanimous in victory. To the contrary, the treaty imposed a vindictive peace, severely punishing Germany by accepting most of the Allied demands for territory, reparations, and war guilt. When the Allies presented the final treaty in June, the Germans predictably balked and asked for modifications. The British, sensing they had gone too far in punishing Germany, agreed to reconsider, but Clemenceau refused. Dispirited, Wilson agreed with the French, fearing the time had passed to seek the idealized peace he craved. House also concurred, believing he had done everything possible to achieve a "just peace." In the end, Wilson told his delegation to stand down. The treaty would remain as written.

On June 28, 1919, the world powers signed the Treaty of Versailles. House attended the ceremony in the palace, and he later went out on the terrace with his wife, Loulie, and the four Allied leaders to see the garden fountains turned back on for the first time since the war started. The president left for home that evening, not wanting to wait a minute to start the hard work of securing Senate passage. House accompanied his friend to the train station.

Their final conversation on the platform played out true to form, as if scripted. House urged Wilson to approach the isolationist Senate in a "conciliatory" manner. "House," the president replied, "I have found one can never get anything in this life that is worthwhile without fighting for it." In what would be his final rejoinder, the Colonel reminded Wilson that "Anglo-Saxon civilization was built on compromise. I said that a fight was the last thing to be brought about, and then only when it could not be avoided." Minutes later, when the train whistle sounded, the president turned toward House and "with a stern look, said coldly 'Goodbye, House.'" It was the last time the two men would ever see or talk to each other.

The peace treaty Wilson and House had worked so hard to shape would be vilified by history, blamed for many of the woes of the twentieth and twenty-first centuries. Its harsh terms ultimately gutted Germany of 13 percent of its territory, 10 percent of its population, and all its colonies. Whether in the end Wilson and House could have constructed a more just peace will never be fully known. House for one doubted it, believing that given the profound wreckage of the war, "history could guide us but little in the making of this peace." A better settlement, House believed, could only have come from "an unselfish and idealistic spirit which was… too much to expect of men come together at such a time and for such a purpose."

But the Treaty of Versailles also marked the first moment of American ascendancy on the world stage. By bringing the country into the war, and then leading the negotiations to end it, Wilson and House had introduced an activist, muscular approach to how America viewed its role in the world. Their strategy—"Wilsonian democracy," as it came to be known—would become the norm for a succession of presidents as they exported American values and capitalism to all corners of the world. It would reign for a century, through another world war, a cold war, and a war on terrorism, only to retreat, if temporarily, during the one-term Trump administration.

The four years Woodrow Wilson had left on earth would be unhappy ones, consumed with crippling illness and legislative defeat. That fall, in the midst of a bone-weary, cross-country trip to sell the treaty above the heads of senators, Wilson collapsed. He had suffered a massive stroke from which he would never recover. He returned to the White House incapacitated and unable to carry out his presidential duties. Edith seized the moment, serving as his stand-in without ever acknowledging to the country her husband's dire condition or her newfound power. She ruled through little notes, issued with the words "The President wishes..." to cloak her own authority. And one thing she most certainly wished was the permanent banishment of House from her husband's life.

House wasn't giving up, though. Throughout the summer and fall of 1919, he continued to maintain the fiction of their friendship. He had no interest in informing the world of their breakup—despite his own prominence, it remained the primary source of his power—but news inevitably leaked. A story that first appeared in the *New York Sun* and later picked up in London broke the news: "The Colonel virtually has ceased to function as the President's unofficial diplomatic agent in Europe." Still, House vigilantly followed both his friend and the Senate's deliberations of the treaty. Throughout the fall of 1919, he sent letters to Wilson urging various strategies to win its passage. Wilson's vengeful wife ignored House's correspondence, not opening a single one.

On November 19, 1919, the inevitable happened. Presented a treaty with and without Senator Lodge's reservations—concessions the president refused to support—the Senate voted both down. Ironically, a majority of senators supported the concept of American participation in a League, but as Neu notes, Wilson and Lodge's "rigidity" doomed its creation. Yet even in the face of defeat, House wouldn't give up. He sent another letter to Wilson urging him to resubmit the treaty so it could be ratified in whatever form that would preserve their League. Again, Edith refused to consider House's idea, shutting out his counsel at the last moment it could have saved her husband's legacy.

By the spring of 1920, Edith had accomplished her mission: The rift with House was complete, leaving the Colonel in despair. The press amplified the sensational news of their breakup—news Edith did nothing to tamp down. Forlorn, House made one last attempt to reach Wilson through his wife. This time he heard back, but his friend's terse response left House disappointed. He resigned himself to the new reality. "I shall accept the letter as the end of our relations or, at least, the end of our official relations," House concluded in his diary.

On the morning of February 3, 1924, Wilson died at his home in DC at the age of seventy-eight. When House learned the news, he called former Wilson colleagues to inquire about the funeral arrangements, only to be told he wasn't invited. Edith had exacted her final revenge. Instead of sharing in the intimacy of the two funerals Edith had planned, House sat with ten thousand other people in an overflowing memorial service at Madison Square Garden.

By the time Wilson was laid to rest, a fight had already unfolded to determine who deserved blame for the failures of Paris and the breakup of their legendary relationship. The controversy pitted Wilson's large army of loyalists against House and his young biographer. Girding himself for battle, House had enlisted a former member of his Inquiry team, Charles Seymour, to go through his papers and diary and condense them into a publishable memoir. In 1926, the first two volumes of *The Intimate Papers of Colonel House* were published. On balance, the book presented a damning portrait of Wilson. Throughout the 979 pages, House came across as the more knowledgeable, sophisticated actor on the global stage, while Wilson was reduced to a secondary player, a man consumed by prejudices and slow to act in the face of growing threats. Volumes three and four, covering the war years and the peace conference, came two years later. Only at the very end of volume four did House address his excommunication: "My separation from Woodrow Wilson was and is to me a tragic mystery, a mystery that now can never be dispelled, for its explanation lies buried with him." These were the only public words he uttered of the most famous breakup in political history since Hamilton and Burr.

The opposing side boasted a more formidable team: Grayson, Tumulty, Edith Wilson, and Ray Stannard Baker, the former press secretary now turned historian. Baker had criticized House's diplomacy in Paris, but he also harbored an enduring fascination for the man. After a visit to House's New York home before Wilson's death, he recorded in his diary a devastatingly colorful and apt description of House's personality and relationship to Wilson:

> [House] has a kind of common-sense (not wisdom) which grows out of his knowledge of what human beings are. His intellectual equipment is small: he has no real mind of his own.... He compromises everything away in order to preserve "harmony" & keep people liking one another.... I think the Colonel understood the President better than most men: & wanted to serve him well: but got too little... human sympathy and encouragement.... It was perhaps because these two men were at opposite poles of temperament: one cold & negative, the other warm & positive, that they so flew together, each recognizing in the other what he lacked.... [House] lives always in a kind of warm haze of good-feeling. What a contrast with the grim, bitter, tragic, lonely old man [Wilson].... And yet twenty years from now [House] will be utterly forgotten... except as he was a friend, a helper, of the President: an incident in the President's career & one of the men who reflected for a moment the light from that great figure and then suffered his displeasure.

As fate would have it, Edith Wilson chose Baker to write the authorized biography of her husband. After their visit in 1921, House hadn't had any contact with Baker and grew worried—with good reason—about how he would fare after his attacks on Wilson in his biography. In 1931, after the release of the volumes dealing with the Wilson presidency, Baker skewered House. In Baker's portrait, the Colonel emerged as a preening, vainglorious, and simple-minded supplicant who exaggerated his influence and whose friendship with Wilson was the "crowning achievement of his life." House did not exaggerate in his own review: "[Baker] is belittling me in every way he thinks he can safely do so."

Published at the height of the Great Depression, Baker's scathing book marked a particularly low moment for the Colonel. For the first time in his life, House was forced to worry about money. Christmas that year was so pinched that the Houses decided not to exchange presents.

House at seventy-three had one more act to play before he would permanently rest, and it came with the campaign and election of Franklin Delano Roosevelt. Sensing one final chance at reclaiming the power he had enjoyed a generation earlier, the Colonel began to advise the New York governor. He had known and liked Roosevelt when the latter served as assistant secretary of the Navy early in the Wilson presidency, and those feelings were mutual. House began counseling FDR during his first race for governor, and as Roosevelt geared up for his presidential run, the Colonel helped him deal with such issues as whether America should still join the League of Nations. He gained such influence that he joined Roosevelt's "Brain Trust" two months before the 1932 election.

On election night, FDR called House to discuss the results, but the Colonel "felt none of the excitement that had swept over him . . . when his new friend Woodrow Wilson had won the presidency." The day after the election, House lunched with the president-elect and two other advisors, but he soon realized that there would be no re-creating his former role in the new administration. For one reason, the Colonel lacked the necessary physical energy. But more important, with the country still in economic crisis, FDR planned to remain on US soil for the foreseeable future. With no diplomatic initiatives in the offing and FDR's preference to deal with a range of advisors, House recognized his limited utility. By the time Europe faced renewed conflict in 1934, House felt ill equipped when the president finally floated the idea of him returning to the Continent to analyze the situation. Over the next four years, the Colonel would grow very close to the president and his mother, seeing and speaking with them often, but his days as an active presidential advisor had ended.

As House lay dying in his New York apartment in early 1938, he still agonized over the most consequential failure of his long and storied life: the break with Woodrow Wilson. In the twenty-one years since Paris, House had lived by any measure a full and satisfying life. Until the very end, he maintained his health, enjoyed a blissful family life with Loulie and his two daughters, had a remarkable association with his assistant, Fanny Denton, who kept his diary and organized his domestic life, met and dined with every president who followed Wilson, and enjoyed the homage of every important foreign ambassador who came through New York or Boston.

And yet House couldn't shake the grief he associated with June 1919, when he had said goodbye to Wilson forever. As the Colonel lay on his deathbed, he needed one more conversation with Seymour, now the president of Yale. Looking like a "wax effigy" to his biographer, House recalled those fateful Paris days one final time to make sense of what really happened. He ran through all the possible causes but could find fault only with Edith and her enablers. Wilson had no reason to have "hard feelings against me," the Colonel insisted, "but lacked the strength" to stand up to his wife and his other enemies. Had it not been for them, "my separation from Wilson [would] not [have been] a break."

After exhausting the subject, House turned more philosophical. The Colonel told Seymour he had accomplished all his life goals. He had indeed become a man of consequence, just as his long-ago dreams while gazing out at the Texas prairie had foretold. "My hand," he concluded, "has been on things."

CHAPTER 5

FDR and Daisy Suckley

Alone Together

During the summer of 1939, the American public was increasingly occupied with a looming question: Would Franklin Delano Roosevelt break a tradition that had started with George Washington and run for an unprecedented third term? The president himself repeatedly refused to provide an answer, prompting the press to nickname him "the Sphinx," that mythical creature—half man, half lion—who spoke slyly through riddles. With his serene countenance, FDR betrayed nothing to outsiders. And he seemed to delight in playing this guessing game, telling Treasury Secretary Henry Morgenthau, "You know I am a juggler. And I never let my right hand know what my left hand does."

Roosevelt's evasion was not just due to his guile and cunning; he himself wasn't really sure. For years now, FDR fantasized about retiring to Top Cottage, his private home on Dutchess Hill in Hyde Park, a few miles from his family's Hudson Valley estate. He had already begun planning for his retirement there (he actually drew the preliminary designs for the cottage as an armchair architect) and considering Democratic successors—signs that he was thinking seriously about finally exiting politics.

And yet it was at this dreamed-about retirement retreat that FDR staged his next bold political move, revealing his mindset as the specter of a second world war loomed.

On June 11, 1939, he welcomed King George VI and Queen Elizabeth of England for some "rest and relaxation" at Hyde Park. He claimed that this would be an opportunity for the dignified royals to bask in some "very simple country life."

But the meeting was not merely a pleasant vacation for the king and queen. As Hitler's aggression in Europe intensified, US-British relations had grown strained; some Americans still blamed Britain for dragging the United States into its long and painful involvement in World War I. Now, with Hitler's Third Reich expanding its control over Europe, FDR realized that the time had come to mend Anglo-American ties in case the worst happened.

In a display of his diplomatic savvy, FDR decided that he would throw an old-fashioned picnic at Top Cottage. He planned it down to every last, painstaking detail, from the seating chart to the menu. To win over the American public, Roosevelt believed, the royals needed to seem like "regular people"—the kind of people who dined informally outside on a bright summer day, surrounded by no fewer than 150 fawning guests.

In keeping with FDR's secretive nature, reporters and photographers were barred from the picnic. And yet the *New York Times* found a leak; the next morning's front page blared the shocking headline: KING TRIES HOT DOG AND ASKS FOR MORE. Controversy ensued. Had our patrician president lost his sense of etiquette? How did he have the nerve to offer hot dogs (and beer) to royalty—leaving the queen with no option but to eat hers with a knife and fork? Was he acting too casually, threatening the dignity of our country? And most important, was this a sign that he planned to run for a third term, possibly leading America into a looming war against fascism?

The *New York Times* dug as deeply as it could for the scantest details: what the king and queen wore, what was eaten besides hot dogs, how the royals shook hands with Roosevelt's servants. The article obsessively listed the most honorable guests—those sitting at the first seven tables—then ended by naming the ten women of the White House executive staff singled out by Roosevelt for special introductions.

But one key person was missing from that long list of exalted names: Margaret "Daisy" Suckley. She was sitting only two tables away from the king and queen, close enough to witness the waiters serve them two measly hot dogs on a silver tray. No official report of the picnic ever mentioned Daisy. Yet it was Daisy who knew the answers to many of FDR's riddles. And it was Daisy, at Top Cottage and elsewhere, whom FDR turned to so frequently as a source of solace and support during his darkest hours.

Fifty years later, it was also Daisy—one of only two guests from the original picnic still living—who described that celebrated afternoon to the *New York Times*. In 1939, Daisy had been an invisible presence. But on the picnic's fiftieth anniversary, the *New York Times* took special note of her attendance as a rare link to the past. For while FDR might have been a Sphinx to most people, to Daisy he revealed a side of himself that few had ever seen.

Daisy Suckley (rhymes with "book-ly") was a devoted diarist and prolific letter writer, but nobody knew that until her passing in 1991, just before her one-hundredth birthday. In a well-worn suitcase under her bed, there were thousands of pages of her diary entries and dozens of letters to FDR, along with thirty-eight letters back from him, many of them running for several pages. Four years later, the noted historian Geoffrey Ward would assemble these documents into his definitive book on their friendship. Taken together, Daisy's collection amounted to a profoundly personal—and unequaled—glimpse into Roosevelt's life in the White House during a time of world-changing events. But they also convey a friendship unlike any others in this book and perhaps even in the history of the American presidency.

Different from other presidential First Friends, Daisy didn't officially advise the president. Nor did she speak hard truths to him or play a role in shaping a consequential decision. They weren't equals in power or prestige; indeed, their relationship often revolved almost exclusively on the axis of Roosevelt's needs, interests, and predilections. All of this seeming one-sidedness has led some historians to disparage Daisy's interactions with the president as "worshipful" and "undemanding," as if Daisy lacked the agency to shape the friendship herself. But if being in "the room where it happens" is an important measure of primacy or relevance, Margaret Daisy Suckley was in the room—at the request of the president himself—more than anyone else.

After the passing of seventy-five years, there is no one alive to clarify why a distant cousin with no obvious portfolio would grow to command such intense interest and affection from the most powerful man on the planet. All we have left to judge comes from Daisy's diary entries and their correspondence. And what these documents seem to suggest is this: Theirs was a deep and loyal friendship that filled an emptiness in the life of a man who, as Daisy observed in her diary, "has no real 'home life' in which to relax, & 'recoup' his strength & peace of mind." As incidental as she might have appeared to outsiders, to FDR she proved essential. She possessed the exact qualities he most desired and often needed as president: intelligent, perceptive, loyal, discreet, thoughtful, poetic, conscientious, and caring. She was his confidante, cheerleader, companion, and later archivist. As he wrote to Daisy in 1938, he could tell her things that would sound "cuckoo" to others but that only she understood. At the same time, she intuited things about him that no one else could.

Most vitally, she balanced FDR's life, which switched constantly between either intense scrutiny or solitary independence. As Roosevelt once remarked to Daisy after a particularly grueling day fulfilling the duties of the presidency, "I'm either Exhibit A, or left completely alone." Many presidents have commented on this paradox of their position—at once surrounded by endless streams of people and activity, yet uniquely alone in bearing its awesome responsibility. Daisy provided an antidote to that loneliness. She did not merely serve as an outlet for FDR's ever-shifting moods. She also actively shaped a parallel private world that buttressed FDR's ability to shepherd the nation through depression and world war.

"He was wired for this relationship," historian Jonathan Alter says. "His emotional landscape required that he have Daisy in it. He would have been a more unsettled and less natural president had he not had Daisy with him."

Daisy was the fifth child and first daughter of Robert Bowne Suckley and Elizabeth Phillips Montgomery. Like FDR, she was born into the landed gentry of the Hudson Valley. Her family's estate—Wilderstein—was perched majestically on the east bank of the Hudson River outside the village of Rhinebeck, just ten miles north of Roosevelt's in Hyde Park. As a young girl, she became known to most people as Daisy, a common nickname for Margaret. Ten years younger than her cousin Franklin, Daisy was eighteen when she first caught sight of him at a New Year's gala at a neighboring estate. She watched with wonder as the strikingly handsome, six-foot, two-inch Roosevelt commanded the dance floor with an array of partners, the very image of grace and verve.

Even beyond the dance floor, Roosevelt was a man most at home in the company of women. Throughout his life, he would surround himself with powerful women who provided him with emotional and intellectual ballast at crucial moments. His wife, Eleanor, would garner the most attention for the groundbreaking contributions she made to the country during his life and to the world after his death. But there would be many others: Frances Perkins, the first woman to hold a Cabinet position (secretary of labor) and who became the architect of many of the most important back-to-work New Deal programs; Missy LeHand, the first woman to serve as secretary to the president, a dominant voice in FDR's professional and personal matters (so dominant that she graced the cover of *Time* in 1934 and FDR later named a frigate after her), who may or may not have been his mistress for a time; and Grace Tully, who succeeded LeHand as his secretary and delighted the president with her loyalty.

Roosevelt's preference for the company of women can be traced to his childhood. Roosevelt's father, James, was fifty-four when Franklin was born, and he already had a twenty-eight-year-old son from a previous marriage. As Franklin entered his teens, James became increasingly distracted by his failing health. So Franklin's care and upbringing was left mostly to his mother, Sara, a powerful personality whom Franklin adored but who could frustrate him at times by aggressively inserting herself into his affairs. He basked in her attention, seeking her approval—qualities he also drew upon from Daisy. Daisy came to recognize FDR's near-total dependence on his mother shortly after Sara's death in 1942, writing in her diary that to Sara, Franklin "was always 'my boy' and he seemed to me often rather pathetic, and hungry for just that kind of thing."

Dismissed later as a "feather-duster" by Alice Roosevelt, Franklin's cousin and Teddy Roosevelt's acerbic daughter, Roosevelt was never "one of the boys," observed Michael Reilly, chief of his Secret Service detail. More specifically, FDR had never been an athlete, never had a gang of male friends, and, most punishingly for the status-conscious young man, never got into Porcellian, the elite, all-male Harvard social club to which his father, Teddy Roosevelt, and Teddy's sons all belonged. FDR later described the rejection from his male classmates as "the biggest disappointment of my life." Women, however, took a more adoring view of the up-and-coming aristocrat with a winning smile and rugged good looks. If FDR didn't have a crew of men with whom to relax or recreate, he was always surrounded by women who delighted in his conversation and company.

When Franklin started courting his distant cousin Eleanor Roosevelt, his mother strenuously objected—so much so that she forced the couple to keep their engagement a secret for a full year. Her protests and distractions failed to pry the two apart; Eleanor and Franklin finally wed in 1905. They had six children together (five of whom survived to adulthood), but after thirteen years of marriage, their relationship had become transactional, much more of a calculated partnership than a loving marriage, a deftly cultivated façade of civility to conceal the increasing emotional and physical distance between them.

It had been like this from the moment Eleanor learned of Franklin's long-running romance with Lucy Mercer, Eleanor's part-time social secretary since 1913. The affair began in the summer of 1916 and continued as America entered World War I in 1917. In the fall of 1918, Franklin, then the assistant secretary of the Navy, had taken a long trip to Europe to assess the state of the US Navy for himself. On his return trip aboard the USS *Leviathan*, Roosevelt and scores of others on board were stricken with the Spanish flu, an epidemic that would kill more than twenty million worldwide. Roosevelt fell seriously ill, fighting not just the virus but also double pneumonia. He was terribly weakened but managed to pull through. When the ship docked in New York, FDR was carried to an ambulance and taken to the family town house on East Sixty-Fifth Street in Manhattan.

Unpacking his suitcase, Eleanor discovered a bundle of love letters from Mercer. "The bottom dropped out of my world," Eleanor later wrote. "I faced myself, my surroundings, my world, honestly for the first time."

Though Roosevelt was deeply in love with Mercer, he and Eleanor remained married—reinforced by Sara's threat to disinherit her son if they divorced—allowing them to maintain the appearance of propriety, spare the children from a public scandal, and protect FDR's political future.

Over the summer of 1921, FDR contracted polio, forcing him into a wheelchair at the age of thirty-nine. Just a year before, he had been nominated as the Democratic candidate for vice president. Although the Democrats lost the race, Franklin acquitted himself well, and to most observers his future seemed boundless. Now, hearing the news that his chances of ever walking again were minimal at best, he became distraught. For a man who had always enjoyed ascendance, albeit with a few minor setbacks, he felt his future, as James Tobin writes, "being stolen—the everyday pleasures of sailing and golf... of riding horses with his children, the plans for new campaigns, the glowing hope of the presidency. It was all in the gravest doubt." A man used to shaping his own fate was now at the mercy of a disease that "threaten[ed] to rob him of that pleasure."

At one point during his rigorous rehabilitation in Hyde Park in the summer of 1922, Eleanor returned to Manhattan to be with their five young children. Under the care of his domineering mother, FDR yearned for company that would bring him "good cheer," as he put it to her.

Sara Delano heeded her son's wish by picking up the phone and calling Daisy Suckley, inviting her to join them at Springwood, the Roosevelt estate. Although they hadn't seen each other much in the twelve years since Daisy first spotted Franklin on the dance floor, Sara sensed Daisy would offer good company for her recovering son. They shared the same privileged background, a love for the Hudson Valley, and could gossip about local matters. Sara also knew that the unmarried Daisy had some time to spare; if they clicked, as Sara hoped, Daisy could become a kind of stand-in for the now-departed Eleanor.

Daisy accepted Sara's invitation and became a frequent visitor that summer, spending afternoons with Franklin as he rebuilt his body and spirit. As they sat on the verdant Springwood lawns, Roosevelt would exercise his upper body with a bar erected over his chair. "I'm not going to be conquered by a childish disease," Franklin told her, even though the most quotidian physical tasks now presented a challenge.

Daisy proved to be the perfect companion. Refined and witty yet reticent, she was mature beyond her years, with a social ease among older people more than her own peers. She and Franklin established a playful repartee. They related easily to each other, with Daisy displaying "a sharp mind and wicked wit," especially when the topic turned to local gossip, as it often did. They became so comfortable together that FDR even recited a tall tale he loved to share with intimates: how he had been subjected to blackmail eighteen years earlier by a woman claiming to be a baroness who lured him and a friend into a compromising situation. The more times he told the story, the more colorful it grew. Nevertheless, Daisy loved the intrigue of the outlandish story, so alien to her own cloistered life at Wilderstein. FDR opened up a new world to her while she entertained him through tedious and dark hours.

She had her own dark hours. When Daisy was five, her father fell into financial ruin and took the family to Switzerland to flee the shame. For ten years there, her only companions were her siblings; by the time she returned home in her mid-teens fluent in three languages, she had no American friends at all, and that remained largely true into her late twenties. She pleaded to attend college but ran into resistance from her mother, who wanted her home instead to help care for the mass of relatives who regularly descended on their vast estate. They managed to reach a compromise: Daisy would study at Bryn Mawr but return home after only two years. Discouraged by her parents from marrying, she rejected every one of her many suitors. Of her five siblings, only one—her younger sister—would ever marry.

Tragedy also likely compounded Daisy's loneliness and sense of limitation. In 1917, her oldest brother, Henry, was killed in Greece by a German bomb that hit the Red Cross ambulance he was driving. Four years later, her father died suddenly, leaving her, as she confided to her diary, an "inadequate creature." The time she spent with Franklin may have distracted and strengthened her at a time of great personal loss.

Daisy was just one of many people to experience the power of Roosevelt's innate ability to transmit his "internal strength to others"—a jaunty optimism that would become the hallmark of his presidency. Frances Perkins once described leaving an interview with the president feeling better, not because the president solved her problems but because he had given her greater strength and good cheer. One can thus imagine the uplifting effect he had on Daisy as he worked tirelessly to regain his strength. And as for Franklin—whose spirit would later inspire a nation in the ashes of the Depression—he drew sustenance from the quiet simplicity of his friendship with Daisy during a harrowing time in his own life.

The cousins stayed in regular touch through the rest of the 1920s and into the start of the next decade when FDR, encouraged by his wife, reentered the political arena to become governor of New York and then president of the United States. They exchanged scores of letters during this period, with each one of hers signed "your affectionate cousin." Their correspondence, as historian Joseph Persico writes, "indicated both her understanding of him and his need for someone to whom he could unburden himself." While Roosevelt resurrected his career, however, Daisy continued to flounder, receding into a world of books and fantasy. "I live," she told a friend, "mostly in dreams." But with FDR's ascension to the presidency in 1933, Daisy's fears of "falling away into a gray world of castles in the air" were instantly extinguished. She stood on the cusp of a new life, one filled with the bright colors of the most consequential figures and events of the twentieth century.

It began with an invitation: FDR asked Daisy to attend his inauguration in 1933, bestowing her with a seat of honor at the parade. Her tickets didn't arrive at her hotel in time, so she listened spellbound to his iconic address on the radio, as FDR invigorated a nation wearied by three years of economic depression: "The only thing we have to fear is... fear itself—nameless, unreasoning, unjustified terror which paralyzes needed efforts to convert retreat into advance." Later that afternoon, Daisy sat behind FDR as he watched the parade, then attended a White House reception while FDR, wasting no time, convened his first Cabinet meeting. Within a year, she would become a fixture in the president's new life, part of his innermost circle both in Washington and Hyde Park, as well as the keeper of some of his most closely-guarded secrets.

After winning the 1932 election in a landslide against Herbert Hoover, FDR faced a nation crippled by the Great Depression—an economic crisis without precedent in the country's history. Between 1929 and 1932, ten million people had lost their jobs and breadlines had become a ubiquitous feature of the national landscape. The stock market had plunged nearly 90 percent, mirrored by a precipitous drop in national morale. For many Americans then, FDR's election felt like sorely needed relief, a challenge to the orthodoxies that had led the country to this dismal state.

Roosevelt wasted no time in attempting to steady the nation through decisive federal action or, in his words, "bold, persistent experimentation." At his request, an emergency session of Congress began on March 9, only five days after his inauguration. Thus ensued FDR's First Hundred Days, a period of swift lawmaking aimed at rebuilding the banking system; providing unemployment relief; and transforming the nation's approach to agricultural policy, industrial recovery, and mortgage financing. By the end, fifteen groundbreaking bills had been passed, designed to reactivate the ailing economy.

In the words of historian Arthur Schlesinger Jr., this flurry of activity brought about "a presidential barrage of ideals and programs unlike anything known to American history." Soon enough, critics began attacking the New Deal for being either dangerously radical or heartlessly insufficient. But few could disagree that in little more than three months, the Roosevelt administration had laid the groundwork for the American welfare state.

After the First Hundred Days had passed, FDR needed a brief summer respite. Some five months into his presidency, in August 1933, he returned home to Springwood and Daisy came for tea at Eleanor's invitation. Before Daisy returned home, and without Eleanor's knowledge, the president asked her to visit again a few days later and go for a drive with him. FDR loved driving his roadster, which was equipped with hand-powered controls for him to operate the gas and brakes.

Daisy arrived back at Springwood and they were soon off, motoring through the leafy roads tailed by four detectives in a state-trooper cruiser. It must have been exhilarating for a man with paralyzed legs to experience such independence—riding through the countryside, seemingly free of his disability. They ended up spending most of the day together, with Franklin sharing his favorite books and illustrations and including her in a picnic with his family and the press. That night, an elated Daisy wrote in her diary, "The President is a man—mentally, physically & spiritually. What more can I say?" She soon became his favorite driving companion, ultimately spending more time with him in his roadster than anyone else.

As wrapped up as he was in bringing the New Deal to fruition, FDR still kept Daisy on his mind. In October 1933, after she had complimented one of his "fireside chats" on the radio, he wrote saying how much he missed her company and asking her to visit again:

> Dear Daisy—
>
> That was dear of you to write me about the Sunday night talk & I'm glad you liked it because that means so much more from a very understanding person like you... I count on that visit soon—
>
> Affectionately yours, FDR

He didn't have to wait long. Three months later, in January 1934, Daisy came to Washington to celebrate the president's fifty-second birthday. She visited the city for five days, much of it spent at the White House. At one point, she noted that "Mrs. R was evidently surprised" to see Daisy with her husband. For the next month FDR, ever on guard after the Mercer affair, never acknowledged to his wife the growing intensity of his friendship with Daisy.

What followed was a week of dinner parties, receptions, and late-night conversations in the upstairs Oval Room. In a rare moment of immodesty, Daisy confided to her diary, "I begin to feel that I am quite important at the White House!" Roosevelt welcomed her fully into his world and openly confessed to her that he "does get mentally tired and that is terrifying to realize." He then carefully added that he would admit this "to very few, and that it was not for quotation!" as she recalled in her diary.

FDR's comfort with showing Daisy his vulnerable side allowed them to share a playful rapport during these times together. Once, as he made his halting way past her during a formal diplomatic reception in the White House Blue Room, Daisy recalled, "Franklin looked at me, winked & laughed. I smiled circumspectly! In the afternoon before, he said he was sure I would laugh at him as he went by in the procession, and I said I would *try* to behave properly. I did!"

But Daisy had more to offer than frivolity; her sensitive nature made her an astute observer of Washington goings-on, which she both shared in her diary and often with FDR when alone. For example, she sensed (correctly) that Alice Roosevelt's omnipresence at the White House had more to do with intelligence gathering for her beloved Republican Party than affection for her cousin the president. And after listening to the president describe a conversation he had with a prominent Japanese man who laid out his country's expansionist plans, she offered her own commentary: "It is a plan looking a century ahead, a thing we Anglo Saxons can't do, and in considering what has happened so far, since 1900, they seem to be carrying out this plan." Then, almost as an aside, she added presciently: "We must watch coming events!" Witness to numerous dinners and meetings throughout his presidency, she could also be piercingly perceptive and biting about those who underwhelmed her. At one dinner with FDR, Harry Hopkins, and his wife, Louise, she noted how Louise "isn't interesting enough or amusing enough to warrant all that talking she does to F, and he can't help looking a little tired at making the extra effort."

They shared a special, unspoken bond when together, but when apart, their correspondence was also tinged with warmth and tenderness. In one letter to Daisy in October 1934, Roosevelt informed her of his plans to travel to Hyde Park in time for election day. "I hope to have a real four days without political thoughts—isn't that a grand idea for the period immediately preceding an important election? Come & tell me about chips and cabbages & Kings—the mythological kind—but not about *sealing* wax—that would be too much like the State Department—it will be nice."

After a drive in his roadster during that trip, FDR acknowledged the effect she was having on him: "I think you added several years to my life & much to my happiness." During another outing in June 1935, FDR thanked her for "that *bestest* of afternoons—I told you there were a million things I wanted to talk about and I think I only talked about a dozen—so if you will work out 12/1,000,000 you see how often you will have to come again."

Later that summer in Hyde Park, they took a succession of driving trips that suggest the progression of their relationship. On the first, they took shelter beneath a tree on what the two friends began to refer to as "Our Hill"—the future site of Top Cottage, where Roosevelt dreamed of a quiet life post-presidency. In a letter she wrote later to FDR, Daisy sounded like a woman falling in love: "I am afraid I am getting myself in very deep! Almost like an intrigue and it's so completely foreign to my nature!"

Then, on the afternoon of September 22, 1935, something happened that Franklin, three years later, described as the beginning of "a voyage." The president and Daisy were again driving in the countryside, and again stopping at "Our Hill." No letters or diary entries reveal what intimacies were exchanged on the hill that day, but their correspondence immediately afterward suggests that something meaningful did occur. In a note to FDR later that night, Daisy exclaimed how "OUR HILL" is "without exception" the "nicest Hill" before assuming a more serious tone: "You remember that little verse by Maria Mulock on Friendship? On the blessing of being able to *talk* freely to one's friend? Shouldn't there be another verse, on the silent moments, where often more is said—*without* words than with them?"

During that outing, the president had also implored Daisy to join him on a long train trip west on which he would depart that very night. Daisy declined, writing to FDR after his departure: "Do you realize the amount of will-power that was necessary to refuse a certain invitation...? A slightly *righteous* feeling, I find, gives *no* satisfaction whatsoever—only irritation!"

For the next month, Roosevelt adopted a distinctly affectionate tone in his letters to her, regretting that she had decided not to accompany him. Writing from his train as it hurtled west, he opened up to her: "Do you know that you alone have known that I was a bit 'cast down' these past weeks. I *couldn't* have let anyone else know it—but somehow I seem to tell you all those things and what I don't happen to tell you, you seem to know anyway." Nearly a week later, after dedicating the Boulder Dam, he was even more blunt: "[T]here is no reason why I should not tell you that I miss you *very* much—it was a week ago yesterday." He continued to mark the time since they had last seen each other on September 22. One month after their trip to the hill, still in planning mode for Top Cottage, FDR wrote: "I think a one-story fieldstone two-room house...one with very thick walls to protect us...Do you mind—then—if I tell you fairy stories till it gets very late?"

It remains unclear what to make of this string of uniquely intimate letters exchanged during a small slice of time in 1935. But one other clue shows how deeply their care for one another had grown by then. FDR frequently addressed his letters to "MM," or My Margaret. Daisy signed her letters "YM." Whatever the level of their intimacy, there seems little question that by the third year of his presidency, Roosevelt held MM closer to his heart than most anyone.

Whether the two shared a physical or just deeply emotional relationship has long been a matter of debate. In 2012, the movie *Hyde Park on Hudson* was released, starring Bill Murray as FDR and Laura Linney as Daisy. The movie leaves little to the imagination: FDR is on the famous car ride to Top Cottage, stops the car, releases his security detail, and then, as the camera pulls back from the car, begins to seduce an eager Daisy. The movie was panned for its thin story line and for taking liberties with historical fact. But those who know Roosevelt only through their history textbooks (and know nothing of his seventh cousin) are left believing they were lovers.

Historians have been more circumspect in their conclusions. Geoffrey Ward says today: "I don't believe there was ever a physical relationship between them. Theirs was a flirtation, not an affair. Their mutual delight in it intensified, I think, by the fact that it could never actually be consummated."

Daisy herself carefully defined the non-sexual nature of their relationship after what may or may not have been that hilltop kiss.

> Do you mind if I do a little thinking aloud—on paper? The subject is Friendships, and the way they start and grow—An introduction, a shake of the hand, a few casual words to begin—and then, by various stages, sometimes slowly and sometimes remarkably quickly, the friendship is established—That's the usual way, and the friendship is tested in its different stages, and usually finds very definite limits not so far from the surface.
>
> On rare occasions, however, it seems to start in the deepest depths, where the important elements are—and in these rare cases, the superficial elements are completely unimportant. They can be however, a source of interest and amusement—a never-ending voyage of discovery to strange and distant lands—with never a feeling of fear, because of the safe & solid ship one knows is underfoot—

Daisy claimed not to be bothered by gossip about her and the president: "I have argued to myself & with members of the family as to whether whatever gossip about us there may be, is justified," she noted in her diary. "Since there is nothing but good in my desire to help him, & since he seems to feel I do help him, I have long since made up my mind that that is the important thing. Only those who wish to find evil in our friendship, will do so—and I, for one will not have my life ruled by that sort of person."

Ward goes even further, saying he believes Daisy never had a physically intimate relationship with *anyone* during her lifetime, let alone the president, and would have been mortified at the suggestion she had.

With millions finally back to work in New Deal programs and a growing sense that the worst days of the Depression were over, Roosevelt knew by early 1936 that his chances of re-election were promising. Still, he felt a gnawing sense of uncertainty for several reasons. He was facing a wave of labor unrest not seen since 1919. And though his Republican opponent, the millionaire Kansas governor Alf Landon, posed little competition, there were other leaders of formidable movements who blasted FDR with undisguised contempt, including "radio priest" Charles Coughlin and Louisiana senator Huey Long. Even worse, a mounting fascist threat seemed to be sweeping across Europe: Adolf Hitler in Germany, Benito Mussolini in Italy, civil war in Spain.

Amid such challenges and pressures, FDR's enthusiasm for the job could waver, especially after the death of his close friend and advisor Louis Howe in April 1936. In unusually frank language, he vented to Daisy: "Why did I come back—why this endless task—why run again—why see the endless streams of people—why the damned old basket of mail which is either full & hanging over my head or just emptied & ready to be filled." Daisy responded with calm encouragement, reminding him that what he was doing through "the medium of that mail basket & those endless conferences is *so* wonderful."

In 1936, Roosevelt easily won reelection in a romp over Landon, capturing a record 98 percent of the Electoral College vote and the highest share of the popular vote since the uncontested election of James Monroe in 1820. Meanwhile, the cousins continued their elaborate planning for Top

Cottage, right down to selecting books for what they called "OL"—Our Library on "Our Hill," as Daisy began referring to it. The president was just as enthusiastic. Such projects with Daisy proved to be a delightful distraction for the president, who was nursing ever-growing concerns about Hitler's designs on Europe and his threat to the Western world.

One way that FDR dealt with these crushing burdens was to convene what he called "the Children's Hour," a gathering at the end of the day in a second-floor study of the White House where he could unwind with close friends and associates. The cardinal rule of the Children's Hour, which often lasted well into a second hour, was that *no* important work be transacted while FDR mixed martinis, which he served and refilled. Whenever Daisy visited Washington, which was often, she was an integral part of this gathering. Writing about one such "hour" later in his presidency, Daisy observed, "[It was] when the P. seems to relax. He casts off his heavy responsibilities talks nonsense, teases etc. as he mixes cocktails." One person who did not attend was Eleanor, who wasn't wired for small talk and couldn't refrain from using whatever time she had with her husband to press the issues important to her. "The P.," Daisy noted, whenever "Mrs. R. is here . . . gets tense & concentrated again."

Even when Daisy wasn't at Children's Hour or in his presence, she remained privy to some of the most intimate moments of FDR's life. In late summer 1938, Roosevelt's son James needed emergency surgery to remove gastric ulcers. Both Eleanor and Franklin traveled to Minnesota for the surgery. While tending to his son, Roosevelt wrote Daisy on September 14: "Oh! I wish so that C.P. were here." By then, the two had developed their own parlance to describe their relationship, "C.P." standing for "Certain Person."

That exceptional closeness was also made clear by the front-row seat Daisy occupied at the most famous "picnic" in American history, when the king and queen visited Hyde Park in June 1939. After the weekend's festivities, "F" related to Daisy some of his insights on the royal couple, including that the king was "grand" with an almost "American sense of humor," while the queen was humorless. He also recounted four separate episodes after Daisy departed during which his jittery servants committed faux pas directly in front of the royals, including dropping trays full of glasses and breaking brand new china ordered especially for them.

In colorful, fast prose that could have doubled as a script for an *I Love Lucy* episode, Daisy recorded in exquisite detail each of the four episodes FDR joyfully recounted to her. "Later in the evening, a butler carried a tray with 6 ginger-ale bottles & a few tall glasses. He caught his heel on the top of the steps leading to the library, lost his balance & the whole tray went flying into the room, with him after it. The King remarked: 'That's number 2, what will be the next?'" Her observations capture both the banal and memorable moments of the weekend, even including whimsical drawings of the main characters at the picnic and a diagram of where they sat.

Most surprising to FDR, the queen had "not the *slightest* idea" he couldn't walk, he told Daisy. The royals apparently thought he used a cane. Their ignorance reflects just how well FDR had succeeded in keeping his infirmity an international secret. He had an unwritten understanding with the media and others that no one would ever capture an image of him in his wheelchair, not even the ubiquitous cameramen who covered his public appearances. As of five years ago, of the four known photographs that survive of him sitting in his wheelchair, two were taken by Daisy Suckley.

Despite FDR and Daisy's apparent delight in daydreaming about a post-presidential life at Top Cottage, the idea that he would soon retire to Hyde Park after his second term and spend sweet, unhurried afternoons with "MM" appeared increasingly unlikely as the world inched closer to war. Daisy's letter to FDR on September 1, 1939—the day Germany invaded Poland—reveals a significant shift in the conversation, from plans for "us" to a future for "you."

This change in focus reflected the daunting moment that Roosevelt faced, no doubt with some measure of trepidation. In his fireside chat after Hitler's invasion, Roosevelt implicitly acknowledged that the Great War had been a cautionary tale, a tragic mistake that had failed to secure stable peace and democracy. Now, with another world war looming, he vowed to maintain American neutrality. But he sent a mixed message, expressing his belief that the country must still confront the grim task of mobilization.

With FDR now the leader of a country that would likely be pulled into overseas hostilities, the tenor of their letters changed. "What an excellent idea for *you* to have a 'Retreat' on the top of *your* wooded hill," Daisy wrote. Nevertheless, Daisy would remain a constant presence in Roosevelt's life, both through her unwavering friendship and the gift of a beloved pet—a welcome diversion that added some levity to the bleak moment. In the summer of 1940, Daisy presented Roosevelt with a four-month-old Scottish terrier, whom he named Murray the Outlaw of Falahill, in honor of a Scotch ancestor. "Fala" would become perhaps the most famous canine in American history (and a favorite four-letter answer for crossword-puzzle writers). Daisy trained Fala herself, teaching him to sit, roll over, and jump.

FDR loved him.

Less than a year later, Scribner's offered Daisy a contract to write a children's book on the make-believe life of Fala. With FDR's approval, she dove into it, "getting all worked up about my Story of Fala!" In a letter to FDR she proposed a working title:

> "The True Story of Fala"
> By [Daisy] and underneath
> "This *is* the True Story of Fala"
> F.D.R.

Speculation over whether FDR would run for a third term and buck a 143-year tradition reached a feverish pitch by the summer of 1940. As noncommittal as he was at the Hot Dog Picnic a year earlier, he was just as coy now, in part because he was still unsure of his plans. Most assumed, given the war in Europe, that he would break with the two-term norm, but the decision was far from inevitable. By 1940, FDR had already made specific plans to retire to Hyde Park, where construction had begun on his presidential library and work on Top Cottage was complete. On every trip back to Hyde Park that spring and summer, he brought with him material that would be housed in the library. But anyone who knew Roosevelt wasn't counting him out quite yet, no matter how elaborate his retirement planning.

It turns out neither Roosevelt nor his legions of supporters were ready for him to retire to Top Cottage, especially with tensions flaring in Europe and party sentiment that America could ill-afford a change in commander in chief at this perilous moment. The president was overwhelmingly nominated for a third term at the Democratic National Convention in Chicago in July of 1940, after crafty operatives sparked a spontaneous "draft Roosevelt" campaign among the delegates—aided by the fact there were no other viable candidates in sight. Hitler's blitzkrieg across Europe in the spring and summer finally resolved the matter. The so-called "phony war" had definitively ended, and World War II began in earnest. Even though a Gallup poll revealed that 93 percent of Americans still viewed the war as a European problem, Roosevelt knew that he could not abandon the nation at this pivotal stage, just as it began to boost its defenses and to reinitiate the national draft.

Running a cautious campaign against the Republican nominee, Wendell Willkie, a New York corporate executive, Roosevelt won 54.8 percent of the popular vote, his smallest-yet margin of victory, but took thirty-eight states in an Electoral College landslide. He had shattered precedent—all with the future of the United States and the world in the balance. As one historian dramatically put it, Roosevelt's pursuit of a third term was "one of the most consequential presidential decisions of the twentieth century."

During that time, Daisy remained a crucial witness to the most pivotal—and covert—moments in history. In early August 1941, as he set out for a clandestine summit with British prime minister Winston Churchill off Newfoundland, the president told neither Secretary of State Cordell Hull nor Secretary of War Henry Stimson—nor even Eleanor—where he was going. Pretending to be off on a ten-day fishing trip along the New England coast, FDR went to great lengths to deceive the press and hoodwink the German U-boats that patrolled the North Atlantic. The president departed from New London, Connecticut, on the USS *Potomac*, a presidential yacht. From there, Roosevelt stealthily transferred onto the battleship *Augusta*. As the *Potomac* continued through the Cape Cod Canal, hundreds of well-wishers waved to the "president," being played by a Secret Service agent, who waved back.

One of the few people who was clued in to FDR's whereabouts was Daisy. Throughout the secret trip, Roosevelt sent her a steady stream of letters from the day he transferred onto the *Potomac* on August 5 until he arrived home on August 15. "Even at my ripe old age I feel a thrill in making a get-away—especially from the American press," he wrote. After his first day of meetings with Churchill on August 9, Roosevelt described him as "a tremendously vital person & in many ways is an English Mayor [Fiorello] LaGuardia! Don't say I said so! I like him—& lunching alone broke the ice both ways." His meetings with Churchill produced what would become the Atlantic Charter—setting out the joint US-UK goals for the postwar world—in which the leaders pledged that "all men in all lands may live out their lives in freedom from fear and from want." Though the country was not yet at war, FDR was doing everything he could short of committing troops to provide morale and material support to its ally.

The imminent war was Roosevelt's chief preoccupation that summer and fall, but it wasn't his only concern. As he returned to American soil, he learned of Daisy's increasingly dire financial straits. For years, Daisy had earned a meager income by taking care of an elderly aunt. She had been forced to work after her family had squandered their fortune in trade and shipping through bad investments and even worse luck. By the beginning of the Depression, Daisy didn't even have enough money to maintain the wardrobe she felt defined her. Still, as she confessed to her diary, she liked to call herself the "prim spinster," a joke that Roosevelt laughed about with her. Now, though, her fortunes had worsened, and she desperately needed a new source of income.

The timing couldn't have been more fortuitous. FDR just happened to be seeking an archivist for his newly opened Presidential Library in

Hyde Park. At tea at her house a month after returning from his trip, he offered her the job. She accepted—no longer just a witness to history, but an active recorder of it.

The idea to open a presidential library was a novel idea. While other presidents, beginning with George Washington, had gathered their papers (usually to bring home with them), no president had ever attempted to centralize all the papers from his presidency in a single library—what is today a common practice. A collector since his youth, Roosevelt had been carefully planning his library since first taking office. He raised the money, consulted historians for advice, and pushed Congress to pass legislation to make it happen. Now, two months after its opening, Roosevelt needed someone to help with the assemblage and organization of the millions of documents that were accumulating, and Daisy was the obvious choice given her intimate knowledge of FDR's world and the mountainous pile of newspaper clippings she had already amassed.

The day after Daisy's job was formalized, FDR's mother, Sara, died, at the age of eighty-six. Just two months earlier, his de facto chief of staff, Missy LeHand, suffered a stroke from which she would never recover, ultimately dying in 1944. In quick succession, two of the women closest to Roosevelt had been stripped from his life. Daisy remained. For the rest of the war, she would split her time between the library (where FDR kept an office) and Washington, and play an increasingly greater role in his life, which would soon get more complicated.

At 1:30 p.m. on December 7, 1941, Roosevelt was in his study on the second floor of the White House talking with advisor Harry Hopkins when Navy Secretary Frank Knox called with stunning news: Japan had just launched an attack on the US naval installation at Pearl Harbor. Eventually, 2,403 naval and military personnel would die in the surprise raid. A few hours later, FDR kept his calm as he methodically began dictating what would become the preamble to his famous "Day of Infamy" speech the next day in Congress: "Yesterday... December 7th... 1941... a day which will live in world history... the United States was simultaneously and deliberately attacked...." He agonized over every word of the speech, intent on ensuring that it conveyed the urgency of the moment. Minutes before delivering the speech the next day, he crossed out "world history" and inserted "infamy," immortalizing the word forever. The subsequent vote was almost unanimous—388 to 1—and shortly after noon on December 8, the United States had officially entered World War II.

Two weeks later, Roosevelt summoned his military commanders to the White House and issued a dire command: The United States must now start planning a massive bombing raid on Japan. Later that night, as his generals pored over maps next door at the War Department and drew up bombing routes, Roosevelt took a break to honor Daisy with an intimate White House dinner for two to celebrate her fiftieth birthday. Afterward, in the president's study, they took pictures of each other: he in his evening clothes and she sitting on a lion-skin rug gifted to FDR by Ethiopian leader Haile Selassie.

As the strains of the war multiplied, Daisy's regular presence continued to provide a much-needed source of comfort for the president. White House aide and son-in-law John Boettiger would later tell Daisy that of all the people in the White House during Roosevelt's twelve years there, she "contributed probably more than anyone, in allowing him to relax, and think of completely different things." She was a careful listener as well as an inquisitive questioner, and FDR often brought up his most pressing issues while they worked or relaxed together. Over Thanksgiving weekend of 1942, Roosevelt revealed that he had been "thinking ahead to the shape of the world" after the war and asked Daisy to go with him to Top Cottage for a picnic to discuss his thoughts. "Our conversation was momentous," Daisy said, recalling the president's description of a postwar world in which just four nations—the United States, the United Kingdom, the Soviet Union, and China—would dominate global politics.

Daisy was also a witness to FDR in his most unguarded, raw moments when the pressures of his office manifested themselves in unusual ways. One night while staying over at the White House, she was awakened by "blood curdling sounds" emanating from Roosevelt's bedroom. The president was "calling out for help." At breakfast the next morning, FDR told her, "I thought a man was coming through the transom and was going to kill me." When Daisy asked why the Secret Service hadn't rushed in at the sounds of his cries, he confessed that they had already grown "quite accustomed to such nightmares."

Luckily, though, the nightmare of war began to give way to brighter news. In January 1943, in the midst of Germany's first major defeat at the gates of Stalingrad, FDR secretly set out to Casablanca, first by train and then by plane, to meet with Churchill and their respective military planners. Before leaving, as Daisy recounted in her diary, the president shared his "mixed feelings" about the physical dangers posed by the trip. But his fears would not deter him from accomplishing a crucial objective: to discuss with Churchill the next phase of the war and how to leverage Russia's unexpected victory.

Roosevelt kept an almost daily diary of his activities that he then shared in letters sent back home to Daisy. Over the course of five hectic days of travel and midnight meetings, FDR recounted for Daisy how Churchill tried to bring French general Henri Giraud and future French leader Charles de Gaulle together but failed because of de Gaulle's hatred for Giraud. While de Gaulle, then in exile in London, expected to lead the Free French Forces in Africa, Giraud was FDR's choice to do so. When FDR asked Churchill who paid de Gaulle's salary, "W.S.C. beamed—good idea—no come—no pay!" De Gaulle came. Daisy learned not just about these consequential calculations, but also about more trivial details. Throughout the trip, de Gaulle became a favorite object of FDR's derision, and he described the Frenchman to Daisy as a "headache" who "yesterday [said] he was Jeanne d'Arc & today that he is Georges Clemenceau!" He also joked about how his correspondence had been delayed due to "the Winston hours"—a reference to Churchill's propensity for late nights of talking and drinking that robbed Roosevelt of much-needed sleep.

Throughout that spring of 1943, as the war continued to favor the Allies and speculation began to build over whether he would seek a fourth term, Franklin confided in Daisy about his hopes for a future "peace organization" that ideally he would chair instead of continuing on as president. He mused that the project could be done "simply," with no big building and just a small staff of two assistants, housed on an island like Horta in the Azores. He would have a place on the island, "not very large," where he would live and work. Another small group of houses would be occupied by the staffs of the other member nations. "It's all very exciting, & perhaps it will happen," Daisy replied. "If the P. keeps his health & strength."

Daisy's diary entries for the final three years of Roosevelt's life reveal that he wrote, called, or saw her in person every few days. And despite the demands on his attention, Daisy seemed never far from his mind. One afternoon, as Daisy rested in the Lincoln bedroom, she heard a knock on the door: The president wanted to see her in the doctor's office downstairs. FDR apparently worried that Daisy's eyesight wasn't what it should be. She was given a visual exam as the president looked on (her prescription was right). They also frequently shared lunches and dinners together, took their regular motor drives, and reviewed materials for the library at both the White House and Hyde Park, where FDR maintained an office at the new library. And Daisy was often invited when the president had to entertain foreign dignitaries, Churchill being her favorite.

When the prime minister had made his first visit to Hyde Park back in June 1942, Daisy had joined the small group invited to dine with him and the president. "Both seemed a little tired and absent-minded though this might not have been noticed by anyone who doesn't know the P. as well as I do," she wrote. Thereafter, whenever "WSC" (whether alone or with his family) would visit the United States, FDR would always include Daisy. After each visit, she would insightfully record her observations of the two leaders and their entourages: "The P.M. recognizes in P. a man with a greater soul & a broader outlook than his own—It is very evident to a person who has had such wonderful opportunities to see them as I have."

She considered Churchill a "great man," but as she explained in her sometimes cryptic style, one who "has not yet achieved the spiritual freedom of F.D.R." On another "memorable day—but how casually I take it," Daisy described how Roosevelt drove his roadster up to her house and, with Churchill in the passenger seat, had her and Fala squeeze in for a drive through the woods to a pool party, where they donned swimsuits and spent the day relaxing on the lawn. She also acted as tour guide to Churchill's daughter, Mary (a woman of "American blood and easy manner"), and his wife, Clementine ("very English and reserved"), and she became so much a part of the two first families that after one visit, Churchill asked her to "come along" with them as FDR himself drove them to their train. As the train departed, the prime minister's last words were: "Goodbye, Miss Suckley, and thank you so much."

Toward the end of 1943, with the tide of the war turning decidedly in the Allies' favor, the plan for its end kicked into high gear. On November 8, "the P.'s worst day," FDR had twenty-two separate meetings, culminating in dinner with just Daisy. They sipped sherry and dined on ptarmigan from Iceland while they discussed his upcoming trip to Cairo, Basra, and Tehran, where the president would meet in succession with Churchill, Chiang Kai-shek of China, and, for the first time, Soviet premier Josef Stalin. Daisy noted in her diary: "It is certainly not in the simple & natural course of the life of a Suckley to be seeing, at first hand, the very core & hub of world history—It is fantastic—But here I am."

The meetings proved a major success, culminating in the Tehran summit and the fateful decision to launch a cross-Channel invasion of northern France—Operation Overlord—to engage the German forces on a second front. The day Roosevelt returned, one of his first calls was to Daisy. It was the week of her fifty-second birthday, and each day he presented her with a new gift from his travels, including a Persian prayer rug and a painted piece of ivory.

FDR was so consumed traveling the world and managing the war that he scarcely had time to tend to his own affairs, especially his health. If he was ignoring it, Daisy most certainly was not; by early 1944, she was gradually coming to the realization that FDR was in rapid physical decline. Many of her diary entries expressed worry over the fragile state of his health: "The flu has left him rather miserable" or "The P is feverish &

generally miserable." Roosevelt often sought to calm her. "I thought you might read in the paper that I am sick and I had better tell you, first," he assured her one day.

FDR's daughter Anna—who had grown close to Daisy—was equally alarmed by her father's declining health, and she pressed his team of doctors to conduct what would become his first thorough physical examination in years. It was fortunate that she did; a new cardiologist brought in for the examination found he was suffering from congestive heart failure, with an enlarged heart, shortness of breath, and extreme hypertension. His blood pressure was an astonishing 218 over 120.

Given how sick he was yet how vital he needed to appear as the nation's wartime commander in chief, the physicians hesitated to tell him the severity of his condition. Their reluctance was coupled with FDR's own lack of curiosity after the examination: He never asked a single question during the afternoon of testing. Within weeks, however, FDR had figured out the reality for himself and confided it to Daisy while they were spending time at financier Bernard Baruch's plantation in South Carolina: "He found out that they were not telling *him* the *whole* truth & that he was evidently more sick than they said! It is foolish of them to attempt to put anything over on *him*!" Now that FDR realized his dire condition, his doctors put him on a low-calorie diet and instructed him to cut back on his smoking and drinking, as well as on the constant influx of visitors and dinner guests. Roosevelt mostly complied, but the diet in particular made him miserable. Eating well was one of his great pleasures.

Daisy made it easier for him to bear the new restrictions on his life and to continue plowing forward with as much normalcy as possible. In mid-May of 1944, they were sitting at Top Cottage when FDR confided in her a secret few in Washington knew: the coming invasion of Normandy—D-Day. In her diary entry that night, without any trace of irony, Daisy mentioned one of the most consequential military operations as casually as the scenery and foliage: "We put a couple of chairs in the sun, north of the porch, & just talked, quietly, about the view, the dogwood, a little about the coming invasion in Europe."

FDR's confidences went beyond military secrets to include political musings as well. Later that month—only two months before the Democratic convention of 1944—he and Daisy retreated to their hill, where they sipped tea and toasted some of FDR's favorite bread. Daisy asked if he had chosen a running mate yet. "I haven't even decided if I will run myself," he replied. Unlike how he had approached the question in 1936 or 1940, Roosevelt now framed his answer in terms of his health, not politics: "... If I know I am not going to be able to carry on for another four years, it wouldn't be fair to the American people to run for another term." Daisy pressed: "But who else is there?" Roosevelt then confided another secret: "I have a candidate—but don't breathe it to a soul—there is a man, not a politician, who, I think, I could persuade the country to elect. There would be such a gasp when his name was suggested, that I believe he would have a good chance if he were 'sold' to the country in the right way!"

FDR was referring to Henry J. Kaiser, the private-sector shipbuilder whose leadership in building Liberty ships had caught his eye back in 1942. Daisy pressed again: "How would he get on with the Churchills, Stalins etc." The president responded: "He's more like them than I am." Daisy leaned in once more: "But your strength lies in the fact that those men look up to you. Just another man like themselves, will bring the whole International problem down a peg, to the usual materialism." Roosevelt didn't answer at the moment, but he later assured her that if Kaiser were elected he would seek FDR's "teaching guidance," a prediction that finally seemed to satisfy Daisy, ever protective of the president.

Only a few days later, on the night of June 5, they were together again in the White House residence when Roosevelt announced that Rome had fallen to Allied forces. Daisy kept the radio on as she prepared for bed, knowing the D-Day invasion in Normandy was imminent. The initial bulletins that crackled over her radio at 12:49 a.m. were from Germany. More news followed all night long. At 9 a.m. Daisy entered the president's bedroom and delivered what she thought were the first reports to him on the success of an invasion that would hasten the end of the war. "I told him all that I had heard over the radio, & for once, knew the details before he did!" she noted. "It was a novel experience for him." Whether the president was actually surprised or just feigning ignorance is unclear, though it's impossible to imagine FDR sleeping through the night without at some point learning of the invasion's progress.

That evening, Roosevelt delivered a prayer for the soldiers who had stormed the beaches in what he called "a mighty endeavor." It came with unfathomable cost, but in its wake, the war began steadily turning in the Allies' favor, a shift that persuaded Roosevelt that he should run for an astounding fourth term. However weak his health, he concluded that the country needed him to oversee the war's end and the world's crucial transition to peacetime.

Roosevelt spent election day in Hyde Park, a ritual that had begun with his first victory in 1932. That afternoon, he drove his roadster to the library, where he picked up Daisy and took her and a group of other people to Top Cottage for tea. They then settled in at the Big House for cocktails, dinner, and the long night of election returns. When Republican candidate Thomas Dewey conceded at 3:45 a.m. on November 8, the only three-term president in the history of the United States now became the first president elected to a fourth term. Daisy was one of only six people who sat at the long table with FDR when he heard Dewey's early-morning concession call.

Following the election, the president headed to his retreat in Warm Springs, Georgia, where for twenty years he had sought the curative powers of its hot pools. Daisy, of course, belonged to the traveling party. They were joined there by Lucy Mercer Rutherford, FDR's lover from a quarter century earlier, who was now recently widowed. The instant and completely frank friendship Daisy formed with Lucy should further cast doubt on the suggestion Daisy and FDR were romantic partners.

After Eleanor had discovered their affair in 1918, she had forbidden Franklin from ever seeing Lucy again. Yet through the intervening years, FDR defied her, maintaining their relationship through secretly arranged liaisons. Unbeknownst to Eleanor, Lucy had attended FDR's first inauguration, picked up by a White House car and stationed a safe distance from the proceedings. Twice in 1941, White House logs suggest she arrived under a pseudonym to see her former lover. After Lucy's husband died in 1944, Roosevelt asked his daughter Anna, who was then managing social affairs at the White House, to help arrange another visit, again without Eleanor's knowledge. From then on, Lucy and Franklin would see each other often at the White House when Eleanor was away. On his way from Washington to Hyde Park for a September 1, 1944, meeting with Churchill, FDR and Daisy made a secret detour to Lucy's late husband's estate in New Jersey for a sit-down lunch. As Daisy perceptively recorded in her diary after the lunch, "The whole thing was out of a book…with all the characters at that lunch table, if one counts"—she mischievously added—"the absent husbands and wives."

Together now in Warm Springs, Lucy and Daisy, the two women closest to the president, shared their emotions and concerns for him. Lucy told Daisy she "felt for years that he has been terribly lonely." Daisy recalled in her diary that the two women wept on each other's shoulders and acknowledged how grateful they were to have one another to support him. But Daisy was by no means resigning herself to his death, at least not yet. She had arranged to have a massage therapist, Lenny Setaro, work on FDR's body three times a week. He claimed to possess a "gift" from God and Daisy, desperate for any solution, enlisted him. Some close advisors to the president deeply resented Daisy's intervention as unnecessary quackery, but she remained undeterred. After one session with Setaro, the president reported movement in a big toe for the first time in years, and later said he felt "tingling sensations in his hips and legs." But the progress was ephemeral.

Roosevelt kept his fourth inauguration celebration on January 20, 1945, understated—held on the South Portico of the White House instead of the usual setting on the Capitol steps. Those closest to him, including his doctors, suspected his days were numbered, and not in years or even necessarily months. Roosevelt himself seemed to acknowledge his looming mortality when he asked that each of his thirteen grandchildren be present for his swearing-in. His fourth inaugural address marked the last time he stood before the American people. His strong voice belied the weakness of his body. Woodrow Wilson's widow, Edith, attended the ceremony and noted, "He looked exactly as my husband looked when he went into his decline." Bowing to his infirmity, Roosevelt kept his remarks to only five minutes—537 words—the second shortest inaugural address in US history (second to George Washington's 135-word speech in 1793).

As the ailing president began his final term, the war was moving to a swift end. The Allies continued to squeeze the teetering Axis forces: After liberating France and Belgium, the troops headed into Germany for one final assault. As the prospect of peace finally arose, Roosevelt celebrated his sixty-third (and final) birthday before heading to the Yalta Conference in Crimea, where he, Churchill, and Stalin hashed out the postwar plan for Germany and the world.

The most devastating war in the annals of humankind was nearly finished—a reason for great celebration. Yet anyone who saw FDR at Yalta or afterward knew how very sick he was, and it soon became harder to camouflage. An unidentified senior administration official sent an order to the Secret Service asking it to beef up its security of FDR's new vice president, Harry Truman. For some, the question was no longer *whether* Truman would succeed FDR, but how soon.

A restless FDR dove back into the presidential business that had piled up during his absence overseas. But he looked—and felt—completely worn out, and he knew that he needed another getaway to his "Little White House" in Warm Springs. On March 30, he arrived there with a small circle of companions, including Daisy and his eccentric cousin Polly Delano. He attended Easter service in a small Presbyterian chapel and then went for a car ride, seemingly regaining a bit of strength. But Daisy was still concerned enough to have regular talks with the president's cardiologist, Dr. Howard Bruenn, who was also at the Warm Springs compound. On the night of April 6, FDR complained of being cold, even under blankets. Daisy nursed him, pulling up the covers and feeding the president spoonsful of porridge. Roosevelt "put on his little act of helplessness! It amuses him to be fed, and I love to feed him," Daisy recorded affectionately in her diary, as if trying to convince herself to remain hopeful. "On paper it sounds too silly for words and it *is* silly—but he's *very* funny and laughs at himself with us." When they were finished, she kissed him goodnight and left him "relaxed and laughing."

The next day, Lucy Mercer Rutherford arrived, bringing with her an artist friend, Elizabeth Shoumatoff, whom she had commissioned to paint a portrait of FDR. Daisy, along with Lucy and Polly, went for a two-hour ride in the country with the president, an outing that delighted him; car rides remained his favorite pastime. Noticing that Roosevelt was shivering, Lucy draped her sweater around his legs. Daisy admonished him, "You need to lead as dull a life as possible until you get your strength back." It had become her refrain. FDR didn't disagree, even acknowledging to Daisy that he was considering retiring from office in 1946 after getting "the peace organization well started."

FDR awoke to a beautiful spring day on Thursday, April 12, but he didn't feel well, with a headache and stiff neck. Dr. Bruenn rubbed his neck and ordered a hot water bottle to further loosen it up. Early in the afternoon, Roosevelt was posing for his official portrait with Shoumatoff. Daisy remained nearby on a sofa crocheting, until a few minutes before one o'clock. She looked up and saw the president's head pitch forward, his hands fumbling and his face contorted in pain. She rushed to his side and looked anxiously into his face, "Have you dropped your cigarette?"

His forehead taut and furrowed, he looked at Daisy and said, "I have a terrific pain in the back of my head." Daisy grabbed the phone and summoned Dr. Bruenn. Meanwhile, Daisy held his right hand, while Lucy tried to revive him. "I had a distinct feeling that this was the beginning of the end," she later wrote. Two hours passed; the doctors cleared the room. Dr. Bruenn was on the phone with FDR's doctor in Washington when the president took his last breath. Daisy looked at her watch. It was 3:35 p.m.

That night, Daisy wrote in her diary: "What this means to me, and to all who knew him personally, is impossible to put into words. What it means to the world, only the future can tell."

Within an hour of his collapse, Lucy had fled the house: Eleanor was on her way. "We must pack and go," Lucy yelled at Shoumatoff, appreciating immediately how embarrassing her presence would be if later discovered by Eleanor or the press. She only learned of her lover's death later when they stopped at a hotel and were told by an operator as they tried to place a call back to Warm Springs. Hearing the news, Lucy "sat motionless and remained utterly silent."

Adding a final diary entry that night, Daisy mused on the paradoxes of the Roosevelt marriage: "Poor E.R.—I believe she loved him more deeply than she knows herself, and his feeling for her was deep & lasting. The fact that they could not relax together, or play together, is the tragedy of their joint lives."

Just like the train which carried Lincoln's casket eighty years earlier, the train returning FDR's body to Washington was slowed by millions of mourners lining the tracks. Daisy and Polly sat with the casket throughout the ride. Walking into the White House one last time later that night, Daisy mourned, "Every item speaks of him & when the thought crosses one's mind that he has permanently left them in other hands, it is almost unbearable."

Franklin Delano Roosevelt was laid to rest at Springwood, his family home in Hyde Park, on April 15, 1945.

Not too long after that, his daughter Anna happened upon a stack of envelopes tucked into FDR's stamp box. Inside those envelopes were all his letters from Daisy. Anna asked if Daisy would like to have them back. Daisy thanked her and said yes, adding with her vintage self-effacement that FDR no doubt found it easier to "toss them into the stamp box rather than bother to tear them up & drop them into the waste-paper basket!"

What Daisy probably appreciated more than anyone was how precious the stamp box was to FDR: Wherever he went during his presidency, he brought along the stamp box so he could "work over [his stamp collection] during the evenings."

Devastated as she was, Daisy resolved to soldier on at the Franklin Delano Roosevelt Library, honoring the memory of the president she revered and the man she adored. She continued to work as the library's photo archivist for another eighteen years, until she retired in 1963. Archivists and librarians today hold her in high regard for her groundbreaking work on the nation's first presidential library.

For the next twenty-eight years after her retirement, Daisy lived alone at ramshackle Wilderstein, its original paint still dating all the way back to 1910. She eventually allowed the public to tour the home, even narrating a video to accompany them. When historians came knocking to look for fresh material on the Roosevelt presidency, she dismissed her role as nothing more than his "dog walker." Asked if she ever kept a diary, she countered with characteristic modesty: "What makes you think *I* would keep a diary?"

She maintained that ruse until her hundredth year, when she died at home on June 29, 1991.

By keeping her trunkful of letters and diaries stowed away safely beneath her bed, Daisy must have known that some day after her passing, that trove of material would be discovered. She could have destroyed it all as her days dwindled. But—archivist that she was—thankfully she did not.

Perhaps imagining that one day historians would pore through her papers and struggle to understand their friendship, she described it herself in the final entry of her diary—in candid words that must be respected on their own terms:

> My friendship with FDR was one of those very rare relationships (outside of marriage), which is so simple, so completely clean and straightforward, that only a person who has experienced it can believe it and understand it. I never felt any self-consciousness or embarrassment, or any inhibitions, when with him. I could say or think what I wanted—He never needed to worry about hurting my feelings—He answered, or did not answer, my questions without my insisting on an answer or without my feelings hurt when he didn't answer. He knew that I knew there were many things he could not answer.

In the end, it may all be as simple as that: FDR—a lonely man shouldering the burdens of his office at a critical juncture in history—drew solace and strength from Daisy's steady devotion, loyalty, and discretion. For Daisy, FDR opened the door to his world and made her feel cherished within it.

On May 1, 1945, Margaret "Daisy" Suckley returned by herself to Top Cottage. It was no longer "Our Cottage" on "Our Hill." Daisy thought of all the hours she had spent there with her beloved "F." The pain of her loss was enormous, but she found comfort in walking over to Franklin's grave. It was covered in ivy, fresh roses, pansies, and forget-me-nots, which Daisy had planted herself.

"I think he loves it as it is now, because it has been fixed by the hands that love him."

CHAPTER 6

Harry Truman and Eddie Jacobson

Beshert

In 1899, fifteen-year-old Harry S. Truman penned an essay on courage that opened with his favorite quote by Ralph Waldo Emerson: "Behavior is the mirror in which each man shows his image." For the young Harry, that quote seemed to capture his life's mantra. It echoed the Horatio Alger myths he grew up reading, those rags-to-riches stories about humble boys working hard to achieve lives of middle-class comfort. Like Alger, Emerson affirmed a kind of pioneer positivity that Truman worshipped: the conviction that personal behavior could change the course of history; that right and wrong existed purely and unambiguously; and that by displaying a certain gutsiness, a man could create an image he'd be proud of.

Two years later, Truman was forced to put these juvenile musings into actual practice. Ever since the Spanish-American War erupted in the summer of 1898, he had dreamed of becoming a professional soldier. With the neighborhood boys, he formed a drill company that trooped through the streets, camped in the woods, and shot at chickens. By his second year of high school, he began preparing for the US Military Academy by taking special lessons in history and geography.

But after graduating from Independence High School at age seventeen, he faced an unexpected setback: his poor eyesight torpedoed his candidacy into West Point. The sinking of his dream coincided with yet another obstacle. His father, John Truman, suffered calamitous financial losses in the commodities market, a crushing blow that meant the family did not have the means to send Harry to *any* college with a tuition bill attached. Amid these troubles, Truman recalled his essay from two years ago, when he had defined true courage as a quality that emerged "in taking care of those at home." Now "those at home" needed him, and Truman perceived an opportunity to prove his mettle, to be an Emersonian kind of man.

Decades later, reflecting on those hard times, Truman admitted, "It took all I received to help pay family expenses and keep my brother and sister in school." Over the next two years, the teen held a succession of small gigs, never considering any job beneath him. Though he dropped out of business college after one semester, he cleverly used that short-lived experience to secure work as a timekeeper at the Atchison, Topeka & Santa Fe Railway, forced to sleep in camps along the rail lines. Next, he turned to a series of clerical jobs, including a lowly position at the *Kansas City Star*. Then in 1903, at nineteen years old, he heard about a promising position as a clerk at the National Bank of Commerce in Kansas City, Missouri, the largest bank west of the Mississippi.

With his eyes on the prize, Truman set out to establish his image as a disciplined go-getter. In the employment application, under a section labeled "Habits," Truman was asked, "Have you any tastes or habits extravagant in proportion to your means?" "Don't think so," the applicant replied. Truman listed his favorite pastimes as "theatre and reading," and confessed that he typically spent his evenings and Sundays "at home."

Dr. G. T. Twyman, the Truman family physician in Independence, enthusiastically supported the application. "I have known Harry Truman since infancy," the doctor wrote. "He is a modle [*sic*] young man worthy of all confidence being strictly sober, truthful and industrious."

Truman easily landed the job, securing a starting weekly salary of $20, which soon doubled. His performance proved Dr. Twyman right; in his annual review, A. D. Flintom, Truman's supervisor at Commerce, wrote: "He is a willing worker, almost always here and tries hard to please everybody. We never had a boy in the vault like him before. He watches everything very closely and by his watchfulness detects many errors which a careless boy would let slip through. His appearance is good and his habits and character are of the best."

In the next review, Flintom went even further: "I do not know of a better young man at the bank than Trueman [*sic*]."

Though he only worked at Commerce for two years, Truman made his mark as a dedicated young banking clerk. He moved into a boardinghouse (where his housemate was Arthur Eisenhower, brother of Dwight) so his commute would be a manageable walk down a long hill. He gained valuable experience learning what it took to make it in the workaday world, meeting with customers who came in to make deposits and withdrawals.

One of those customers was a fifteen-year-old high school dropout, also helping to support his own struggling family. He worked at Burger, Hannah, Monger, a dry goods store housed in a sprawling brick building a few blocks from the bank. The youngster would regularly visit the bank with a bag of cash to deposit. Soon enough, he grew friendly with the vault clerk, Harry, who was seven years older but much closer in age to him than the other bank employees. The young customer's name was Edward Jacobson, but everybody called him Eddie.

Over the next few years, this routine transaction evolved into something much more meaningful, with vast historical implications. As Jacobson's daughter later stated, "Harry Truman was [my father's] closest friend—there is no doubt about that." More so than any other First Friendship, the bond between Truman and Jacobson illustrated the power of happenstance, the fortuitous way in which timing, place, and talent intersect. For both these men, history would intervene at multiple points in their lives, pressing them to rise to the moment.

Truman would become known for his endless contradictions: someone with deep-seated insecurities yet outsized ambitions; the most powerful leader in the land who never earned a college degree; a hard-drinking, poker-playing pugilist who was acutely sensitive to public opinion; a man who used racial and anti-Semitic slurs but who also made civil rights a federal priority and who recognized the state of Israel. For that latter point in particular, it was Eddie Jacobson who played a crucial role in encouraging Truman to be the man he had long aspired to be.

As one of Truman's closest aides, Harry Vaughan, once said, Truman was "one tough son-of-a-bitch of a man.... And that was part of the secret of understanding him." No one better than Jacobson—a businessman without any formal political involvement—grasped that secret. Though far less is known about him than about Truman, Jacobson undoubtedly held his own tacit power. Decades later, the nation's first Cold War president would critically need someone like Jacobson to remind him of his roots and of their shared ideals.

As president, Truman would keep on his desk one of his favorite maxims by Mark Twain: "Always do right. This will gratify some people and astonish the rest." That maxim perfectly echoed the one Truman had cited at fifteen, hailing the lone individual who acted virtuously to control his destiny and impress the world. Deep down, however, Truman knew that however much he loved such pithy phrases, they oversimplified. On one of his most consequential decisions—the recognition of the state of Israel—he knew it was shaped as much by the quiet influence of his dearest friend Eddie as it was by his own personal mantra to always do right. As an immature teen, Truman idealized the image of the self-reliant trailblazer. But as the emergent leader of a post–World War II world, at a defining moment, he would depend on the hidden counsel of someone he'd known for more than half his life.

Beginning with those casual noon encounters at the bank, Truman and Jacobson embarked on a rich and varied friendship, one that spanned over fifty years and encompassed National Guard service, boot camp, the battlefields of France in World War I, a business partnership, poker games, hunting trips, lunches in downtown Kansas City, a historic meeting in the Oval Office, and frequent letters on White House stationery that the president always signed off in the same way: "Harry."

Despite the fact that over twenty-four million Americans would later elect him president of the United Sates, Truman himself was the first to admit that he grew up unpopular, someone who struggled to win the respect of his peers. Decades later, he recounted, "The popular boys were the ones who were good at games and had big, tight fists. I was never like that. Without my glasses I was blind as a bat, and to tell the truth, I was kind of a sissy. If there was any danger of getting into a fight, I always ran." The glasses—prescribed to him for his misshaped cornea—indeed posed a handicap for the young Truman, especially in a boyish world where athleticism counted more than anything. Even at the age of sixty-five, he would describe his poor vision as a "deformity," one that undermined his already shaky sense of self.

The bulky eyewear also didn't make it easier for six-year-old Harry to adjust to life in a new town, Independence, where his parents had moved so their son could get a better education. Truman had spent his infancy at four different locales, mostly growing up at his grandmother's six-hundred-acre farm in Grandview, Missouri, surrounded by pastures and ponies. Independence was different—a town only ten miles east of the budding metropolis of Kansas City. When the Truman family moved there, Independence lacked even the basic markers of habitability: water systems, paved roads, electricity. Yet it seemed to be emerging from its rough frontier roots into the modern twentieth century, promising countless opportunities for any ambitious entrepreneur. The spunky Truman had already decided he would be one of those entrepreneurs. To make a little pocket money, he began serving his Jewish neighbors as a "Shabbos goy," someone who performed tasks for them on Sabbath—his first informal job in what would grow into quite a long list.

In the fall of 1892, newly fitted with a pair of thick, expensive glasses, Truman started the first grade. From his teacher Myra Ewin, along with a succession of other single Victorian women, Truman absorbed the values of diligence, obedience, punctuality, and respect. Perhaps most important, he discovered what he believed to be the key to success in life. "Whenever I entered a new school room I would watch the teacher and her attitude toward the pupils, study hard, and try to know my lesson better than anyone else." As Myra Ewin recalled, "He just smiled his way along," doing whatever it took to land in the good graces of his superiors.

This yearning for praise and attention burned most strongly at home. Truman always suspected that his father favored his younger brother, Vivian, a mischievous child who hated school and whose passion for the outdoors and livestock trading endeared him to his father. Harry, gentler and protected by his mother, could not have been more different from Vivian, a fact that John Truman tried to offset by impressing upon his older son the need to be a fighter. His method was tough love. When a young Harry fell off his pony one day, John Truman told him any boy who couldn't stay upright at a walking pace didn't deserve to ride. So he made Harry walk his pony home. Seventy years later, Truman tried to frame the episode in his usual rosy way: "In spite of my crying all the way to the house, I learned a lesson."

John Truman remained a caring patriarch, though, keeping a stern but loving eye on his bright young son. In 1900, drawing upon his ties to local politicians, he secured a job for Harry at the Democratic Convention in Kansas City. He arranged for Harry to work as a page, running errands and delivering messages to and from delegates.

Harry served as little more than a glorified gofer, but he didn't mind. The work was a significant upgrade from his current job, swabbing floors, dusting bottles, and churning the ice cream machine at J. H. Clinton's Drug Store in downtown Independence.

That Kansas City was selected by the Democratic Party as the convention site—the westernmost location it had ever been held in—was the source of much civic pride, validation of the city's status as an emergent riverside boomtown. With the completion of the Hannibal Bridge over the Missouri River and a new east–west rail link, Kansas City had become a meatpacking hub and major shipping and distribution center. It also boasted a burgeoning garment industry. A town of just over thirty thousand people at the end of the Civil War, Kansas City's population had grown fivefold by 1900. Still, not all Democratic delegates were enthralled with the convention's site selection. Kansas Citians had to endure a barrage of snarky comments from convention goers about how they would have to dodge gunfights at every street corner and be on the lookout for cattle stampedes.

Such observations surely annoyed the sixteen-year-old Truman, the beginning of a lifelong insecurity about how his rough roots reflected on his own image as a man. But overall, he was simply too spellbound by the convention's throbbing energy and soaring spectacle to care about outside perceptions. Everything about the moment stirred him: the seventeen thousand Democrats packed into the Convention Hall and especially the thunderous oratory of William Jennings Bryan, who won the nomination for a second consecutive time.

Though the convention marked the birth of Truman's political consciousness, any fresh dreams had to be put on pause. Easing his family's financial desperation took first priority. Truman would spend the next seventeen years focused on nothing more glamorous than honest, hard work. And at this precise time, while he faced his first real challenge, his life intersected with Eddie Jacobson's.

Eddie was the son of a poor Jewish shoemaker, the fourth of six children born to David and Sarah Jacobson, both of whom fled religious persecution in their Lithuanian homeland to arrive in New York City around 1880. The couple married in New York and settled into the rough-and-tumble tenements of Manhattan's Lower East Side. David struggled to make a living, and Sarah's health teetered on the edge. Since Sarah had a sibling in Leavenworth, Kansas, the family packed their bags and moved once again.

The transition to the Midwest had its challenges at first; several of the Jacobson boys had a knack for getting into mischief, and their mother's native language—Yiddish—did not allow for many fruitful discussions with the Leavenworth sheriff. Still struggling to make ends meet, the Jacobsons—like the Trumans—kept their eyes open for any opportunity that seemed better than the last. Twenty-five miles to the southeast was the bigger metropolis of Kansas City, which had a robust economy and a much larger Jewish community. And so the Jacobsons uprooted themselves for a third time and headed to Kansas City, settling into a small home on East Thirty-Sixth Street.

In Kansas City, Eddie dropped out of school at fifteen years old and went to work for Burger, Hannah, Monger, "deciding in my boyish unwisdom that an education doesn't buy bread," as he would write later in an autobiographical sketch. Already, Jacobson exhibited the qualities that would ultimately draw him to Truman: pragmatic, sensible, and entrepreneurial, with the same up-from-the-bootstraps discipline that defined Truman's early life on the frontier. These characteristics bound someone like Jacobson to someone like Truman: Though one would go on to become president, both shared a lack of formal education alongside a hard-earned wisdom about the real world. Eddie didn't stay with Burger, Hannah, Monger for long, but he did stick with the clothing business, moving on to the Baltimore Shirt Store in Kansas City, working variously as a stock boy and an all-around helper.

During this time, Eddie briefly fell out of touch with Truman, who by then had left the city at his father's request and returned to Grandview to help run the family farm—grinding and unrelenting work that led him to forever characterize himself as a farmer. "Prosperous farmers make for a prosperous nation, and when farmers are in trouble, the nation is in trouble," Truman would later say. As president, Truman proudly identified with Thomas Jefferson and Andrew Jackson, champions of "the people" who worked the nation's farms.

Tracing his presidential lineage to Jefferson and Jackson certainly made sense to Truman in hindsight. But in 1906, quitting his banking job, abandoning the city's cultural excitements, and ignoring his simmering political interests was no easy decision. Reluctant to disappoint his father, the twenty-two-year-old Truman moved back to his childhood stomping grounds, without direction and about to face eleven years of grueling labor.

It would seem, then, that Eddie and Harry had embarked on separate paths unlikely to ever intersect again: the businessman in the city and the farmer in the country. Once again, however, history conspired to bring them together.

Truman likely would've remained on the farm, but the outbreak of the Great War brought another call of duty, and an improbable reunion with the young customer from his banking days. A National Guard veteran, Truman wasn't obligated to enlist for World War I. He was thirty-three years old and had not been active for years. But when President Woodrow Wilson declared war on Germany, Truman felt compelled to join the cause. The decision testified to his sense of patriotism and represented a modest fulfillment of his teenage military aspirations. After reenlisting in June 1917, he was made a first lieutenant and assigned to Missouri's

Second Field Artillery, a National Guard outfit eventually folded into the Army's 129th Field Artillery.

Moved by the same call as Truman, Eddie Jacobson enlisted and, by pure coincidence, was assigned to the Second Field Artillery as well, reuniting the men after more than a decade apart. In yet another coincidence, the regiment established barracks in Kansas City's Convention Hall—the same place where Truman had made his first foray into politics as a lowly page for the 1900 Democratic Convention.

Truman and Jacobson seized the moment to show their ingenuity and pluck. As the enlisted men drilled in preparation for war, Private Jacobson took note of the drab fare the soldiers were being fed and went to Lieutenant Truman with an idea that would allow for the purchase of an occasional steak, ice cream, and other meal upgrades.

"While we are out on maneuvers, firing our guns and going through our mock battles, why not record the whole thing in movies?" Jacobson said. "Then, when we return, we could show the movies at Convention Hall and follow them with a dance." Jacobson figured that with all the soldiers hailing from the Kansas City area, many friends and relatives would buy tickets to the event. It would become a fund-raiser—and a spirit-raiser—and bring in money that would allow the troops to eat better.

Truman loved the idea. It not only honored the values of comradeship that had motivated him to join the Artillery; it also enabled him and Jacobson to work together as a team.

"You go ahead and make all the arrangements. I'll back you one hundred percent," Truman promised.

Delighted to hear of his superior's support, Jacobson asked Truman for one more favor. Taking care of the logistics and promoting the event would require Jacobson to be all over town. It would be much easier if he had access to a car. Truman, Jacobson knew, had a red convertible Stafford roadster. Eddie asked if he could borrow it, and Harry agreed.

Jacobson and a sergeant took care of all the pickups and the publicity work, motoring productively around town until one day, they got into an accident. When they returned to the barracks, a sheepish Jacobson told Truman what happened. The lieutenant took it well, all things considered.

"Your show better turn out well and make a lot of money for the boys, or I know two candidates for the guardhouse," Truman joked. The event proved to be a rousing success, clearing $2,600, "enough to keep our outfit in steaks for months to come," Jacobson remembered. Truman dropped the guardhouse threat.

Several months later, the 129th Field Artillery was dispatched to Camp Doniphan, a sprawling tent compound on a dusty plain outside Lawton, Oklahoma. Doniphan had been established in 1917 to help ready more than twenty-five thousand National Guardsmen for war, drilling them on the operation of seventy-five-millimeter cannons and other weaponry. It was a desolate place notorious for its dust storms, the wind whipping over treeless tundra, gritty red dirt flying everywhere. In a letter to his future wife, Bess Wallace, Truman wrote, "A tent fifty yards away is invisible. Dust is in my teeth, eyes, hair, nose, and down my neck. The cook next door brought me a piece of apple dumpling...when I ate it there was a grinding sound.... I ate it anyway, sand and all."

No amount of dust and dirt could dim the partners' continued motivation to improve camp life. One of Truman's responsibilities as a lieutenant was to run the regimental canteen, the base store stocked with soda, cigarettes, candy, and other sundries coveted by young soldiers. Jacobson's success with the movie and his demonstrated business acumen made him the obvious choice to help. So Truman promoted Jacobson to sergeant and made him his aide-de-canteen. From the outset, Jacobson noticed flaws in the canteen operation, overstaffed (with eighteen men working the small store) and not a single cash register—just a collection of cigar boxes to hold the receipts. "I've always believed that most people are honest and I know that Harry Truman always goes on that assumption, too—but there's such a thing as offering too much temptation," Jacobson said.

Truman and Jacobson convinced their commanding officer to sign off on a $700 investment in cash registers. Then they collected two dollars from all 1,100 soldiers in the regiment and raised $2,200, which enabled them to stock the canteen with a variety of goods. Soldiers were reimbursed almost immediately, and within six months the canteen had made $15,000—the only one in Doniphan to be in the black. In light of the robust canteen business he built, Truman earned a promotion to captain. But he credited the success almost wholly to Jacobson. In a letter to his future wife, Truman wrote:

> I have a Jew in charge of the canteen by the name of Jacobson, and he is a crackerjack.

His fellow officers took note, referring to him as a "lucky Jew" and "Trumanheimer." Truman remained unabashed. "I guess I should be very proud of my Jewish ability," he said.

A successful canteen is one thing; surviving war together quite another. Truman left for France in March 1918, to undergo additional training in field artillery school. He was put in charge of Battery D of the 129th, a notoriously incorrigible group that Truman forged into a war-ready battalion. His skillful leadership left a deep impression on his soldiers and especially on Jacobson, who though posted to a different battery shared the details he had gleaned years later in an interview with the *Kansas City Times*:

> Battery D had been bracketed by enemy fire. German shells fell to one side of the battery's position and then, equidistant, to the other, in range. The next round would find the battery. One of the sergeants went chicken and hollered, "Every man for himself." Captain Truman was standing nearby, studying fire-order reports and preparing to make counterbattery on the enemy positions. He heard the sergeant yell, whipped out his automatic and shouted, "I'll shoot any xxxx xxxx xxxx xxx who leaves his gun!" The men went back to their jobs, and we got the German battery in the next few minutes.

Under Truman's firm (and profanity-laden) command, Battery D pulled off a remarkable feat: Not a single man was lost during the final six weeks of the war, even when it came under heavy assault from German forces during the Meuse-Argonne Offensive. Truman had entered the war a mild, reserved man, unsure of his abilities and still craving respect. He would return home with a reputation for bravery and decisive leadership. His grateful charges even gifted him an ornamental drinking cup to mark their deep appreciation.

Five months after the war's armistice, on April 9, 1919, Truman, Jacobson, and more than 1,300 other officers and soldiers from the 129th Field Artillery departed France for New York City on a steamship named *Zeppelin*. It wasn't an easy passage; Truman reported feeling terribly seasick for most of the long voyage. But he could take comfort in one thing: He now realized that he truly did possess courage, the sort of audacity he had waxed lyrical about as a mere fifteen-year-old. Until that point, he had never been involved in any fights, the "sissy" whose mother had kept him from roughhousing because of his glasses. But after enduring the horrors of war, Truman saw that he could genuinely lead people on the strength of his own gifts.

In the immediate moment, though, more practical matters dominated Truman's thoughts. After the strains and stresses of war, he and Jacobson wanted nothing more than to restore a sense of normalcy. When they finally made it back to Missouri, their first order of business was to marry their sweethearts. After a courtship that spanned more than a decade and one rejected proposal in 1911, Harry Truman finally won the hand of Bess Wallace, a high-society girl from Independence, marrying her on the steamy afternoon of June 28, 1919, in Trinity Episcopal Church. On that same day, the Versailles Treaty officially brought World War I to an end. Six months later, Eddie Jacobson followed his friend by marrying Bluma Rosenbaum in Kansas City's oldest reform temple, B'nai Jehudah. The two friends could now say with confidence that they had experienced the best and worst together.

No longer bachelors, Eddie and Harry now turned to their second priority. Bolstered by the profitability of the canteen operation, Truman and Jacobson had already, before reaching shore in New York, hatched a plan to go into business together. With Jacobson's extensive experience in the garment industry, the men decided to open a haberdashery in downtown Kansas City, their mutual trust so great that the partnership was made strictly with a handshake. They signed a lease for a space inside the lobby of the stately Glennon Hotel at Twelfth and Baltimore, across the street from the Hotel Muehlebach, a palatial, newly built, twelve-story property that would become a destination for Ernest Hemingway, Helen Keller, and a procession of presidents, including Theodore Roosevelt, Woodrow Wilson, Herbert Hoover, and Truman himself (who would stay in the Presidential Suite so often it came to be called "White House West").

With gleaming glass displays and polished tile, Truman & Jacobson Haberdashery specialized in silk ties and shirts, hats, belts, and other upscale furnishings. It flourished from the start, thanks to a steady stream of well-heeled guests from the Muehlebach and the Glennon, as well as regular visits from Truman's loyal men in Battery D. The partners hit the ground running, working six days a week from 8 a.m. until 9 p.m. Behind the scenes, Jacobson handled the buying and Truman kept the books. They sunk $35,000 into inventory to get started and sold $70,000 worth of goods their first year. Business stayed strong for the next year and a half, the partnership worked, and the future looked secure.

But in late 1921, a collapse in grain prices hammered the local economy, and soon the country confronted a full-blown depression. For Truman, the downturn must have conjured up dark memories of his father's own failed business ventures. He and Jacobson held on as long as they could—even borrowing more money to keep the failing store afloat—but would-be customers no longer had the means to buy their merchandise, and so they closed their doors in 1922, never to reopen. The partners declined to file for bankruptcy protection that would've wiped out their $35,000 in debts.

"No creditor of ours ever lost a cent," Jacobson later said, though he himself would be forced to declare bankruptcy three years later.

If grain prices had held that year, it's highly likely no one outside of Missouri would have ever known the name Harry Truman. But through yet another twist of fate, they didn't. So Truman would be forced to find a new line of work, starting him on a path that would inexplicably lead him just two decades later to the highest office in the land.

After the collapse of their business, Truman and Jacobson's friendship diverged again. The first time they drifted apart, Truman had withdrawn to the country and Jacobson had remained in the city. This time, Truman's fortunes led him irrevocably into politics, while Jacobson remained closer to home.

Truman's last vivid memory of Missouri politics dated all the way back to his small role as a page at the fiery Democratic Convention in 1900. His curiosity had been sparked then, only to be quickly snuffed out by his family's financial struggles. But this time, one of Truman's Army buddies from the 129th Field Artillery happened to be Jim Pendergast, the nephew of none other than Tom Pendergast, the notorious Democratic boss who controlled Kansas City and Jackson County. The Pendergast machine was just that: a highly disciplined operation that plowed through local elections like a tractor in a field, winning loyalty by handing out patronage jobs and government contracts. Pendergast consolidated his wealth by taking care of folks (many of them poor immigrants), who would in turn take care of Pendergast-favored politicians at the ballot box.

In a surprising turn of events, Truman's political future now depended on the Pendergast machine. In 1922, Jim Pendergast brought his father, Mike, a wingman to big brother Tom, to meet Truman at the haberdashery. Mike asked Truman if he would be interested in running for a "judgeship" in Jackson County, actually an administrative job based in Independence. Truman agreed. With female voters on the electoral rolls for the first time, Truman won a bruising Democratic primary by 279 votes, then won an easy victory in November, along with all the other Democrats in the region. Thus began Truman's political ascent, an unblemished record of electoral victories save for one setback, in 1924, when he lost his reelection campaign for judge to an Independence harness maker, Henry Rummel—the only man in history to win an election over Harry Truman.

After losing his judgeship, Truman supported his family by selling automobile-club memberships, but a few years later, in part driven by a vague sense of inadequacy over his lack of education, he enrolled in law school. He got through the treacherous first year, survived a second, but ultimately never got his degree when the chance to run again for chief judge in Jackson County presented itself. He won, going on to serve two four-year terms before earning the surprise backing of the Pendergasts for US senator in 1934. Truman again prevailed in a tight Democratic primary and coasted to victory in the election, despite being derided as a political lightweight in some corners and as "the Senator from Pendergast" in others.

It wasn't an ideal linkage—between someone who liked to model himself as an honest, homespun hero and one of America's most corrupt political bosses. After Pendergast's conviction for tax evasion, Truman would spend much of his time trying to dodge accusations that he had been under Pendergast's thumb. He largely managed to escape the taint of corruption and to establish his reputation for personal integrity. But the gnawing insecurity about being a rube among sophisticates lingered. Truman often questioned how a small-town kid with little formal education and scant political experience would fare in his daunting new position. James Hamilton Lewis of Illinois, the Senate's majority whip, reassured him, "Harry, don't start out with an inferiority complex. For the first six months you'll wonder how the hell you got here, and after that you'll wonder how the hell the rest of us got here." Those words could not have been better timed, as Truman stood on the brink of gaining national prominence.

Eddie Jacobson, meanwhile, stuck with the business he knew best: clothing. He took a job as a traveling salesman for a shirt and pajama company, spending the next twenty years mostly on the road, visiting his accounts in Missouri and Kansas. His wife, Bluma, assumed most of the responsibilities of raising their two daughters, but Eddie remained a doting, playful father. According to his oldest daughter, Elinor, her gregarious father "would've laughed his way through life" were it not for the financial pressures of supporting his young family, particularly after the onset of the Great Depression.

The extent of Jacobson's affection surfaced in even the smallest ways.

One Friday, after a week on the road, he returned home and said to Elinor, "C'mon, it's springtime, we have to plant a garden. What would you like to grow in the garden?"

She replied that she wanted to plant flowers, so they went to a nursery, chose seeds, and carefully planted and watered them.

Early the next morning, Eddie entered Elinor's bedroom and shook her awake. "Come here and look what happened!" he exclaimed. After his daughter went to bed, Eddie had planted artificial flowers all through the garden.

"My garden was blooming already!" Elinor said. "[My father] was the happiest thing in the world."

Just like Eddie's willingness to maintain a certain level of fantasy for his child, Truman displayed a similar devotion to his daughter—though perhaps of another magnitude. In one well-known episode, Truman threatened bodily injury to the *Washington Post*'s music critic, Paul Hume, after Hume criticized Margaret Truman's singing abilities. Truman's December 6, 1950, reply did not hold back:

> It seems to me that you are a frustrated old man who wishes he could have been successful. . . . Some day I hope to meet you. When that happens you'll need a new nose, a lot of beefsteak for black eyes, and perhaps a supporter below!

Though planting fake flowers and writing enraged letters were entirely different undertakings, they hint at a common thread running through the lives of both men as fathers. They remained exceedingly loyal to their loved ones, to each other, and to their Missouri heritage. Because of this shared foundation, they stayed in touch even as they moved in very different orbits. Whenever they had spare time, they would share lunch at Dixon's Chili Parlor at Fifteenth and Olive in Kansas City. Periodic reunions of the 129th Field Artillery also brought them together to reflect on old times. They enjoyed countless poker games, usually in Jacobson's wood-paneled basement, where one ironclad rule was that no females were allowed. Elinor would bring refreshments to the basement door, but under no circumstances would she be permitted to walk downstairs. Other times, the poker games would be held at the home of Eddie's brother Abe or at the Oakwood Country Club.

When they longed for more substantial escapes, they retreated to nature. An avid outdoorsman, Jacobson often invited Truman on hunting and fishing trips. They and a few pals would head to a hunting shack on the banks of the Missouri River, just a short ride from Independence. Jacobson also had a camp on a lake where he and his friends would go, Truman always among them, even though he never hunted; it wasn't an activity he ever warmed to, especially due to his poor eyesight. While his buddies roamed the woods with their guns, Truman would bring a big stack of books and catch up on his reading. When everyone returned, Truman would then serve as the camp cook.

By 1944, fate intervened once again. Truman was becoming a national figure at the very moment that FDR began searching for a new vice presidential running mate. With the war grinding on, the Senate decided to investigate gargantuan military contracts in the hopes of exposing waste and corruption. Truman chaired the Senate committee that would ultimately save the government $15 billion (equivalent to $220 billion today), an accomplishment that landed him on the cover of *Time*. Meanwhile, rumors started swirling that Franklin Delano Roosevelt might jettison Vice President Henry Wallace, whose liberal views and personal eccentricities had become a distraction and liability. Though Truman did not seek out the nomination, he ended up on the very long list of replacement candidates—a natural choice given his growing acclaim. Still, many New Dealers joked that Truman as vice president would be the "second Missouri Compromise." They viewed the country bumpkin with disdain, describing him as "a small-bore politician of country courthouse caliber only."

Amidst this storm of speculation, praise, and condescension, Truman returned home to Missouri. At this critical moment, he had no interest in engaging in the power struggle, instead seeking out the comforts of his best friend's Missouri home. Truman spent the time playing the piano alongside Gloria, Jacobson's fourteen-year-old daughter. They took turns performing solo numbers, then shared some duets. When the piano playing ended, Truman confessed to his friend, "Honest to gosh, Eddie, I don't want to be vice president. I think I can do a better job where I am, in the Senate."

Truman's wish did not come true. When he was nominated for vice president at the Chicago convention in July 1944, President Roosevelt sent him a telegram with his "heartiest congratulations." Truman wired a copy of it to Jacobson, writing by hand at the bottom:

> To Eddie Jacobson, my friend, buddy + partner in whom I repose the utmost confidence.
>
> Harry Truman USS Mo.

Four months later, an ailing FDR was reelected to an unprecedented fourth term, along with his new running mate, the former haberdasher from Kansas City. Jacobson and other close friends threw a celebratory bash for Truman at the Hotel Muehlebach, across the street from the former site of Truman & Jacobson. Jacobson brought along Elinor and her fiancé, Joe Borenstine, a major in the Army, who had just proposed in the same wood-paneled basement where Harry, Eddie, and pals played their poker games. Jacobson wanted Truman, the newly elected vice president, to give Elinor's marriage his approval before he gave his own. Truman took a moment to size up Borenstine. "Major, I think it's a good idea," Truman concluded. With that, the young couple went out ring shopping. "The marriage was approved by Truman. Otherwise it wouldn't have taken place," Elinor Borenstine recalled.

As celebrations resumed, the friends switched from settling Elinor's future to pondering Truman's own. "I really meant it when I said I didn't want to be vice president," Truman told Jacobson candidly. "But now that I have the job, I promise you I'll do the best I know how."

Harry Truman was vice president for only eighty-two days. His tenure ended on April 12, 1945, when President Franklin Delano Roosevelt died of a cerebral hemorrhage in Warm Springs, Georgia. As the nation mourned, Truman was administered the oath of office by Chief Justice Harlan Stone at 7:09 p.m. Truman's first act as president was to kiss the Bible that he'd placed his right hand on as he was sworn in. The next morning, in Kansas City, Eddie and Elinor Jacobson went to temple to pray for the new president. Elinor said the only other time she and her father had made such a special trip was when they prayed for the soldiers who had landed on the coast of Normandy on D-Day.

In the nation's 169-year history, with the possible exception of Washington or Lincoln, no president had taken office under so much pressure, or with so many matters requiring his urgent attention. While the war in Europe would soon end—Adolf Hitler's suicide came just eighteen days later—the Pacific theater was still far from won, with top Allied strategists predicting that Japan would not surrender for at least another year.

Truman had been president for all of twelve days when Secretary of War Henry Stimson came into his office and handed him a note. It said, "Within four months we shall in all probability have completed the most terrible weapon ever known in human history, one bomb of which could destroy a whole city." Advisors soon presented a detailed report on the so-called Manhattan Project to Truman, who had heard nothing about it while vice president. Stimson asked if he could empanel a select committee to explore all facets of the weapon and the likely consequences of employing it. Truman agreed. A little more than three months later, on the morning of August 6, Truman broadcast a message to the American people. It began:

> Sixteen hours ago, an American airplane dropped one bomb on Hiroshima.... It is an atomic bomb. It is a harnessing of the basic power of the universe.

Three days later, the United States dropped a second bomb on Nagasaki. Five days after that, Truman received word from Japan that it agreed to an unconditional surrender, thus ending World War II. Truman called his mother at the farm in Grandview. "I'd known he'd call. He always calls me after something that happens is over," Martha Truman said.

As massive a relief as it was for Truman to have the war over, the postwar challenges facing the president were no less daunting. The US economy had to be transitioned from wartime to peacetime. Critical decisions on how to mobilize the Marshall Plan to rebuild the war-ravaged European continent had to be made. Moreover, relations with the Soviet Union, an erstwhile ally against Germany and Japan, seemed to grow more tenuous by the day: Stalin was steadfastly setting out to expand the Soviet bloc and establish what would become known as the Iron Curtain. Containment became the foreign policy watchword, as manifested in the Truman Doctrine, which called for the United States to provide economic and military support to Greece and Turkey and other nations under siege from authoritarian forces.

With no electoral mandate, Truman struggled to find a core constituency and to muster support for his policies, particularly with a Republican-controlled Congress. As the 1948 election year approached, these factors made it that much more difficult for Truman to grapple with one of his most vexing geopolitical issues: the "puzzle of Palestine," as Undersecretary of State Dean Acheson called it.

Palestine was home to Arabs and Jews, and from 1929 on, almost unending strife. The land had been controlled by Great Britain since 1918, when they took it over from the failed Ottoman Empire, but was scheduled to be turned over to the United Nations in 1948, amid deepening discord and mutual distrust. Since Theodore Herzl first conceived of creating a Jewish state in the land of Israel in the late 1890s, oppressed Jews worldwide had longed for a state they could call their own, a place where they could exercise their religious and political rights without fear of persecution. In the half century between the founding of Zionism and the end of the Second World War, hundreds of thousands of Jews had emigrated to Palestine, building cities alongside their Arab neighbors while bringing to life vast tracts of land once thought uninhabitable. After Hitler's war machine slaughtered six million Jews, and tens of thousands of Jews who survived the Holocaust came to Palestine in search of a new home, pressure to create a Jewish state heightened. The issue of a Jewish state could no longer be postponed. A resolution would have to be found, now, and Truman would be the decision-maker.

The plight of Jews fleeing from Nazi Germany had attracted Truman's interest during his time in the Senate. In a 1943 speech in Chicago, Truman proclaimed, "Today—not tomorrow—we must do all that is humanly possible to provide a haven and a place of safety for all those who can be grasped from the hands of the Nazi butchers. Free lands must be opened to them." As World War II came to a close, he again underscored the urgency of the matter, pushing for more Jews to be permitted to emigrate to Palestine, describing it as "the most distressful situation that has happened in the world since Attila made his invasion of Europe."

A devout Baptist who had read the Bible cover to cover while still a teenager, Truman was well aware of the Old Testament narrative that the Jewish people should one day have their own homeland. After two thousand years of exile, this was exactly what the Zionists were pressing for, but in practicality the matter was complicated by a thicket of strategic, economic, political, and moral concerns. FDR, for his part, spent years essentially playing Palestine down the middle, trying to appease both Arab and Jewish leaders. However, with the British and their forces withdrawing and the United Nations set to determine Palestine's fate, Truman didn't have this luxury. Truman's own State Department, led by General George Marshall, a World War II hero and a man almost universally revered, adamantly opposed the idea of partitioning Palestine into Arab and Jewish states, believing it would push the Arab world into the Soviet sphere. Marshall also argued that such a move would imperil American access to Arab oil, and almost certainly require the presence of US troops to contain the violence.

On November 29, 1947, the UN, with US support, voted to adopt a plan to partition Palestine into an Arab state and a Jewish state. Jews were ecstatic, but the Arab nations said the vote meant war. The British, about to withdraw their fifty thousand troops, thought the partition plan was untenable and that violence, if not full-blown war, was inevitable. Positions hardened all around. State Department officials kept reminding Truman how devastating it would be for the US economy should the Arabs get payback by withholding oil. And what if the Arabs, in their quest to drive the Jews out, enlisted military support from the Soviets?

While the debate over the effects of partition raged, the White House began receiving cards and telegrams by the hundreds of thousands in support of a Jewish state. The question became whether the United States would continue to support the partition plan or, if that failed, recognize an independent Jewish state once it was declared. Truman had supported the partition, but now he faced even greater pressure, and he seemed to be wavering. Zionist leaders, fearful that Marshall and others in the State Department would persuade Truman to change his mind, grew increasingly aggressive advocating for their cause. Truman started getting barraged with demands from such Zionist leaders as Stephen Wise, co-chairman of the American Zionist Emergency Council, and Rabbi Abba Hillel Silver of Cleveland, a man who at one point pounded a fist on Truman's desk and shouted at him. Another account told of a wealthy New York garment-district businessman who showed up at a meeting in Washington with wads of cash tucked inside an umbrella, which he then opened, scattering bankrolls everywhere and announcing he was ready to do business if the president supported Israel.

"Tell the bastard to go to hell," Truman reportedly replied. Already on record as supporting a Jewish state, Truman felt increasingly annoyed by what he considered the Zionists' over-the-top zealotry.

"Jesus Christ couldn't please them when he was on the earth, so how could anyone expect that I would have any luck?" he said when the subject of the Zionists came up in a Cabinet meeting.

Believing that the most important matter in the history of their people—the creation of a Jewish state—was at stake, the Zionists pressed for Truman to meet with Dr. Chaim Weizmann, the renowned scientist and venerable leader of the world Zionist movement, a man whose commitment to the Jewish state went back decades. During the First World

War, Weizmann had developed a process to mass-produce acetone, a key component in the production of gunpowder. His discovery was later credited with helping the Allies win the Great War. In appreciation, the British government asked Weizmann what he wanted. "A national home for my people," he boldly replied. The government thereafter issued its famous Balfour Declaration, committing Britain to the establishment of a Jewish state in Palestine. Now seventy-four years old and in failing health, Weizmann was seeking to realize his life-long dream. He had met Truman before and impressed him deeply, the president calling him "a wonderful man, one of the wisest people I think I ever met."

In the hope of securing a meeting with Truman, Weizmann traveled from London to New York in late February 1948 despite being in poor health. Truman remained so put off by Zionist pressure that he declined to meet with anyone, even Weizmann.

Fears mounted among Jewish leaders that if Weizmann—their most persuasive and authoritative voice—returned to Israel without meeting Truman, the chances of Truman recognizing a Jewish state would disappear as fast as Weizmann himself. Frank Goldman, the national president of B'nai Brith, then (and still) one of the most influential Jewish organizations in the country, grew desperate. Having exhausted all other options, he decided his last option was to contact Truman's best friend, Eddie Jacobson.

The late-night phone call on February 20, 1948, jarred Jacobson from his sleep, but he was already deeply familiar with the issue and the urgency of the historical moment. Jacobson was committed enough to the cause to have brought small groups to the White House to lobby the president. After arranging one such visit to see the president with a New York rabbi and a clothing company executive, Charles Kaplan, Jacobson told reporters, "Kaplan sells shirts, I sell furnishings, and the Rabbi sells notions." When Truman was mulling whether to support the UN partition plan earlier that fall, Jacobson had made two separate trips to the White House to urge his friend to vote yes, even sending a two-page wire following one visit to lay out his rationale. Goldman now explained to a sympathetic Jacobson that Weizmann had come all the way from London to see Truman, and it would be most unfortunate if this trip had been made for naught. Goldman's hope was that Jacobson's longtime friendship with Truman might forge a change in the president's thinking.

Goldman's call roused Jacobson into action. Knowing that Truman would soon depart for vacation in Key West, Jacobson wired a letter via the president's appointments secretary, writing, "Mr. President, I have asked you for very little in the way of favors in all our years of friendship, but I am begging of you to see Dr. Weizmann as soon as possible." Jacobson anxiously awaited a reply. Almost a week later, Truman responded from Key West. He remained as cordial as ever with his old friend, but insisted that a meeting with Weizmann would change nothing.

"This situation has been a headache for me for two and a half years," Truman wrote bluntly.

> The Jews are so emotional and the Arabs are so difficult to talk with it is almost impossible to get anything done. The British . . . have been completely noncooperative in arriving at a conclusion. The Zionists, of course, want us to take a big-stick approach and have naturally been disappointed when we can't do that.
>
> I hope it will work out, but I have about come to the conclusion that the situation is not solvable as presently set up; but I shall continue to try to get the situation outlined in the United Nations resolution.
>
> I hope everything is going well with you.
>
> Sincerely yours,
> Harry Truman

It was a disappointing reply, but Jacobson remained undaunted. As much as he understood his old friend's quandary, he would not accept anything less than affirmation. So he decided to fly to Washington to deliver his appeal in person. Without even securing an appointment beforehand, Jacobson traipsed up the White House driveway on the morning of March 13 and into the West Wing office of Matt Connelly, Truman's appointments secretary and gatekeeper. Connelly knew Jacobson and the close bond he had with the president and immediately granted the meeting, but still implored Jacobson not to bring up Truman's least favorite subject: Palestine.

Jacobson entered the office, shook hands, and sat down. He was heartened to see that Truman looked recharged from his time in the Keys. They exchanged pleasantries and gave family updates, and Truman, like always, wanted to know how business was going for Jacobson, who had recently opened a new clothing store at Thirty-Ninth and Main in Kansas City. Jacobson, who regularly sent shirts, ties, and even pajamas to the White House (never including a bill), proudly reported on the store's thriving success. Then, when the moment arrived to turn to the matter at hand, Jacobson paused while looking his friend straight in the eyes. To Truman, the pause seemed interminable: "I finally said 'Eddie what in the world is the matter with you. Have you at last come to get something from me because you never have asked me for anything since I've been in the White House and since we've been friends.'" Finally, Jacobson broached the topic Truman least wanted to confront:

"You must see Dr. Weizmann; you must support an independent Jewish state."

In an instant, Truman's face hardened and his demeanor changed. Jacobson had never seen or heard Harry Truman acting this way. He appeared brusque, almost unreachable. He didn't want any dialogue on the matter, whether pertaining to a Weizmann meeting or anything remotely connected. Jacobson persisted, reminding Truman of the esteem in which he held Weizmann, employing every argument he could think of, from the plight of refugees to the biblical roots of a Jewish homeland.

Truman remained unmovable, hectoring Jacobson about how "disrespectful and mean" certain Jews had been to him.

At that moment, Jacobson later wrote, he felt for the first time that "my dear friend, the President of the United States, was... as close to being an anti-Semite as a man could possibly be."

But Jacobson persisted. Like a defense lawyer trying to sway a jury, he searched his mind for another tack to take, some way to break through. He looked around the office for a moment and spotted a bronze equestrian statue of Andrew Jackson, a replica of the one Truman had commissioned for the Jackson County Courthouse back home in Independence. Truman adored Jackson's strong, pioneering spirit, and Jacobson well knew that Truman loved to compare himself to his predecessor. In his *Memoirs*, published in 1955, Truman praised Jackson for being an outspoken leader for plain folk: "People knew what he stood for and what he was against." Now, Jacobson seized on those connections, highlighting this as a moment for Truman to take his own stand, to show his naysayers that he was no sissy from rural Missouri but an Emersonian pioneer who now held the power to determine the fate of the Jewish state:

> Harry, all your life you had a hero. You are probably the best read man in America on the life of Andrew Jackson. . . . I, too, have a hero, a man I never met but who is, I think, the greatest Jew who ever lived. . . . I am talking about Chaim Weizmann. He is a very sick man, almost broken in health, but he traveled thousands of miles just to see you and plead the cause of my people. Now you refuse to see him because you are insulted by some of our American Jewish leaders, even though you know Weizmann had absolutely nothing to do with these insults, and would be the last man to be party to them. It doesn't sound like you, Harry, because I thought you could take this stuff they have been handing out. I wouldn't be here if I didn't know that if you will see him you will be properly and accurately informed on the situation as it exists in Palestine.

When Jacobson had finished his appeal, Truman "began drumming his fingers on his desk." He swiveled his chair away from Jacobson and looked out at the Rose Garden, gazing through the window that was just beyond the photos of his mother, wife, and daughter. The Oval Office resounded with silence. To Jacobson, it seemed that this silence lasted "for centuries." Finally, Harry Truman swiveled his chair back around.

"You win, you bald-headed son of a bitch. I will see him," Truman declared.

An utterly relieved Jacobson described these as "the most endearing words I ever heard from his lips."

Truman buzzed Connelly to set up the meeting time with Weizmann. Jacobson thanked his former partner and departed, walking happily up Sixteenth Street to the Statler Hotel, where he was staying. He stopped at the hotel bar and ordered two double bourbons. He had never done that before in his life.

Chaim Weizmann arrived at the White House after dark on Thursday, March 18. He entered through the East Wing to attract as little press attention as possible. Truman informed nobody about the visit, not even his secretary of state; this meeting would be completely off the record. It lasted forty-five minutes, and by all accounts it went well. The men held each other in high regard, and Truman made a point to reassure Weizmann that he supported partition and wanted to do whatever he could to minimize bloodshed. To Weizmann, the meeting marked a complete triumph, but the relief the Zionists felt was short-lived. The next day, Warren Austin, the United States' ambassador to the UN, announced that the US was reconsidering the partition plan and wanted to invoke a temporary UN trusteeship over Palestine to allow for more time to consider all options.

It was a stunning reversal, leaving Jacobson blindsided. Jacobson was soon fielding calls from people accusing Truman of being a duplicitous scoundrel and a traitor to the Jewish cause. Heartbroken, Jacobson took to his bed for the entire weekend: "There wasn't one...who expressed faith and confidence in the word of the President of the United States." Still, Jacobson refused to believe the President had betrayed him until he heard the words from Truman directly. The truth was that while nobody at the State Department knew about Truman's meeting with Weizmann, let alone his vow of support, the president had never authorized Austin's back-tracking statement. In fact, the president felt betrayed by a group of men he called "the striped-pants boys" in the State Department who he believed were out to sabotage him. Now, with the May 14 expiration of the British Mandate over Palestine looming, this mess needed to be straightened out quickly.

Weizmann wrote to Truman on April 9, seeking to underscore the high stakes:

> The choice for our people, Mr. President, is between statehood and extermination. History and providence have placed this issue in your hands, and I am confident that you will yet decide it in the spirit of moral law.

On a follow-up trip to the White House shortly after the tempest, Jacobson sought to clarify where things stood. Truman reaffirmed his support for statehood, saying that nothing had changed in the substance of what he'd told Weizmann. Jacobson, immensely relieved, then told his friend how vital it was for the United States to publicly recognize the new Jewish state when it was finally declared. Jacobson wrote later that Truman "agreed with a whole heart."

Two days before the British Mandate was set to expire, Truman convened an Oval Office meeting to hear final arguments on whether to recognize the new and as yet unnamed Jewish state. Days before, knowing time was running out and that his most revered Cabinet member, George Marshall, remained opposed, Truman had asked Clark Clifford to prepare the argument *for* recognition, as if he were arguing a case before the Supreme Court. A lawyer by training and now White House counsel, Clifford went to work, studying everything from the text of Deuteronomy to the horrors of the Holocaust to compile his most persuasive arguments. But instead of preparing for nine Justices, he would effectively have an audience of one: George Marshall. His goal wasn't necessarily to convince the war hero to accept recognition but to ensure that he wouldn't resign in the event the president did decide to recognize the Jewish state. Truman understood how damaging Marshall's resignation would be to his re-election prospects, and was determined to avoid that danger.

The tension was palpable in the Oval Office as Marshall and three State Department aides quietly took their seats to Truman's right. To his left sat Matt Connelly and one other White House aide. Directly in front sat Clifford. Truman opened with a noncommittal statement, then turned to Marshall for his view. Marshall's deputy, Robert Lovett, made their case: Recognition would be premature and counterproductive. The more prudent course would be to continue the UN trusteeship of Palestine until a truce and an enforceable plan could be put in place. Marshall's core point, Clifford would say later, was that "there were twenty or thirty million Arabs as compared to a million and a half Israelis and the Israelis were going to end up being pushed into the Mediterranean." Factoring in the importance of Arab oil and the strong likelihood that the Soviets would align themselves with the Arabs, Marshall insisted siding with the Jews constituted both dangerous and foolish policy. He also insinuated that the only reason they were even debating the idea of an independent Jewish state was to secure both the Jewish vote and the financial backing of prominent Jewish businessmen.

Truman then called on Clifford to deliver his argument in favor of recognition. Unbowed by what he had just heard, Clifford upped the stakes: America should not only recognize the new Jewish state in forty-eight hours, but also beat the Soviets by being the first country to do it. For fifteen minutes, speaking fluently and in perfectly structured sentences, Clifford asserted that there were effectively Jewish and Arab states in Palestine already, and with the Mandate ending, the Jews could wait no longer. Moreover, with six million Jews having been murdered by the Nazis, and refugees desperate for a place to live, the only humane option was to support a Jewish homeland. The longer Clifford talked, the redder Marshall's face became. At one point Marshall asked why Clifford, a domestic affairs advisor, was even in the meeting. "General, he is here because I asked him to be here," Truman said. The tension in the office was palpable. Now fully agitated, Marshall delivered the coup de grace: If the president followed Clifford's advice, he would vote against him in November. "That brought the meeting to a grinding halt," Clifford later remarked, adding it was the "sharpest rebuke" of Truman's presidency. When the meeting ended, Marshall departed without even looking at Clifford.

The ultimate decision belonged to one man: Harry S. Truman. As much as he admired and respected Marshall, Truman had to heed what was in his own heart—and what Jacobson had persuaded him to do. Now was his chance to fulfill that Mark Twain maxim that sat on his desk, to "gratify" the nation and "astonish" the world. The next day, after Lovett informed Clifford that the secretary wouldn't publicly oppose Truman's recognition, the path was cleared.

At midnight the next evening in Jerusalem, David Ben-Gurion declared the new Jewish state of Israel. Eleven minutes later, at 6:11 p.m. in Washington, DC, came this statement from President Harry Truman:

> This government has been informed that a Jewish state has been proclaimed in Palestine, and recognition has been requested by the provisional government thereof. The United States recognizes the provisional government as the de facto authority of the State of Israel.

The United States thus became the first nation to extend de facto recognition to Israel. To later American diplomats like Dennis Ross, it had enormous consequences, not the least conferring on the fledgling new state "standing internationally when it would otherwise not have had it. Psychologically, that was huge, effectively signaling American support. It also undercut the messages that the State and Defense Departments had been sending to the Europeans and the Arabs that the US opposed the advent of the state."

As jubilant Israelis danced in the streets of Jerusalem, Jacobson celebrated in Kansas City. Within a day, he was headed to New York to meet with the new president of Israel, Chaim Weizmann. Three days later, he arrived at the White House to be received as Israel's "temporary, unofficial ambassador."

May 14, 1948, was one of the most heartening days of Harry Truman's tenure as president. If professionals at the State and War Departments found his decision bewildering and his decision-making sloppy, the public and the press supported him. Isaac Halevi Herzog, the chief rabbi of Israel, visited the White House soon thereafter and told Truman, "God put you in your mother's womb so you would be the instrument to bring the rebirth of Israel after two thousand years." The words brought tears to Truman's eyes.

Eddie Jacobson always downplayed his "small part in this historic event." He said his role came down to *beshert*—a Yiddish expression that means "destiny." To Harry Truman, the destiny was undergirded by a lifetime not only of trust and friendship, but also of humor, laughter long being a staple between them. When Jacobson was named one of the directors of a prominent Kansas City bank after news emerged of the pivotal role he had played, Truman wrote to him, "You and I seem to be getting up in the world—you a Bank Director and me the president of the United States."

Jacobson's stock had indeed risen in the world. In 1949, Jacobson traveled to Israel as a personal emissary of Truman's. Over the course of four weeks, he was feted by both Prime Minister David Ben-Gurion and Israeli president Chaim Weizmann. Upon his return, one Kansas City rabbi even floated the idea that Jacobson should succeed Weizmann when he retired, a suggestion Eddie promptly rejected. Truman, for his part, joined the debate, saying that while he hoped Jacobson wouldn't take it, "Israel couldn't nominate a better man."

Jacobson had no hidden agenda, no singular self-interest beyond being a Jewish man who wanted to "do right" by his people. He loved Harry Truman, and the feeling was mutual. Across decades of friendship, Jacobson made it his business not to intrude on Truman's time or trade on his closeness to the man. They were Harry and Eddie, Eddie and Harry, and that never changed, even when Truman was writing him on stationery that said "The White House" on top.

"When the day came when Eddie Jacobson was persuaded to forego his natural reluctance to petition me and he came to talk to me about the plight of the Jews... I paid careful attention," Truman wrote years later. He called Jacobson's involvement of "decisive importance," the one man who had spoken truth to power and who did not sacrifice his friendship along the way. Truman once said that reading history taught him "that a leader is a man who has the ability to get other people to do what they don't want to do, and like it." Based on that definition, it was Jacobson—even more than Truman—who operated as a silent leader on one of the most fraught issues in US foreign policy.

To more than a few observers of Truman's life and political career, he stood as an unlikely candidate to champion the cause of Jewish statehood. Truman was known periodically to traffic in Jewish stereotypes; when referring to Jews, he also often resorted to slurs not uncommon in the Midwestern world in which he'd grown up. He made the "crackerjack Jew" comment about Eddie when he was doing such a "splendid job with the canteen," and he once wrote to Bess that he had little use for Miami because it was nothing but "hotels, filling stations, Hebrews, and cabins." In a 1947 diary entry, Truman assailed Henry Morgenthau, the former secretary of the Treasury, who had appealed to him on behalf of Jewish refugees.

"The Jews I find very, very selfish," Truman wrote. "They care not how many Estonians, Latvians, Finns, Poles, Yugoslavs or Greeks get murdered or mistreated as D[isplaced] Persons as long as the Jews get special treatment."

On a more personal level, as close as Jacobson was to Truman, he and his wife, Bluma, were never invited into the Wallace family home, where Harry and Bess lived with Bess's mother, Madge Wallace. Madge was widely thought to have a strict no-Jews policy in her home. Elinor Borenstine said years later in an interview with the Truman Library that Bess Truman and daughter Margaret adhered to a similar, if unstated, attitude.

"We felt they didn't care for Jews or want any part of them so, you know, we didn't care," Borenstine said. "We knew Harry was alright with us, but we also knew Bess was not. After all, she was raised at her mother's knee. They were the first family of Independence, Missouri for God's sake, this big place! So, that was alright, we didn't care. We didn't miss 'em."

And yet, in his long friendship with Jacobson, and in his words and deeds in both the Senate and in the White House, Truman advocated passionately and tirelessly on behalf of the Jewish people and their statehood. As a Christian senator, he lent his name to the American Palestine Committee, a Christian Zionist group. He even supported the Committee for a Jewish Army, a group that advocated for Jews taking up arms against the Nazi war machine. Publicly, his words and deeds did not reflect the feelings of an anti-Semite. Nevertheless, decades after his death, there is still that open question: Was Truman an anti-Semite?

In an interview with the *Washington Post*, Sara Bloomfield, director of the US Holocaust Memorial Museum, tried to provide context for understanding Truman's views. She ascribed Truman's private commentaries on Jews as "typical of a sort of cultural anti-Semitism that was common at that time in all parts of American society. That was an acceptable way to talk." That doesn't make his comments any less alarming or offensive, but people who knew Truman and his character best—count Eddie Jacobson and Chaim Weizmann among them—would rightly argue that his actions were far more meaningful than his asides. David Holzel made precisely this point, writing in *Washington Jewish Week* in 2018:

> Truman was an imperfect man with imperfect views. The unfavorable regard he had for Jews does not negate his many contributions to the Jewish community or the country as a whole. One should judge Truman on his actions, not on a few unflattering comments.

Eddie Jacobson's health started to falter in 1950. His heart was weakening. When Truman heard the news, he told Jacobson what a privilege it was to have such a good and loyal friend, and he admonished him to take good care of himself. "I sure don't want to send flowers to Mrs. Jacobson for you," Truman said in a handwritten note. Their correspondence was steady and always heartfelt. When Truman announced that he would not run for reelection in 1952, Jacobson was among the first to congratulate him.

Truman returned to his beloved Independence, and the handsome Victorian home at 219 Delaware, where Bess Wallace Truman had grown up. He would get together regularly with the boys from the 129th Field Artillery, and he continued to be the resident reader and chief cook on annual hunting and fishing outings with his buddies. His friendship with Eddie Jacobson only got stronger. In June 1955, Truman suggested they take a long trip with their wives, traveling to London, Holland, and France, meeting the leaders of each country, and proceeding on to Italy, for an audience with the Pope. Then they would take a ship to Israel, and follow that with visits to Turkey and Greece. Truman wanted to do this in the fall of 1955, but Bess Truman needed some extensive dental work done, so they had to put it off until the spring of 1956. On October 25, 1955, Eddie Jacobson suffered a heart attack and died en route to the hospital. He was sixty-four years old.

Harry Truman visited the Jacobson family as they sat shiva in their Kansas City home. He was so overcome with emotion he could barely speak. When Elinor Borenstine asked him to sign copies of his memoirs, he began to sob. He said he would gladly sign the copies but could not do it at that moment.

"Eddie was one of the best friends I had in this world," Truman said later. "He was absolutely trustworthy. I don't know how I am going to get along without him."

Just over a year after Eddie Jacobson's passing, his closest friends held a memorial service in Kansas City, launching a foundation in his name. The featured speakers were Abba Eban, Israel's ambassador to the United States, and President Harry Truman, whose friendship with Eddie Jacobson spanned a half century. Truman struggled with how to capture the richness of their friendship in just a few remarks. He knew nothing he would say that morning would do it justice, but he tried. His voice quivering with emotion, Harry Truman began:

> Eddie was one of those men that you read about in the Torah. If you read the articles in Genesis concerning two just men [Enoch

> and Noah] you'll find those descriptions will fit Eddie Jacobson to the dot.

Truman continued: "I don't think I've ever known a man I thought more of, outside my own family, than I did of Eddie Jacobson. He was an honorable man. He's one of the finest men that ever walked on this earth, and that's covering a lot of territory."

CHAPTER 7

Jack Kennedy and David Ormsby-Gore

A Special Relationship

Twenty-one months into his term in the White House, the youngest elected president in American history found himself facing a crisis so grave that it threatened not only his political life but also humanity itself.

John Fitzgerald Kennedy was sitting in the dining room of "the Suite of Presidents" in Chicago's historic Blackstone Hotel, eating a bowl of the hotel's famous Boston clam chowder while he scanned the local newspapers. It was Saturday, October 20, 1962, what would later be known as Day 5 of the Cuban Missile Crisis. The night before, he had headlined a fund-raiser for the Cook County Democratic Party. Now he would fly off for a day of vigorous campaigning for Democratic candidates in the upcoming midterm elections. As Kennedy began reviewing the day's schedule—which would take him to five states, starting in Milwaukee and ending in Seattle—a phone call came in from his brother Bobby, the attorney general. He had ominous news. After four intensive days of deliberations, the Executive Committee of the National Security Council (ExComm) had agreed on two options for the president to take in response to the discovery days earlier of Soviet ballistic missiles in Cuba. The first was to launch an air strike, the second to impose a naval quarantine with the threat of future military action. Either one could result in a nuclear confrontation with America's most formidable enemy.

Kennedy instantly scrapped the day's campaigning and prepared to return to Washington to meet with the ExComm. But since the public still knew nothing about the existential threat just ninety miles from Florida, the president needed an excuse for heading home early. So he turned to the oldest trick in the schoolkid playbook: fake an illness. As Kennedy boarded Air Force One, the country was told that his doctor had found him running a low-grade fever and ordered him to return home forthwith. The patient obliged, even donning a borrowed gray fedora for only the second time in his presidency to demonstrate he was taking all necessary precautions.

Once back in Washington, Kennedy made four decisions. First, he called and asked his wife, Jackie, to come back from their weekend getaway in Virginia. He wanted her and their two children, Caroline and John Jr., within the safe confines of the White House. The president then scheduled a national television broadcast for Monday night, when he would reveal the crisis at hand and explain how he intended to address it. Third, after a heated debate with his ExComm, Kennedy opted for the less aggressive strategy of a blockade to keep Soviet ships from delivering their missiles. And finally, early on that Sunday morning, he called one of his closest friends and asked him to "come unseen" to the White House shortly before lunch. For nearly a quarter century, the president had been having an ongoing conversation with this friend about leadership and decision-making in the midst of crisis. But this time the discussion no longer dealt with hypotheticals. If ever Kennedy felt a need for the wisdom, counsel, probity, and friendship of David Ormsby-Gore, it was now.

A few hours later, Ormsby-Gore was ushered into the Yellow Oval Room in the second-floor residence. There he met the president, who was grappling with how to manage a complicated military operation and then explain it to the nation in a speech the following evening. The two men recognized that the stakes would never be higher: Just one false step could set off a nuclear war. That night over dinner and afterward, they labored over the words Kennedy would employ the next night. Then, over the six days and nights following the address, Kennedy and Ormsby-Gore would draw deeply on their twenty-five-year conversation to help guide the young leader through the worst crisis of his presidency. Deliberating in the Cabinet Room, taking meals in the residence, and talking late into the night, they finally had an opportunity to *demonstrate* what true leadership should be in the crucible of conflict.

That Kennedy would choose Ormsby-Gore as one of his key confidants is testament to the fullness of a bond forged at the outset of World War II and deepened over the ensuing two decades. More remarkable still is the fact that the man the president entrusted with such sensitive information during the Cuban Missile Crisis was neither a member of his government nor even a citizen of the country he led. He was the British ambassador to the United States, a lord-in-waiting, a cousin by marriage to a sibling, and a man of exquisite social grace and fierce intellectual firepower (Kennedy often told friends that next to McGeorge Bundy, Ormsby-Gore was the most brilliant man he had ever met). Naturally, then, Kennedy often called him for support during trying times and for company during more relaxed moments.

Bundy, Kennedy's national security advisor, later reflected that no one could overestimate "how intimately and how completely" the two friends discussed matters. Ormsby-Gore, Bundy continued, "was probably in the [White] House more than any other person with a serious concern for affairs" during Kennedy's presidency. And no couple spent more time on weekends with the First Couple—in Hyannis Port, Palm Beach, Glen Ora, or at the White House—than David and Sissie Gore, a tribute to their intellectual and social verve. Barbara Leaming, who in *The Education of a Statesman* first unearthed Ormsby-Gore's critical role in Kennedy's life, perhaps summarized it best: "The friendship would prove among the most important of Jack's life and have immense historical ramifications" during his dramatic years in the White House.

John Fitzgerald Kennedy never wanted for friendship. Witty, urbane, and handsome, a man from a prominent family and with a hunger for intellectual stimulation, Kennedy made friends easily and, with few exceptions, kept them. His life was short, only forty-six years, but his list of friends ran long—so long that as president he felt no need to add to it. "The presidency is not a good place to make new friends. I'm going to keep my old friends," he quipped.

Kennedy had what historian and presidential advisor Arthur Schlesinger Jr. called "the gift of friendship." His world was filled with friends culled from every aspect of his life—his family, the elite schools he attended, the Navy, and even his extensive travels abroad. His speechwriter Ted Sorensen said the perfect Kennedy friend was someone "cheerful, amusing, energetic, informed and informal." He gravitated toward those who could make him laugh and, in particular, execute a sophisticated prank. Kennedy himself loved to prank, and he never stopped even when he got to the White House. With his love of quick banter and good jokes, Kennedy also thirsted for gossip, the more salacious the better, especially when it concerned the affairs of politicians, reporters, and friends that he could then mischievously trade for more. "Who does Castro sleep with?" the president once asked a stunned journalist from *Look*. "I hear he doesn't even take his boots off." Above all else, Kennedy cherished loyalty. He returned that loyalty by giving his friends unfettered access to his life of glamour, action, and purpose.

As open to friendship as he was in his personal life, Kennedy was equally wary of it in his public life. He served in Congress for over half of his adulthood, yet in those fourteen years, with the exception of George Smathers of Florida, he never forged a single real friendship among his fellow House members or senators. Reflecting on this oddity after his death, Jackie believed he subscribed to the Palmerston theory, which held that in politics there are no permanent friendships or alliances, only permanent interests. Whether consciously or not, Kennedy realized early on that to get overly invested in politicians was a waste of time, because interests shifted daily. A friend one day could become a foe the next. So he preserved his equanimity by keeping his personal distance from Hill colleagues.

Much like how the *New York Times Magazine* would depict Bill and Hillary Clinton's lives a generation later, Kennedy's vast world can be visualized as a galaxy of individual planets rotating around a single sun.

The planet that orbited closest to him was his immediate family: his parents, Joe Sr. and Rose; his three brothers, Joe Jr., Bobby, and Teddy; and his five sisters, Kathleen, Eunice, Rosemary, Pat, and Jean. From their birth, Joe Sr. had instilled in all of his children a fierce protectiveness of the family, which fostered a closeness among them that would last their lifetimes. But, as in any family, Jack had his favorites. He bonded most easily with his oldest sister, Kathleen, known to all as "Kick," though the sibling he would ultimately be closest to was his younger brother Bobby.

To those who knew the brothers growing up, it wasn't always obvious this would be the case. Jack was eight when Bobby was born. Slight of frame and small in stature, Bobby was described by his father as the "runt of the litter," while his mother worried he would grow up to be a "sissy." On the contrary, he matured into a highly skilled and ruthless political operative who, starting from 1952, would manage every one of Jack's campaigns. Few would deny that "as much as any single person alive, it was Bobby Kennedy who made Jack Kennedy president." As president, Kennedy would rely on his brother—the country's youngest-ever attorney general—for counsel on every major decision he made.

Lem Billings occupied his own planet. He visited the White House so often that, depending on the source, he was either given his own room or at the least allowed to keep his belongings in a third-floor guest room. Kennedy's sister Eunice described Lem's friendship as a "complete liberation of the spirit" for her brother, who especially delighted in the elaborate practical jokes he could play on Lem. In the summer of 1962, Billings became fast friends with the actress Greta Garbo. He came back to the White House filled with details of their enchanted adventures across Europe. Immediately inspired, the president soon invited Garbo to the White House for an intimate dinner with Jackie and her new close friend Lem. Garbo arrived first and spoke with the president, who gave her special instructions for the evening. Then Lem came in, "glowing with anticipation," and opened his arms: "Greta!" A ghastly pause followed. Garbo looked at Lem blankly. She then turned to the president and said, "I have never seen this man before."

The next half hour was excruciating for Billings. He rattled off all the places they had visited, the friends they had met, and the meals they had shared. Nothing worked. Embarrassed and befuddled, Billings never considered the possibility that her amnesia was contrived by none other than the president. The actress kept up the ruse until the second course. Later, Billings would remember the dinner as "one of the worst things I ever went through in my life."

Next came the "Irish mafia," most notably Dave Powers and Kenny O'Donnell, both fiercely loyal men who met Kennedy in the 1940s and would serve him unflinchingly until the last day of his life. There were also his Navy friends, men like Red Fay and James Reed, who experienced the crucible of the Second World War with him and lived to tell, and retell, their heroic exploits.

And then there were the intellectuals, men like Schlesinger, Bundy, and speechwriter and aide Ted Sorensen, who quenched the president's thirst for knowledge. Schlesinger and Bundy managed to straddle the worlds of ideas and glamour, and they typically made the cut of the most sought-after social invitations. Sorensen with rare exceptions didn't get invited, a rejection that rattled him. Jackie Kennedy later admitted she kept him away because of the persistent rumors—rumors she blamed Sorenson for instigating—that he was the real author of *Profiles in Courage*, the book that won Kennedy a Pulitzer Prize for biography in 1957. Worse, she acknowledged what every socially ambitious staffer in the White House feared most: "As [Jack] and Ted had the problems all day, that would be the last person you would invite at night."

And finally there were his friends from the press, such as Ben Bradlee, Charlie Bartlett, and Joseph Alsop, who amused the president with an intoxicating blend of gossip, tales of backroom machinations, and the skepticism that came from having spent their careers covering Washington politics. Of the three, Bradlee came to the party the latest but grew closest to him during his presidency. Kennedy loved to gossip—according to Bradlee, "It was one of his all-time favorite subjects." Blessed with Kennedy's good looks and as clued-in as anyone, *Newsweek*'s DC bureau chief never failed to satisfy the president's need for the latest buzz.

Out of Kennedy's numerous friends, only one transcended all these groups—able to move seamlessly among family and staff, around the intellectuals and the media luminaries, with the Irish crowd and the Navy pals. Kennedy himself seemed to recognize this adaptability when he described Ormsby-Gore as "a companion for every mood."

As British prime minister Harold Macmillan later put it, "You see, the President had three lives; he had a smart life, dancing with people not in the political world at all, smart people, till four in the morning; then he had his highbrow life, which meant going to some great pundit...and discussing his philosophy; and then he had his political life. And David belonged to all three." David Ormsby-Gore wore that distinction with modesty, never seeking to leverage his relationship for personal fame or professional aggrandizement. Secure in himself as well as in his duty to his country and to Kennedy, his only goal as confidant was to advance ideas and policies he thought best served the interests of his friend, his native country, and the "special relationship" between Britain and the United States.

Kick Kennedy's entry into polite British society in the early spring of 1938 was proving far more difficult than she had ever anticipated. The eldest daughter of America's brash new ambassador to the UK, she arrived shortly after her eighteenth birthday with the intention of staying at least until the fall. During that time, she would follow the rituals of well-heeled English daughters by being presented at court and having her own debutante party. But two things weren't working, leaving Kick sorely frustrated: The most sought-after boys weren't laughing at her jokes, and she wasn't thrilled by the few girlfriends she had managed to make.

All that changed one magical weekend in April that year when Kick attended her first weekend party at a proper English country house and met young David Ormsby-Gore, an Oxford University student a month away from turning twenty. He too stood at a crossroads of sorts. David was the second son of Billy Ormsby-Gore, the seventh-generation Gore to sit in the House of Lords as Lord Harlech, baron and owner of the family's extensive landholdings in Wales and Shropshire. At various points in David's youth, his father would play prominent roles in Britain's foreign affairs, including serving as a member of the British delegation to the Paris Peace Conference in 1919. In 1933, as Britain's delegate to the League of Nations and an unabashed supporter of Zionism, his father made international headlines when he bucked official British policy by denouncing Hitler's racial theories and attacking *Mein Kampf.* David's mother, meanwhile, was the granddaughter of Lord Salisbury, a prime minister under Queen Victoria.

As part of the London aristocracy, David followed the traditional path of attending Eton, where he became known more for his pranks and wit than for his academic mastery. One day a fellow student committed suicide, and, as the story goes, the housemaster called an assembly and asked the boys if anyone knew why. Ormsby-Gore raised his hand and asked, "Could it have been the food, sir?" During the year before his last at Eton, David's older brother Gerard died in an automobile accident. Under the rules of primogeniture, David as the second son would now inherit the Harlech barony and the new title of "lord-in-waiting." Instead of settling into the modest and private life he longed for, family tradition dictated that Ormsby-Gore enter the House of Commons prior to assuming the title—a public life he neither wanted nor felt suited him.

When David met Kick that spring evening, whatever unease each may have felt vanished almost instantly. Though innately shy, Ormsby-Gore in the right environment was a man who loved to talk—and then talk some more. That evening, armed with knowledge derived from a youth spent reading, David, his first cousin Andrew Devonshire, and his friend Hugh Fraser regaled Kick with their quick minds and wit; and Kick, enchanted and amused, reciprocated with equal verbal velocity. By the end of the weekend, Kick had found the squad that would sustain her in Britain for the following decade. With her older brother Jack due to arrive in London any day, Kick couldn't wait to show them off. And by the time he left three months later, Jack, like Kick, would have his own London social circle, with David Ormsby-Gore at its center.

Precisely how, when, and where Kennedy first met Ormsby-Gore remains lost to history. Several accounts suggest they linked at a dinner party at the ambassador's residence or at the Epsom horse races. The novelist Evelyn Waugh had a different recollection, saying they met "over supine bodies in a squalid basement bottle-party." What *is* certain is that once Kick sparked their connection during the early summer of 1938, Jack's attraction to Ormsby-Gore and his fellow Brits would prove as strong for him as it had been for her.

Jack by this time felt almost magnetically drawn to London. Even before he met David Ormsby-Gore, Andrew Devonshire, Hugh Fraser, and many others, he already knew a great deal about their family lore, including the stately homes they owned, the major scandals they endured, and even their quirky legacies. His studies at Harvard over the past two years had been entirely consumed with English and European history (he claimed to be reading up to twelve books on the subject weekly), and now his father was the US ambassador to England. Kennedy had spent the previous summer traveling across Europe, trying to better understand the prospect of war facing the continent. Earlier, he had studied briefly at the London School of Economics after graduating from Choate. Settling down in London now for another summer, Kennedy planned to focus his time understanding what Hitler's threatening agenda might portend for the rest of the world.

For his part, while at New College, Oxford, Ormsby-Gore closely followed the current political scene and could parse complex public issues with anyone. Later on that summer with his new friend in tow, he would attend House of Commons debates, fascinated by the discourse over how and when Britain should confront Hitler's rising menace. Still, Ormsby-Gore believed he lacked that singular drive—that killer instinct—to be a politician himself, a sobering thought for a man expected someday to succeed his father and sit in the House of Lords. At a time when his friends were starting to get more serious about their futures, he felt directionless, more consumed by his obsession for fast cars than thoughts of how he would make it in the world.

As Kennedy and Ormsby-Gore discovered during that summer of 1938, they shared much in common. Both were second sons and viewed by their fathers as the lesser. Both were highly educated—each studying at prestigious universities—yet not quite sure how to apply their book knowledge to the real world. Both were good-looking, though David in a less classic sense. Toothy and angular, with a prominent nose and a shock of black hair, David didn't possess the chiseled features of his friend Jack, but he more than compensated for it with a debonair, confident style. Both liked to have a good time. When they weren't on dates squiring women around London, they were often together—either on the golf course, at the racetrack, or in underground nightclubs, engaging in spirited conversations that typically included a fair amount of drinking (mostly by David) and gossip. Their speaking styles and sensibilities suited one another as well: Jack, easily bored, wanted to get to the point; David also talked fast, with plenty of color and wit. Their conversations were "swift and sharp," just as both liked them. And increasingly that summer, those discussions grew more and more substantive.

One question in particular riveted the two men: What does it mean to be a true leader in a democratic society? It was an issue they would return to time and time again over the next twenty-five years, culminating with the future of the world at stake.

This critical question of how leadership should be wielded intensified that summer with the publication of Winston Churchill's book *Arms and the Covenant*, a collection of his speeches since 1932 advocating for rearmament in the face of German militarization. Churchill's polemics forced Brits like Ormsby-Gore to confront the question of whether the previous six years—a period when Germany seized territory, proclaimed its master-race superiority, and strengthened its military while England stood still—had been squandered. Churchill called them the lost "locust years," a stinging indictment of Stanley Baldwin, Neville Chamberlain's predecessor as prime minister. In Churchill's depiction, a weak Baldwin refused to address the growing threat of German militarization because he capitulated to a British electorate adamantly opposed to intervention. Baldwin later defended his inaction by arguing that had his government betrayed public sentiment and rearmed, the pacifist Labour Party would have swept into power—leaving the country even weaker.

This schism between Churchill and Baldwin "posed large questions for the young men about the role of leadership in a democracy," as historian Fredrik Logevall writes. "Should a leader pursue a course of action, that, however meritorious on strategic or ethical grounds, might cause his political downfall? How much should public opinion matter in policy-making? Should a leader take care not to get too far ahead of the electorate, as Baldwin seemed to argue, or was Churchill right to insist that he must speak his mind, must educate the public, whatever the consequences to his own standing?"

Ormsby-Gore and his British friends firmly sided with the Churchill camp, convinced that a true leader must take action to preserve and protect the greater good of the nation, regardless of the whims of the public. Chamberlain's submission at Munich later that fall and Hitler's subsequent violation of the pact reached there only cemented their opinion. Kennedy, however, refused to take a firm position that summer, in part because his father's increasingly pacifist views put him in conflict with Churchill. And for much of the next twenty years, Kennedy's actions on this question would remain nuanced. He criticized Britain's appeasement of Germany in his senior thesis, *Why England Slept*, but refused to place the blame on either Baldwin or Chamberlain, instead faulting the entire British political system for failing to meet its responsibilities. Sixteen years later, in his Pulitzer Prize–winning *Profiles in Courage*, he celebrated eight US senators who had demonstrated Churchillian leadership, risking their political careers to pursue causes they thought just. Still, even as he aspired to govern guided by Churchill's ethos, Kennedy often struggled to apply it in his public life, veering, as Barbara Leaming writes, "between Baldwin and Churchill, between politician and statesman." Only when he reached the presidency, and came face-to-face with the greatest existential threat the world had ever faced, would he finally and fully resolve this question—with Ormsby-Gore at his side.

Jack returned to Harvard that fall while Kick remained in London. Whatever early doubts she had about her suitability to blend into the city's rarefied social scene had long since abated. To the contrary, she now blossomed at its center. She had fallen in love with David's best friend and first cousin, Billy Hartington, himself a lord-in-waiting to one of England's most important dukedoms and one of London's most desired bachelors. Given the taboo then against marriage between Catholics and Protestants, their families both fiercely objected to the romance—but to no avail. David, a Protestant, also fell in love at roughly the same time to a Catholic, Sissie Lloyd Thomas. Further cementing Ormsby-Gore's connections to the Kennedy family, Sissie had become Kick's best friend in London, and she would remain so for the rest of her life.

The London that Jack returned to in mid-1939 was a changed city from the one he had left the previous fall. The fear of imminent war with Germany was as pervasive as the resolve of young Brits like Billy and David to serve when war arrived. Billy by then had enlisted in the Coldstream Guards, an active frontline regiment. David wanted to do the same but was blocked by his father, who feared losing another son. Instead, David joined the Territorial Army where, as his father hoped, he would likely never see combat.

As sentiment among his children's friends grew for a muscular response to German provocations, Ambassador Joe Kennedy continued to insist that Britain would be annihilated if it went to war. One evening that summer, Kick invited David, Billy, and a few other friends to dine with her father and Jack at the embassy residence. After dinner, as he often did, the ambassador decided to show a movie. The former Hollywood studio owner typically would screen a light movie. This night, he had a different objective in mind; entertainment wasn't it. He showed instead a movie about the horrors of war, with World War I as his example. Soon his guests were viewing some of the most gruesome images from the Great War. Joe Kennedy's intent couldn't have been more obvious. "That's what you'll all be looking like in a month or two," he shouted, as scenes of British soldiers being mowed down played before their eyes. But if he had hoped to convince the young men of the folly of war, his one-man show actually accomplished the opposite. Their British reserve kicked in—none made a fuss—but Kick, noticing their displeasure, later apologized for her father's insensitivity. Jack "sat impassive throughout," never uttering a word of opposition to his father's diatribe. If he was embarrassed by his father's intemperance, he wasn't going to display it to outsiders, even those as close as David and Billy.

By then Jack was much more of a realist about the likelihood of the British going to war than his father, observing the rise of German militarism with the same cool detachment that would later characterize his approach to other moments of crisis. With David in tow, he went to Germany in the late summer of 1939 to assess the situation for himself, and he concluded that war was fast becoming inevitable. He suspected that

Hitler was badly misjudging Britain's resolve—this time to fight, not appease. On September 1, 1939, the Germans finally tested that resolve by invading Poland. When the British, as Jack predicted, honored their pact with Poland and, joined by France, declared war on Germany two days later, armed conflict again swept across the world.

Once the war began, Joe Kennedy wasted no time moving his family back to New York and an ocean away from Hitler's menace. The ambassador, however, remained at his embassy post on Grosvenor Square. As the German blitzkrieg rained missiles all around him in London, Kennedy sent cable after cable back to Washington predicting England's demise and urging the United States to stay neutral. The more he advocated for isolationism, the more isolated he himself grew from President Roosevelt and the State Department. By the summer of 1940, it was clear he needed to go; when Roosevelt won reelection to a third term that fall, Joe Kennedy resigned in disgrace.

Of all the Kennedy children, Kick had put up the biggest fight to remain in London when her father moved the family home. By 1943 she finally prevailed, returning into the arms of Billy Hartington despite threats from her mother that she would disown her. In May 1944, the two were married in a small civil ceremony. The only Kennedy to attend was her brother Joe.

The war years kept Ormsby-Gore and John Kennedy apart, each occupied with serving his country and, in the case of David, marrying Sissie and raising a family that now counted two young children. While Ormsby-Gore avoided any live combat in the Territorial Army, Kennedy became a war hero, saving his *PT-109* crew from near-certain death after a Japanese cruiser sliced his boat in half. If the circumstances of the ramming left some wondering whether it could have been avoided, no one doubted Kennedy's heroism afterward. Of his twelve crewmates, ten survived, many because of Kennedy's will and physical exploits over five excruciating days while they awaited rescue. For his heroism, Kennedy would receive the Navy's highest award for gallantry, the Navy and Marine Corps Medal. He also received a Purple Heart.

But the war would also bring tragedy to both families. In the late summer of 1944, Kennedy lost his older brother, Joe, when the plane he was piloting blew up over East Suffolk, England. His father took the loss especially hard. According to one of his closest friends, Arthur Krock, Joe Kennedy was overwhelmed not only by grief, but also by guilt. In Krock's retelling, Joe came to believe that his son took on the dangerous mission that killed him not to outdo his younger brother's heroics, as most assumed, but to disprove the image his father had created of the Kennedys as cowards and capitulators. Then, just three weeks later, Jack lost his brother-in-law and Ormsby-Gore his best friend and first cousin when Billy Hartington was killed by a sniper in Belgium. In rapid succession, the two men suffered terrible loss. In time, however, they would come to mitigate these losses through their own enduring friendship.

With the war finally over, a saddened but newly motivated Jack Kennedy returned to London in the spring of 1945, his first visit in six years. Though still gaunt from his serious war injuries, Kennedy eagerly delved into his new work as a journalist for the Hearst Newspaper Group, assigned to cover the British general election pitting the war hero Churchill against Labour Party leader Clement Attlee. Most afternoons when he returned from reporting, he would hole up in his Grosvenor Hotel suite, where Ormsby-Gore and a few other British friends would join him for drinks and spirited political debate. To perceptive friends like Ormsby-Gore, it was clear Kennedy was observing the campaign as much "with an eye to his own political future" as to how the British would vote (they shocked themselves—and the world—by voting out the war hero). The overwhelming impression Ormsby-Gore and others had of their American friend was that he had become a grown-up—a more serious, sober, and substantive man than the one they remembered.

Soon the newly reunited men fell right back into their familiar patterns of rapid-fire gossip. As close as they were before, the two friends were now even more solidly bonded as a result of Billy Hartington's death. After his passing, David and Sissie deepened their relationship with both

Kick and, by extension, Jack. To David, Jack became another "cousin" to be counted among their large clannish family, which in the world of British aristocracy was "no small matter."

One reason Jack's friends suspected he was eyeing a political future was the opening that came with his older brother's death. While shattering, Joe's death was also liberating, freeing Jack to pursue a political career once thought reserved only for the eldest son. In truth, Jack had never been especially close to his older brother, and they often competed for the spotlight. At a fifty-fifth birthday party for Joe Kennedy Sr. two years earlier, a close friend, after toasting the guest of honor, had offered a second toast to the absent ambassador's second son, "our own hero, Lieutenant John Kennedy of the United States Navy." Ignored was Joe Jr., seated right next to his dad and who in mere days would himself set off for war. Later that night, the snubbed son was heard sobbing in his bed: "By God, I'll show them." Now, in Joe's absence, Ormsby-Gore could sense from those late-afternoon talks Kennedy's ambition to emerge from his brother's long shadow.

Ormsby-Gore, on the other hand, remained as baffled about his future as he had been in 1938. The war years had given him a family but not a career. "I hadn't got a clue what I wanted to do in life," Ormsby-Gore later reflected on these postwar years. While other close friends were standing for seats in the Commons, Ormsby-Gore defaulted to spending time with his father learning how to manage the family's estates.

Ormsby-Gore's observation about Jack's political aspirations was prescient. Returning home that fall, Kennedy decided he would rather shape events than cover them as a journalist. He carefully weighed several potential races before deciding to run for an open seat in Congress from his hometown of Boston. Despite having left the city almost twenty years earlier, his family still maintained strong political connections to the district. Jack put that network—and his father's fortune—to immediate use, bombarding the district with paid advertising and get-out-the-vote efforts while enlisting his sisters to organize teas for female voters dazzled by the handsome young war hero. He was a patrician candidate campaigning in the blue-collar saloons and docks of a district that should have been repelled by his family and his wealth. Yet in a field of ten that included two prominent longtime Boston pols, Kennedy outhustled and outsmarted his competitors, convincing skeptics that he had the grit, guts, and substance to represent their interests in Congress. On primary day he won handily, doubling the vote total of his next closest competitor. In the general election he won in a rout. Observing Kennedy's success, Ormsby-Gore found it both "fairly remarkable" and "impressive and somehow a little difficult to take seriously"—reactions perhaps as much tinged with envy as with memories of their cavorting through London as carefree youths.

Even in good times, however, tragedy never seemed far away. By 1948, Kick had fallen in love again, this time with Peter Fitzwilliam, a soon-to-be-divorced Protestant aristocrat she planned to marry—again over her parents' strenuous objections. On May 13 of that year, the couple was flying from Paris to the Riviera when their storm-tossed plane went down into the hills of the Rhone Valley, killing them instantly. Kick Kennedy was only twenty-eight years old. Her death left Jack so distraught that even after he had flown to New York to board the plane to her funeral in England, he couldn't summon the strength to continue the trip. Shattered themselves, Ormsby-Gore and his wife were among the mourners. Six weeks after Kick's passing, Jack finally made the trip to London to tend to her affairs. When the moment came to visit her grave, he still couldn't leave London to do it.

"True freedom means pushing oneself to the full all the time, always knowing of one's approaching end," Kennedy wrote to Ormsby-Gore later that spring.

Jack's electoral success coupled with Kick's sudden death seemed finally to shake Ormsby-Gore from his decade-long lethargy. In 1950, he won a seat in the House of Commons—almost by accident. Filled with ambivalence, Ormsby-Gore had taken the baby step that summer of putting his name on a list of Conservative candidates for the seat. He never expected to be chosen, but the committee selected him thanks to his social status and his experience overseeing the family estate. Later, the voters elected him to Parliament.

A few months after Ormsby-Gore's surprising ascendance, Kennedy arrived in London to see his old friend newly absorbed in his own role as a public official. For this trip, in addition to the usual briefing papers on British defense policy, Kennedy brought with him a brown paper parcel filled with food, nylon stockings, and other wares he dispensed to Ormsby-Gore and friends suffering from shortages caused by an English economy in free fall. In addition to the usual rounds of dinners, golf, and afternoons at "drafty country houses," they spent the bulk of their time talking about foreign policy, seeking to shape themes they had pondered together in their youth into cogent worldviews. Both by then were staunch anticommunists and believed that only a unified Europe, with a strong US-UK alliance, could act as an effective bulwark against an expansionist Soviet Union. They would translate that shared conviction into practice many times over the next dozen years.

As the 1950s advanced, so too did the public careers and private lives of the two friends. In 1952, thirty-five-year-old Kennedy was elected to the Senate, narrowly defeating the incumbent Henry Cabot Lodge. Meanwhile, Ormsby-Gore swiftly rose up the hierarchy of the Commons and the British Foreign Service, due in no small measure to the mentor he found in Selwyn Lloyd. When Churchill was reelected prime minister in 1951, he appointed Lloyd minister of state for foreign affairs, the effective deputy to the foreign secretary. Lloyd needed a parliamentary private secretary and offered the position to Ormsby-Gore; accepting it changed Ormsby-Gore's life. At the UN General Assembly session that fall in Paris, where the topics included Soviet-bloc containment and disarmament, Ormsby-Gore quickly established his expertise in both realms, putting him on a path that would have profound benefits for both his own career and that of his friend in the US Senate.

A year after becoming a senator, Kennedy became a husband, marrying Jacqueline Lee Bouvier before eight hundred family members and friends at St. Mary's Roman Catholic Church in Newport, Rhode Island. No fewer than five priests took part in celebrating the wedding mass.

With a larger prize than a Senate seat in his sights, Kennedy now turned his attention to the issues that would give him added credibility and position him as a future presidential candidate. Once again, he confronted the question of what constitutes leadership in a democracy, this time in the context of the Cold War. In an essay for the *New York Times Magazine* published a year after his wedding, Kennedy argued that weapons of mass destruction now in the possession of the two world superpowers made the decisions of its leaders more consequential than ever before. Poor decisions by leaders in the past could cost millions of lives. Poor decisions today might imperil "the very existence of mankind." Consequently, Kennedy argued, the *duty* of a leader was "not to pander to people's false beliefs in an effort to win votes, but rather to take steps to educate and enlighten public opinion." Sixteen years after first debating with Ormsby-Gore about the disparate approaches of Baldwin and Churchill, Kennedy at least for the moment had moved decisively toward the Churchill camp—a shift made abundantly clear in the way he advocated for strong, unwavering diplomacy as a response to the Soviets, rather than the overly confrontational approach that many Americans were then demanding.

When it came to actually negotiating with the Soviets, few people in the world boasted more experience or skill at the craft than Ormsby-Gore, who had spent three excruciating years across the table from them. He possessed the unique ability to bring seemingly irreconcilable parties to agreement around positions they once thought unimaginable but, through his persuasion, now believed they had a stake in.

A week after the publication of his article, Kennedy invited Ormsby-Gore to spend the weekend with him and Jackie at their home in Hyannis Port. It was not only David's first visit to the compound, but also the moment that Jack's "twenty-five year conversation with British friends shifted to American soil." Ormsby-Gore told Kennedy that Stalin's recent passing in 1953 had rendered the Soviet leadership more pliable, making worthwhile negotiations possible. In Ormsby-Gore's view, negotiating wasn't a tactic out of Chamberlain's appeasement playbook but a "strategy to bring about the downfall of Soviet Communism." If Kennedy really wanted to lay the tracks for the Soviets' eventual demise, Ormsby-Gore argued, the United States must *engage* with them in disarmament talks. This might have seemed like a counterintuitive argument, but it clicked with Kennedy. As Jackie recalled: "From then on, Jack started to say in his speeches that it was a disgrace that there were less than a hundred people working on disarmament in Washington."

Leaming, who wrote a biography of Jackie in addition to her account of Kennedy's evolution as a statesman, later captured how Jackie viewed Ormsby-Gore's influence over her husband: "Jackie loved in Jack the man he wanted to be, and David was the man helping him, in her eyes, to be the man Jack wanted to be."

Kennedy would return to the issue of disarmament many times in the future, but first he had pressing health concerns to address. Despite appearing vigorous and healthy, Kennedy at thirty-seven was anything but. Ever since childhood, Kennedy had battled debilitating health conditions that often required extensive stays in hospitals. Never showing a hint of his struggles in public, Kennedy at various times suffered chronic pain borne of a degenerative back, Addison's disease, and severe intestinal ailments. Now in 1954 he was facing his second back operation in a decade, this time a delicate spinal fusion. Ormsby-Gore went to New York with Jack and Jackie for the surgery. In one of the pre-op meetings, with Ormsby-Gore by his side, the doctors told Kennedy he had a fifty-fifty chance of surviving the procedure. "I'd rather be dead than spend the rest of my life hobbling on crutches and paralyzed by pain," he told his friend.

Kennedy survived the surgery, barely, coming so close to death that a priest came to perform last rites. After yet another operation and then a long recuperation, Kennedy regained enough strength to travel back to England the following year.

Through the remainder of the decade, both Ormsby-Gore and Kennedy would enjoy meteoric rises within their respective political establishments. In 1956, Kennedy lost the vice presidential nomination but gained national stature as a rising political star with Hollywood appeal, a rare commodity during a time of gray political personalities. His constant health battles had one decided upside: With so much time spent on his back convalescing, Kennedy could write his Pulitzer Prize–winning book, which brought him additional fame and gravitas. In many ways, *Profiles in Courage* was a paean to Churchill's conception of leadership. Meanwhile, Ormsby-Gore also experienced his own notable run of professional success, having been promoted to replace Lloyd as minister of state.

Kennedy and Ormsby-Gore took full advantage of each other's growing prominence, consulting on crises and acting as sounding boards for one another. During Kennedy's successful Senate reelection campaign in 1958, he used the race to test out themes he and Ormsby-Gore had been debating for twenty years. Comparing President Eisenhower to Baldwin a generation earlier, Kennedy argued that Eisenhower had wasted the last several years while the Soviets rebuilt their military capabilities. The result, he warned, was an imminent "missile gap" in which the United States would lose its nuclear superiority. His appropriation of Churchill's pre–World War II rhetoric helped him win an overwhelming victory and notice as a formidable new national candidate.

By 1959, as Kennedy contemplated launching a bid for the presidency, Ormsby-Gore began sharing details of his continuing talks with the Soviets about ending nuclear weapons testing. Kennedy understood it wasn't enough just to fearmonger over a looming "missile gap": He also had to offer Americans a practical solution. He began pressing his friend on how such a treaty limiting arms could be achieved. Ormsby-Gore responded with a memorandum laying out in detail the process and substance by which the United States could secure a historic agreement. It so resonated with Kennedy that it became a standard talking point in his writings and speeches. By combining tough talk now with diplomatic outreach, Kennedy could present himself as a hawk who would nonetheless pursue a realistic path to peace. In typical understatement, Ormsby-Gore recalled his influence on Kennedy's "carrot and stick" approach: "I noticed in certain speeches . . . that he did make it quite a theme."

Later that year, Kennedy made another trip to Britain, during which he had his first face-to-face encounter with one of his heroes, Winston

Churchill. Ironically, the meeting took place on Aristotle Onassis's 325-foot yacht *Christina*, on which Kennedy's widow nine years later would live for months at a time as Onassis's wife. That night, Kennedy wore a tan mess jacket with a black tie. Churchill by then was showing signs of aging, physically and mentally, and often failed to recognize even prominent people. One witness recounted that as the Kennedys were leaving, Jackie half-kiddingly told her star-struck husband, "I think he thought you were the waiter, Jack."

Once Kennedy declared his candidacy for president in early 1960, he made a disquieting discovery about his foreign policy team: Like other young candidates who came before and after him, he found his reputedly wise men either condescending or too fixed in their views to have a meaningful conversation. They most assuredly didn't align with the Kennedy campaign's "New Frontier" themes of innovation and imagination. With his relative lack of experience in foreign affairs, Kennedy needed someone with the requisite wisdom, experience, and humility to counsel him throughout the campaign.

And so a scion of British royalty became a highly placed—and highly unofficial—foreign policy advisor to a candidate for the American presidency. Kennedy would call Ormsby-Gore often for quick input on a foreign policy issue, and when they got together in person, said Hugh Sidey, a journalist and Kennedy friend, "The two men were sometimes closeted together for six hours or more completely enraptured by the mutual intellectual challenge of the moment." In his oral history for the Kennedy Library, Ormsby-Gore recalled one such moment before the Wisconsin primary when they stayed up late into the night talking "arms control and disarmament issues" before the senator flew off to greet workers at a Milwaukee factory gate. Dave Powers later remembered how the bone-weary candidate, with no sleep and one bad cup of coffee, still managed to shake every last hand. Kennedy won the primary and went on to sweep enough of the remaining contests to secure a first-ballot victory at the Democratic National Convention in Los Angeles that summer.

As the general campaign unfolded, Ormsby-Gore kept Kennedy abreast of developments in arms talks and provided sharp insight into the status of Soviet military might. He confidently told Kennedy that the Soviet nuclear arsenal did not exceed that of the United States, as Kennedy himself knew. But Ormsby-Gore also realized that the so-called missile gap remained a politically potent issue among American voters, and so he was willing to overlook his friend's bending the truth to gain electoral advantage. By constantly invoking the "missile gap" and vowing to surpass the USSR in nuclear capabilities, Kennedy could thwart the efforts of his Republican opponent, Richard Nixon, to paint him as soft on communism.

And that is what he did, reprising the strategy he so successfully employed in the 1958 election. In effect, Kennedy channeled the Churchill of the 1930s, even employing the words "locust years" as he called for America to rearm. But this time he coupled his bellicosity with language promising he would also pursue diplomacy to achieve a breakthrough arms control treaty. Guided by Ormsby-Gore's astute offstage counsel, Kennedy managed to thread the needle and find a way to present himself as the candidate of both peace and military strength.

It was deft messaging, and it worked. Kennedy edged Nixon to become America's youngest-ever elected president, at the age of forty-three years, 236 days. Less than a week after Kennedy's election, Ormsby-Gore as minister of state formally requested Foreign Office approval to approach the president-elect as a representative of the British government. More than a few officials back in London thought Ormsby-Gore was overreaching and blocked him. What they failed to appreciate was the true depth of the men's friendship. Before the Foreign Office even made a final decision, Kennedy had silenced their skepticism by reaching out to Ormsby-Gore first. They met a week later for a ninety-minute lunch at the Carlyle Hotel in New York.

At 12:20 p.m. on the bitterly cold afternoon of January 20, 1961, John F. Kennedy took the oath of office as America's thirty-fifth president.

His inaugural address—one of the shortest in history, at a brisk fourteen minutes—stirred the world as he spoke of how "we shall pay any price, bear any burden, meet any hardship, support any friend, oppose any foe to assure the survival and success of liberty." The new president's British friends, those who had known him back in the summer of 1938, expressed the most astonishment. "It was as though one had gone to sleep knowing Jack as a charming young student or promising political apprentice and woken up to find him the most powerful man in Christendom," Selwyn Lloyd marveled.

The President and Ormsby-Gore had his first extended sit-down five weeks after the inauguration. Over dinner in the residence of the White House, Kennedy told Ormsby-Gore of the four consequential foreign policy decisions he would soon have to make—all leftovers from the Eisenhower administration. To frame and then address these issues, he and Ormsby-Gore returned to their familiar paradigm: choosing between boldness and caution.

This night, however, Kennedy had ample reason to feel emboldened: He had just learned that his approval ratings after his first month in office were four points higher than Eisenhower's at a comparable period. The question Kennedy now debated with Ormsby-Gore was whether to use that popularity to do what he thought right: admit Communist China into the UN and not support the anti-communist forces fighting in Laos—positions he knew Eisenhower and a majority of the public opposed. Carefully weighing both sides with Ormsby-Gore reassured Kennedy his instincts were right. He would delay a decision on China while remaining neutral on Laos. As the men continued to talk past midnight they also agreed that the upcoming nuclear test ban talks held the promise of a groundbreaking treaty both desperately sought.

There was one topic, though, that Kennedy could not be forthcoming about: what he planned to do in Cuba, where communist Fidel Castro had led a successful revolution two years earlier. The president was weeks away from approving a flawed invasion plan in which the CIA would dispatch fourteen hundred half-trained Cuban exiles to the Bay of Pigs to topple Castro's regime. That night he could only hint at the troubles he faced, since Ormsby-Gore was a British official. Despite the president's absolute trust in his friend, even their friendship faced hard limits when it came to the CIA's clandestine operations. So Kennedy had to conceal his profound doubts about Eisenhower's leftover Cuba team and the poorly planned scheme he would soon authorize. One can only speculate that had Kennedy enjoyed the benefit of Ormsby-Gore's informed judgment, history might have turned out differently. Instead, in April 1961, twelve hundred American sympathizers were either killed or captured on the beaches of Cuba, dealing Kennedy a humiliating loss.

Two months later, heavily medicated for his back pain and other ailments and demoralized by the Cuban debacle, Kennedy had his first meeting with Soviet leader Nikita Khrushchev. At his February dinner with Ormsby-Gore, Kennedy had raised the idea of an informal summit with Khrushchev as an opportunity for the two men to get to know one other. Wary from years studying the combative Soviet leader and negotiating with his team, Ormsby-Gore bluntly told Kennedy the idea was "premature" and bound to fail: Khrushchev wasn't one for small talk and would want to use the time, whatever the president's intentions, to press his own agenda.

Ormsby-Gore proved right. The Vienna summit was a disaster by all accounts, including the president's. "Worst thing in my life," he vented to a *New York Times* reporter. "He savaged me." Kennedy felt browbeaten and belittled, and he left Vienna convinced Khrushchev thought him weak and America vulnerable. By the time he got to London, Kennedy looked "worn out," remembered Ormsby-Gore. Before beginning his official duties, the president and First Lady went to Jackie's sister's home near Buckingham Palace. There, among a few of Kennedy's London intimates, Ormsby-Gore found his friend in "great pain.... There is no doubt that Khrushchev made a very unpleasant impression on him. That's what he said to me.... That Khrushchev obviously tried to browbeat him and frighten him. He had displayed the naked power of the Soviet Union."

The next morning Kennedy was scheduled to meet with Prime Minister Macmillan and his senior advisors. The avuncular British leader immediately sensed the president's distress. As the American motorcade pulled up to the Admiralty House, according to notes taken of the moment, Macmillan took one look at Kennedy, put his arm around his shoulder, and, scrapping the larger meeting, took him upstairs for a private chat that would last two and a half hours. Despite the early hour, the prime minister offered him a stiff drink—"which was accepted." At the president's request, Ormsby-Gore joined the two leaders at the end of their marathon talk, and he later described the one-on-one meeting as "the beginning of a much closer understanding" between the two leaders and a stronger relationship between the two countries.

In the early afternoon, the president put aside his physical and emotional pain to lunch with Ormsby-Gore and various other British friends. Afterward, the president and his friend talked alone, deliberating on how to position the failed Vienna summit the next night in Kennedy's address to the American people. The president was determined not to repeat the mistake Chamberlain had made in 1938 when he returned from Munich to famously and falsely proclaim "peace for our time." Ormsby-Gore urged him to speak with complete candor, telling the nation the hard, unpleasant truths that he had learned from Vienna and not to sugarcoat anything. Kennedy agreed. The next night, when Kennedy delivered the address, he struck a notably subdued tone, telling the American people of a "very sober two days" during which no progress had been "either achieved or pretended."

There was never any doubt that—at the first opportunity—Prime Minister Macmillan would appoint David Ormsby-Gore to the post of British ambassador to the United States. Both sides saw the urgency and advantages of having so close a friend to the president helping oversee the special relationship between the two countries. Meeting with Kennedy in Key West, Florida, in March 1961, Macmillan asked the president if he had any views on a suitable new ambassador. As Selwyn Lloyd later recalled, the president gave "that dazzling smile of his, like a boy in a toothpaste advertisement," and said, "I'd like David." He got David.

At Ormsby-Gore's White House investiture six months later, Kennedy happily expressed what everyone in the room knew to be true: his great pleasure at the United Kingdom's decision to "appoint you, an old friend, as her representative." Almost immediately, Ormsby-Gore became, in Macmillan's words, an "invigorating new spirit" in the Atlantic alliance. Not only did no other ambassador in Washington have a closer relationship to Kennedy; no senior White House, State Department, or Pentagon officials did either—much to the dismay of Secretary of State Dean Rusk, who complained the president saw more of "that man" than any of his own top advisors.

This closeness benefited both men. In December 1961, Kennedy and Ormsby-Gore met for one of many private dinners over the course of Kennedy's thousand days in office. As they settled into their seats, Ormsby-Gore told the president that he had just heard from Macmillan that the British government could fall if the UN continued to threaten sanctions against British-backed troops in the Congo. Without delay, the president picked up the phone and called both the State Department and his UN ambassador to request a total reversal of US policy in the region. "I have got David Gore sitting beside me here. He will explain what it is the British government wants done, and I want it done," he told them. By the next morning, the threat of sanctions was lifted. The Macmillan government held.

Kennedy could possibly afford to be generous to his friend because at that moment no vital US interest was at stake in the Congo. Nevertheless, as Ormsby-Gore later said, the president was "wonderful. He threw the full weight of his authority behind getting the results that [we] required."

Later, reflecting on the outsized influence Ormsby-Gore had on his brother, Robert Kennedy said the ambassador was the only diplomat with whom the president "really had a close relationship at all. My brother would rather have his judgment than that of almost anybody else.... He was part of the family, really." If anyone doubted that claim, they need only notice the black ambassadorial Rolls-Royce parked most days at the White House.

By the time Ormsby-Gore walked into the White House "unseen" on Sunday morning, October 21, 1962, Kennedy was six days into the Cuban Missile Crisis, with the United States and the Soviet Union eyeball-to-eyeball in a standoff that seemed to be inching terrifyingly close to nuclear engagement. The night before, Kennedy had finally decided on a blockade as the military approach he would take, overruling generals like Curtis LeMay who favored bombing Cuba. Still, the president sought the input and reassurance of the man whose judgment in such situations he trusted most. As Ormsby-Gore later recalled, he had "a pretty good idea of what was already happening" from the CIA reports shared with the British, but he knew none of the particulars.

Unlike during the Bay of Pigs, the president this time eagerly filled in Ormsby-Gore on all the details of the looming showdown. He shared satellite photos of the missile sites, then laid out the bombing or blockade options that had been presented to him. Measured and thoughtful, Ormsby-Gore argued for a blockade, believing bombing would only escalate matters. The rest of the world wouldn't understand such overt aggression, he said, and it would also likely compel the Soviets to move against West Berlin. But Kennedy countered: Isn't this our best chance to take the strongest possible action to deter Castro from ever trying to do this again?

The conversation went back and forth this way for an hour. In unusually passionate language, Kennedy declared that the mere existence of nuclear weapons made "a secure and rational world impossible." Ormsby-Gore had rarely heard his friend speak so openly and emotionally. Perhaps all their discussions around test bans and disarmament had taken root, Ormsby-Gore thought. Later that night, when he and his wife, Sissie, returned to the White House for dinner, the president and Ormsby-Gore continued to debate the language that Kennedy should use to announce the blockade to the American people the following evening. The decision had been made, but Kennedy was still agonizing over it.

Two nights later, the Ormsby-Gores—along with Andrew Devonshire and his wife, as well as two other British friends from their World War II days—returned to the White House for a long-planned dinner with the president and Jackie. The poignancy of the moment wasn't lost on any of them. A quarter century before, they had shared similar meals, wondering whether bombs would soon be raining down on them. At the end of the dinner, with Soviet ships fast approaching the quarantined zone, the president excused himself and took Ormsby-Gore to the Long Gallery to further strategize the imminent showdown. Over brandy and cigars, the two men began discussing how poorly Kennedy's speech the night before had been received in Europe. The president had declared that the launch of Cuban nuclear missiles on *any* nation in the Western Hemisphere would be viewed as an attack on the United States, requiring a swift and full retaliatory attack on the Soviets. Ever suspicious of the CIA, Europeans remained deeply skeptical over whether the Soviet missiles were as threatening as Kennedy described or even existed in Cuba at all.

Ormsby-Gore offered a solution: Why couldn't the United States release some irrefutable evidence such as U-2 photos of the missile sites? Intrigued, Kennedy asked for photos to be brought up to him. Jackie later recalled walking in on the two men "squatting on the floor" looking at satellite pictures, trying to determine the best ones to release. And when they were made public the following day, each photo included a "clear explanatory" note—just as Ormsby-Gore had recommended.

After resolving this problem, Kennedy told Ormsby-Gore that his brother Bobby had learned earlier in the evening about the Soviets' plans to have their ships "go on to Cuba" right through the blockade. That news led Ormsby-Gore to question the current perimeter of the quarantine zone itself. Looking at a map that put the zone at eight hundred miles from Cuba's shoreline, Ormsby-Gore asked the obvious question: Was that the right point to intercept the Soviet ships? Without any instructions at all from his government, Ormsby-Gore began to argue "rather strongly" that the perimeter needed to be shifted closer to Cuba "to give the Russians a little bit more time" to consider the gravity of breaking the blockade. Intrigued again, the president called Defense Secretary Robert McNamara and asked why the perimeter had been set at its current point. The answer Kennedy received—if the perimeter was moved in closer, Cuban planes would be able to intervene in any confrontation—failed to satisfy him. He pushed back. That night, the blockade line changed to five hundred miles, exactly the distance that Ormsby-Gore advised. As important as Ormsby-Gore thought it was to give the Soviets the extra three hundred miles to turn back, he nevertheless reinforced to Kennedy the importance of showing resolve. Vienna still weighed on both men's minds. If Khrushchev had any inkling that he could bully the president, the situation would prove "disastrous," Ormsby-Gore reminded him.

That night and throughout the thirteen days of the crisis, Kennedy obsessed over every strategic detail. At some point, Ormsby-Gore recalled a particular concern the president suddenly raised: What if all the military aircraft massing in Florida were "drawn up in their usual lines" and the Cubans decided to strike? They could all be knocked out by just one Cuban fighter strafing down the line. With painful memories of Pearl Harbor still fresh two decades later, Kennedy wasn't going to let that mistake be repeated under his command. Getting on the phone again with McNamara, he asked for a photoreconnaissance flight to ensure the dispersal of the planes. "No need," McNamara assured the president, "they've already been scattered." Kennedy insisted on double-checking. "They flew over and all the planes were in line up and down the runway," Ormsby-Gore later recounted.

Ormsby-Gore would remain a presence at the White House for the next six days. His proximity to the seat of power did not go unnoticed. Vice President Lyndon Johnson complained that "the limey" was seated "front and center" at a meeting of a steering group that week in the White House Situation Room, while he himself was "down in a chair at the end, with the goddamned door banging in my back." Afterward, Jackie described Ormsby-Gore's presence then and later as "indispensable," adding: "If I could think of anyone now [after Jack's death] who could save the Western world, it would be David Gore."

With Ormsby-Gore's counsel, Kennedy stared down Khrushchev, and this time he didn't blink, securing a settlement that eliminated the offensive Soviet missiles from Cuba in return for a guarantee—not made public at the time—that the United States would remove its own missiles from Turkey. When the crisis had passed, Ormsby-Gore sent a handwritten note to the president expressing his "admiration for the superb manner" in which he conducted himself throughout the crisis despite the "mass of conflicting advice you received." Kennedy kept the letter in the Resolute Desk in the Oval Office for the remainder of his life.

With Cuba behind them, the two friends shifted their focus back to a nuclear test ban treaty—the single best way in their minds to deescalate a Cold War that might drive the world to extinction. Their first hopeful sign that after the fits and starts of the previous twenty-four months a pact could now be achieved came while they were vacationing in Palm Beach with their families just before Christmas in 1962. The Soviet premier sent a letter indicating his willingness to negotiate not just a test ban treaty but one with verifiable inspections. Kennedy and Ormsby-Gore were jubilant. Just three months earlier, they had barely averted a nuclear war. Now in mid-January 1963, they were starting bilateral negotiations in New York to rein in those very weapons. A week later, with Kennedy's approval, Ormsby-Gore joined the talks as the British observer, and work got underway. That very day, in a signal to the Russians of his full commitment, Kennedy postponed already scheduled underground nuclear tests for up to three weeks while the negotiators met.

That single move proved to be a bridge too far for those still skeptical of the Soviets' intentions. As soon as Kennedy postponed the tests, Republicans began to attack him for appeasement. The most stinging criticism came from the one Republican he most feared politically—New York governor Nelson Rockefeller, who said Kennedy's concessions "threatened the future security of the U.S. and the world." The adulation that had enveloped Kennedy after the missile crisis—the resolute, confident leader who stood up to the Commies—soon gave way to fears for his reelection in 1964.

Kennedy and Ormsby-Gore retreated to Palm Beach in late February 1963 to assess the president's quandary. Kennedy, convinced that a treaty with the Soviets would not survive a Senate vote, was not willing to take on a major political risk that might threaten his electoral prospects—no matter how much he believed in the treaty's merits. A shaken Ormsby-Gore used every argument he could to move Kennedy away from his Baldwin-like mindset, but for once his efforts seemed futile.

One man who emphatically would not give up, however, was Prime Minister Macmillan. Having seen the horrors of world war firsthand, he refused to let the chance of averting an even more deadly one elude him. The prime minister grasped, even appreciated, the political risks Kennedy faced in advocating for the ban. But he nonetheless believed this was *the* moment to take such a risk. Ensuring peace, Macmillan believed, was too important to be left to the whims of politicians and their electoral prospects. He circled back to Ormsby-Gore with a question: How can we reengage the president and change his mind? At his ambassador's suggestion, Macmillan wrote a thirteen-page letter that addressed all of Kennedy's concerns in language he knew from Ormsby-Gore would resonate with the president. The prime minister appealed to his sense of duty as a leader, invoking the predictable Churchill references about finishing the work while time remained. The test ban treaty, Macmillan wrote, represented the "most important step" they could take as leaders.

The president and Ormsby-Gore met five days later to discuss the Macmillan letter. In this moment, would Kennedy emerge as a disciple of Baldwin or of Churchill? Would he do the right thing—what he *knew* needed to be done—no matter the political consequences? Ormsby-Gore homed in again on the essence of duty, emphasizing Macmillan's deeply held belief that leaders were called to "change the course of history and guide it in a direction which would be of benefit to our peoples." Kennedy wanted to be that sort of leader, but he couldn't escape the hard political realities at play. If he advocated for a treaty and then lost the election to someone like Rockefeller, nuclear testing worldwide would continue indefinitely. However, as Ormsby-Gore pointed out flatly to his friend, that was the same morally weak argument Baldwin had used against rearming, when he told critics he might be replaced by the spineless Labour Party if he took such a route. Still, the conversation ended without a decision.

Then fate made a timely intervention. In the midst of Kennedy's anguished deliberations, the United States granted Winston Churchill honorary citizenship. The president commemorated the occasion with a Rose Garden ceremony broadcast nationally as well as in Britain. Too frail to travel, Churchill sent his son Randolph, an old friend of Kick's, to accept the honor. After downing a full bottle of Beefeater Gin, Randolph (whose drinking problem was well known) read out loud to the gathered dignitaries his father's remarks, including his call for a robust British role in shaping the new Cold War world: "Let no man underrate our energies, our potentialities and our abiding power for good." Kennedy listened with surging emotion. Hearing the words of Churchill's son—whose preface to *Arms and the Covenant* had first laid out the Baldwin-Churchill divide twenty-five years earlier—finally convinced him that he had to do what was *right*. Kennedy pulled Ormsby-Gore aside later at the reception to tell him the treaty was back on.

Two days after the ceremony, the president called Macmillan to tell him that Averill Harriman was headed to the USSR as his personal emissary to secure a test ban agreement with Khrushchev. For the next two months, Kennedy would become the evangelist in chief, devoting significant political capital to selling the test ban to a skeptical public and Senate. Soon, his message that America must move from a "strategy of annihilation" to a "strategy of peace" started to gain traction with a public weary from years of nuclear brinkmanship.

In the midst of his test ban barnstorming, Kennedy took a detour to Germany to make a series of speeches. One of them became the famous "Ich bin ein Berliner" ("I am a Berliner") address—widely regarded as the most audacious speech of Kennedy's presidency and perhaps of the entire Cold War era—in which he personally identified with the city's valiant struggle against communism. On his way to London afterward for an official visit with Macmillan, the president made two unscheduled, unannounced trips. First, he visited Shropshire, David Ormsby-Gore's home county, spending just enough time to attend a church service and then to walk through the center of town. The visit was so low-key that it only became known in 2013. From there, he flew to the tiny town of Edensor where the president visited, finally, the grave of his sister Kick. Descending in a US Army helicopter, Kennedy made his way to the Devonshire family estate, Chatsworth, where in 1944 Billy Hartington had been laid to rest, followed four years later by his wife, Kick. Fifteen years earlier, Kennedy couldn't overcome his grief to visit her grave. Now standing before it, her favorite brother prayed in the rain for several minutes before laying down a simple wreath. Ormsby-Gore and other family members stood by silently.

The president left London exultant over the success of his trip and looking forward to making further progress on the test ban treaty. As Harriman flew to Moscow to nail down a deal, Kennedy spent the weekend with his old friend in Hyannis Port, where Ormsby-Gore had first laid out his vision for disarmament nine years earlier. Now the two men were about to witness their grand dream become reality. With a pregnant Jackie taking notes, the two men talked, then talked some more. They golfed and monitored the deliberations in Moscow, then returned to Washington with guarded optimism.

Within ten days, Harriman had worked out a treaty that included a full ban on tests underwater, in the atmosphere, and in space (but not underground), with seven annual on-site inspections. Kennedy and Ormsby-Gore called Macmillan to relay the good news; he cried upon hearing it. The following day, the president made a national address announcing the pact, hailing it as the first step toward ending the Cold War. Two days later, with the Ormsby-Gores in tow, the Kennedys retired again to Hyannis Port to celebrate the monumental achievement.

As it turned out, it would take another twenty-five years before the Soviet Union would start to open up and a full thirty years before the Cold War would end. Still, there is no denying that the Limited Test Ban Treaty proved to be a historic milestone for peace in that long struggle.

The two friends had achieved much in the few short years of the Kennedy presidency. From safely navigating the Cuban Missile Crisis to securing the Limited Test Ban Treaty, they shifted the dangerous dynamic between the two superpowers to make the world a safer place. Thanks to the abiding trust and deep friendship shared by Jack Kennedy and David Ormsby-Gore—and their twenty-five-year conversation about leadership—the president of the United States did what was best for the country in the face of enormous political risk.

The morning of November 23, 1963, broke rainy and dreary in Washington, DC. David and Sissie Ormsby-Gore arrived at the White House, but instead of heading straight upstairs to the residence, as was their usual custom, they waited in a somber East Room with family and only a few other close friends for Jackie to come downstairs with her children.

They were there to offer prayers of thanksgiving for the life of Jack Kennedy, who the day before had been assassinated while riding through Dealey Plaza in Dallas. His flag-draped coffin sat on a bier in the middle of the room, surrounded by men representing the five branches of the military, rifles held at their sides. Shortly after ten o'clock, Jackie walked in with Caroline and John Jr. and a short mass commenced. Many people wept openly, and a few, like Ben Bradlee, were so overcome with emotion that they had to leave the room. "Jackie held up the longest," Ormsby-Gore recalled. Afterward, the young widow walked around the room to say a word of comfort to every person there. When she got to David and Sissie, Jackie was so distraught she could barely speak. Still, in her whispered voice, she confided something they had never known in the three months since the Kennedys had lost their third child, Patrick, only days after his birth. Had the baby lived, she told them, Sissie would have been his godmother.

The death of Jack Kennedy affected Ormsby-Gore and Sissie profoundly. In its aftermath, Sissie would ruminate on the dinner she and David had at the White House a few nights before Jack and Jackie left for Dallas. "I told Jack he should have the roof up on the limousine when he drove through Dallas, but he said he couldn't because he didn't want people to think he was scared or hiding," her eldest daughter, Jane, remembered her mother obsessing over afterward. For David, "the sun has gone down and Washington seems desolate and dull in comparison with the still so recent past," he wrote to the recently resigned Macmillan, two months after the assassination.

A few months after vacating the White House for a home in Georgetown, Jackie sent Ormsby-Gore a reminder of his unique place in her late husband's life: a book of poetry by Percy Bysshe Shelley, taken from JFK's personal library and containing his presidential bookplate. Kennedy loved poetry—"What government corrupts, poetry cleanses," he once declared—and Shelley was among his favorite poets. In a note accompanying the gift, Jackie wrote: "I wish I could give you the most precious thing that belonged to him—as precious as your friendship was to him—but nothing tangible could ever express that."

The thrill of his post extinguished, Ormsby-Gore resigned as ambassador during President Lyndon Johnson's second year in office. He returned to England, where he began a second career as a television executive, starting a Welsh television channel with the famed English actor Richard Burton that is still on the air today. In his absence, relations between the two countries suffered, losing "the finesse" that had marked the Kennedy/Macmillan/Ormsby-Gore years.

The people of Great Britain shared Ormsby-Gore's grief. In May 1965, some five thousand people gathered at Runnymede to express their appreciation for what President Kennedy meant to their country. On the sacred ground where in 1215 King John signed the Magna Carta that led to England's constitutional system of government, Queen Elizabeth II granted three acres to the US government on which to erect a memorial honoring the late president's memory. It was an extraordinary and unprecedented gesture by the British government to a foreign leader. Accompanying the queen as she emerged to dedicate the memorial that day were Jackie and her two children, Jack's remaining siblings, and David Ormsby-Gore.

David Ormsby-Gore would live another twenty years after that glorious afternoon. He became the fifth Lord Harlech upon the death of his father, inheriting the vast lands of the barony he knew so well from his wilderness years before entering Parliament. But heartbreak continued to stalk him. His wife, Sissie, with whom he had five children and a loving and happy marriage, would die in a car accident in June 1967—ironically, the same way he had lost his older brother in 1935. Jackie and Robert Kennedy flew to England to attend her funeral and burial.

After Sissie's death, Jackie's friendship with Ormsby-Gore deepened as they sought consolation in their mutual bereavement. Correspondence between the two, saved by Ormsby-Gore in two locked dispatch boxes only discovered in 2017, revealed that the friendship culminated in Ormsby-Gore asking Jackie to marry him. Gently deflecting the proposal in October 1967, Jackie wrote: "If I can ever find some healing and some comfort—it has to be with somebody who is not part of all my world of past and pain.... I can find that now—if the world will let us." A year later, she stayed true to her word by marrying the Greek billionaire Aristotle Onassis. Forlorn but determined to move on himself, Ormsby-Gore too would find a new spouse not within his prior world of pain. In 1969, he married Pamela Colin, an American magazine editor.

But loss would never escape him. Over the next sixteen years, two of David and Sissie's children would also suffer tragic deaths: Their oldest son, Julian, would die from gunshot wounds, an apparent suicide, in 1974; and in 1985 their daughter Alice, who was engaged to guitarist Eric Clapton, died of a heroin overdose. Their two remaining daughters, Victoria and Jane, survive. Jane was rumored to have had an affair with Mick Jagger (all she will acknowledge today is that they are "great friends"), and most still consider her the inspiration for the Rolling Stones song "Lady Jane." His second son, Francis, became the sixth Baron Harlech and sat in the House of Lords until 1999. He died in 2016.

On a winter night in January 1985, David Ormsby-Gore—Lord Harlech—crashed his car while driving over Montford Bridge in Shropshire, England. He had spent his final full day interviewing potential Kennedy scholars who hoped to attend Oxford under a program Ormsby-Gore had helped create and endow after Jack's death. He died the following morning in a nearby hospital—eerily killed just as his brother and wife were. He was sixty-six years old.

His funeral and burial were held in the tiny parish of Ardudwy, Gwynedd, in northwest Wales, home to the Harlech barony. Among the ninety family and friends who crowded into the small church to witness his funeral were Jackie Kennedy Onassis and Senator Edward Kennedy. During the service, the Reverend Robert Hughes eulogized Ormsby-Gore as "a citizen of the world, equally at home in the fertile beauty of Shropshire, the sophistication of London or the special jungle of international diplomacy." Afterward, Ted Kennedy remembered Ormsby-Gore as "the most intelligent man he had ever known." Jackie Onassis "fought back tears" as she left the burial.

It marked the final verse in a long and very special friendship between John F. Kennedy and David Ormsby-Gore, perhaps best described in the words of Percy Shelley, whose book of poetry Jackie had given to Ormsby-Gore shortly after JFK's death:

> *Friendship... a dear balm. A smile among dark frowns; a beloved light:*
> *A solitude, a refuge, a delight.*

CHAPTER 8

Richard Nixon and Bebe Rebozo

Silent Partner

On the night of November 8, 1960, Vice President Richard Nixon settled down in his fifth-floor suite in the Ambassador Hotel in Los Angeles for what he knew would be long, anxious hours in front of his television sets. After campaigning in all fifty states, Nixon could now do little more than wait for the ballots to be counted to determine whether he or Massachusetts senator John Kennedy would be the nation's thirty-fifth president. Nixon's immediate family was down the hall, and political aides were sequestered a floor below. Nixon took out his yellow legal pad; the pad was what one aide later described as his "true" best friend. Nixon started taking notes on the results trickling in from around the country. All three broadcast networks that night were trotting out their newest computer technologies for quicker and more accurate projections. Early in the evening CBS was saying that Nixon was headed toward a big victory while ABC, then a less robust news operation, interrupted its election reporting to show Bugs Bunny cartoons and *The Rifleman* before predicting a more narrow victory for Nixon. At midnight, NBC's RCA 501 computer projected Kennedy would win with 51.1 percent of the vote. As the hours ground on, the flickering black-and-white images on the TVs a few feet away from Nixon were all telling him the same thing: It was going to be an agonizingly close election.

A loner since childhood, Nixon wanted only one other person by his side that night, the most important of his life. Remarkably, Nixon had known him for only nine of his forty-five years, but in that short time they had formed a bond unlike any other in his life. The two rarely if ever talked politics, didn't share the same party affiliation, and often spent large chunks of time together in silence. But there was something in this man's soothing and calm presence that gave Nixon comfort, almost a reassurance that the world wasn't quite as hostile as his paranoid mind told him.

Nixon's friend wasn't judgmental, didn't often if ever challenge him, and never brought up unpleasant topics. They both came from modest backgrounds but through dint of hard work and sharp instincts had become successes in their respective fields. The only man in the country to witness the torment Richard Nixon suffered over losing the closest general election in presidential history—100,000 votes out of 65,000,000 cast—was a banker and businessman from Florida who met Nixon on a boating excursion off of Key Biscayne. His name was Bebe Rebozo, and over the next fifteen years, he would become one of the most famous First Friends ever—as much for his ubiquitous, dapper presence as for his role in the most infamous scandal in presidential history.

Charles Gregory ("Bebe") Rebozo was born two months before Nixon, on November 17, 1912. He was the youngest of nine children in a family of Cuban emigres that traced their ancestry to the Canary Islands. He acquired his nickname, Bebe, from a brother who couldn't pronounce his name, resorting instead to the Spanish word for "baby"—*bebe*—which stuck for life. Young Bebe grew up first in Tampa and then in Miami. He helped add to his father's modest earnings by delivering the *Miami Herald*. In the fifth grade he took on a second job, killing and plucking chickens for a local poultry market. "I had never killed a chicken before and I've never killed one since, but it was the only job I could get at the time," he later said.

Bebe had big ambitions. He wanted to be an entrepreneur, without knowing yet what the word meant. Still in high school and slinging newspapers, he was beginning to think more boldly about what he could do with his modest delivery savings. He settled on real estate—putting down $25 for a small lot in a nearby town. He never actually saw or even took possession of the property, and lost it during the Depression after failing to make timely payments. But Rebozo was learning, most important, that the best way for him to succeed in school and in business was to be modest and unobtrusive—smiling a lot while speaking little. More charming than scholarly, he was known best for the white suits he wore and the deft moves he made on the dance floor. His fellow classmates voted him the best-looking boy of his senior class.

Just after graduating, Rebozo married his high school girlfriend, Claire Gunn, the sister of his best friend. By 1933, the marriage was annulled, with Claire claiming it had never been consummated. Nine decades later, that fact would be used in part to suggest Bebe was gay and that the basis for his relationship with Nixon was sexual somehow, but no evidence ever emerged to support either claim. In fact, in the thirties, lawyers often counseled clients to use that reason as an easy and quick way to obtain an annulment in state courts.

In 1930, Rebozo secured a job with the fledgling airline Pan American as one of its first ten stewards assigned to the sea planes that flew between Miami and the West Indies as well as to Panama. During his year as a steward, he saved enough money to buy a gas station in Miami. A year later, he closed the business and made his living driving tourists around the city. But his fortunes began to turn when he was able to open, in 1935, a new service station—Rebozo's Service Station and Auto Supplies. This time business was good. Months before the Japanese attack on Pearl Harbor, he added a new feature to the station—recapping tires—on the advice of a silent investor and friend who had inside information from his government job that with war looming there would be rubber shortages.

Rebozo spent the war as a Pan Am navigator on loan to the US Army while one of his eight brothers ran the service station. When his friend's tip proved right, Rebozo's tire business exploded, returning him to civilian life a wealthy man. He used his newfound status to make inroads into Miami's elite. His experience as a steward provided him with the manners to assimilate into a world that had once been beyond his reach. Rebozo learned to fly and bought a small plane. He became more involved in the community, sponsoring baseball and bowling leagues and making major commitments to the Boys' Club and Junior Achievement. Meanwhile, he smartly spotted the opportunity to capitalize on the hot real estate market of postwar Miami and began buying "every good property I could afford"—including large lots in Biscayne Bay such as the one that would become known in the Nixon years as "the winter White House." All the while, Rebozo kept building businesses, buying a single laundromat that quickly turned into a chain and seeding two finance companies where he served as a principal. With his wealth, he bought a new house on Key Biscayne's most expensive street and a new boat that he loved to skipper. He also remarried his ex-wife, Claire.

By his forty-second birthday, Bebe Rebozo had made it. He was known around town as a successful businessman with impeccable style, an easy-going grace and a gift for telling jokes. He was also a flirt. After divorcing Claire a second time, in 1950, he became known for squiring different women around town to Miami social events. He would remain a bachelor for the next twenty-one years until remarrying in 1971; he never had any children. But if lasting love eluded him, he was lucky in most everything else: Fun, empathetic, rich, charming, Rebozo was the companionable man required when, on a warm January morning in 1951, an anxious and exhausted US senator-elect from California arrived looking for some rest.

Richard Nixon was coming to Florida that December weekend to "chase the sun." He was trying to alleviate some stress after conducting one of the ugliest Senate campaigns in US history. A month earlier, Nixon had beaten Helen Gahagan Douglas in a race so nasty it earned him the enduring moniker "Tricky Dick." Nixon accused Douglas of being "pink right down to her underwear" as part of a relentless, vitriolic, red-baiting attack on her supposed communist sympathies. He ran a flawless if ugly campaign, garnering the widest margin of victory of any Senate winner that year; his victory also generated enormous national prominence. And yet fame gave him no peace of mind. Nixon had long been fighting demons real and perceived that left him at heart a lonely and emotionally fragile man devoid of close friends. In a letter to his new wife, Pat, shortly after he enlisted in the Navy in 1943, Nixon wrote: "I'm anti-social, I guess, but except for you—I'd rather be by myself as a steady diet rather than with most people I know. I like to do what I want, when I want. Only where you are concerned do I feel otherwise."

Like Rebozo, Nixon grew up in modest circumstances. His parents were Quakers, strict disciplinarians who exhibited little affection to their five boys. Many years later, his secretary of state, Henry Kissinger, said: "Can you imagine what this man would have been had somebody loved him?" Friends and relatives remember a young boy "lying by himself in the grass, staring up at the sky, or wandering past the clusters of playing boys, lost in his own thoughts." Nixon's thoughts typically revolved around dreams of greatness. In his eighth-grade autobiography he wrote, "My plans for the future if I could carry them out are to...study law and enter politics for an occupation so that I might be of some good to the people." Above his bed throughout his youth was a poem from Longfellow, "A Psalm of Life," that speaks of "great men" who upon departing "leave behind us Footprints on the sands of time."

When Nixon was twelve his younger brother Arthur died. It was a crushing loss. He cried every day for weeks. But he persevered, as would be his nature throughout his life. He learned to use his innate ambition, that constant drive, to conquer the emotional pain that so often burdened him. And he was learning he could overcome his often powerful feelings of loneliness and despair by exerting power and control over others. Shortly after Arthur's death, he ran for his first office, the eighth-grade presidency, and won. When his older brother, Harold—whom Nixon looked up to—died during his junior year at Whittier College, Nixon suffered another breakdown. But again, it wouldn't overwhelm him. Despite being an underdog and lacking any close friends on campus, he won the race to become student body president.

After Whittier, Nixon headed east to Duke Law School on a full academic scholarship. Despite graduating at the top of his class, none of the top New York City law firms hired him. Dejected by what looked like Ivy League elitism to him, he returned to Whittier and bided his time as a small-town lawyer.

He was luckier in love, marrying Pat Ryan, a student at USC whose beauty had earned her bit roles in Hollywood movies. He met her at a play rehearsal in 1938 and discovered he "could not take my eyes away from her." Before their first date he declared. "Someday I'm going to marry you." She laughed. It took more than a year of relentless pursuit (Nixon often drove her to Los Angeles for dates with other men, just so he could spend time with her) before Pat decided she too was in love with Dick. They married a year later. In 1941, the newlyweds moved to Washington, DC, where Nixon landed a job as a government lawyer. He despised the work and escaped within a year, enlisting in the Navy, where he became a lieutenant and saw combat in the Pacific. A steady stream of letters back and forth to each other during the war are poignant reminders of how deeply in love the two were during this period. Afterward, depending on the historical source, the feeling would vary between cool and hostile.

Home from the war and back in the government job he loathed, Nixon knew he needed to do something more exciting and important with his life. His deliberations became much easier when Republican leaders from Whittier began looking for a new face to take on Jerry Voorhis, a five-term Democratic incumbent running for reelection to the US House of Representatives. A cold call from a party leader to Nixon asking if he was interested was all that was needed to start him on his way. With no political experience beyond his eighth-grade and Whittier College wins, Nixon nevertheless impressed party elders at his audition with his command of the issues and political acumen. His general election campaign was ugly, foreshadowing the campaigns he would run for the next twenty-six years: under-the-table money from oil interests, unrelenting smears against his opponent, lying about his opponent's record. Nixon's desperation—"I had to win," he later told a friend—resulted in an overwhelming victory. Four years later, in 1950, riding the fame won from leading the House Un-American Activities Committee's pursuit of Alger Hiss and his spying for the Soviets, Nixon beat Douglas to win a seat in the US Senate.

His takedowns of Voorhis, Hiss, and Douglas came at a high cost, however. He established his bona fides as an anticommunist crusader and a reliable conservative, but in the process he alienated a generation of left-of-center journalists, influencers, and voters with his win-at-all-costs approach to campaigning and governing. His increasing number of opponents never forgave him and, in a sign of just how raw a nerve Nixon touched, would haunt him for the next quarter century.

Part of the cost of victory was also the emotional toll it exacted on the senator-elect. He was a man in need of a break. In his own curious way, he would soon get the respite he so desperately needed. But in the process, he would acquire something far more valuable and sustainable: a lifelong First Friend.

Nixon's trip to Florida at the beginning of 1951 came at the suggestion of George Smathers, a Florida Democrat who had also won his first Senate campaign that fall and feared Nixon was having a "nervous breakdown" from the stress of the campaign. Known as "the Collector" because he acquired so many friends, Smathers had been a high school classmate of Rebozo and remained friends with him. After being elected to Congress in 1946, Smathers began luring political friends like John Kennedy and Lyndon Baines Johnson down to Florida with promises of afternoons fishing on Bebe's boat and evenings carousing in Miami's clubs. Nixon agreed to come down, Rebozo agreed to host, and the trip was on.

Smathers's campaign manager, Richard Danner, picked Nixon up at the airport. "He was tired, worn out and wanted to relax," Danner recalled. The senator-elect was also dressed for winter, so Danner took him to buy suitable clothes before driving him to the Key Biscayne Hotel, where Rebozo was waiting in the bar. Nixon gave Rebozo a polite brush-off and went straight to his room.

The next day didn't go much better. Nixon went out on Rebozo's thirty-three-foot Chris-Craft houseboat called the *Cocolobo*, but in a dramatic departure from every other trip Bebe had hosted with Washington pols, his new guest showed no interest in fishing and he made no effort to hide it. Instead of socializing with the other guests, Nixon stayed apart, catching up on paperwork. After the boat trip, instead of joining in the other planned activities of golf and tennis, drinking and carousing, Nixon again stuck to himself and his yellow legal pads. Rebozo was so put off by

Nixon that he immediately afterward wrote to Smathers: "Don't ever send another dull fellow like that down here again. He doesn't drink whiskey; he doesn't chase women; he doesn't even play golf."

If Bebe thought his friend shared his same disappointment with the weekend, he was pleasantly surprised a few days later to receive a gracious thank-you note from his guest. Years later, now close friends, Rebozo would remember his first encounter far more charitably: "He had a depth and genuineness about him which didn't come through because of his shyness, but I saw it."

Nixon continued his rapid political ascent, becoming at age forty the second-youngest vice president in US history in 1952, when the Republican ticket led by Dwight D. Eisenhower won an overwhelming victory over former Illinois governor Adlai Stevenson. His new status only enhanced his relationship with Rebozo. The trips to Florida became more frequent as the two men developed a natural rhythm; Nixon needed a place to unwind where he could fish (he overcame his earlier reluctance), eat well, drink martinis (Nixon's initial abstinence was an anomaly—they would consume enormous quantities of alcohol together the rest of their lives), and sit quietly on the houseboat. An extraordinary friendship took root. For the next forty-two years it would remain a constant in both men's lives.

In Nixon's 1990 memoir, *In the Arena,* he devotes a chapter to "friends," which begins with the quote, erroneously attributed to Harry Truman, that "if you want a friend [in Washington] buy a dog." Like his predecessor Jack Kennedy, Nixon's concept of friendship distinguished between the personal and the political. He too subscribed to the Palmerston theory that to have a political friend required shared interests. Since a politician's interests typically changed depending on the issue at hand, Nixon, like Kennedy, found it hard to maintain a genuine, longstanding friendship with any of his professional peers.

Sadly, Nixon appeared to have very few friends in *or* outside of politics. One day during his vice presidency, his boss, President Eisenhower, went to visit him in the hospital. When he returned to the White House, Eisenhower remarked to his secretary how lonely Nixon had seemed. "How could that be?" Eisenhower wondered aloud. How could a grown man—no less a man at the absolute top of his profession—have so few friends? For the handful of friends he could claim, Nixon believed all that was required was shared "values." In his memoir's brief chapter on friends, Nixon never directly addressed why he had developed such a close relationship with Rebozo or what values they shared. That vacuum leaves the reader to speculate what "values" they allegedly held in common. On the surface, what they seemed to share the most was unspoken, unswerving loyalty. Both were self-made men; neither needed nor asked for anything from the other except for reliable and true companionship (and the accoutrements that made it possible). It seemed, at least on the surface, to be as simple as that.

On a deeper level, their relationship is more enigmatic. Was it a friendship between equals, for example, where each gave as much as he received? Based on most public accounts, it seemed one-sided, with Rebozo in a subservient role. He was always the one reading Nixon's mood to determine when to speak or to be silent. It was up to him to provide the entertainment: the boat, the barbecue, or whatever else his friend might like to do that day. Rarely would an observer get a sense of what *Bebe* wanted or derived from the friendship. Was it just the thrill of being close to power? Was Nixon as accessible to Rebozo as Rebozo was to him? Nixon liked being around Rebozo because—at a minimum—he gave him companionship without demanding much from him in return. But why did Rebozo like being around Nixon? He never spoke or wrote in any detail about his friendship to answer these questions, but it certainly must have been enough to keep them so close for more than four decades.

A close relative to the president who witnessed their relationship over more than a quarter century saw a logic to why an intellectual like Nixon would want as his best friend an "intense, careful non-intellectual" like Bebe: "The president's mind was always churning, whether he was writing, reading, or just looking at the expanse of the sea." Bebe's unique gift was his ability to provide "structured frivolity" that could "break [Nixon's] intensity with just the right anecdote or joke at just the right moment" that then allowed him to return to his thoughts with renewed energy. The close relative added: "The president had plenty of writers and thinkers at his disposal to consult with when he wanted intellectual sustenance. That wasn't Bebe. He never interrupted him with a thought or an argument. He was very careful not to exercise his own ego or talk about things he knew nothing about."

Viewed from this insider's perspective, Bebe became in essence a human sounding board for Nixon. "Bebe doesn't present Nixon with any intellectual problems, so Nixon doesn't feel threatened," one mutual friend later wrote. Pat Nixon put it more sharply: "Bebe is like a sponge; he soaks up whatever Dick says and never makes any comments. Dick loves that." Years later as president, Nixon called Lyndon Johnson at his ranch in Texas just two weeks before his predecessor would die of a heart attack, describing Bebe as the perfect tonic: "[He's] a great guy to have around; he cheers people up, you know, he never brings up any unpleasant subjects." Smathers, for one, interpreted Bebe's approach to the friendship in far more cynical terms: "Bebe's level of liking increased as Nixon's position increased."

If Smathers's cynicism was right, then Bebe's level of liking rose to new heights in the summer of 1960 when Nixon became the Republican nominee for president. Bebe threw himself into the race, accompanying the candidate on trips while he helped secure Florida for the Republicans at home. He even engaged in a little skullduggery, paying a private investigator to dig up dirt on Kennedy. The damaging material he passed on about Kennedy—that he had married once in 1947—was ultimately based on forged documents and went nowhere. For much of the general election campaign, Nixon seemed to have the edge in a race where the two candidates competed to see who could be tougher on the Soviets. But Kennedy took advantage of the new medium of television and the introduction of televised national debates that year to narrow the gap, and as election day neared the race looked to be a dead heat.

So there they were on November 8, 1960: Nixon and Rebozo, alone in a suite at the Ambassador Hotel in Los Angeles watching Nixon's early lead slide away as Tuesday turned to Wednesday morning. When the final returns came in from Illinois, Kennedy had won by 0.2 percent of the overall vote. Bebe was in the room that Wednesday afternoon when Nixon picked up the phone and conceded the election to Kennedy. Later, Nixon would ponder a series of what-ifs to try to make sense of his loss: "I can think of a hundred things I could have done or said that might have changed the result," Nixon wrote to a friend shortly after the election.

When everyone else futilely warned Nixon against challenging incumbent California governor Pat Brown in 1962, Rebozo moved at great financial sacrifice to Los Angeles to support his best friend's losing campaign. The morning after that election, Rebozo was at his side again when Nixon famously declared to the press, "You won't have Nixon to kick around anymore, because this is my last press conference." Of course it would not be his final press conference. Whether the reporters believed it, the colorful quip gave them an irresistible opportunity to write his political epitaph, and they did so enthusiastically.

Throughout Nixon's wilderness years, Rebozo remained close, and the devotion went both ways. In 1964, when Rebozo chartered his new Key Biscayne Bank, Nixon showed up for the official groundbreaking, shovel in hand. "*Where other banks have branches, we have roots*," was the bank's slogan, and Nixon became its first and most famous depositor. Rebozo even had a bust of Nixon installed in the bank's lobby, where it remained until the bank was sold. Just over five years later, when Nixon became president, he divested all his stocks and bonds, depositing the proceeds in Rebozo's bank.

The fact that Nixon was making deposits in Rebozo's bank showed that—for the first time in his life—he was making real money. After his loss to Governor Brown, Nixon moved the family to New York City, where he became the lead partner in the Wall Street law firm of Nixon, Mudge, Rose, Guthrie & Alexander. From 1963 to 1968, he pulled down a six-figure income, all the while ingratiating himself with New York's monied elite in case he ever returned to politics. He was one of the firm's primary rainmakers, taking full advantage of the fact that corporate titans loved to tell friends and colleagues that the former vice president was now their lawyer. To get their business, all he had to do was regale them with political insights. Privately, he was more biting. "I just got $25,000 for telling a bunch of stupid jerks something they could have learned from the newspapers."

In addition to all this extra income, for the first time in twenty-five years Nixon was enjoying a relatively uncluttered personal calendar. That meant more time with his Florida friend. The trips down to Key Biscayne became more frequent. They found a new favorite haunt, the English Pub, with its wooden booths and hundreds of pewter mugs hanging from the ceiling—including two bearing the names Bebe Rebozo and Richard Nixon. Nixon would almost always order chop steak (medium rare), and just as surely Rebozo would pick up the tab, tip generously, and ask the staff to say nothing to the few journalists who sometimes snooped around, looking for a scoop.

Their matchmaker, Smathers, who often joined the men in Florida, was especially attuned to the unusual quiet of their relationship. Others marveled at it, too. When Nixon was president, John Dean, Nixon's young White House counsel, remembers being approached by the Secret Service when they became concerned that Rebozo, not their agents, was driving the president around—a major breach of protocol. Dean worked out a compromise with Rebozo whereby the Secret Service would always drive the cars, but when it came time to captaining Bebe's Florida houseboat, an agent would sit up top above the boat while Bebe took the helm. On his first outing, the agent became concerned after hearing only silence from below for the first hour of their trip. He climbed down and peered into the stateroom to see two men sitting in total silence, both looking out at the sea. The agent continued to watch for the next hour and still heard not a peep. He came back to Dean and expressed his confoundment: "They didn't exchange two words to each other." Intrigued, Dean went back to the Secret Service and asked what they witnessed when the president took beach walks with Rebozo. He heard the same thing: They walk in silence. "I suppose they were just so comfortable with each other that they could often occupy each other with literally no words," Dean said in an interview fifty years later.

Monica Crowley, Nixon's foreign policy assistant for the final four years of his life, spent dozens of hours with the two men, including on what would be Nixon's final trip to the Far East. What Crowley observed was "two different but very complementary personalities." As she described the two friends: "It wasn't that Nixon didn't like people—he did, very much—but he also found constantly being around a lot of people somewhat draining, and he needed time to recharge, emotionally and physically. Bebe was an extrovert; he loved people, was always gregarious, hilarious, a shoot-from-the-hip wisecracker. Nixon loved all that in him and that's why he enjoyed being around him so much."

One aspect to Rebozo that became especially attractive to Nixon during this time was his skill at generating wealth, especially for a man who lived on a public salary for much of his adult life. Rebozo, a gifted moneymaker, began to offer Nixon opportunities to make investments in his real estate projects. Nixon proved smart entrusting his investments to Rebozo: In 1967, Nixon took out loans from two Miami banks to purchase 199,891 shares of stock in a company Rebozo had created to develop Fisher Island in Miami Beach, today one of the wealthiest enclaves in America. Others around Nixon—including his secretary, Rose Mary Woods; his valet; and his speechwriter, Pat Buchanan—also bought stock, all at $1 a share. Two years later, the now-president Nixon sold his shares back to Rebozo at $2, doubling his initial investment. At the same time, on Rebozo's recommendation, Nixon purchased two vacant lots in Key Biscayne for $38,000. Right after his reelection in 1972, he sold the lots for a profit of $111,000. Years later these profits would become public and raise a furor in the press.

For the time being, though, Nixon and Rebozo freely mixed money with friendship—or, more accurately, family. Childless and again single, Rebozo became almost an extension of the Nixon family, growing especially close to Nixon's two daughters, Julie and Tricia. As Julie Eisenhower wrote, he seemed "more like an uncle" to her and Tricia than just their father's friend. A decade later, Tricia's fondness for her adopted uncle was so great she made him a godfather to her son Christopher. He was the only non–family member invited to celebrate the Nixons' twenty-fifth wedding anniversary and, right afterward, Nixon's only companion on an extended trip to South America.

So when Nixon began contemplating another run for the presidency in late 1967, it was only natural that Rebozo would be among the few who knew. From the very start, Rebozo was a vocal opponent of the idea. As much as anyone, including the family, Rebozo had witnessed the rawness of Nixon's emotional pain after his losses in '60 and '62. Normally reticent to take such strong positions, Rebozo stepped out of character because he feared what failing again might do to his friend—and to Pat and the girls. Evidence emerged decades later that Nixon's pain may have been so great following his '62 loss that he physically abused Pat—"blackened her eye"—according to former Nixon campaign aide John Sears's account of a conversation he had with a Nixon lawyer right after the election. Sears maintained that the incident was so serious that Pat threatened to leave Nixon afterward. Investigative journalist Seymour Hersh claims to know from informed sources of at least "three alleged wife-beating incidents" Nixon inflicted on Pat. Julie Eisenhower has firmly denied the charge.

Whether true or not, Nixon evidently shared Rebozo's reticence about re-entering the political arena. After his annual Christmas party, he retreated to the quiet of his library late in the evening of December 22. At the top of a fresh legal pad, he wrote, "I have decided personally against becoming a candidate." He then listed all the reasons that supported his decision, agreeing with Rebozo that "losing again could be an emotional disaster for my family." But ultimately he surprised himself when he wrote, "I don't give a damn." Because he in fact *did* give a damn. As he recounted in his memoir *RN*, "I *did* want to run. Every instinct said yes." He knew if he was ever going to "leave footprints in the sand," as Longfellow had silently exhorted him, this was his time. Still, he agreed with Rebozo's assessment that the cost of losing, especially to Pat and his daughters, would be great.

Paralyzed with indecision, Nixon decided to fly down to Florida right after Christmas for some "concentrated thinking." With Rebozo "silently" at his side ("I already knew what he thought," Nixon wrote), he walked along the beach, mulling his decision. It happened that the Reverend Billy Graham was in Miami that week recovering from pneumonia, and he joined Nixon and Bebe on their first day there. Nixon and Graham by then already knew each other well, and Nixon respected Graham's judgment and wisdom. The reverend wasted no time appealing to Nixon's sense of destiny. He pulled out his Bible and, reading from Romans, shared the same message Nixon was coming around to himself: This *is* your moment. Seize it. By their third day together, Graham had shed any pretense of impartiality: "Dick, I think you should run.... It is your destiny to be President." In the end, the First Preacher had trumped the First Friend. The race for the presidency was on.

Rebozo put all his reservations aside once Nixon formally announced his candidacy in mid-January 1968. Apart from raising money for the candidate, Rebozo also changed his lifestyle in deference to his friend's new circumstances and his own rising national visibility. Since his divorce from Claire in 1950, Rebozo had become known in Miami as a consummate ladies' man, squiring an ever-changing cast of women around town as he moved from one social engagement to another. Now, he decided, it might be better to act with more caution. He started an exclusive relationship with Jane Lucke, his lawyer's assistant and a twice-divorced mother of two. They would marry a few years later, though Jane always knew where she ranked in her new husband's life: "Bebe's favorites are Richard Nixon, his cat, and then me," she later remarked. They would remain married until Bebe's death in 1998.

The general election pitted Nixon against Vice President Hubert Humphrey and the segregationist third-party candidate George Wallace. Nixon ran a much better campaign than in 1960, but like his 1950 Senate campaign, it was ugly—built on a "law and order" message that set Black people against whites, city dwellers against suburbanites. His primary strategy was to appeal to older white voters seeking to restore the traditional social order, and everyone else who despised the progressive policies of Johnson's Great Society. It was an "us versus them" gambit, and it worked—though just barely. By the time Illinois (again) finally certified its results at noon on Wednesday, November 6, Nixon had secured 301 of 538 electors and won the popular vote by half a million ballots. Nixon could barely conceal his joy when taking the podium to claim victory on his second try for the White House: "I can say this—winning's a lot more fun," he said.

Later that day, the president-elect and his family boarded an Air Force jet provided by President Johnson and flew to Key Biscayne. It took only minutes once the plane landed for Nixon to appreciate how different life would be on this modest barrier island. As the president-elect, he was now trailed by the Secret Service and a large national press contingent. Once ignored by the locals and tourists, Nixon and his family suddenly found themselves hounded. Nixon soon realized big changes were needed. He decided to sell his New York apartment and to buy two lots right next to Bebe's home for $250,000, equal to half his declared net worth at the time. The idea was to create a winter White House—an enclave during the winter months where he could move his office into the sun for his "perfect day," as daughter Julie described it in her memoir: "Reading in deck chairs, looking out over the glassy calm toward the city . . . a morning and afternoon swim, always a walk on the beach, [ending] the day with Bebe's delicious steak and Cuban black-bean dinners."

Within a month of becoming president, Nixon pressed Rebozo into service. He had vast new powers at his disposal, and he wasted no time enlisting intimates in his schemes, legal or not, to keep himself firmly in power. Twenty-eight days after an inaugural speech in which the president spoke of "the better angels of our nature" and "building a great cathedral of the spirit—each of us raising it one stone at a time, as he reaches out to his neighbor, helping, caring, doing," H. R. Haldeman, Nixon's chief of staff, wrote a confidential memo to John D. Ehrlichman, another top aide to the president:

> Bebe Rebozo has been asked by the President to contact J. Paul Getty in London regarding major contributions. Bebe would like

> advice from you or someone as to how this can legally and technically be handled. The funds should go to some operating entity other than the National Committee so that we retain full control of their use. Bebe would appreciate your calling him with this advice as soon as possible since the President has asked him to move quickly.

Until this moment, there exists no record of Nixon ever asking his friend to do anything beyond the customary parameters of their friendship—certainly nothing as nefarious as routing a campaign contribution outside the normal channels of the party so he could "retain full control" of it. And while there is no evidence that Bebe ever acted specifically on this request, it is the first of Nixon's presidential efforts to draw Rebozo into his dark view of the world—an attempt that would one day succeed, with painful results.

For Nixon, always paranoid, always an introvert, the new strains of being president seemed only to exacerbate his darker instincts. From his first days in office, he was seeing enemies at every corner and plotting retribution in response. Like his campaign, his presidency quickly descended into an "us versus them" operating mode—the few whom he perceived were with him versus the hordes he believed despised him. "He had no personal ability to get control," media advisor Roger Ailes recalled. "He has to live in a drama—in a Western: Nixon against the world."

The ultimate power of his office, rather than emboldening him, seemed to exacerbate his feelings of unworthiness. On a trip to California a few months after becoming president, Nixon took Rebozo and Henry Kissinger, his new national security advisor, on a tour of his hometown. "As he was talking softly and openly for the first time in our acquaintance, it suddenly struck me that the guiding theme of his discourse was how it had all been accidental," Kissinger wrote. "There was no moral to the tale except how easily it could have been otherwise.... He never was certain that he had earned it.... He could not find the locus of his achievements."

Nixon's untethered ambition, combined with paranoia, ultimately forced many of those closest to him to choose between their loyalty and their conscience. For Rebozo, a private citizen who until now had enjoyed a relatively simple relationship with the president, the conflict could have been especially vexing. But it wasn't, and one reason might have been his own history of shady dealings—details that were just then coming to light among law enforcement officials in Washington.

By the late 1960s, FBI agents investigating criminal syndicates had identified Rebozo as a "non-member associate of organized crime figures." Their conclusion arose from Rebozo's numerous and long-standing business ties with well-known mob leaders from across the country, relationships that in some cases created real estate opportunities not only for Rebozo but also for Nixon. For one, the FBI now had reason to believe the Key Biscayne lots Nixon had purchased were owned by a business associate of Rebozo's connected to organized crime, who sold them to the then-aspiring candidate at bargain rates. The FBI also focused closely on Rebozo's Key Biscayne Bank, and in particular Rebozo's role in selling stock that earlier had been stolen by a crime syndicate and deposited in his bank. Even the English Pub they loved to frequent in Key Biscayne was now off-limits to the president because of the FBI's concerns over its involvement with organized crime. How much the president knew about these Rebozo connections, if anything, has never been firmly established.

The best retelling of Rebozo's central role in Nixon's life and work comes from Bob Haldeman's exquisitely detailed diary. Every night for the nearly four and a half years he served as Nixon's chief of staff, Haldeman would dictate an account of his day, which more often than not was spent at the president's side. What becomes abundantly clear from Haldeman's diary is Nixon's near-total reliance on Rebozo for companionship—no matter whether the location was the White House, Camp David, Key Biscayne, or San Clemente. One entry from early 1969 described a typical Southern White House day, "The P [the President] generally spent most of his time working alone, relaxing alone with family, or with Bebe." When the president decided to have a "stag party" for his closest friends—all six of them according to Haldeman—Rebozo was guest number one. When Nixon planned to give a major national television address and wanted emotional support, he would ask Haldeman to get his friend up to the White House. And if Haldeman needed help convincing the president to take more relaxation time away from the White House, there were only two people to call who could make sure it happened: Rebozo or Billy Graham.

Within the White House, Bebe played an equally prominent role in the social life of the First Family. Though Lucy Winchester had the official role of White House social secretary, Rebozo was the de facto secretary—often choosing the First Family's movies and entertainment while playing an active role in revamping the White House kitchen. Whenever he flew on Air Force One, which was often, Rebozo proudly wore a blue flying jacket emblazoned with the presidential seal. At the Rose Garden wedding of Tricia Nixon and Ed Cox in 1971, Rebozo was the Nixons' houseguest for the weekend. Knowing how much his friend liked bowling, Rebozo even paid to install a bowling alley in the White House basement.

On numerous occasions, the president would enlist Rebozo on delicate matters he wouldn't entrust to his staff or thought his friend could uniquely handle. One of Nixon's first initiatives as president was to resume the CIA's activities to destabilize Fidel Castro and Cuba. A second-generation Cuban-American, Rebozo shared Nixon's hatred for Castro and was tasked by his friend to devise new covert efforts to undermine his control. When the president fretted over how to silence an increasingly erratic and alcoholic Martha Mitchell, wife of his good friend and attorney general John Mitchell, Nixon urged Rebozo to take her on "frontally." In 1971, Nixon wanted revenge on the *Washington Post* for printing the Pentagon Papers. The Graham family, which owned the *Post*, also controlled television stations, so the president asked Rebozo to organize a group of pro-Nixon businessmen to challenge their FCC television station licenses. In the end, the challenge to the *Post* broadcast properties never cost the company its licenses, but it did cost the company a lot of its market cap when its stock tanked on news of the challenge.

And there were the absurd moments involving the two friends, often fueled by alcohol, that got wide play within the White House complex. In one oft-repeated story, the president and Rebozo were enjoying a weekend alone together at Camp David in April 1970. The issue consuming the White House at that time was whether to commence the bombing of Cambodia. As the two men sat down for a dinner of steaks and multiple martinis, Kissinger and his national security team were at the White House planning various scenarios. Every few minutes, Nixon interrupted them, calling with orders and then promptly hanging up. An incredulous Kissinger "rolled his eyes each time," an observer later recalled. After one call Kissinger turned to his colleagues and finally told them, "Our peerless leader has flipped out." But Nixon wasn't done. Later, after watching his favorite movie, *Patton*, the president called again. By now he was slurring his words as he barked even more orders at Kissinger. Finally, Nixon said, "Wait a minute. Bebe has something to say to you."

Rebozo got on the phone. "The president wants you to know if this doesn't work, Henry, it's your ass," Rebozo told the future secretary of state.

In truth, Rebozo was much more comfortable in his role of loyal companion than provocateur. From his second inaugural through his resignation twenty months later, the president took sixty separate trips to Camp David, Key Biscayne, or San Clemente with Rebozo as his sole friend. In spite of his proximity to power, Rebozo never sought to advance an initiative or espouse a cause. Nor did he ever appear to enjoy or seek any fame at all as the president's best friend. For its cover story in the summer of 1970, *Life* magazine sent a reporter to shadow Rebozo in Key Biscayne for almost two weeks. The closest the reporter got to him was on the other side of a window at Rebozo's Key Biscayne Bank. The reporter waved, and Rebozo waved back. When the reporter then entered the bank and asked to speak to him, a secretary came out to tell him her boss wasn't in.

On June 18, 1972, readers of the *Washington Post* awoke to a front-page story about five men getting arrested for breaking into the headquarters of the Democratic National Committee in the Watergate complex, a cluster of luxury residential and commercial properties on the banks of the Potomac. Nixon and Rebozo were relaxing on a private island off of the

Bahamas owned by Robert Abplanalp, the multimillionaire inventor of the aerosol valve and perhaps the only other person Nixon considered a close friend. The reporter, Albert E. Lewis, who covered local crime, began his story this way:

> Five men, one of whom said he is a former employee of the Central Intelligence Agency, were arrested at 2:30 a.m. yesterday in what authorities described as an elaborate plot to bug the offices of the Democratic National Committee here.

Nixon and Rebozo were down by the sea that morning when a Secret Service agent came out to the shoreline to tell the president about the reported break-in.

"What in God's name were they doing there?" asked Nixon, according to an account Rebozo gave in 1990, adding:

"We laughed and forgot about it."

The men continued their swim, but the laughter would not last long. Both men by the time of the Watergate arrests were well aware of the nefarious acts (if not specifically of the DNC break-in) already underway in support of Nixon's reelection efforts. But neither could have known that a little more than two years later, this single act of brazen foolishness a thousand miles to the north would unspool the greatest presidential scandal of our time, forever changing their lives. For Nixon, of course, it would lead to resignation and disgrace. For Rebozo, it would mean notoriety bordering on ignominy as his own involvement in Watergate became national news. Over the next twenty-four months, the scandal would thrust him into the national spotlight, embroil him in expensive and embarrassing investigations, and, fairly or not, forever brand him as the president's bagman.

The first inkling that the press was catching on to some of the dirty acts being engineered out of the White House surfaced nearly a year before, in August 1971. Jack Anderson, a syndicated columnist known for breaking major news stories, wrote an item alleging that Howard Hughes, the reclusive Las Vegas billionaire and famous germophobe, had given Bebe Rebozo $100,000—all in $100 bills—who then put it in a Florida safe deposit box. The money was delivered by Richard Danner, the same Smathers aide who had picked Nixon up on his first visit to meet Rebozo in 1950 and now worked for Howard Hughes.

Anderson's news raised eyebrows at the time but not much more. A few months later, though, a Nevada publisher, Herman Greenspun, followed a hard lead suggesting that the Hughes money had actually gone from Rebozo to Nixon to purchase his home in San Clemente. When Greenspun tried to confirm it with the White House, aides realized the story could spell trouble. And in fact, in January 1972, Nixon and his aides were sent into a panic when Anderson reported he now had "evidence" that Rebozo had indeed received the money from Hughes.

The questions raised were troubling: Why would Howard Hughes give Rebozo $100,000? Was it a loan or payment of some sort? Was it a campaign contribution, and if so, why wasn't it sent immediately to a proper account instead of sitting in Rebozo's safe-deposit box?

By then too many people knew that Hughes in fact had a direct financial interest in wanting to see Nixon reelected: He needed a favor, and it was a big one. Already a major casino operator in Las Vegas, Hughes was eager to purchase another one, the iconic Dunes Hotel. The problem was that seeking to own two casinos would certainly generate concern from lawyers at the Antitrust Division of the Department of Justice. Hughes's hope was that timely support of Nixon would convince the president to get the DOJ to back off and help him gain approval for the acquisition. In this context, all the parties understood that the line between a loan or a campaign contribution and a bribe was about as thick as Richard Nixon's skin.

The trail from Hughes to Rebozo to Watergate threaded through one formidable man, Larry O'Brien. A former senior aide to President Kennedy, O'Brien had helped run Humphrey's campaign in 1968 before becoming chairman of the Democratic Party in 1972. But in between those two jobs, O'Brien worked briefly for Howard Hughes as a highly paid public relations consultant, right around the time Hughes had given the $100,000 to Rebozo. As the theory goes, Nixon and his top aides were fully aware of this, and their fear was twofold: First, O'Brien might know how the cash was intended to be used; and second, he could now be preparing to make it all public and ruin Nixon's reelection chances.

All this caused a serious case of déjà vu to descend on the president. In the 1960 presidential campaign, word had leaked out of a $205,000 loan from Hughes to Nixon in 1956 that Nixon long believed had led directly to his defeat. He vowed now not to let that happen again.

So at the start of this reelection campaign, the president acted. Nixon impressed upon his senior aides his fears about the Hughes money, and they then translated those fears into an illegal plan of action: They would break into O'Brien's new offices at the Democratic National Committee and wiretap his office and phones to find out what he knew about Hughes's $100,000 cash payment and what he might be contemplating to do with such information. At the same time, they hoped to collect incriminating information about O'Brien's own connections to Hughes that they could then use offensively to attack the chairman and the party he led.

On May 28, 1972, Nixon's men broke into the Watergate offices of the DNC, sifting through files, taking photographs, and planting bugs, including one they thought was on O'Brien's phone that failed to work. When they started to listen to their handiwork, they soon realized that not only did the bug (allegedly) on O'Brien's phone not work, but they had also bugged the wrong phone and office. The bumbling team returned three weeks later, this time to reinstall a wiretap that would work and on phones in the right suite. But a piece of tape on the outer door of the office complex alerted the security guard on duty that a break-in was in progress. Minutes later, off-duty DC detectives entered the office and caught the five men red-handed. Watergate was born.

Whether Hughes's cash was the main driver—or even among the reasons—for the Watergate burglary is far from settled history. Watergate investigators spent two years probing the matter without reaching a consensus. John Dean, Nixon's former White House counsel, scoffed at the suggestion when asked about it in 2020. He and others still believe the impetus for the break-in was a more general interest in learning how the Democrats planned to win the campaign and what they knew about Nixon's own illicit acts to defeat them. But a report of the Senate Watergate Committee unsealed after Nixon's resignation built a circumstantial and theoretical case that the White House's motive was indeed fear that the disclosure of the Hughes-Rebozo transaction would damage the president's chances for reelection in 1972.

In his own testimony before the Watergate grand jury in 1973, Nixon offered some support for the committee's theory: "O'Brien was giving us a rough time, he was the only effective pro that [DNC presidential candidate George] McGovern had working for him, and he was worrying us." But then he added: "The Howard Hughes organization at that time was under intensive public investigation as well as private, with regards to payoffs, and here Larry O'Brien had his hand in the till." In that testimony, Nixon himself outlined a clear rationale for the break-in and wiretaps—keeping O'Brien from exploiting the Hughes-Rebozo connection by threatening to expose evidence of his own corruption.

Of course it wasn't only the break-in itself that caused Nixon's downfall but instead his later attempts to cover up the crime. Whether Nixon himself had plotted the actual burglary or even knew of it beforehand has never been established. Nevertheless, as the Watergate scandal began to unravel, it would inevitably close in on the president, and on his best friend.

Despite news of the break-in, the public largely ignored the story in the summer and fall of 1972, and Nixon for once enjoyed a relatively stress-free campaign. He was riding high from his foreign policy triumphs, opening up relations with China and signing a series of nuclear arms control agreements with the Soviets. Détente was working, the economy was humming, and in McGovern, a liberal senator from South Dakota, he was facing one of the weakest candidates the Democrats had put up in decades. McGovern made the contest even easier for Nixon by running one of the most disorganized, blundering general election campaigns in party history. All of Nixon's concerns at the beginning of the year—worries that precipitated Watergate, other similar break-ins, and off-the-books fund-raising—proved needless.

Voters returned him for a second term in the biggest landslide in American history, with 60 percent of the popular vote and a record 520 electoral votes.

Ten days after Nixon became the second person in American history to be inaugurated four times (FDR being the first)—twice as president and twice as vice president—a jury returned a guilty verdict against two of the Watergate burglars. If the country hadn't focused on the scandal before, it did now, accelerating efforts by investigators and journalists to better understand the impetus for the break-in and how far up the hierarchy the conspiracy climbed. Nobody pursued the story more relentlessly than two young *Washington Post* reporters, Bob Woodward and Carl Bernstein, who would earn Pulitzer Prizes and lasting fame for their investigative work. It took three more months for the press to link the burglars to people deep inside the White House. Testimony from Dean before the Senate Watergate Committee directly implicated the president's two top aides in covering up the crime. For their involvement, Haldeman and Ehrlichman were forced to resign. A despondent Nixon told them he would rather "die in the night" before asking for their resignations. But a few hours later, the president appeared on national television announcing their departures from the White House. For blowing the whistle, Dean was rewarded with a swift firing.

Weeks before Haldeman and Ehrlichman were officially let go, the president had begun to focus on how their inevitable testimony before grand juries and congressional committees would affect *his* future. To that end, the president organized an outing with his best friend on the *Sequoia*, the 104-foot presidential yacht that boasted a mahogany hull and a rich history. It was on board the *Sequoia* that FDR and Churchill had drafted plans for the D-Day invasion, and where Nixon, who made eighty-eight trips on the yacht (more than any other president), negotiated the SALT I nuclear arms treaty with Soviet leader Leonid Brezhnev.

Nixon's aim this night wasn't quite as noble. As the boat set out on the Potomac, Nixon laid out a set of grim facts to his friend. Within weeks, Haldeman and Ehrlichman would be unemployed and under indictment from federal prosecutors for crimes related to their involvement in the

Watergate cover-up. Neither man had the means to pay for proper counsel, a concerned Nixon told Rebozo. Now he got to the point of the voyage: Could Rebozo discreetly raise a slush fund to pay for their defenses? If he paid for their counsel, the president likely reasoned, he could have greater visibility into their defenses and possibly blunt the worst of their testimony.

Without hesitation, Rebozo told a relieved president that he and Robert Abplanalp could raise several hundred thousand dollars without trouble. Within weeks he fulfilled his promise. On the transcript of a White House tape from April 30, 1973, Nixon told his two departing aides about the existence of the slush fund raised for their defense.

"No strain," Nixon said. "Doesn't come outta me. I didn't, I never intended to use the money at all.

"As a matter of fact, I told B-B-Bebe, uh, basically, be sure that people...who have contributed money over the contributing years are, uh, favored and so forth in general."

The existence of this secret fund was reconfirmed for Watergate investigators by Lawrence Higby, Haldeman's top aide, who testified under oath that Haldeman had told him that "the president indicated that Mr. Rebozo did have some funds that could be made available to Mr. Haldeman and...Mr. Ehrlichman for the purpose of assisting in a legal defense." The Senate Watergate Committee's final report concluded that Rebozo's secret fund amounted to about $400,000.

As Rebozo was setting up his slush fund, he was also appearing under subpoena before the Senate Watergate Committee. The committee wanted to hear directly from Rebozo why the Hughes money was given in the first place, where if anywhere it was disbursed, and what if anything was left of it. In sworn testimony before Senator Sam Ervin's committee, Rebozo said the $100,000 he received from Danner had remained in the original safe-deposit box until, under Nixon's direction, he returned the money untouched to Hughes. The president, he said, believed it would be wrong to use the money because it was a campaign contribution. He also testified that Nixon advised him to talk to Herbert Kalmbach, Nixon's personal attorney, about how best to handle the matter with the IRS. Without evidence that Rebozo was lying, the committee tabled the matter, though not for long.

Later that fall, six days after the "Saturday Night Massacre" (when Nixon in quick succession fired his attorney general and deputy attorney general for failing to fire Special Prosecutor Archibald Cox) set the machinery of impeachment in motion, Nixon was questioned at a press conference about Rebozo's handling of the Hughes cash payment. In a defiant tone, the president backed up Rebozo's spring testimony to the committee, saying that the funds had never been touched and all had been returned to Hughes in the same manner in which they'd been delivered. "I think that is a pretty good indication that he is a totally honest man, which he is," Nixon insisted.

At another press conference three weeks later to quell the rising clamor for his impeachment, Nixon tried to assure the nation *he* was still an honest man: "People have got to know if their president is a crook. I am not a crook."

But the Senate remained skeptical. All that summer and fall, Watergate investigators were developing sworn testimony that directly contradicted Nixon's assertion that Rebozo was a "totally honest man." Most damningly, Kalmbach revealed to Terry Lenzner, the committee's chief investigator, that Rebozo had directly told him he'd parceled out much of the $100,000 to Rose Mary Woods, Nixon's longtime secretary, and to the president's brothers, Ed and Donald, along with a few others. Once Rebozo found out about Kalmbach's devastating testimony, he knew he had to act swiftly to protect himself and the president from being implicated any further. On March 21, 1974, Rebozo and his attorney asked to meet with committee chair Sam Ervin, the crusty old North Carolina senator and now national celebrity as a result of the highly rated and riveting hearings he had led the previous summer. Ervin insisted Lenzner be in the meeting, too. The men entered a small side room in the Capitol. Rebozo proceeded to put his briefcase on a table, open it up, and reveal two stacks of $100 bills, each bundled with a rubber band.

"I remember Ervin's astonished expression—his busy eyebrows fluttered up and down, and he gasped," Lenzner wrote in his book, *The Investigator.* "The cash," Rebozo's lawyer announced as he pointed to the stacks. With all eyes riveted on the money before them, Rebozo's lawyer assured Ervin and his investigators that his client had left the money "untouched" in order to return it to the Hughes organization. This was their attempt to prove, Lenzner later wrote, that the money had not been used.

There were a few problems with this account from Rebozo and his lawyer, however. Most troubling, Kalmbach had already testified that Rebozo told him he'd disbursed the funds. If that was true, what was the source of this $100,000 that Ervin was gaping at? A forensic accountant stepped in to investigate. Every bill released by the Federal Reserve has an index number that is tied to its date of release. The accountant soon discovered, according to Lenzner, that more than thirty of the bills had been issued *after* Danner had given the money to Rebozo, meaning that the original bills had gone elsewhere. Making matters worse for Rebozo, the stacks contained an extra $100, making for a total bundle of $100,100 in the briefcase. To Lenzner, who described Rebozo as an "uncooperative" and "arrogant" witness who "acted as if he could get away with anything," the discrepancy of the serial numbers and the extra bill meant that the committee needed Rebozo to re-testify. It issued another subpoena to him, and Rebozo promptly left the country. He never testified again before the committee.

In 2005, a *60 Minutes* segment on CBS attempted to answer the riddle of the Hughes cash. The piece offered some tantalizing new clues, including a chart prepared by Senate investigators that had not been included in their final report. Tracing the money through various bank accounts, Lenzner could now assert that $46,000 of the Hughes money went directly to Nixon's Key Biscayne house for such distractions as a putting green and a pool table. Lenzner came to an unequivocal conclusion: "This was a bribe...in effect through Mr. Rebozo to the President." Lenzner recalled that he had written an entire section laying the blame for Watergate on the Hughes bribe, but for reasons he didn't disclose, his explanation was never included. One theory later propounded for its omission was that Democrats had also received Hughes money and didn't want to draw more attention to it.

And did O'Brien in fact know about the money, warranting the wiretap put on his phone? CBS interviewed Hughes's right-hand man for eighteen years, Bob Maheu, who had been directly responsible for making sure the money got to Rebozo thirty-five years earlier. Asked if he ever told his then PR consultant O'Brien about the loan, Maheu scoffed: "Never, never. I had no reason to tell Larry. Why the hell would I tell Larry about this?"

The break-in that would take down a president may have all been for naught.

By the summer of 1974, a pervasive gloom hung over the White House. Nixon's last chance to save his presidency seemed to rest on the US Supreme Court. After US District Court judge John Sirica demanded the president turn over tapes of his private White House conversations, Nixon appealed on the grounds of executive privilege in *Nixon v. U.S.* On July 24, the Court ruled 8–0 (Justice William Rehnquist recused himself) that the president must surrender the tapes to the Watergate investigation. Days later the House Judiciary Committee adopted three articles of impeachment. The transcript of the tapes was not yet public, but Nixon knew that the entry recorded on June 23, 1973, would seal his fate. For nearly two years, the president had been telling the country that he'd known nothing about an attempt to cover up the Watergate break-in. But in that recorded conversation a week after the break-in occurred, Nixon and Haldeman talked in detail about how they could scuttle the FBI investigation by having the CIA pretend it was a national security matter.

On the night of August 2, the president, his family, and Rebozo again boarded the *Sequoia* for what would be a somber voyage. On a yacht that in times past had given the president such solace, Nixon decided that he was going to become the first man in history to resign as president of the United States. Rebozo, who had flown up from Miami the day before, tried to dissuade him.

"You can't do it. It's the wrong thing to do. You have got to continue to fight. You just don't know how many people are still for you," Rebozo urged.

Four days later, on August 6, the *Washington Post* carried the latest, and biggest, story based on the now public June 23 tape. "President Nixon personally ordered a pervasive cover-up of the facts of Watergate within six days after the illegal entry into the Democrats' national headquarters," the story began.

Despite this damning revelation, Nixon's family made the same entreaty as Rebozo. "Go through the fire just a little bit longer," Julie wrote in a note she left on her father's pillow. "You are so strong! I love you. Millions support you." Nixon saw his daughter's tender note in the early hours of August 7, but in his mind and heart the decision was already made. He had to resign. His impeachment was inevitable. Earlier Arizona senator Barry Goldwater had delivered the news that Nixon knew sealed his fate: Once impeachment reached the Senate for trial, he could count at best on only ten votes for acquittal. As much as he relished a good fight, Nixon knew that his options had run out. It would be better for him, for his family, and for the country to leave. That night, speaking to the nation from the Oval Office, Richard Nixon resigned as the thirty-seventh president.

Nixon, his wife, and his daughters flew back to California and their oceanside estate in San Clemente. Rebozo and Abplanalp visited the president in those first days of exile, as they would regularly for the next twenty years. As much as Howard Hughes's $100,000 cash contribution to Rebozo had abetted his downfall, Nixon could never fault his old friend for it. Rebozo ultimately was not charged by the Justice Department for putting the money to personal use, although a subsequent IRS investigation did find he underreported his taxable income for 1970 and 1971, forcing Rebozo to repay more than $50,000 in back taxes and interest. In the end, all Rebozo could be accused of was excessive—even blind—loyalty to Nixon.

A half century after Nixon and Rebozo stepped off center stage, there are still puzzling aspects to their forty-year friendship that defy logic. For such a public relationship—one intensely scrutinized amid an electrifying scandal—questions still come more readily than answers. Why would such an intellectual as Nixon choose a nonintellectual for his best friend? How could they derive such satisfaction from a friendship that was so often spent in silence? Was it all based on unwavering loyalty?

With few definitive answers, differing theories, from the benign to the salacious, still compete for acceptance: The rags-to-riches Rebozo thrilled just being in the room as history unfolded; Nixon valued him because he aided and abetted his nefarious side, secretly plotting and then executing some of his most unsavory acts; they were gay lovers; or that Nixon needed Rebozo to fill an emotional void left by an intensely complicated marriage, one that swerved between periods of closeness and alienation, affection and possibly physical abuse. Or the most likely: that Nixon, even beyond his loveless marriage, found in Rebozo a level of comfort and intimacy otherwise absent from his life.

Ultimately, no sure answers exist. Discreet to their core, neither man ever divulged so much as a glimmer of what bonded them so tightly beyond the occasional bromide. All that we really know is that Rebozo served as an intimate witness to Nixon's greatest triumphs and his most bitter defeats—frequently the only witness. And that they felt comfortable enough in each other's presence to spend more time together than with anyone else, including their own wives.

Perhaps in the end what that unloved young boy from Whittier needed most in life was someone to shield him from the world. A paradox to be sure, Nixon was a public man with the heart of a loner—aloof, uptight, and nursing grievances against enemies both real and imagined. With Rebozo by his side, he could focus on how best to build on his successes while moving past his all-too-painful failures. Bolstered by a friend who gave him respite, a steeled Nixon emerged better equipped to face what life threw at him. He could be kicked around, again and again, but with Rebozo's steady presence, he could still get up and plow forward. The basis of their special dynamic may be as simple as what Nixon sparingly describes in *In the Arena*: a friendship in which neither asked anything of the other beyond just being there.

Even as the friends reached their ninth decades, their devotion to one another remained as strong as ever. In 1990, nearing his seventy-seventh birthday, Nixon made his final visit to Miami—this time as a favor to Rebozo. He agreed to be the guest speaker at a sold-out, $250-a-plate benefit for the Miami Boys' Club, the same charity Rebozo had started supporting a half century earlier. In a rare interview with the *Miami Herald* to help promote the event, he continued to protect his notorious friend, still vouching for Nixon's essential goodness. When the subject of Watergate arose, Rebozo blamed the scandal on others, never on the president himself.

"I know that in the beginning he was just appalled by it," said Rebozo, without a hint of doubt. "I was convinced that he was the last to know what was going on."

CHAPTER 9

Bill Clinton and Vernon Jordan

Two Brothers of the South

Shortly after graduating from Yale Law School in 1973 at the age of twenty-seven, Bill Clinton took out a pen and piece of paper and wrote down his most important life goals. "I want to be a good man, have a good marriage and children, have good friends, make a successful political life, and write a great book." Assessing how he fared decades later against those five missions, he was unequivocal with respect to the third: "No person I know ever had more or better friends."

Although he would call upon many of those friends, one man in particular gave him the emotional life he most needed when he became the youngest ex-governor in American history. In 1980, the voters of Arkansas rejected Clinton's bid for reelection to the office he loved. He was only thirty-four. His vision of a grand political career—which so many others believed would carry him to the White House—now appeared to be in tatters. He became depressed, convinced his career was over. Until one morning a few weeks later, when his new friend came down from New York to talk some sense into him. Three hours later, his spirits lifted, William Jefferson Clinton would be back in the game, emboldened by the wise, encouraging, and empathetic words of the man who would one day become his First Friend, Vernon Eulion Jordan.

Defeat was an alien experience to Bill Clinton, and the 1980 gubernatorial loss left him devastated. Until then, with few exceptions, he had always found a way to win. From childhood, despite living in a dysfunctional home with an alcoholic and abusive stepfather, Bill Clinton seemed destined for great things. He was junior class president at Hope High School, Boys Nation senator going into his senior year (which led to his shaking President Kennedy's hand at the White House), and a drum major in the marching band. At Georgetown University on financial aid, he was elected class president his freshman and sophomore years, and he went on to win a coveted Rhodes Scholarship to study at Oxford University—even if, as his mother conceded, he was "gawky and not quite coordinated enough" to be proficient in any sport, usually a necessity for capturing a Rhodes.

At Oxford, Clinton carried a black notebook wherever he went. When he met someone new, he would jot down their key biographical information. One night someone asked why he was writing this all down: "I'm going into politics and plan to run for governor of Arkansas, and I'm keeping track of everyone I meet," Clinton replied. Oxford led to Yale Law School. His ability to conceptualize complex legal theories allowed him to sail through his studies while spending big chunks of time helping manage two political campaigns. One was a Connecticut senate race by an antiwar ordained minister, Joe Duffy. The other was George McGovern's 1972 Texas general election campaign where Clinton had the improbable task of wooing regular Democrats from the old LBJ machine at county courthouses. Even though his candidates lost, these provided more opportunities for mentors, contacts, and strategies—carefully stored away for the next challenge.

As he shuttled between academics and politics, Clinton was rarely without the companionship of a serious girlfriend. He fell especially hard for a fellow Yale law student named Hillary Rodham. They first spotted each other in the reading room of the Yale law library. He spent so much time looking across the room at her that Rodham finally walked over to him. "If you're going to keep staring at me and I'm going to keep staring back, we should at least introduce ourselves," she said. By the time they graduated in the summer of 1973 and left New Haven—he back to Arkansas, she to Washington to work for the House Judiciary Committee as it considered Richard Nixon's impeachment—they were in a committed relationship.

Returning home, Clinton was happy with what he'd been able to accomplish. He had outshined the top students at the most prestigious educational institutions in the world, proved himself a gifted political organizer, amassed a vast network of friends and associates who would form the backbone of his next agenda, and would soon marry a woman who was his intellectual equal yet generous enough to tolerate his weaknesses. And in a decade when many of his peers were physically and spiritually wounded by serving in Vietnam, he had obtained a deferment from the draft, never imagining it might someday become a political issue.

Back in Arkansas, it took Clinton only four years to reach the pinnacle of power. On his brief journey to the governor's mansion, he suffered but one setback, when he lost his maiden run for political office—a seat in Congress in 1974—by just four thousand votes, or two percentage points. Once again, Clinton won by losing, proving his political bona fides after starting with little name recognition and no organization. He was now a political wunderkind on par with the state's most popular leaders. He had begun teaching at the University of Arkansas Law School in 1973 (after convincing skeptical interviewers he really wanted to be a law professor, not a politician) but resigned in early 1975 to run for state attorney general, which he won with no meaningful opposition. Proving the adage that a state AG looks in the mirror and sees a governor in waiting, Clinton wasted no time announcing his campaign for governor after the sitting governor decided to run for the US Senate. Nine months later in November 1977, he won with 63 percent of the vote. At just thirty-two years of age, Bill Clinton had become the youngest governor not just in Arkansas history, but in the United States.

But just two years later, Clinton's fledgling political career was in jeopardy. Even before the polls opened in November 1980, Clinton knew that two of his own decisions had imperiled his reelection bid: a steep new license tax he enacted that enraged every car and truck owner in the state; and his reluctant acquiescence to President Jimmy Carter's decision to transfer Cuban refugees from the Mariel boatlift into northwest Arkansas. Nightly television reports led with the ensuing rioting and lawlessness, further alienating voters.

Ten minutes after the polls closed, Clinton knew his tenure was over.

The voters of Arkansas had rejected him, but this time he could find no silver linings. It was catastrophic politically and deeply wounding to his psyche. Clinton was now convinced his life fit the classic joke they make about Rhodes Scholars upon leaving Oxford: someone with a great future behind them. "He was flailing, in utter shock," remembered Terry McAuliffe, who met Clinton right after his loss when he began interviewing to run the Democratic National Committee. "He screwed up, and now didn't know what to do with his life." In the early weeks after his defeat, Clinton tried to make sense of how everything had come undone so quickly. In dozens of calls to friends and acquaintances, he heard plenty of support and commiseration. But that didn't change his view: His perfect career had been knocked off its trajectory. This time, he felt too depressed to chart a comeback.

Vernon Jordan had watched the returns from his Fifth Avenue apartment in New York City on election night 1980. Ronald Reagan and his conservative Republican coalition swept the nation, winning the White House, flipping the Senate, and ushering in a generational realignment of American politics. Jordan was one of the nation's most prominent civil rights leaders, and he was concerned what that rightward shift would mean for the future of a movement to which he'd dedicated much of his life. Amid all the carnage, one race in particular saddened him: the defeat of his new friend Bill Clinton in Arkansas.

The two men had met only three years earlier at a banquet for the National Urban League in Little Rock. Clinton then was the state attorney general, and Jordan was in town to raise funds for the powerful civil rights organization he had led for nearly a decade. Jordan had known of Clinton for years through Hillary, whom he met in 1969 minutes after Hillary had given a speech at an activist conference in Colorado. She was sitting on a park bench, going over the rest of the day's schedule with Peter Edelman, a former Robert Kennedy aide, when "into my eyesight came a pair of highly polished shoes and a voice that said, 'Well Peter, aren't you going to introduce me to this *earnest* young woman,'" Hillary remembered. "I looked all the way from his shoes up to the head of this very attractive man. We started talking and instantly I was struck by his intelligence, his charisma and mannerisms. Just an incredible public presence. From that day forward we stayed in touch with each other until I introduced him to Bill years later. It was a mind meld between them from the get-go."

Forty-three years later, Bill Clinton vividly recalls the first time the two met:

> The Urban League banquet was in a big school setting, inside a big gymnasium. We had a heck of a crowd there and he was a big star. The emcee for the evening was this woman who was one of our best TV anchors. She wore a beautiful dress that was high collared but had no back. Vernon and I were sitting on either side of the lectern where she was speaking, and her back was visible to Vernon. And he said to me after we were walking out, he said, "She's a very attractive lady and that was a beautiful dress. It's too bad they ran out of fabric before they finished it."

And so began Bill Clinton's closest adult friendship—fittingly, in laughter, and not surprisingly about women, which would become a frequent topic of conversation. Over time, the bond would play a pivotal role at the most important moments of Clinton's political and personal lives. When he thought about quitting politics, Jordan talked him out of it. A decade later, when he considered running for president, Jordan told him he was ready. Once in office, Clinton only had to say "Get Vernon" and Vernon would appear, asking for nothing in return. And then, when a sex scandal nearly ended Clinton's presidency, Jordan was there to save his marriage and bolster his defense. He not only counseled Hillary to stay with her husband at the nadir of their relationship, but also found the seam that allowed Jordan to remain loyal to his friend without telling falsehoods.

That single exchange back in 1977 presaged thousands of conversations and asides, some serious, others better left for the locker room, that would keep Clinton and Jordan engaged and entertained for the next four decades. Their banter would play out at Thanksgiving at Camp David and during Christmas Eve parties at the Jordans' DC home; on Martha's Vineyard for summer vacations and on golf courses across the country; in the Oval Office and upstairs in the White House residence. That America's "first Black president"—the moniker bestowed on Clinton by writer Toni Morrison in 1998—would choose as his First Friend a Black man from the South is neither surprising nor a coincidence. They were two halves of a whole. As one former aide said, "They complemented each other perfectly: Both were extremely smart and charismatic; both were larger-than-life guys, with big appetites to do big and important things in life."

One important goal both were determined to effect was the dismantlement of systemic racism in their native South. Jordan grew up in the deeply segregated city of prewar Atlanta. Every day, he felt deeply the degradation of being a Black person in the schools he attended, the restaurants he could eat in, or the fountains he could drink from. A decade his junior, Clinton grew up in the equally segregated city of Hot Springs, where his grandparents ran one of the few grocery stores that served Black customers. His mother, Virginia, would come home from the hospital where she worked as a nurse and rage about the injustice of seeing Black patients deprived of proper health care because they couldn't afford insurance. "There's no role for prejudice in our lives," Virginia Clinton preached to her son, often with his best childhood friend, David Leopoulos, seated nearby. One night when Bill was at Leopoulos's house, David's mother came home from an Episcopalian church meeting. The issue that night was how the church would react if a Black person applied for membership. "If we even have to ask the question, I don't want to be a part of it," she told the two boys. "So I just quit." Years later, a few weeks before his inauguration as president, Clinton pulled David aside and said, "You don't know how powerful that moment was for me."

Both Clinton and Jordan became transformational forces in their fight for racial equality: Clinton through sweeping reforms in the Arkansas legislature, Jordan through his legal and voter registration efforts in his native Georgia. Both men then made their mark on the national stage:

Clinton as a progressive Southerner, Jordan as a moderate bridge builder to the White community.

As Clinton grew into adulthood, he realized more and more how culturally at ease he felt with Black people, especially those from the South. Years later, Michael Waldman, Clinton's chief speechwriter for the last six years of his presidency, recalled flying on Air Force One to Little Rock for the fortieth anniversary of the 1957 desegregation of Little Rock High School. Several of Clinton's closest Black Arkansan friends were on the flight. As the plane got closer to Little Rock, Waldman recalled, "Clinton visibly relaxed, his drawl deepened, there was more laughter." At the same time, he also knew as a progressive Southern Democrat that to win elections he had to build a multiracial coalition between Black voters and white working-class voters. In later years, on the national stage, that led to his efforts to connect with "Reagan Democrats" in the Midwest and to talk to them in the same terms in which he talked to people in Detroit's inner city.

"I could see that he was aggressive, sure of himself and genuine," Jordan wrote of their first meeting. "It was clear that he had a deep, caring concern about race, and so there was an immediate affinity between us." And Clinton saw in Jordan those same beliefs, along with the political acumen and infectious personality to advance Black interests across all aspects of American life.

Their shared commitment to racial equality was what initially united them, but the easy rapport and love of the game—especially politics and sports—took the Clinton-Jordan friendship to another level. The person who witnessed the friendship the most—Hillary Clinton—said that Jordan intuitively understood what "Bill, and any president needs—someone they can just totally relax with, tell stories with, share a joke with, someone to just go out on the golf course with and not talk about anything of any significance if that's what they choose. That's what I thought was the incredible gift Vernon gave us over all the years we've known him."

Both of them were operators, players. They knew how much each of them had benefited from their boundless charm and confident bearing. At six foot two and six foot five, with broad shoulders and radiant smiles,

Clinton and Jordan were keenly aware how much they lit up whatever room they occupied. When they turned those powers on each other the first night they met, the chemistry was electric. When Clinton later used that same magnetism on an intern in the White House, the effect would be equally electric but with devastating consequences, imperiling his presidency, shaming his paramour, and thrusting his best friend into the uncomfortable center of a national scandal.

By the time he dialed his defeated friend in December 1980, Jordan knew the soon-to-be ex-governor needed a stern talking-to. Hillary answered the phone to a booming baritone of a voice. It was Jordan. "You got any grits down there?" Jordan asked. "I don't know how to make grits, but you come on down," Hillary told him. A few weeks later, Jordan stood in the tiny kitchen of the Clintons' small yellow-framed house where they had just moved into after vacating the governor's mansion. Awaiting him was a piping hot plate of instant grits Hillary had purchased that morning.

When he entered the cramped kitchen in his tailored three-piece suit and saw the young couple with their one-year-old daughter, Chelsea, Jordan could feel their despondence, especially from the ex-governor. Gone was the confidence and verve that had so enchanted and impressed Jordan at their first meeting. He now saw sitting before him a diminished man carrying an overwhelming if irrational sense of rejection. Worse, he seemed lost, searching for direction but lacking will or a compass to steer himself.

Over the next two and half hours, Vernon Jordan's regal presence dominated the small room. If ever there was a moment for Jordan to show his stuff, it was in that kitchen, at that table, as Bill Clinton wrestled with what to do next. Jordan knew he needed some straight talking. So he gave it to him in blunt, direct terms: Stop pitying yourself and appreciate what others see in you. You're a man of immense promise who suffered a single setback, not a career-ending defeat. You have too much talent, too much commitment to the causes you care about, too much support to step off the stage and give it all up.

"He knew that I had just become the youngest former governor in the history of the country. And that my epitaph had been written," Clinton recalled. "He told me: 'You and Hillary, you got a lot of talent, and your heart's in the right place; it's going to come out all right.' "

"Nobody else was saying that to me," Clinton remembered forty years later. "That wasn't the storyline."

Jordan's message resonated with Clinton at the very moment when he was seriously beginning to entertain offers out of state that would have given him better financial security and less heartache. "He told me I needed to stay in the game," Clinton said. By this point, Clinton had been approached about becoming the head of the World Wildlife Federation, chief of staff to Governor Jerry Brown of California, chairman of the Democratic National Committee, or president of the University of Louisville. Then Jordan appeared as the lone voice in the wilderness. "You're not done, and you shouldn't think you're done," Hillary remembered Jordan saying as Clinton ticked off the opportunities he was considering. "He made a big impression on him in that moment."

Eventually, his message sank in. "I just took a deep breath and instead of being miserable, after that, it all began to sort of fall into place. And I began to just think about the rest of my life and try to live in the present and for the future."

"That conversation was a milestone in Bill's decision to stay in Arkansas, stay in politics, and ultimately to run for president," Hillary said.

Before leaving for the Little Rock airport, Jordan offered one more piece of advice—for friend Hillary Rodham: She needed to start using "Clinton" as her last name. If Bill was going to make a political comeback someday, as he hoped, and do it in Arkansas, Hillary needed to accede to the conventions of the time and tone down her feminist rhetoric. As Clinton recalled, "Vernon said to her, 'I'm older than you are. I think keeping [the Rodham] last name is bothering a lot of older black people and we need them all.' And Hillary thought if Vernon believed she could do it and maintain her integrity and be who she was, it made her think she could do it." Hillary agreed: "It was important to have his voice in that decision. I respected his intelligence and political experience, and really paid attention to what he told me."

On the heels of that pivotal conversation, Clinton went back to the voters of Arkansas, asking for their forgiveness and for another chance. Two years later, on January 11, 1983, Bill Clinton, with Hillary Rodham Clinton by his side, took the oath of office as the forty-second governor of Arkansas. Amid the sea of thousands of onlookers massed at the front of the Capitol to see Clinton restored to power as the state's favorite son was a smiling Vernon Jordan.

Vernon Jordan's role in shaping the path of the forty-second president of the United States testifies to his own remarkable journey over four and a half decades. During that time, he traveled from the deeply segregated public housing projects of Atlanta to the most prestigious boardrooms in America as one of the country's most prominent civil rights leaders and sought-after board directors. Nothing tells that journey better than Jordan's 2001 autobiography, *Vernon Can Read!*, which recounts how a young Black boy growing up in "unreconstructed, unrepentant Georgia" could lift himself up, with the help of a loving mother—"unlettered, unlearned, but with a Ph.D. in life"—and make his way in a world not built for him.

Jordan was born in 1935 in a state governed by Eugene Talmadge, one of the nation's most virulent segregationist politicians. Talmadge declared that a Black man's place was "at the back door with his hat in his hand." When Jordan was one year old, there were six lynchings in Georgia.

Still, Mary Belle Jordan, the daughter of a sharecropper, had big ambitions for Vernon and his two brothers, just as she had for herself when she took a job running the kitchen concession of a military facility and—through hard work and some good old Southern home cooking—became the owner of one of the most popular catering businesses in Atlanta. Mary Belle's business thrived among the city's most elite white lawyers and business executives. Every week, she made sure to expose Vernon and his younger brother Windsor to the posh homes and opulent banquet halls where she plied her trade. There they would wash dishes, tend bar, serve meals, and, most important, *observe* her well-heeled clientele—a side of Atlanta otherwise inaccessible to the impressionable teenagers. What they learned, Windsor later recalled, was "there were two worlds, two life-styles. And the idea was to get to that other style."

Vernon's aptitudes as a student became immediately apparent to his teachers in the segregated public schools he attended through high school. He shot to the top of his class, moving as far and as fast as he could. But living behind an "iron curtain" of state neglect and deprivation limited his abilities to compete in a white-dominated society. His grades were good enough for him to gain acceptance to nearly all-white DePauw University, but when he attended a pre-orientation conference in the summer of 1952 (he would be the only Black freshman among five Black students overall) and took tests to determine his standing, the dean of admissions gave him sober news. Not only would he be miserable and out of place socially, but he also wouldn't make it academically. He simply lagged too far behind the other students. The dean's message was clear: Don't enroll here. And don't think you can be a lawyer. Become a high school social science teacher instead.

Undeterred, Vernon attended DePauw that fall. His parents and younger brother helped move him in. When it came time for his parents to say their goodbyes, his normally taciturn father, a postman, pulled him aside:

"You can't come home."

"What do you mean I can't come home?"

"I mean you can't come home. You know those tests say that you don't read as fast as these boys and girls. When they've finished the book you may still be reading. But you just can't come home."

Feeling exposed, Vernon asked: "Well, what should I do, Daddy?

"Read, boy," he said. "Read."

Vernon took his father's words to heart. He not only learned to read faster, but to talk with stirring cadences and language that would enthrall ever-larger rooms with his oratorical gifts. He won every major speaking contest in Indiana during his college years, earning him renown on campus as well as at home in Atlanta. His preternatural skills also firmed his resolve:

Despite the dean's warning four years earlier, he *could* be a lawyer, and a good one at that. Yet he also had a nagging interest in using those same skills to become a minister. In the end he realized that both his lifestyle and his personality were better suited to a legal career. He declined a seminary offer by telling the admissions office "half-kiddingly" that he had "discovered sin and liked it." Instead he chose Howard University Law School, the nation's premier all-Black school in Washington, DC, and the alma mater of civil rights lawyer and future Supreme Court justice Thurgood Marshall. If college meant learning to live and thrive on foreign land, Howard represented a chance to return to safety—to a place of comfort where he found "a wife, a career, and a reaffirmation of my faith in the mission of black people."

With his wife, Shirley, and newborn daughter, Vickee, twenty-five-year-old Jordan came home to Atlanta in 1960 to find a community as racially divided as when he had left eight years before. He soon saw firsthand the intractability of racial injustice in his state. Just three days after graduating from Howard, he was clerking for one of Atlanta's most prominent civil rights attorneys, Donald Hollowell, known then for successfully litigating many of the cases that desegregated Georgia's colleges. When Hollowell opened his practice in 1952, he was one of only fifteen practicing Black lawyers in the whole state. That number had swelled, but conditions for Black people who found themselves on the wrong side of the law remained deplorable.

As Hollowell's only legal assistant, Jordan was thrown right into the frenzy and tedium of his office—researching cases, fact-checking citations, talking to witnesses, and driving him to and from his appointments. He was hamstrung by the meager pay—$35 a week—requiring him to take a night job waiting and bartending for his mother's catering business. It made for an uncomfortable scene: The lawyers he worked alongside during the day he would now serve at night. He persevered because he liked the casework, especially the highly publicized case of two Black students who were denied admission to the University of Georgia because of their race. Jordan found the key piece of evidence—a white woman with the exact same credentials as his clients had been accepted—that tilted the case in favor of the plaintiffs. The university was forced to desegregate, and the day his clients enrolled, a throng of angry white students confronted them. Jordan accompanied one of the Black students—Charlayne Hunter—to the registrar's office through a "howling mob... just unbounded hatred and fear on open display." Later, as one of America's most prominent Black journalists for *PBS NewsHour*, Charlayne Hunter-Gault would remember Jordan's "poise in the midst of chaos" as he walked her though a sea of vile racial epithets. The message he conveyed—to Gault and to millions of others watching transfixed that day on television—was: "I have humanity and dignity, and you will have to deal with that because I'm not going anywhere."

In winning Hunter's case, Jordan actually lost the chance to practice law in Georgia ever again. Serving dozens of subpoenas on university officials had made him a marked man. "You need to be taught a lesson," the state attorney general told him after the desegregation order came down. To Jordan, his message was clear: They would alter if necessary the results of his upcoming Georgia bar exam to make sure he was never admitted to the bar. When he learned he had failed, he concluded, rightly or not, that the powers that be had made good on their threat (he would ultimately pass the Arkansas bar exam in 1973 but not practice law again until 1982).

But even just a year of practicing civil rights law instilled in him a desire to spend the next two decades working to advance the interests of Black Americans in every sphere of life: education, politics, business, and culture. Over that twenty-year period, Vernon Jordan would employ his skills as an orator, a writer, a lawyer, a fund-raiser, and a diplomat to rise through the ranks of mainstream civil rights organizations: as Georgia field director for the NAACP; head of the Southern Regional Council's Voter Education Project; executive director of the United Negro College Fund; and head of the National Urban League from 1971 to 1981, the post that would cement his status and power in the movement and in the larger world.

Over those two decades, Jordan's work had a sweeping impact, both directly and indirectly. It led to the registration of millions of new Black voters and the training and election of thousands of Black officials. It brought an infusion of millions of dollars into historically Black colleges, hastened the end of de jure segregation and employment discrimination based on race, and accelerated the integration of institutions and structures previously reserved only for whites, including corporate boardrooms. Along the way, he became known as one of the most effective and dynamic leaders of the movement—gracing the covers of almost every major national magazine during the 1970s with his broad smile and intense eyes. Every president from Johnson to Reagan would come to know and work with him.

Metaphorically, if the civil rights movement of the 1950s and 1960s had been about conferring on Black patrons the right to check in to any hotel in the country, as Jordan believed, the 1970s was about having the financial means to check out and pay the bills. That meant opening up economic opportunities that had traditionally been denied to Black people, a feat that required the active cooperation of the white corporate and philanthropic elite. His first entrée into corporate America came in 1966 when he was invited to President Johnson's White House Conference on Civil Rights and met hundreds of Fortune 500 CEOs, many of whom would become precisely the kind of friends who could help create those opportunities.

Jordan proved masterful at playing both the inside and outside game to benefit his cause. First at the United Negro College Fund and then at the National Urban League, he would use his immense powers of persuasion to attract crucial financial support while offering counsel to white CEOs trying to make better connections with Black America. In part to solidify the corporate support he attracted, Vernon agreed to serve on some of his biggest donors' corporate boards, including Bankers Trust and Xerox. At the peak of his influence later, he would serve concurrently on thirteen corporate boards, including such blue chip companies as Monsanto, American Express, Calloway Golf, Revlon, and Dow Jones; in all but one, he was the only Black director. Black people in total at that time held only 222 seats on the boards of the *Fortune* 1000. Jordan occupied a staggering 6 percent of those seats.

Henry Louis Gates, the celebrated Harvard literary critic, credits

Jordan as the man most responsible for breaking down the color barrier in corporate America: "Vernon did more to integrate the corridors of power on Wall Street than any other Black leader. Historians will remember Vernon Jordan as the Rosa Parks of Wall Street."

Despite his coziness with big business, Jordan also spoke his mind when he sensed that his corporate patrons were reneging on their responsibilities to the Black community. One day in the late 1970s, Jordan was in Florida to deliver a speech before the New York Savings Association. He planned to lambast the association for failing to do what their charter required: "reinvest funds in the communities where they made money." They were instead taking money they raised from Black communities and investing it into rich white communities where they could generate better returns, places like Boca Raton, where he stood that very night. Minutes before he was to speak, bank officials confronted him: They told him he couldn't give the speech because it was too incendiary. Speechwriters stood ready to modify it.

Defiant, he informed them if that was what they wanted, he would leave immediately and release the speech as written on his way back to the airport.

The bank backed down, and he gave the speech exactly as he had drafted it.

The episode was vintage Vernon Jordan, a man who believed racial reconciliation could be best achieved through moderation and cooperation, but never at the expense of principle.

Early on the morning of May 30, 1980, at the height of his prominence and impact, Vernon Jordan's life came within a hair's breadth of ending.

He was in Fort Wayne, Indiana, returning from a late dinner at the home of a supporter—a white woman—after delivering a speech earlier in the evening at an Urban League dinner. As investigators would only learn a year later, he was noticed by a white racist who became enraged at his transgression: a Black man driving in a car with a white woman. The punishment: a single bullet into Jordan's back that would lead to five operations within the first sixteen days of the shooting, and 104 straight days of hospitalization in Fort Wayne and New York City. Had the bullet entered just a quarter inch to the left, it would have hit his spine and killed him. Surprisingly, Alabama governor George Wallace was the first person to send him a telegram when he came out of his initial operation. An avowed segregationist—who in 1963 used his body to block two Black students from entering the University of Alabama—Wallace had himself been the target of an assassin's bullet in 1972 when campaigning for president.

Despite their vastly different outlooks on race, Wallace wanted Jordan to know that he too would recover, but the road ahead wouldn't be easy. "I appreciated that wire," Jordan recalled in a speech years later at his college alma mater. "It said to me that it is possible for the deepest of divisions to be subordinated to common humanity." When they later met in person, the wheelchair-bound Wallace asked Jordan for a hug: "The governor of Alabama, a mean old racist who once stood in the schoolhouse door to keep black people out, could no longer stand at all yet he wished he could stand, not to set himself defiantly or athwart history, but rather to embrace me as a brother."

When he finally emerged from New York Hospital in September, he had lost fifty-five pounds but gained a new perspective on his life: He had been spared for a reason.

For twenty years, Vernon Jordan had taken care of others. Now he understood it was time to take care of himself and his family.

Once he decided he was ready to leave the Urban League and practice law, the choice was easy. He accepted a partnership at the prestigious Washington, DC, law firm Akin, Gump, Strauss, Hauer & Feld. One man sealed the decision for Jordan: Robert Strauss, Washington's most renowned power broker and insider. Strauss had watched Jordan's ascent over the previous decade. He knew instinctively the skills that had made Jordan so successful fighting for civil rights could be seamlessly transferred to his well-heeled corporate clients fighting for advantage within the private sector. So he watched and waited. As soon as Jordan expressed interest in joining, Strauss hired him.

Jordan's transition to the private sector started slowly. His first few years he performed below expectations. But then he hit his stride, and by the end of the decade he had become exactly what Strauss always envisioned: a Washington power broker, rainmaker, and political fixer in his own right. A lawyer in the traditional sense he most certainly was not. "If you ever see me in the library here tap me on the shoulder," he once told a young associate. "For you will know that I am lost." Instead, his main if amorphous responsibility, as one partner described, was to counsel clients "who have problems in which Washington plays a substantial role." For his work, he annually earned more than a million dollars in legal fees and another half a million dollars from his board directorships, offering him financial security for the first time in his life.

In moving from the front lines of the civil rights movement to the front of the white corporate boardroom, Vernon became the first "crossover artist," providing an example to a generation of Black businesspeople that they could not only succeed but also thrive in the world of big business. "He didn't just open up doors for Blacks in business; he guided them to success," American Express CEO Ken Chenault remembered. "His invisible hand was always there, mentoring people from all walks of life. So many people today will say it was 'Vernon who made the difference' in their [lives]."

Chenault added: "And when white CEOs started asking *him* to introduce *them* to other white CEOs, that's when I knew Vernon arrived."

But amidst all his new success, Jordan suffered a deep personal loss. In 1965, just seven years into their marriage and two years after their daughter, Vickee, was born, Jordan's wife, Shirley, had been diagnosed with multiple sclerosis. A decade later she was confined to a wheelchair, but she never gave up trying to be as independent as she could. Many of Jordan's intimates like Skip Gates still recount the moving image of Vernon wheeling Shirley into rooms big and small to ensure she remained a vital part of his life. In 1985 she lost her valiant battle. Within a year Jordan married Ann Dibble Cook, a former professor of social work at the University of Chicago and a power broker in her own right; he also became a stepfather to her three children, Janice, Mercer, and Toni.

As he began a new chapter of his personal life, his public life was thriving. By 1991, as the nation's focus started to turn to next year's presidential election, Vernon Jordan was as powerful and adored as anyone in America who worked at the intersection of politics and business.

Every year, Vernon Jordan traveled to Europe to attend the Bilderberg Meeting, a gathering of the world's elite who met to discuss issues threatening the US-European alliance. It was also a chance for leaders and would-be leaders from both sides of the Atlantic to see and be seen. Jordan had been invited to join the group back in 1968 at the behest of Richard Neustadt, a Harvard historian and presidential advisor who saw him as an up-and-coming civil rights leader. In 1991, Jordan extended that same invitation to another up-and-comer: Governor Bill Clinton.

The timing was perfect for the restless Clinton, now in his fifth term as governor of Arkansas. Clinton was raring to ascend more rapidly the national political ladder. One rival politician, Georgia senator Sam Nunn, openly mocked him as "the only politician to be a rising star in three decades." After winning back the governor's office in 1983, Clinton mastered the art of governing a small state—adding jobs, training its workers, and improving its schools. Voters took notice, reelecting him each time with comfortable margins. Confident in his secure base, the ever-ambitious Clinton was spending more and more of his time outside of Arkansas working on national issues. He toyed with running for president in 1988, pulling back only the morning of his intended announcement. At the Democratic National Convention that year, Clinton gave a widely panned thirty-two minute prime-time speech on behalf of the party's nominee, Michael Dukakis. It bombed, both at home and in the hall, where his only cheer—a Bronx one—came at the end when he said, "In closing..." But once again, Clinton found a way to turn defeat into victory. Three days later, he went on *The Tonight Show* and joked with host Johnny Carson that his horrendous speech was all part of a plan—to make Dukakis look good by comparison. Once he picked up the saxophone and did a passable rendition of "Summertime" with the show's band, the audience—and America's fickle voters—had been won over.

Clinton soon emerged as one of the leading voices of moderation in a party that had lost three straight presidential elections, in part because voters thought it had moved too far to the left. In a 1991 speech to the Democratic Leadership Council's national convention in Cleveland, Clinton laid out a vision that encapsulated all that he had learned in seventeen years of politics. The party needed to embrace both opportunity and responsibility in order to find relevance again. It was no longer enough to advocate for a cleaner environment or for better schools, Clinton argued. The party also had to embrace economic growth and educational excellence at the same time. The audience loved Clinton's message, showering him with a long standing ovation. He returned to Arkansas more convinced than ever he had found the winning message for Democrats to recapture the White House in 1992.

Watching his friend from his law office in Washington, Jordan had arrived at the same conclusion. Progressives to their core, both men realized that the only way to attain and keep power was to moderate their views and appeal to the center. For Clinton, that meant reframing divisive issues like affirmative action and welfare reform in terms that wouldn't scare away more conservative white voters; for Jordan the civil rights leader, that meant at times abandoning the strident rhetoric and tactics of some of his more activist colleagues, like John Lewis or Jesse Jackson, and working collaboratively with the white power establishment. Now, as a private lawyer and political advisor, it meant lending his imprimatur to politicians like Clinton who shared his urgency to advance the Black agenda and possessed the political and oratorical skills to translate electoral success into progressive reforms.

But Jordan also believed that Clinton needed some international exposure and foreign policy gravitas to become a more credible candidate. Bilderberg presented a perfect opportunity. "Vernon called me and said 'I think you ought to go,'" Clinton said. "'It'd do you good to get exposed to them and you'll learn something.'" In June 1991, the two arrived in Baden-Baden, Germany, for a few days of high-level talks with European leaders like Gordon Brown, the future British prime minister, as well as senior members of the Bush administration. They then proceeded to Russia, giving Clinton a chance to witness for himself the country's dramatic transition to a market-driven democracy. They were there the night Boris Yeltsin was elected Russia's first president, then visited a newly opened McDonald's that seated 850 people and where everyone young spoke English.

As they flew home, both men agreed that Clinton had performed well. Jordan viewed the experience as Clinton's "coming out party." Without question, Clinton possessed the maturity and intellectual breadth to be president. But there was one problem: President Bush's approval ratings, sky-high after the first Gulf War, still remained in the 70s. To most observers, the president looked invincible. But not to Clinton. He had recently seen factories close in his home state and sensed a vulnerable spot in Bush's popularity, telling Jordan as their plane crossed the Atlantic: "I'm out here living in the real America and Bush's popularity is based on the Gulf War. But the economy is in much worse shape than people know.... There's a lot of anxiety here. And I really believe that I need to look at this."

Jordan was more cautious. He knew how ruthless the Bush political operation could be; he had seen campaign manager Lee Atwater's infamous and racist Willie Horton ad against Dukakis.

"Are you tough enough to handle this?" Jordan asked his friend.

"If I'm not, then I'm not tough enough to be president," Clinton replied.

The trip to Bilderberg accomplished its purpose. Clinton sized up his opponents and concluded he could beat them. "Bill listened to representatives of the Bush administration give answers to questions about domestic policy, economic policy at Bilderberg," Hillary remembered, "and he thought their answers were so weak that I knew he came out of it very fired up and thinking maybe he would actually run that year. It was very important to his decision to run."

Four months later, standing on the steps of the old Capitol in downtown Little Rock, Bill Clinton announced his candidacy for president of the United States. Just a decade removed from his kitchen debate with Jordan about whether to leave politics for good, Clinton now stood as one of only five credible candidates—still a long shot but with a clear path to the nomination if everything went right. And everything seemed to be going right by the middle of January 1992, when he outraised, outhustled, and outsmarted his opponents. *Time* put him on its cover, with the blurb "Is Bill Clinton for Real? Why both hype and substance have made him the Democrats' rising star."

He had gained real momentum. But then two stories emerged that nearly derailed his candidacy. First, Gennifer Flowers, a singer from Arkansas, came forward to allege a twelve-year extramarital affair with Clinton. He admitted "causing pain in my marriage" on *60 Minutes* with Hillary by his side; his momentum stalled as voters processed yet another sex scandal after damning revelations had derailed the 1988 campaign of another front-runner—Gary Hart. Then things got worse when letters surfaced revealing that Clinton had initially sought a Vietnam draft deferment despite his claims to the contrary. In a letter written to his ROTC recruiter in 1970—which the Clinton campaign made public in February 1992—twenty-two-year-old Clinton thanked the recruiter "for saving me from the draft" but said that he ultimately "decided to accept the draft in spite of my beliefs for one reason: to maintain my political viability within the system." With just three weeks to go before the crucial New Hampshire primary, a once-promising campaign was fighting for its survival.

His friends—literally hundreds of them—stepped in to rescue him.

No president in modern presidential history accumulated a larger and more diverse collection of friends than Bill Clinton. "It keeps life from being unbearable," he said when asked why. He liked those who were "fundamentally good-hearted, who care about other people and can identify with people, even those very different from them," Clinton explained. "I like people who are there in the storms as well as in the sunshine, the 'stickers.' "

Clinton himself was one of those "stickers," vacuuming up friends wherever he went. David Gergen worked in senior staff positions for four presidents, including as counselor to President Clinton in 1993–1994; he is among the most astute observers of the presidency and how presidents govern effectively. "He's one of the best I've ever seen at friendship—it's one of his single greatest talents," Gergen said. "Whether he was doing it consciously or not, I think he knew early on that practicing the art of friendship was good practice for the art of politics and would help his political career." Gergen also observed: "Everything, everyone, was fodder for his political narrative. The most amazing thing about his mind was his ability to pull together disparate facts, stories, and experiences and weave them into that compelling narrative. His friends helped him do that." A consummate storyteller, Clinton took from every friendship details both large and small to animate his political tale.

But he did not just craft those tales for utilitarian reasons; he displayed genuine loyalty to his oldest and closest friends. No matter how high or how quickly he ascended the political ladder, he maintained a populist attachment to his roots. Of all other presidents, Gergen found this quality especially powerful in Clinton: "As he moved into more select and elite worlds he always maintained his connection to the real people he met and befriended. Even as he evolved over the twenty years he was in Arkansas, he never removed himself from them. He was a star from a little state, he was going places, going to the White House, but he never left them."

The more Clinton tried to explain the damning allegations, the less voters believed him. Back in Little Rock, Clinton and his advisors searched for a way to dispel those doubts. They needed a message to reassure voters that Clinton was a good, honest, God-fearing man who cared about people and their struggles. The solution was to tap into the "FOBs," or Friends of Bill, as they famously became known: the hundreds of Arkansans he had grown up with, befriended, and had come home to serve. Within days, more than a hundred FOBs were enlisted and dispatched to New Hampshire, led by his oldest friend, David Leopoulos, who had drained his savings to drive to the Granite State and spend two weeks doing radio interviews and campaign appearances. "Some of his friends from outside, like Mickey Kantor and Harry Thomason, and all of his friends from

Arkansas—they literally showed up and dragged him out of the depth of his political oblivion in New Hampshire so he could survive," Hillary remembered.

Even today the former president expresses awe over how his friends pulled together to save his candidacy:

> I didn't know anything about it in advance, but six hundred people took out an ad in the *Manchester Union Leader* and said, "Don't believe all the stuff they tell you about our governor. If you want to know about him, call us." All six hundred of them had their phone numbers and said, "Call us collect. We'll pay for the call." A hundred and something of them left their lives and drove to New Hampshire and put out a hundred thousand little baggies on doors in New Hampshire with the old-fashioned Betamax campaign film in a cup holder. I don't think there's a way in hell I'd have made it without them. I'm probably the only guy that ever got elected as president because of his personal friends.

Those years of studying names and making connections indeed paid off. Clinton survived New Hampshire, finishing a better-than-expected second to Senator Paul Tsongas from neighboring Massachusetts. Christening himself "the Comeback Kid," Clinton turned that second-place finish into a victory that resurrected his presidential campaign and propelled it forward. He swept the next two months of primaries. By the end of April, he was the party's presumptive nominee.

The biggest question facing Clinton now was whom to pick as his vice presidential running mate. He knew he needed someone with superior discretion and judgment to help guide the process. Surprising no one, he chose Vernon Jordan to cochair the committee delegated with selecting the nominee.

The committee operated off two lists: the official list of forty or so potential candidates that the committee (chaired by future secretary of state Warren Christopher and staffed by five junior lawyers) would consider; and the private list known only to a handful of Clinton intimates.

On that list were the candidates Clinton was *really* interested in, the ones who, without any vetting, he had already decided would be his strongest choices. Clinton quietly asked Jordan to determine who on that very short list was ready to run with him.

Interestingly (and never disclosed before), the man Clinton ultimately picked, Senator Al Gore of Tennessee, was not on that short list.

As Clinton recalled, "The first person I was interested in was Bill Bradley because I had known him a long time." With Jordan, Clinton called Warren Christopher to set up a clandestine meeting in Philadelphia. Christopher made the pitch to the New Jersey senator and former New York Knick, but as both men later confirmed, he took his name out of consideration right from the beginning. He wasn't interested.

Clinton then asked Jordan to call West Virginia senator Jay Rockefeller. He and Clinton had worked closely together as governors, and they shared a passion for health care. Clinton thought the promise of passing comprehensive health care reform might be enough to attract Rockefeller's interest, but he was wrong. Rockefeller told Jordan he was sure Clinton was going to lose the general election. When he did, Rockefeller planned to run for president himself in 1996.

With both Bradley and Rockefeller nixed, Clinton directed Jordan to make one last call to his friend Colin Powell, Bush's chairman of the Joint Chiefs of Staff and a hero of the Gulf War. Clinton always believed Powell was a long shot: "I never really thought he'd do it because he was made a general under President Reagan and had a good relationship with President Bush," Clinton said. "He also probably thought of himself as a liberal Republican before it became a vanishing, extinguished species. But I felt that I had to ask because I thought the country was so divided. If we could have had a national unity ticket, it would be good." Powell was immune to Jordan's argument and declined, citing his wife Alma's fear for his safety.

The short list exhausted, Clinton turned to his longer list. Gore immediately shot to the top, but as a fellow Southerner from the baby boomer generation, he didn't offer the geographical, biographical, or even ideological diversity tickets usually valued. Plus, Clinton wasn't sure the two would mesh personally. On the day of his interview, Gore traveled in a tinted Ford Bronco to meet Clinton secretly at the Capitol Hilton Hotel. Only then did they discover that they actually liked each other. Greeting each other stiffly in suits and knotted ties, they started talking at nine in the evening and, soon enough, one hour turned into two and then three. Ties came off, shirttails dangled, beer bottles emptied; each time an aide reminded the governor of the time, he was shooed away. By the time the meeting finally ended at midnight, the two men were sprawled out on couches, spent from talking but aware they had just made a historic match.

Late in the evening on July 6, Clinton placed a call down to Carthage, Tennessee, where Gore was hiding from the press, and offered him a place on the ticket. The men would enjoy a productive and healthy partnership until 1999, when they had a bitter falling-out after Clinton's impeachment for lying about his affair with Monica Lewinsky and Gore's seething assessment that it had cost him the presidency in 2000.

Of all the roles Jordan would play throughout his friend's presidency, helping navigate the treacherous waters of presidential personnel was among the most important. No one could equal the size or quality of his Rolodex, his judgment of human character, or his ability to persuade. "His genius was his charm," George Stephanopoulos, one of Clinton's closest aides during the campaign and through the first term, said. "His smile, his voice, his size, his looks, his capacity to pay attention to you, all of it in combination could just get you to do anything without realizing it was really him that was pushing it. He wasn't unlike Clinton in that way, but more."

According to Stephanopoulos, "Vernon would make you feel you were being taken into his confidence and you could trust him, that he wasn't going to screw you. Even when he got me to do something I absolutely didn't want to do, he could make me feel like he had my back. He did it with such grace that no one on the receiving end ever felt suspicious or resentful." In short, Jordan embodied the idealized version of Clinton's "sticker" friend, someone who knew how to cultivate loyalty in a city full of transient relationships.

Bill Clinton was still in his jogging clothes when the first encouraging returns started trickling in at 6:30 p.m. on November 3, 1992. A few hours later, with his family and the Gores surrounding him in the living room of the governor's mansion, the networks declared him the winner. Though he beat President Bush with only 43 percent of the vote—the smallest winning percentage in eighty years due to the strong showing of third-party candidate Ross Perot—he won the Electoral College easily with 370 votes. Three days later, in a nod to just how much he trusted and valued his best friend, Clinton used his first official announcement as president-elect to announce Vernon Jordan as chairman of his Presidential Transition Committee. Jordan later described that announcement as one of the proudest moments of his life, the first person of color ever to serve in that role. He also became the first person of color to hold the unofficial distinction of First Friend to an American president.

As he and Jordan got down to the work, the president-elect was adamant about one thing: "I told [Vernon] right away I want a diverse administration," Clinton recalled. "And in America that means a lot of Latinos. It means we have to find some Asians to participate. They were then a much smaller percentage of our population than they are now. And it means I want people with disabilities. I want people who have the ability to serve in these positions and you, Vernon, you got to find me people who are good." By the end of his first term as president, Clinton with Jordan's help would make good on his promise, appointing more people of color and women to the Cabinet and other high-level positions than any other previous president.

When Clinton laid out his ambitious plan, he didn't have to say out loud what both already knew: that he desperately wanted Jordan in his Cabinet. From the start, both Clinton and Hillary had made it known that they envisioned their attorney general to be a person of color or a woman. The previous seventy-seven AGs had all been white men. Almost immediately, Jordan faced pressure from the president-elect, his wife, former colleagues in the civil rights movement, and friends to be the one to break that barrier. Lloyd Cutler, a dean of the Washington bar, told him he *needed* to take the job because "black teenagers would look up to him."

Wasting little time, Clinton asked Jordan to come to Little Rock to talk about the potential appointment. Meanwhile, lawyers back in Washington rushed to compile any public information available to informally preclear Jordan's name for consideration.

The friends met on the back porch of the governor's mansion just as the late November sun began to set. The president-elect had two big questions to discuss. He started first with whom to appoint as secretary of state. Clinton knew Warren Christopher desperately wanted the post, but both Jordan and Clinton agreed that Colin Powell would be the stronger secretary. After Powell had turned down the vice presidency, however, both knew he was unlikely to accept a Cabinet post, and so they acquiesced to moving forward with Christopher. Clinton then got to the main event. Without preamble, he bore in: "Will you be my attorney general?"

Clinton could see hostile forces gathering to oppose him in the Republican Party; he was especially aware that night of the ascendance of a young Georgia congressman named Newt Gingrich. "I saw what they were going to try to do to weaponize the courts. They were already well on their way to doing then what's second nature to [attorney general] Bill Barr now," Clinton said in 2020. Clinton believed Jordan was the one to keep Gingrich's conservatives at bay: "I knew that Vernon was respected enough, wise enough, and tough enough to do the right thing and that he had enough of a foothold in the Washington press establishment that they would respect him when he said what needed to be said."

Like the lawyer he was, Jordan had come ready with his rebuttal. Twenty of the previous thirty years he had worked as a civil rights activist, at relatively little pay. Now he was making real money, and he liked the lifestyle it provided. Beyond the pecuniary considerations, he thought he could be a more effective transition chair if he wasn't in contention for a job himself. But he also knew saying no to his best friend could complicate a friendship he treasured: "There was no way to know where my decision might take our friendship," Jordan said.

Jordan took a few moments before he answered Clinton. The president-elect could tell he was giving the matter serious reflection. Finally Jordan spoke.

"I'm just not going to do it," he stated.

"Why?" Clinton asked.

"I like my life now. I like being a private citizen. I like the business things I do. I like not having a hassle with the political press."

Jordan offered a persuasive alternative:

> The main thing is, I've watched a lot of presidents and you need me more as a friend than in the government. I'll be way more good to you being there always, 24 hours a day to tell you what I think and not have to worry about running some department and the latest controversy, everything. It's best for you. And I know it's the best thing for me.

Clinton knew Jordan so well by then that he recognized what he could and couldn't talk him into. When Jordan played the friend card, Clinton knew he had lost the argument:

> Remember this guy had had a fascinating life, but also a tough one. His first wife came down with MS and was bedridden for most of their marriage. Ann in many ways saved his life and they created this blended family with all the kids together. And he just didn't want a job where he had to be on the road and under fire all the time. And I realized that it was deep. And I also realized how dependent I had grown on him, just because we got each other. He got me, I got him. You didn't have to explain the history of the world.

One thing Vernon and Ann Jordan *did* have to explain to Bill and Hillary Clinton during the transition was how to navigate the shark-infested waters of the city they would soon make their home. Of all the modern presidents-elect, only Jimmy Carter rivaled Clinton in how little he was known, understood, or even liked by the Capitol's elite—many of whom suspected he was coming to town "to make war on them." Clinton knew the establishment had the power to make or break a presidency. And he knew that as much he and Hillary were outsiders to this community, Vernon and Ann were consummate insiders.

Jordan took the lead, telling Clinton shortly after the election that he and Hillary "needed to come to Washington and have some dinners." Jordan sensed in particular that Clinton needed to forge better relations with a national press corps that viewed him at best with skepticism and at worst with disdain. If Clinton wanted to enjoy the honeymoon period typically accorded new presidents, Jordan believed, he needed to work the press, their owners, and their most important readers as assiduously and as carefully as he himself did.

Just a year earlier, with Clinton mulling whether to run for president, Jordan had taken him to the Jockey Club in the lobby of Washington's Ritz Hotel. At tables around them were a who's who of Washington's elite, including Tom Foley, then the Speaker of the House, and Pamela Harriman, one of the city's great hostesses and wife of billionaire W. Averell Harriman. "That's who you need to be having dinner with if you want to run for President," Jordan told Clinton.

Two weeks after the election, Bill and Hillary jetted up to Washington for a day and a half of meetings and meals arranged by Jordan and Ann. This time, the luminaries he longingly observed a year earlier were now angling to have dinner with him. The Jordans hosted the first dinner at their home. Seated around their dining room table were many of the most powerful people from politics, journalism, and business, including Senator Bill Bradley, ABC anchor Ted Koppel, and businessman James Wolfensohn, chairman of the Kennedy Center.

Reflecting back on that night, Clinton had regrets: "I didn't spend enough time personally working the press like Vernon did. The young people in our press operation were gifted, but they were always trying to keep me away from them." The dinner—and the one the following night Vernon and Ann cohosted with Pamela Harriman at her Georgetown town house—were opportunities to leverage Vernon's charm and goodwill to reset Clinton's often rocky press relationship and provide the honeymoon he desperately wanted. "Everybody who should have been there was there," Bruce Lindsey, Clinton's closest aide for twenty years, remembered of the first evening. "Vernon got up and told the story about how he stood on the shoulders of people who came before him. It was one of the better dinners of the transition. We thought coming out that everything would be rosy. It didn't turn out so rosy."

As the president settled into the White House, a certain routine developed between him and his First Friend. Whenever a critical moment arose or a key decision had to be made, aides always received the same instruction: "Call Vernon." And Vernon was indeed called, countless times, from supporting the "Don't Ask, Don't Tell" policy (which allowed gays to serve in the military so long as their sexual identity remained hidden) to reluctantly endorsing the appointment of an independent counsel to investigate Whitewater ("the worst decision of my presidency," Clinton rued twenty-five years later). As one former Clinton confidant said, "He wanted Vernon because he had the best political advice of anybody in the West Wing, the best natural instincts of how something would roll."

Typically when Clinton needed Jordan's input, they conversed by phone, in one-on-one meetings in the Oval Office, or in the residence. On the rare occasions when he would sit in on Clinton's larger Oval Office gatherings, which included the gaggle of young press and policy aides who populated the White House during the first term, Vernon would hang on the periphery, silently observing the discussion around him. Then the room would clear of everyone except Vernon. "Only then would he offer his opinion," the confidant explained. "The president realized at some point early in his first term he didn't have enough adults in the room. Vernon was so much more authoritative and seasoned than anybody else there. He would come in and just talk it through with Clinton. They saw each other as equals, standing shoulder to shoulder. There was never any bullshit when they talked. They talked straight and honestly with each other."

Clinton knew too that when Jordan came to dispense advice on a certain matter or individual, he wasn't just getting his consigliere's judgment, but a distillation of all the intelligence Vernon had synthesized from his vast network. Bruce Lindsey still marvels at how crucial that intelligence network was to the president. "No one knew DC better than Vernon. He knew everybody, and was constantly picking up intelligence from them. So when he goes to see the president to talk about an issue, he knew more about what was going on—who was for it, who was against it, who would be a problem—than anyone else in the room," Lindsey recounted. "More importantly, he didn't give it unless he was very confident."

Jordan was also the only one around the president who saw himself as an equal—to the extent anyone can be an equal to the most powerful person on the planet. Joe Lockhart, Clinton's onetime press secretary, believed the president appreciated that Vernon had made his name and fortune long before Clinton became president. As a result, Lockhart said, "Vernon didn't care that Clinton was president, and Clinton liked that. Here was an older guy he didn't have to perform for, unlike most everyone else." It's no surprise that the only other person during those years (or after) whom Clinton felt an equal closeness to was Terry McAuliffe, Clinton's most prolific fund-raiser during his presidency and later a governor of Virginia. Like Jordan, McAuliffe was independently wealthy and neither wanted nor needed anything from the president.

In this singular First Friendship, then, there were no long, brooding silences waiting to be broken by just the right anecdote or joke. No one served the other, nor did one gain more from the other. No money changed hands, no favors extended, no patronage won.

Numerous former aides recall with astonishment how over eight years they never saw or heard Jordan ask for *anything* from Clinton except for one small request—that he attend the 1994 President's Cup golf tournament due to his friendship with Robert Trent Jones, architect of the eponymously named host course. He never asked for time on Clinton's schedule or input on legislation for clients, nor did he seek special favors for himself or for his friends. Of course it didn't hurt Jordan's law practice to be known as the First Friend, but when it came time to cash in for tangible gain, Jordan was his own man.

"People think I needed Bill Clinton to be who I was," Jordan said in 2018, spelling out his words: "My L-I-F-E," he continued, "did N-O-T start when Bill Clinton became President."

On July 20, 1993, Jordan was at a dinner party at the home of Ben Bradlee, the *Washington Post* executive editor, when a call came from the White House: The body of Deputy White House Counsel Vince Foster had just been discovered in a Virginia park, with evidence of a self-inflicted gunshot. Within seconds Jordan excused himself and rushed to the Foster home to console Foster's widow and the president. No answers existed as to why this taciturn, steady man would walk out of his West Wing office to get lunch, only to then drive himself to a remote park and take his own life. Jordan and the president sat together with Lisa Foster and a few others until 2 a.m., trying in vain to make sense of the inexplicable. Then the two of them drove back to the White House where Jordan stayed with the president until the sun rose. "He was wonderful to me that night," Clinton remembered.

Foster's suicide unleashed a new reason for the press to further uncover the details of a failed investment the Clintons had made in 1978 in the Whitewater Development Corporation. Foster had been working on the case for months; his death and a perceived cover-up of its circumstances led to new speculation that his suicide was somehow connected to the land deal. A year that had started with so much promise at Clinton's inauguration had by late summer become mired in grief and rancor.

In the wake of Foster's suicide, the exhausted president needed a vacation. Unlike previous monied presidents who owned seaside compounds or ranches, the Clintons had nowhere to go. A debate ensued at the White House in early August about an appropriate summer getaway. Patti Solis Doyle, Hillary's scheduler then and later her 2008 presidential campaign manager, recalled of the deliberations that "Bill would say, 'I'm the President, I can go anywhere.' Only Vernon was the one to say to him, 'No, you can't go there.'" Finally, at Jordan's insistence, the Clintons agreed to escape to Martha's Vineyard, a tony island off the coast of Massachusetts and a second home to some of the country's most prominent celebrities and business leaders, including Jordan himself, by then a twenty-year renter on the island. For more than a century, the island was known as an especially hospitable place for Black people to vacation, even earning the nickname "the black Hamptons" for its rich history of racial tolerance. Jordan knew Clinton would feel particularly at home there. He was right; with but one exception in 1995, the Clintons would return to the island every summer of his presidency.

For ten days, Jordan and Ann acted as the Clintons' sherpas and social interpreters. Their first night they celebrated Clinton's forty-seventh birthday at the Jordan home with such island luminaries as Jackie Onassis, Katharine Graham, and author William Styron. The revelry went on until 1 a.m. and included a rousing rendition of "Happy Birthday to You" led by Jordan. Solis-Doyle remarked later how at parties then and throughout the Clinton presidency, the two Clintons and the two Jordans "would consciously stand apart in order to spread the wealth of their presence among fellow guests. Each of them was such a star in whatever room they were in that to satisfy the need for their attention they had to separate from each other."

The next nine nights were the same, a blizzard of high-wattage dinner parties all orchestrated by Vernon and Ann to entertain their First Friends and the island elite. During the most memorable night, Clinton and Jordan got up after a small dinner at Katharine Graham's house and gave an impromptu duet of "Lift Every Voice and Sing." Until then Jordan had never realized that Clinton knew the words to the Black national anthem—three long stanzas even people steeped in the movement can't recite—until they rose in song together:

Lift every voice and sing
Till earth and heaven ring,
Ring with the harmonies of
Liberty;
Let our rejoicing rise
High as the listening skies,

Let it resound loud as the rolling
Sea.

It was just another sign to Jordan of how simpatico they were on race, and how empathetic Clinton was on an issue core to Jordan's being. For Clinton, who memorized Martin Luther King, Jr.'s "I Have a Dream" speech as a teenager and took pride in being so close to one of the most significant civil rights leaders of his generation, the night made him feel like he was "a little boy getting a ribbon, it was that important. The man who would live the life he lived could still be free enough to let me in and want to be in my life." Clinton marked the occasion with an inscribed photograph: "To Vernon—from the only WASP who knows the lyrics."

The Vineyard days followed their own natural rhythm, centered around golf, which the two men played nearly every day on the island's two challenging courses. Over Clinton's presidency and post-presidency, the men spent hundreds of hours together on whatever golf course was available to them. Anyone who played with them through the years would attest that it wasn't the competition or a desire to improve their handicaps that kept them coming back, round after round. Neither was much of a golfer. Clinton was better, but only because Vernon refused to take lessons. "All the time I'd say, 'Why in the hell don't you take lessons? You can take fifteen strokes off your game. You could be a single-digit handicapper easily,' " Clinton remembered. "He said, 'I'm just trying to destroy one more stereotype about blacks, that we're all great athletes.' "

What brought them back instead was the release each felt in being able to walk in the open air and not have to perform or even be *on* for anyone. "The times we spent on the golf course were precious to me. It was almost 100 percent distraction. We didn't have serious conversations to speak of," Clinton said.

One topic they did like to indulge, according to numerous people who played with them, was women. Jordan himself acknowledged that fact at a dinner party when asked by someone what he and Clinton talked about on the links. The week the scandal over Clinton's relationship with Monica Lewinsky broke, both *Time* and *Newsweek*, in their otherwise G-rated profiles of Jordan, confirmed the quote and broke the news. "Asked at a party earlier this year what it was he and Clinton talk about on the golf course, Jordan slyly replied: 'We talk pu—y,'" *Newsweek* wrote. *Time* reported the same but did away with all the letters except "p."

A person who often witnessed their banter described it as "highly exaggerated, highly sexualized, mostly playful; it had a nineteenth-hole quality to it." He added: "You have to remember, they were very similar in their personalities, very attractive and sensual people, and also enormously attractive to women." Each was fully aware of his powerful appeal and the stories that naturally flowed from it. The golf course, without any prying eyes and ears, was their private venue to share those stories.

Although of course no transcripts exist of those conversations on the golf course, the general sentiment expressed by Clinton and Jordan confidants was that women were a constant subject of discussion (on and off the golf course) because they liked so much to be around women. This fact presents one of the most difficult aspects to this particular First Friendship. Known to be publicly flirtatious with women, both men were trailed throughout their careers by rumors of dalliances. Clinton's accusers have been well documented, but no one has ever come forward to accuse Jordan of *any* inappropriate behavior. Where fact and law are concerned, the only public record of this dimension to their friendship comes during Clinton's second term in office, from the Office of the Independent Counsel's investigation of the president and his relationship with Monica Lewinsky—including the ambiguous role Vernon Jordan played in that national saga.

For now, however, Jordan's role remained decidedly unambiguous, through moments of both soaring achievement and profound challenge.

In September 1993, Bill Clinton achieved a breakthrough that had eluded his five immediate predecessors: He had brought together Israeli prime minister Yitzhak Rabin and Palestinian Liberation Organization leader Yasser Arafat to sign an accord establishing a process for peace between the Israelis and Palestinians. Rabin and Arafat received the

Nobel Peace Prize in 1994 for what became known as the Oslo Accords. And while the accords ultimately failed to establish a permanent peace, they gave hope for nearly a generation that peace was attainable. The two adversaries, shaking hands for the first time and encircled by the outstretched arms of a beaming Clinton, became an iconic image of his presidency.

Rahm Emanuel, Clinton's senior advisor for six years, organized the event. "I guess they said, 'Give it to Rahm, he's Jewish,'" Emanuel remembered.

> Everything came together quickly in the end so we had to organize the signing on very little notice.... I had brought my father to the signing—as an immigrant from Israel who fought in the war for Israel's independence. The seating at events like that is obviously carefully considered, and like all things in Washington, proximity is everything. When my dad and I went to find our seats right before the signing started, I was pretty pleased to see we were seated in the 10th row, middle seats. Not bad! I stood one last time to scan the area to make sure everything was in place. That's when I spotted Vernon, sitting three rows ahead. Vernon hadn't been involved at all in the negotiations or in planning the event, and I had never seen him in any White House conversations on the Middle East. But there Vernon was, right where it mattered—just as he always was. I looked over at Bruce Lindsey and said, "Do you see Vernon?" Bruce nodded. "No matter where we go in life, Vernon will always be three rows ahead of us," I said, and we laughed.

The Jordan home became a safe haven for the Clintons as their first full year in the White House came to its merciful end. Bill, Hillary, and Chelsea celebrated Christmas Eve at the Jordan home surrounded by their large extended family of children and grandchildren. "They filled a really big need we had at Christmas in 1993," Hillary said. She had lost her father earlier in the year, Clinton's mother, Virginia, was in the final stages of losing her battle to cancer, and the still-fresh Foster suicide continued to haunt them. Beyond their personal tragedies, the First Family felt under siege more generally. That Christmas, and every one that followed until they left the White House in 2001, the Jordan family became an extension of their own. "We were under constant, unfair, inaccurate attacks all the time for all kinds of things," Hillary said. "The press was really difficult, the Republicans under Gingrich were nasty, so having the people who are your true friends around you is one of the ways you carry the burdens of that pretty daunting office of being President or the wife of the President. That Christmas, Vernon really was the First Friend."

As the troubles mounted, Jordan made a point of befriending those around the president. Many of Clinton's closest aides recalled getting a call from Jordan during his first term inviting them to a meal, and then turning that first occasion into regularly scheduled weekly or monthly meetings. Shrewdly, Jordan realized he needed help in looking after the president's interests, which were constantly under siege from all sides. One senior aide remembers Jordan "talking as if he was reading me into the family" at their first meal. He took this aide to lunch, and after discussing some of the substantive issues he was concerned about, Jordan zeroed in on one matter that especially bothered him: "The President needs to dress better." To Jordan, always one of the nattiest dressers in DC, the president needed a serious upgrade in his suits. "In those days his suits were all from the late '80s—wide lapels, baggy pants, not exactly the kind of suits Vernon wore," the aide wryly recalled. Then and throughout his life, Jordan wore only suits by Oxxford, the haberdasher who dressed Clark Gable, and Charvet shirts from France. "He'd tried to introduce him to a tailor but the President wasn't interested, and now he was including me in his mission, as if there was something I could do about it."

Jordan did not just polish how Clinton presented himself to his political orbit; he also controlled who would enter that orbit in the first place. No one inside or outside the White House during Clinton's presidency had more of a hand in orchestrating the chairs around the president than Jordan. Every month, Jordan received dozens of requests from job seekers requesting a good word from him with the personnel office. To streamline the process, he worked out a scheme with Director of White House Personnel Bruce Lindsey, the close Clinton confidant. As Lindsey recalls, "Vernon's plan was: 'If I send you a letter, you can ignore it. But if I call you, it's someone I'm really interested in.' So whenever I was looking at an application, the only question I needed to ask was, did he call?"

When Clinton moved George Stephanopoulos out of his role as White House communications director and into the more amorphous role of senior advisor, Jordan had just the right solution to mollify the popular aide: He quietly arranged for Stephanopoulos to take the office directly next door to the Oval Office, the best parcel of real estate in a cramped West Wing. In a town where proximity to power is everything, news of the move silenced the noise that Stephanopoulos had lost his juice. When Agriculture Secretary Mike Espy came under fire for allegedly accepting improper gifts, Vernon was the one to coax him out. He helped move Clinton's first chief of staff, Thomas "Mac" McClarty, aside in favor of Leon Panetta, and then when Panetta decided to resign, Vernon was the key voice advocating Erskine Bowles to succeed him rather than Jordan's foe Harold Ickes. When Clinton's political mastermind, Dick Morris, committed the unpardonable sin of allowing a prostitute he was frequenting to listen in on his conversations with the president, Jordan made sure he was fired.

Meanwhile, Jordan's good friend Colin Powell continued to be a Clinton obsession. Powell's term as chairman of the Joint Chiefs of Staff had expired in 1994; as Clinton surveyed the Republican field that could challenge him in 1996, his biggest fear was that Powell would run and then beat him. With Jordan as his confidant, the president wrestled with how they could sideline Powell from waging a campaign. One idea was to award him a fifth star in exchange for permanent retirement; upon further thought they realized it would only enhance his appeal as a candidate without guaranteeing he wouldn't ultimately run. They instead decided to offer the four-star general the chance to replace Warren Christopher as secretary of state in 1994. The president called Jordan at seven o'clock on a Sunday morning and asked him to set the plan in motion. Jordan made the exploratory call to Powell, but, like his offer of the vice presidency two years earlier, he was rebuffed again by the popular general, leaving his candidacy an open question as the calendar hurtled toward 1996.

In the end, Powell didn't run, and Clinton won a tough but comfortable victory over Kansas senator Bob Dole. After losing both the House and the Senate to Republican control two years earlier, the victory marked a stunning turnaround. At his nadir in the spring of 1995, Clinton became such an afterthought that he was forced to defend his continued "relevance" as president to a public starting to doubt he had any. But by election day, the public liked the president's new, more centrist approach. Over the last two years, he had reasserted his role by reviving the economy, passing welfare reform, and creating a sensible affirmative action program—"mend it, don't end it"—which Jordan had actively helped shape. The country seemed at peace, the White House more serene, and voters liked their vigorous, youthful leader enough to give him another four years—the first Democratic incumbent since FDR to accomplish that feat.

Throughout it all, Jordan functioned as the "unseen, steadying hand, maintaining the balance of what at times was a rocky situation inside the White House, smoothing over the edges among competing power centers that could have really hurt the President," said Don Baer, Clinton's White House communications director at the time. "His most important influence was to remind people, in his diplomatic but firm way, that they were there only to serve the President and his goals for the country, not to fight among themselves or pursue their own interests."

If Bill Clinton's presidency had ended after one term, his friendship with Vernon Jordan would be a relatively straightforward story for the history books. But it didn't. Instead, the last three years of Clinton's second term became consumed in scandal, with his best friend caught fatefully at its center. In its wake, the narrative arc of their friendship would bend but never break.

On October 25, 1997—Bill and Hillary's twenty-second wedding anniversary—a distraught twenty-four-year-old former White House intern named Monica Lewinsky sat down in the Oval Office to discuss her employment options with the president of the United States. Lewinsky was in a position to make demands on the president because they were having an on-again, off-again affair, all played out in the immediate vicinity of the Oval Office. The dynamics of their relationship were complicated and fraught on multiple levels—not least because of the vast power gap that separated them. Their sexual liaison had started more than two years earlier, when Lewinsky was only twenty-two years old, and continued with just enough regularity that at some point a White House aide had her transferred from the White House to the safer, more distant confines of the Pentagon. But a frustrated Lewinsky had sought to return, only to be rebuffed.

Now she was sitting in the Oval Office asking the president to find her a lucrative job in Manhattan, and she knew just the person who could arrange it. Vernon Jordan had secured a similar safe landing in 1994 for the Clintons' good friend Webster Hubbell, a former top Justice Department official and law partner of Hillary's, after he was accused of stealing from former clients. Hubbell needed money to hire lawyers, and Jordan found him a $63,000 sweetheart retainer at the cosmetics company Revlon on whose board he served. Lewinsky now wanted Jordan to do the same for her, and Clinton agreed to arrange a meeting between the two.

That single request would lead to a year of intense scrutiny and questions about a man more used to solving problems than causing them. During that time, it would test an intimate friendship in a very public forum, forcing Jordan to the brink between loyalty to his friend and concern for his own reputation.

In the ensuing scandal that became a national crisis, two central questions about Jordan's conduct emerged: Did the president's best friend find Monica Lewinsky a job to buy her silence or color her testimony? And did he encourage her to lie about her relationship? These were questions with huge consequences for the future of Clinton's presidency and that of the country. It gave investigators multiple angles to probe, thrusting a man far more comfortable wielding power behind the scenes into a harsh national spotlight.

Ten days after her meeting with Clinton in November 1997, Jordan sat down with Lewinsky at his Akin Gump law office. He agreed to help find her a job—"We're in business," he assured her—but then sat on it for more than a week, not sensing any particular urgency. For years, Jordan had helped people find employment, passing on résumés and, for the lucky few he cared about, making the crucial call. It's what a connector does, and he often found real satisfaction in launching careers, even sometimes for relative strangers. But at this moment—unknown either to him or to his friend the president—tectonic plates were moving that would reshape what may initially have been a banal request of a connector to a much more troubling, perhaps even illegal ask.

The 1978 Whitewater land deal that first surfaced during the '92 campaign, and that preoccupied Vince Foster in the final days before his suicide, had escalated into a multiyear investigation led by Independent Counsel Ken Starr. Starr had spent four years trying to tie the Clintons to shady loans, but he'd found nothing and the investigation was on its last legs. He even resigned, only to be cajoled into returning to his job by conservative media criticism. Now information about Lewinsky was starting to make its way to Starr, and he sensed a chance to revive his flagging case based on this sordid news.

Fortuitously for Starr, a separate sexual harassment lawsuit against the president was gaining traction at the very moment the Lewinsky news began to circulate. An Arkansas state worker named Paula Jones had already accused then-governor Clinton of sexually harassing her in a Little Rock hotel room in 1991. The Supreme Court ruled unanimously the year before that the suit could continue even against a sitting president (it wouldn't take much time or be disruptive, the justices reasoned). After unsuccessful attempts to settle the matter through the years, the case in 1998 was now on track for trial. Just as Lewinsky was asking Jordan for help, Jones's legal team got wind of her affair. Lewinsky had been pouring her heart out to her friend Linda Tripp, a career White House assistant who earlier worked for Vince Foster. And Tripp was sharing all she knew with Jones's lawyers, who in turn later shared what they heard with Starr's investigators.

After piecing the affair together, Jones's lawyers added Lewinsky's name to a list of witnesses they planned to depose before trial, hoping her testimony would help make the case that the Jones incident, if true, formed part of a larger pattern of sexual harassment.

Clinton soon learned from his lawyers that Lewinsky would be among eleven witnesses called by Jones's legal team. Inexplicably, he kept that news both from Lewinsky and allegedly from Jordan for eleven days. During that time, after initially ignoring Lewinsky, Jordan now became her advisor, taking her to lunch while finally making good on his promise to help her find a job. He called some of his best corporate contacts, including Revlon and American Express, another of Jordan's corporate boards. When Clinton finally did inform Lewinsky she was on the witness list in a late-night phone call on December 17—after her lunch with Jordan—the president advised her to file an affidavit denying they were in a relationship: "If the two people who are involved say it didn't happen, it didn't happen," Lewinsky later testified Clinton told her.

Before Lewinsky could file the perjurious affidavit, Jones's lawyers ratcheted up their pressure by subpoenaing Lewinsky, prompting her to return in an anguished state to Jordan's office, this time for help finding a lawyer. Now Jordan was fully aware of her legal predicament, and the legal jeopardy he could be subject to for finding her a job at the very moment she was being pursued by prosecutors. Over turkey sandwiches and Diet Cokes, the conversation this time got more personal, with Lewinsky telling him how she felt about the president, including how frustrated she was with how "he doesn't call me enough or see me enough." Jordan replied, "You're in love, that's what your problem is," suggesting that he did not already know the true nature of their relationship. When he then asked her directly if she and the president were involved in a sexual relationship, she denied it. Jordan knew that if Lewinsky had said yes, finding her a job would be a nonstarter; prosecutors would paint his efforts as an attempt to buy her silence.

Later, Lewinsky told Starr's investigators that she "sensed" Jordan already "knew" the affair was sexual. In his own testimony, Jordan insisted he had no knowledge, either from the president or from Lewinsky, that the relationship was ever sexual—however implausible that may seem, given his long intimacy with Clinton, their proclivity to talk about women, the lengths to which he went to aid Lewinsky, or his innate shrewdness. The question of what he knew and when remains permanently unresolved.

In mid-January Revlon finally agreed to see Lewinsky; she made the trip to New York only to bomb the interview. When Jordan heard, he called the company's chairman, Ron Perelman, and pressed him to make the job offer. It worked, and Lewinsky was hired. Clinton hoped that within a month, if all went well, she would be 230 miles to the north and no longer a threat to him or his presidency.

It wouldn't be that easy. Neither Clinton nor Jordan knew it at the time, but Jones's lawyers were setting a trap. They now understood from Tripp the full extent of Clinton's affair with Lewinsky: They were sure Lewinsky's affidavit, now filed, was a lie, and they were just waiting for Clinton to perjure himself in sworn testimony.

An affair Clinton hoped would disappear as soon as Lewinsky could land a new job in New York was now in jeopardy of blowing up, especially when Attorney General Janet Reno agreed to allow Starr to expand his Whitewater investigation to include the Jones case. And the president's call to Jordan to help her find a job was looking more and more to prosecutors like a potential obstruction of justice rather than a benign request.

Around this time Tripp shared some new information allegedly gleaned from her conversations with Lewinsky that was particularly enticing to Starr's prosecutors: Not only had Clinton counseled Lewinsky to lie about the affair, but Jordan had, too. If Jordan in fact knew the affair was sexual and urged Lewinsky to deny it, as Tripp claimed, prosecutors believed it could subject Jordan to a possible felony charge of suborning perjury.

In the second hour of Clinton's deposition on Saturday morning, January 17, Jones's lawyers pounced: Did Clinton have "sexual relations" with Lewinsky? Did they ever exchange gifts? Had he encouraged her to deny the relationship in the affidavit she submitted to them? Clinton tried to use his legal background and linguistic skills to obfuscate and deny the allegations about Lewinsky, but the grilling unnerved him. As they left the deposition, Clinton's lawyers feared his predicament was about to get much worse.

What became abundantly and suddenly clear to the president and his lawyers was this: A Justice Department investigation into a 1980s Arkansas land deal was now a far-ranging investigation into the president's own sexual conduct. Although the full extent of Ken Starr's appetite for sexually intimate and even lewd details about the president's life was still yet to be revealed, the enormity of Starr's prosecutorial power—and the zealotry with which he intended to pursue it—was coming sharply into focus.

Meanwhile, the press began picking up hints that a major scandal was about to break involving the president and an intern. The first story of the affair was posted at 2 a.m. on January 17—the morning after the deposition—on the *Drudge Report*, a right-wing website known for its muckraking articles. On January 21, it hit the mainstream press, with the *Washington Post* finally breaking the full Lewinsky story under a four-column headline:

> Independent counsel Kenneth W. Starr has expanded his investigation of President Clinton to examine whether Clinton and his close friend Vernon E. Jordan Jr. encouraged a 24-year-old former White House intern to lie to lawyers for Paula Jones about whether the intern had an affair with the president, sources close to the investigation said yesterday.

Three days later, Jordan went before a bank of cameras at a Washington hotel to say "absolutely and unequivocally" that Lewinsky had never told him she was having a sexual affair with the president. Without taking any questions, he added that he never counseled her to lie about her relationship and that in finding her a job he had not sought to buy her silence.

Having laid down his marker, Jordan then retreated from the public eye while his friend fought for his political life. This time there would be no kitchen conversation to buck him up as he flailed. Because of the ongoing investigation, the independent counsel had the legal right to question Jordan about any conversation he had with the president or anyone else around him, so Jordan stayed away, effectively isolating himself from the White House at the very moment his counsel could have been most helpful. Numerous Clinton aides later wondered whether Jordan could have talked Clinton out of his defiant, finger-wagging denial of ever having sex "with *that woman*, Miss Lewinsky." Jordan, they believed, was the only one who might have convinced him instead to confess to the affair and to gamble that the public might forgive him.

With Jordan effectively sidelined, the press went into overdrive trying to discern the impact the scandal would have on their First Friendship. Conventional wisdom held that if Jordan were to desert the president, it would open the floodgates for other, lesser friends to jump ship as well. Speculation reached its crescendo in early February when Jordan's mentor, Robert Strauss, went on *60 Minutes* and said there were limits to Jordan's loyalty to Bill Clinton. "Vernon is a loyal, devoted friend. But Vernon is not a fool. And Vernon isn't a man who does things that he knows to be either conceivably illegal or improper. He doesn't do that."

One of Jordan's greatest attributes was his loyalty: to his family, to the causes he served, to the friends he cared most about. And so the message Jordan ultimately sent through intermediaries back to the White House rang loud and clear: He wouldn't betray the president—but he also wouldn't sacrifice himself or his freedom. If anyone could walk that fine line and find the seam—saving the president without crossing into perjury—it was Jordan.

And that was exactly the tack he took in twenty hours of testimony he gave before the Starr grand jury in early March. Emerging after his first five hours, he left no doubt where his loyalties stood. "As to those of you who cast doubt on my friendship with President Clinton, let me reassure you that ours is an enduring friendship, an enduring friendship based on mutual respect, trust and admiration," Jordan said, speaking slowly to emphasize his words to the gaggle of cameras and microphones. "That was true yesterday. That is true today. And it will be true tomorrow." The remaining fifteen hours would be much the same, a "bravura performance by Mr. Inside," as the *Post* later described it.

Throughout the spring and summer of 1998, Clinton tried valiantly to maintain a façade of normalcy at the White House and in his marriage. The Lewinsky affair was still the stuff of suspicion, not fact. Hillary remained his bedrock, refusing to believe the Lewinsky story and waging her own campaign to discredit a "right-wing conspiracy" she believed was intent on destroying her husband. For much of the spring and into the summer, the public continued to believe Clinton was telling the truth, in large part a result of the White House's aggressive campaign to shame Lewinsky and paint her as a liar.

But by the time Lewinsky began her testimony under an immunity agreement before the Starr grand jury, and the public learned more details of their affair, serious doubts started to creep into the president's defense. On July 17, Starr subpoenaed Clinton to testify before the grand jury. The noose was tightening, especially after Starr's investigators showed up at the White House late one night to draw the president's blood; it soon confirmed that semen found on a Lewinsky dress was his. After eight months of denial, Clinton now had no option but to admit to the affair—first to his wife, and then to the American people. Shortly before testifying to the grand jury, he confessed to Hillary upstairs in the White House residence. One aide who was nearby that morning later described a "shriek—I never heard a sound like that before" coming from the room the moment when he told her of the affair.

The next day, August 17, Clinton testified by video from the White House before the Starr grand jury. As he did at the Jones deposition, the president fell back on legalese to dance around the prosecution's questions. For five hours, prosecutors tried to prove he had perjured himself during the Jones deposition; and for five hours, Clinton employed every trick he knew to deny it. At one point, asked if he had lied in January when he said "there is absolutely no sex" between himself and Lewinsky, Clinton replied:

> It depends on what the meaning of the word "is" is. If the—if he—if "is" means is and never has been, that is not—that is one thing. If it means there is none, that was a completely true statement.... Now, if someone had asked me on that day, are you having any kind of sexual relations with Ms. Lewinsky, that is, asked me a question in the present tense, I would have said no. And it would have been completely true.

That quotation became one of the most famous of his presidency, second only to "that woman." Later that same night, Clinton finally confessed to the American people that he had engaged in a relationship with Lewinsky "that was not appropriate" and "wrong." He admitted he had "misled" people but denied he had ever lied. The reaction to his four-minute speech was vicious. Critics panned him for spending too much time attacking Starr and too little time apologizing to Lewinsky or to the public. Lewinsky later said listening to it made her feel like "a piece of trash."

With the confession now behind him and Hillary (barely) still with him, the Clintons the next afternoon embarked for the sanctuary of Martha's Vineyard. Vernon Jordan was the first person to embrace Clinton when he came off Air Force One. The two men had not seen each other or even talked on the phone since the morning the *Post* published its first big story in January, eight months earlier. But having completed their grand jury testimonies, they could resume their friendship with little legal jeopardy for now. The next ten days would be unlike any other of their four previous Vineyard vacations. There was little socializing—one of the few social events was a quiet dinner with just the Jordans—and even less golf. The president was consumed instead with trying to salvage his marriage.

Although conventional wisdom held that the Clintons would never divorce, two informed sources later confirmed that things got so bad between husband and wife that Clinton dispatched Jordan to talk Hillary out of leaving him.

For the next six months, Clinton continued to fight for his political life. In September, Ken Starr released his salacious report of Clinton's sexual escapades with Lewinsky. For Jordan, the report delivered mostly good news: The prosecutor found no evidence that Jordan attempted to obstruct justice or urge Lewinsky to lie, saying only that prosecutors saw "parallels" between what Jordan did for Lewinsky and what he did earlier for Hubbell. In testimony later included in the final Starr report, Lewinsky admitted she lied when she told Tripp that Clinton and Jordan had advised her to lie about the affair. "I think I told her that—you know, at various times the president and Mr. Jordan had told me I had to lie," Lewinsky testified to the grand jury. "That wasn't true."

"I told her a whole bunch of lies that day," Lewinsky testified.

For Clinton, though, the news was dire. Not only did it include sordid details of his affair with Lewinsky, but it also concluded with eleven possible grounds for impeachment.

In October, the House Judiciary Committee took up impeachment hearings. Two months later, for only the second time in American history, the full House of Representatives approved two articles of impeachment against a sitting president: for lying under oath to the Starr federal grand jury when he swore he'd had no sexual relations with Lewinsky, and for obstructing justice, in part by asking Jordan to secure a job for Lewinsky.

Because of the second charge, Jordan was forced to testify again—and again he employed the verbal jujitsu that distinguished his earlier grand jury testimony. He obfuscated, charmed, and dissembled just enough to steer clear of perjury without implicating his friend. At times his testimony strained credulity, but there was no way to prove it was false—exactly how Jordan probably intended it.

The Senate trial was high in theatrics but low in suspense. By the time of the vote, the country had long since determined that the president's misdeeds didn't rise to the level of either "high crimes or misdemeanors," and public polling showed a clear majority favoring the president's acquittal. When the final vote fell far short of the two-thirds needed to convict him, Clinton's fear of being the first president to be forced from office (without resigning) ended.

Clinton had survived again. And so had his friendship with Vernon Jordan, which the president acknowledged later needed some careful tending to restore to its former state: "I knew he hadn't done anything wrong and hoped someday he would be able to forgive me for the mess I had gotten him into," Clinton wrote.

One person who didn't emerge from the scandal intact was Monica Lewinsky. For the next twenty years she would be branded "that woman," relentlessly ridiculed in the press and on social media for everything from her looks to her clothes to her weight. Only in recent years has she begun to emerge, speaking eloquently to her struggles in the scandal's wake. Today she is lauded as an effective anti-bullying advocate and an inspiration for people who have suffered public humiliation.

Vernon Jordan was getting ready for dinner on a Saturday night in early January 2001 when he received a call from his best friend for an impromptu get-together: "Can you come over for dinner tonight? I'm here alone." A few weeks earlier, George W. Bush had been declared president-elect when the US Supreme Court ruled 5–4 to end a recount of votes in Florida—which decided the closest election in US history. Clinton would leave the White House with a 66 percent job approval rating, eight points higher than when he arrived. Just as he had after the New Hampshire meltdown in 1992, after the shocking midterm losses in 1994 and then the humiliation of being impeached, Bill Clinton had persevered. As he sat upstairs alone in the residence, he wanted company, and he wanted it from the man who had done so much for him, including helping save his presidency just two years earlier.

"I've already got a dinner, but I can come by after, say around nine," Jordan told him, as independent and honest with the president as always.

Jordan pulled up to the South Portico a few hours later in his red

Cadillac convertible and went upstairs to the second-floor kitchen in the White House residence, where the president was waiting. They settled in for what both sensed would be the final night they shared together in the historic house. Jordan asked for some wine; Clinton directed "the only person there from the upstairs staff" to fetch a bottle. When the wine was laid on the table, Clinton remembered, "I didn't pay attention to it, but later I found out it was some super valuable bottle to the White House. I think it was worth $10,000."

Twenty years later, both men described the night as one of the most memorable of their lives. In the intimacy of a nearly empty White House with the finest wine flowing, they let down their guard. "There was nothing we didn't talk about—what happened in that house over the last eight years, all the fun we had together, what it meant to us," Jordan said. Clinton remembered it as a night he could finally feel a measure of peace after subjecting his best friend to the hell of his impeachment mess. It is possible that until that night, the two friends weren't ready yet to have a conversation that would resolve whatever lingering tension existed over the Lewinsky affair.

"It was one of the most wonderful times of my life," Clinton said, "because I realized that he realized that I did not intentionally get him in the middle of all that impeachment stuff. He didn't hold me responsible for somebody else's misconduct. It meant the world to me that he knew that I had no earthly idea that he could be drawn into all that."

After nearly six and a half hours, Clinton walked Jordan down to his car. It was 3:30 a.m. Clinton told him how much he loved him. It was what Clinton always said to Jordan when they parted. Clinton walked back the two flights of stairs to his bedroom while Jordan started down the south driveway toward the illuminated Washington Monument in the distance. His eyes watered. "Here I am, the son of a postman who grew up in the first public housing project in the country for African Americans, and I've just spent the last six hours sharing everything with the most powerful man on the planet," he remembered thinking. Tears started to stream down his face. Halfway down the driveway, overcome, he turned off the engine and rested his head on the steering wheel. Finally, his crying subsided, and Jordan started the car again and headed home.

Even as the friends forged new paths—Jordan to Wall Street, Clinton to all corners of the world on behalf of his philanthropic foundation—the cadence of their friendship remained the same. If schedules ever got too busy that they couldn't connect for a meal or a game of golf, Jordan would call Clinton's chief of staff just to ask, "How's my boy doing?" Publishing houses threw around huge money for Jordan to write a tell-all memoir that would cover his relationship with Clinton. Instead, he wrote *Vernon Can Read* for a small imprint (and an equally small advance), intentionally ending his story in 1992.

In 2008, when Hillary Clinton ran for president against freshman senator Barack Obama, many people naturally thought Jordan would support the first Black candidate with a clear path to the nomination and the presidency. He didn't. After a disappointed Michelle Obama asked why, Jordan candidly told her: "I'm too old to let race get in the way of friendship." To the candidate himself, he was even more direct: You're not ready. But he promised Obama that if he did beat Hillary, "I'll be with you 100 percent." Jordan kept that promise, becoming a friend, Martha's Vineyard golfing partner, and informal advisor to President Obama during his eight years in the White House.

In December 2019, Jordan suffered a stroke from which he would never fully recover. Confined to his home in the Kalorama neighborhood of Washington, DC, he lived long enough to see a Howard University graduate become the first Black vice president of the United States. Then, on March 1, 2021, after eating dinner, Vernon went up to his bedroom and died peacefully in his sleep.

For years, Clinton and Jordan had joked that whoever outlived the other "would have to take the other's back" and "say the right things" at the unlucky one's funeral. Now in the early afternoon of March 9, 2021, that responsibility fell to Clinton.

Jordan's closest intimates were gathered in Crampton Hall at Howard University to bid their farewells to the man they revered. After two and half hours of prayer, song, and testimonials, Bill Clinton finally took the stage to offer the closing assessment of Jordan's life, and the meaning of their friendship.

Few in the world shared as intimate a relationship with Jordan, yet Clinton now found himself grappling with one seminal question: "Who was this guy anyway?" After "a lifetime studying and listening to him," Clinton reflected, "I was [still] always being surprised by him." In the end, Clinton answered his own question: "Vernon Jordan was a 'Man in Full.' " He could be "ambitious for himself and his family, and still care about every single person in his life and use his ambition and success to hold up as a mirror to others of what they could become."

Jordan's real occupation, Clinton said, was "the freedom business." Jordan knew "that if he hated other people, he would never be free—that reconciliation was better than resentment." Vernon "helped us all to be more free, and he did it with the beauty of any classical artist or athlete."

As his eulogy came to a close, Clinton got emotional. "When they closed that coffin today I felt like a part of my heart was going to be pulled out of my body." Still, in his pain, Clinton felt the gift of Jordan's friendship. "God, we were lucky he was here. Lucky he was our friend. Lucky that in this imperfect world, somehow he found us and we found him."

"My friend, you are free," Clinton said as he closed his book. "I miss you. I love you. And I thank you."

Acknowledgments

This book would not have been possible without the support and encouragement of my agent and longtime friend Esther Newberg of ICM. Esther was the very first person I called in the spring of 2018 when I decided I wanted to write this book; her enthusiasm, steadfast support, and advocacy for this project throughout kept me focused and motivated. She read and gave feedback to every chapter, and she even let me call outside her limited "office hours." There is no one better to have on your side (as I know from once being on the other!). I'm also indebted to Esther for introducing me to Wayne Coffey, who helped research and give shape to this book in its formative days.

I feel fortunate to have been in the able hands of my editor and publisher, Sean Desmond. He believed in this project from the get-go and helped save me from too many "clausy" or "purple" constructions. His admonition to "show, don't tell" became my mantra. Any shortcomings are mine alone. His team at Twelve were also a pleasure to work with. Special thanks to Jarrod Taylor for his designs and to Rachel Kambury and Bob Castillo for shepherding me through the tedious stages of copyediting.

It should come as no surprise that someone who chose to write about friendships would himself have many friends to acknowledge for providing useful and at times critical feedback to early and late chapter drafts. A few in particular I owe a special thanks for reading the entire manuscript and displaying enormous patience in answering my many follow-up questions: Lon Jacobs, Liz Bowyer, Alexandra Mousavizadeh, Saul Shapiro, Jodie Balsam, Ken Orkin, and Craig Balsam. Liz in particular took a special interest in a few of the chapters and gave generously of both her time and many skills to help make them better. So many other friends went well beyond what I could have expected by providing notes to chapters when I nervously sought feedback: Richard Siklos, Josh Steiner, Abby Pogrebin, Michael Lynton, David Remnick, Michael Waldman, Richard Plepler, Dan Klores, Howard Wolfson, Blair Effron, Marisa Kayyem, Richard Cohen, Jasper Aaron, Carol Goodheart, Don Baer, Ron Dermer, Jeffrey Toobin, Michael Oren, Charlotte Alter, Olaf Olafsson, Tom Nides, Jake Siewert, Andrew Plepler, Charlotte Alter, Jamie Gangel, Holly Peterson, Michael Kramer, Richard Beattie, Daniel Bonner, Leah Scholnick, Matt Steinfeld, Max Neuberger, Ziad Ojakli, Lila Watts, David Goodman, Kate Bolduan, and Sarah Lubman. All took time from their busy professional and personal lives; I'm grateful for their wisdom, knowledge, and—if sometimes unwanted but always appreciated—candor. I'm blessed in addition to have two sisters, Beth Ginsberg and Marsha Ginsberg, who took an active interest in the book and offered great insights.

I'm also grateful to the cadre of experts I either knew before or came to know during research for this book who made invaluable contributions. Professor and friend Steve Gillon, the eminent American historian, read numerous chapters; his detailed edits and suggestions for new angles to pursue always made them better. He also introduced me to Yale PhD Andrina Tran, who became a researcher, thought partner, and editor for much of the last six months. I couldn't have finished this book on time without her help. She's a real talent with a bright future.

Jeffersonian scholar Peter Onuf offered great insight into the friendship between the third and fourth presidents and helpful suggestions on the finished chapter; likewise Andrew Burstein and Nancy Isenberg, authors of *Madison and Jefferson*, the definitive chronicle of their long friendship. Authors Peter Wallner, who wrote an acclaimed two-volume biography of Pierce, and Richard J. Williamson, who wrote a book about the impact of the Pierce-Hawthorne friendship on politics and the literary imagination, also took the time to offer important context to that friendship. And to my learned father-in-law, Howard Aaron, who first alerted me to their friendship when I broached the idea of my book.

Dr. Charles Strozier, historian, psychoanalyst, and author of *Your Friend Forever, A. Lincoln,* shared his unparalleled knowledge of the

Lincoln-Speed relationship willingly. No account of that critical friendship in American history will ever match what he accomplished with his seminal work. Professor Thomas Balcerski, a scholar of early American history, was also helpful in better understanding how the Lincoln-Speed relationship fit with the social norms of its time. Lawyer James Robenalt awakened me to the virtues of Warren Harding but ultimately steered me to Colonel House. He was generous in sharing his vast trove of House diary entries that were invaluable for the insights they offered. Fortuitously, my history professor at Brown University, Charles Neu, also happened to write the most recent and complete biography of Colonel House. I'm deeply grateful for his time on the phone and his suggestions on how to sharpen my account of House's friendship with Woodrow Wilson.

Without historian Geoffrey Ward, Daisy Suckley's important role in the life of Franklin Delano Roosevelt might well have been lost to history. Fortunately, he saw the value of her letters and diary and organized them into his seminal book. I'm indebted to him for reading the chapter and for his helpful suggestions. FDR historian and friend Jonathan Alter gave me critical edits as well as the idea to focus on the FDR-Suckley friendship. Rabbi Daniel Fellman's authoritative dissertation on the Truman-Jacobson friendship was a useful aid to better understanding their relationship, as were his recommendations for further research. I'm also thankful to author Charles Sanford for his time reviewing the chapter on President Kennedy and David Ormsby-Gore, and to Professor David Greenberg of Rutgers for his detailed feedback on Nixon's complicated friendship with Bebe Rebozo.

Several libraries and archivists were extremely helpful in gathering information for this book and providing deeper insight into the subject matter. Unfortunately, for much of the time I was researching and writing this book, libraries were closed due to the pandemic. While they were open, David Clark, an archivist at the Harry S. Truman Presidential Library in Independence, Missouri, responded quickly and helpfully to a deluge of questions via email and phone, and he was even more vital uncovering a treasure of great information on Truman and Jacobson. Likewise, Matt Reeves, Education and Outreach Librarian for Special Collections at the

Kansas City Public Library, was most generous in his assistance. Caroline Moseley, an archivist at the George J. Mitchell Department of Special Collections at Bowdoin College, was a vital resource on the lives of two of the college's most famous sons, Pierce and Hawthorne.

For the chapter on the friendship between President Clinton and Vernon Jordan—the only one in which I could double as both a journalist and an amateur historian—I benefited greatly from the Clinton alumni network, which remains as vibrant as ever nearly three decades after its formation. I'm especially thankful to Tina Flourney, Vice President Kamala Harris's chief of staff, who filled that role for President Clinton during the writing of this book. She was instrumental both in eliciting from the president his choice of a First Friend and then in securing my interview with him. The one-hour limit we had agreed to stretched to nearly two by the time we stopped talking; I'm relieved she let me exhaust not only her patience but also my long list of questions. Thanks also to my friend and former colleague Capricia Marshall for her help in securing my interview with Hillary Rodham Clinton.

Vickee Jordan and Toni Bush, Vernon's daughter and stepdaughter, were gracious to invite me to join them for lunch with Vernon and Ann Jordan on the day Joe Biden was declared president-elect in November 2020. I'm indebted to them both. Close Clinton friend and advisor Bruce Lindsey patiently answered my many questions and follow-ups, as were so many others close to the former president, including George Stephanopoulos, David Gergen, Joe Lockhart, Nancy Hernreich, Michael Waldman, Doug Sosnick, Don Baer, Patti Solis Doyle, Terry McAuliffe, David Leopoulos, and Kirk Hanlin.

I feel lucky to have great friends who have provided diversions and support throughout: Steve Price, Andrew Hurwitz, Craig Effron, Jeff Zucker, Cheryl Cohen Effron, Andrew Fox, Kerith Arnow, Jamie Lynton, Harry Wagner, Jeff Zients, Jeff Bewkes, Daniel Silva, Kevin Sheekey, John Rogovin, Steve Silverman, Amanda Green, Jef Caplan, my own Bills Mafia (the Kimmels, Duggans, Olshans, Mintzers, and Levys), Rich Caccappolo, and Devon Spurgeon. A special thanks to Teri Pitts for going out of her way to ensure I had a working computer at a critical moment in the process.

A friend and former colleague at Time Warner, Timothy Clifford, became passionate about this project even during his battle with ALS. For the final six months of his remarkable life, I would send him paragraphs and within minutes would get back his trenchant edits, made on his iPhone 6 using the only two digits that still worked—his thumbs. Those two thumbs, his indomitable spirit, and his love for history are reflected throughout. He died far too young on December 8, 2020, the day after I finished this manuscript. I miss him.

Finally, this book would not have been possible (or nearly as much fun to write) were it not for my family—my wife, Susanna Aaron, and our two sons, Sam and Alec. For large chunks of the last year while I completed the manuscript, we were housed under the same roof. There was nothing better than writing amid the fun, clamor, and sometimes chaos of us all being together, and I'll miss it once life resumes its normal cadence. None of them were immune from my annoying queries, especially Susanna, whom I was constantly interrupting from her own studies to tap her impeccable judgment. She still managed to earn her master's degree in urban planning this past winter. To all three, I am forever grateful for the joy of their companionship and for the love and support they provided throughout.

Photo Credits

Courtesy of the National Portrait Gallery: 1, 41, 79. **Alamy:** 113. **Courtesy of the Franklin D. Roosevelt Presidential Library and Museum:** 163. **Courtesy of the National Archives:** 199. **AP Photo/Bob Schutz:** 235. **Corbis Historical/Contributor via Getty Images:** 273. **PGA TOUR Archive/Contributor via Getty Images:** 307.

Bibliography

1. Thomas Jefferson and James Madison: Founding Partners

Brant, Irving. *The Fourth President: The Life of James Madison*. Indianapolis: Bobbs-Merrill, 1970.

Broadwater, Jeff. *Jefferson, Madison, and the Making of the Constitution*. Chapel Hill: University of North Carolina Press, 2019.

Burstein, Andrew, and Nancy Isenberg. *Madison and Jefferson*. New York: Random House Trade Paperbacks, 2010.

Cerami, Charles A. *Dinner at Mr. Jefferson's: Three Men, Five Great Wines, and the Evening that Changed America*. Hoboken: John Wiley & Sons, Inc., 2008.

Ellis, Joseph J. "Founding Brothers." *New Republic*, January 29, 1995.

———. *Founding Brothers: The Revolutionary Generation*. New York: Vintage Books, 2000.

Fleming, Thomas. *The Intimate Lives of the Founding Fathers*. New York: Harper, 2009.

Klein, Lauren F. "Dinner-Table Bargains: Thomas Jefferson, James Madison, and the Senses of Taste." *Early American Literature* 49, no. 2 (2014): 403–433. doi:10.1353/eal.2014.0034.

Koch, Adrienne. *Jefferson and Madison: The Great Collaboration*. New York: Knopf, 1950.

Meacham, Jon. *Thomas Jefferson: The Art of Power*. New York: Random House, 2013.

"The Papers of James Madison." Founders Online, National Archives.

"The Papers of Thomas Jefferson." Founders Online, National Archives.

Rosen, Jeffrey. "America Is Living Madison's Nightmare." *Atlantic*, October 2018.

Wilkins, Lee. "Madison and Jefferson: The Making of a Friendship." *Political Psychology* 12, no. 4 (December 1991): 593–608. doi:10.2307/3791548.

2. Franklin Pierce and Nathaniel Hawthorne: The Cost of Closeness

Bergen, Anthony. "Franklin Pierce and the Consequences of Ambition." *Medium*. November 23, 2015. https://medium.com/@Anthony_Bergen/franklin-pierce-and-the-consequences-of-ambition-577969fc81ca.

Casper, Scott E. "The Two Lives of Franklin Pierce: Hawthorne, Political Culture, and the Literary Market." *American Literary History* 5, no. 2 (Summer 1993): 203–230. http://www.jstor.org/stable/489745.

Hawthorne, Nathaniel. *The Centenary Edition of the Works of Nathaniel Hawthorne*, Vol. 17. Columbus: Ohio State University Press, 1987.

———. *The Life of Franklin Pierce*. Boston: Ticknor, Reed, and Fields, 1852.

Holt, Michael F. *Franklin Pierce*. New York: Henry Holt, 2010.

Lundberg, James N. "Nathaniel Hawthorne, Party Hack." *Slate*. September 14, 2012. https://slate.com/news-and-politics/2012/09/nathaniel-hawthornes-biography-of-franklin-pierce-whyd-he-write-it.html.

Miller, Edwin Haviland. *Salem Is My Dwelling Place: A Life of Nathaniel Hawthorne*. Iowa City: University of Iowa Press, 1991.

Moore, Margaret B. *The Salem World of Nathaniel Hawthorne*. Columbia: University of Missouri Press, 1998.

Nichols, Roy Franklin. *Young Hickory of the Granite Hills*. Newtown, CT: American Political Biography Press, 1931.

Nowlan, Robert A. *The American Presidents From Polk to Hayes: What They Did, What They Said & What Was Said About Them*. Denver: Outskirts Press, 2016.

Wallner, Peter. *Franklin Pierce: Martyr for the Union*. Concord, NH: Plaidswede Publishing, 2009.

———. *Franklin Pierce: New Hampshire's Favorite Son*. Concord, NH: Plaidswede Publishing, 2004.

Williamson, Richard. "Friendship, Politics, and the Literary Imagination: The Impact of Franklin Pierce on Nathaniel Hawthorne." PhD diss., University of North Texas, 1996.

Wineapple, Brenda. *Hawthorne: A Life*. New York: Random House, 2003.

3. Abraham Lincoln and Joshua Speed: Room Over the Store

Cole, Jennifer. "'For the Sake of the Songs of the Men Made Free': James Speed and the Emancipationists' Dilemma in Nineteenth-Century Kentucky." *Ohio Valley History* 4, no. 4 (Winter 2004): 27–48.

Donald, David Herbert. *Lincoln*. New York: Simon & Schuster, 1995.

———. *"We Are Lincoln Men": Abraham Lincoln and His Friends*. New York: Simon & Schuster, 2003.

Goodwin, Doris Kearns. *Team of Rivals: The Political Genius of Abraham Lincoln*. New York: Simon & Schuster, 2005.

"Joshua Fry Speed: Lincoln's Confidential Agent in Kentucky." *Register of the Kentucky Historical Society* 52, no. 179 (April 1954): 99–110. http://www.jstor.org/stable/23373760.

"Kentucky Lincoln: National Heritage Feasibility Study." National Park Service, Department of the Interior, September 2014.

Mathias, Frank F. "Slavery, The Solvent of Kentucky Politics." *Register of the Kentucky Historical Society* 70, no. 1 (January 1972): 1–16.

Sandburg, Carl. *Lincoln: The Prairie Years*. New York: Houghton Mifflin, 1926.

Strozier, Charles B. *Your Friend Forever, A. Lincoln: The Enduring Friendship of Abraham Lincoln and Joshua Speed*. New York: Columbia University Press, 2016.

4. Woodrow Wilson and Colonel House: The Man and the Opportunity

Brands, H. W. *Woodrow Wilson*. New York: Henry Holt, 2003.

Cooper, John Milton. *Woodrow Wilson: A Biography*. New York: Knopf, 2009.

Edward Mandell House Papers (MS 466), Manuscripts and Archives, Yale University Library.

Grayson, Adm. Cary T. "The Colonel's Folly and the President's Distress." *American Heritage* 15, no. 6 (October 1964; originally written 1926).

Hodgson, Godfrey. *Woodrow Wilson's Right Hand: The Life of Colonel Edward M. House*. New Haven: Yale University Press, 2006.

MacMillan, Margaret. *Paris 1919: Six Months That Changed the World*. New York: Random House, 2001.

Neu, Charles E. *Colonel House: A Biography of Woodrow Wilson's Silent Partner*. New York: Oxford University Press, 2015.

Seymour, Charles (ed.). *The Intimate Papers of Colonel House*. 4 vols. Boston: Houghton Mifflin, 1926–1928.

5. FDR and Daisy Suckley: Alone Together

" 'Affectionately, F.D.R.' Franklin D. Roosevelt's Long-Lost Letters to Daisy Suckley." Roosevelt House Public Policy Institute at Hunter College. http://www.roosevelthouse.hunter.cuny.edu/exhibits/affectionately-fdr/.

Alter, Jonathan. *The Defining Moment: FDR's Hundred Days and the Triumph of Hope*. New York: Simon & Schuster, 2006.

Brands, H. W. *Traitor to His Class: The Privileged Life and Radical Presidency of Franklin Delano Roosevelt*. New York: Doubleday, 2008.

Caron, Ali. "Margaret 'Daisy' Suckley" Profile. FDR Presidential Library and Museum website.

"Fireside Chats of Franklin Delano Roosevelt." FDR Presidential Library and Museum website.

Henneberger, Melinda. "FDR-Rated 'Hyde Park on Hudson' Wrongs Roosevelt and His Cousin," *Washington Post*, December 13, 2012.

Lelyveld, Joseph. *His Final Battle: The Last Months of Franklin Roosevelt*. New York: Knopf, 2016.

Meacham, Jon. *Franklin and Winston: An Intimate Portrait of an Epic Friendship*. New York: Random House, 2003.

Moe, Richard. *Roosevelt's Second Act: The Election of 1940 and The Politics of War*. New York: Oxford University Press, 2013.

New York Times, selected articles.

Persico, Joseph E. *Franklin & Lucy: President Roosevelt, Mrs. Rutherford, and the Other Remarkable Women in His Life*. New York: Random House, 2008.

Schlesinger, Arthur M., Jr. *The Coming of the New Deal, 1933–1935*. Boston: Houghton Mifflin, 1959.

Smith, Jean Edward. *FDR*. New York: Random House, 2007.

Tobin, James. *The Man He Became: How FDR Defied Polio to Win the Presidency*. New York: Simon & Schuster. 2013. Schuster, 2013.

Ward, Geoffrey C. *Closest Companion: The Unknown Story of the Intimate Friendship Between Franklin Roosevelt and Margaret Suckley*. New York: Simon & Schuster, 1995.

6. Harry Truman and Eddie Jacobson: Beshert

AIPAC Policy Conference Video. Washington, DC, 2016.

Becler, Hazel. Phone interview with author.

Fellman, Daniel J. "An American Friendship: A Critical Examination of the Life of Eddie Jacobson and His Relationship with President Harry S. Truman." Rabbinical Thesis, Hebrew Union College—Jewish Institute of Religion, 2005.

Hamby, Alonzo. *Man of the People: A Life of Harry S. Truman*. London: Oxford University Press, 1995.

Kansas City Public Library, Special Collections Division.

McCullough, David. *Truman*. New York: Simon & Schuster, 1992.

Ross, Dennis. Emails with author.

Truman Library Archives for background on Truman-Jacobson correspondence, Truman family history, Truman's political rise, and transcripts of Jacobson's autobiographical sketch and interviews with his daughters.

7. Jack Kennedy and David Ormsby-Gore: A Special Relationship

Bartlett, Martha. Phone interview with author.

Billings, Kirk Lemoyne. Oral History Interview. JFK Library.

Bundy, McGeorge. Oral History Interview. JFK Library.

Kennedy, Jacqueline. *Historic Conversations on Life with John F. Kennedy*. New York: Hyperion, 2011.

Leaming, Barbara. *Jack Kennedy: The Education of a Statesman*. New York: W. W. Norton, 2006.

———. *Mrs. Kennedy: The Missing History of the Kennedy Years*. New York: Simon & Schuster, 2001.

Logevall, Fredrik. *JFK: Coming of Age in the American Century, 1917–1956*. New York: Random House, 2020.

Michaelis, David. *The Best of Friends: Profiles of Extraordinary Friendships*. New York: Morrow, 1983.

Ormsby-Gore, Jane. Phone interview with author.

Ormsby-Gore, William David. Oral History Interview. JFK Library.

Sandford, Christopher. *Union Jack: John F. Kennedy's Special Relationship with Great Britain*. Lebanon, NH: ForeEdge, 2017.

Smith, Sally Bedell. *Grace and Power: The Private World of the Kennedy White House*. New York: Random House, 2004.

Tye, Larry. "Bobby and Jack: 2 Brothers, 1 Political Dynasty." Radio interview with Zoe Mitchell and Meghna Chakrabarti. National Public Radio. WBUR, Boston. 23 May 2017.

8. Richard Nixon and Bebe Rebozo: Silent Partner

Ambrose, Stephen E. *Nixon: The Education of a Politician, 1913–1962*. New York: Simon & Schuster, 1987.

———. *Nixon: Ruin and Recovery, 1973–1990*. New York: Simon & Schuster, 1991.

———. *Nixon: The Triumph of a Politician, 1962–1972*. New York: Simon & Schuster, 1989.

Crowley, Monica. Interview with author.

———. *Nixon Off the Record: His Candid Commentary on People and Politics*. New York: Random House, 1996.

Farrell, John A. *Richard Nixon: The Life*. New York: Vintage, 2017.

Fulsom, Don. *The Mafia's President: Nixon and the Mob*. New York: St. Martin's Press, 2017.

———. *Nixon's Darkest Secrets: The Inside Story of America's Most Troubled President*. New York: Macmillan, 2012.

Halberstam, David. *The Fifties*. New York: Ballantine Books, 1993.

Leinster, Colin. "Nixon's Friend Bebe." *Life*, July 31, 1970, 18B–26.

Lenzner, Terry. *The Investigator: Fifty Years of Uncovering the Truth*. New York: Penguin, 2013.

Miami Herald, selected articles.

Nixon, Julie. *Pat Nixon: The Untold Story*. New York: Simon & Schuster, 1986.

Nixon, Richard M. *RN: The Memoirs of Richard Nixon*. New York: Simon & Schuster, 1978.

Reeves, Richard. *President Nixon: Alone in the White House*. New York: Simon & Schuster, 2001.

Robenalt, James. *January 1973: Watergate, Roe v. Wade, Vietnam, and the Month That Changed America Forever*. Chicago: Chicago Review Press, 2015.

Senate Watergate Committee transcripts.

Summers, Anthony. *The Arrogance of Power: The Secret World of Richard Nixon*. New York: Viking Press, 2000.

Swift, Will. "Richard Nixon, Hopeless Romantic." *Politico Magazine*, February 13, 2014.

Thomas, Evan. *Being Nixon: A Man Divided*. New York: Random House, 2015.

Washington Post, selected articles.

9. Bill Clinton and Vernon Jordan: Two Brothers of the South

Baer, Don. Phone interview with author.

Branch, Taylor. *The Clinton Tapes: Conversations With a President, 1993-2001*. New York: Simon & Schuster, 2009.

Caplan, Thomas. Interview with author.

Clinton, Hillary Rodham. Phone interview with author.

Clinton, William J. *Bill Clinton: My Life*. New York: Random House, 2004.

———. Zoom interview with author.

Doyle, Patti Solis. Phone interview with author.

Emanuel, Rahm. Phone interview with author.

Ferrazi, Keith. *Never Eat Alone: How to Build a Lifelong Community of Colleagues, Contacts, Friends, and Mentors*. New York: Doubleday, 2005.

Gergen, David. Phone interview with author.

Harris, John. "Vernon Jordan's Creed: 'Michelle, I'm Too Old to Let Race Get in the Way of Friendship.'" *Politico Magazine,* March 2, 2021.

Hernreich, Nancy. Phone interview with author.

Jordan, Vernon. Interview with author.

———. *Vernon Can Read! A Memoir*. New York: PublicAffairs, 2001.

Lindsey, Bruce. Phone interview with author.

Lockhart, Joe. Phone interview with author.

Maraniss, David. *First in His Class: The Biography of Bill Clinton*. New York: Simon & Schuster, 1995.

McAuliffe, Terry. Phone interview with author.

———. *What a Party! My Life Among Democrats: Presidents, Candidates, Donors, Activists, Alligators, and Other Wild Animals*. New York: St. Martin's Press, 2007.

Newsweek staff. "The Smoothest of Operators." *Newsweek*, February 1, 1998.

New York Times, selected articles.

Pew Research Center. "The Clinton/Lewinsky Story: How Accurate? How Fair?" Undated.

Ronson, Jon. "Monica Lewinsky: The Shame Sticks to You Like Tar," *The Guardian,* April 22, 2016.

Smith, Sally Bedell. *For Love of Politics: Inside the Clinton White House.* New York: Random House, 2007.

Stephanopoulos, George. *All Too Human: A Political Education.* New York: Little, Brown, 1999.

———. Interview with author.

Time, selected articles from 1992 and 1998.

Toobin, Jeffrey. *A Vast Conspiracy: The Real Story of the Sex Scandal That Nearly Brought Down a President.* New York: Random House, 2000.

"Vernon Jordan '57 Delivers a Powerful Statement As He Returns to His Alma Mater for the Presidential Inauguration." DePauw University website. October 29, 2016. https://www.depauw.edu/news-media/latest-news/details/32687/.

Waldman, Michael. *POTUS Speaks: Finding the Words that Defined the Clinton Presidency.* New York: Simon & Schuster, 2000.

Washington Post, selected articles.

Williams, Marjorie. "Clinton's Mr. Inside." *Vanity Fair,* March 1993.

Index

About the Author

Gary Ginsberg grew up in Buffalo, New York, home to two US presidents. A lawyer by training, he has spent his professional career at the intersection of media, politics, and law. He worked for the Clinton administration, was a senior editor and counsel at the political magazine *George*, and then spent the next two decades in executive positions in media and technology at News Corporation, Time Warner, and SoftBank. He has published pieces in the the *New York Times* and the *Wall Street Journal* and was an on-air political contributor in the early days of MSNBC. He lives in New York City with his wife and two sons. This is his first book.